CHILDREN AND THE POLITICS OF CULTURE

EDITORS

Sherry B. Ortner, Nicholas B. Dirks, Geoff Eley

A LIST OF TITLES

IN THIS SERIES APPEARS

AT THE BACK OF

THE BOOK

PRINCETON STUDIES IN
CULTURE / POWER / HISTORY

CHILDREN AND THE POLITICS OF CULTURE

Sharon Stephens, Editor

PRINCETON UNIVERSITY PRESS

PRINCETON, NEW JERSEY

Library of Congress Cataloging-in-Publication Data

Children and the politics of culture / Sharon Stephens, editor.
p. cm.—(Princeton studies in culture/power/history)
"This collection of papers developed from the session 'Children and
the Politics of Culture' organized in connection with the international
conference 'Children at Risk' held in Bergen, Norway, in May 1992
and sponsored by the Norwegian Centre for Child Research"—Pref.
Includes bibliographical references and index.
ISBN 0-691-04329-9 (alk. paper).
ISBN 0-691-04328-0 (pbk. : alk. paper)
1. Children—Social conditions.   2. Children—Government policy.
3. Children's rights.   4. Ethnicity in children.   5. Identity (Psychology) in children.   I. Stephens, Sharon, 1952– .   II. Series.
HQ767.9.C449   1995
305.23—dc20   95-10602   CIP

Marilyn Ivy, "Have You Seen Me? Recovering the Inner Child in Late
Twentieth-Century America," *Social Text* , 37, pp. 227-52. Copyright
Duke University Press, 1993. Reprinted with Permission.

This book has been composed in Galliard

Princeton University Press books are printed
on acid-free paper and meet the guidelines
for permanence and durability of the Committee
on Production Guidelines for Book Longevity
of the Council on Library Resources

Printed in the United States of America
by Princeton Academic Press

1   3   5   7   9   10   8   6   4   2

1   3   5   7   9   10   8   6   4   2
(pbk.)

Contents

Preface

THIS COLLECTION of papers developed from the session "Children and the Politics of Culture" organized in connection with the international conference "Children at Risk," held in Bergen, Norway, in May 1992 and sponsored by the Norwegian Centre for Child Research. Taking as their organizational foundation the United Nations Convention on the Rights of the Child, conference sponsors sought to bring together researchers, policymakers, health professionals, educators, and others concerned with child-related issues around the world to explore the global dimensions of children at risk—that is, children whose fundamental rights to physical safety, health, education, self-expression, and other Convention-defined rights are not respected and protected by responsible adults in families, communities, and states.

Initially, our session was conceived as an exploration of children variously at risk in relation to "the child's right to cultural identity." Investigation of the complex and potentially contradictory framing of the "fundamental elements of identity" in the Convention itself led to questions about what notions of culture and identity underlie these universal-rights discourses, and about the difficulties that arise when children become the focal points for diverse and often contradictory identity claims.

As I discussed these issues with colleagues at the Norwegian Centre for Child Research, the session gradually evolved from an exploration of "the child's right to (a) cultural identity" (and the myriad forces threatening this right in particular social contexts around the world) to a more wide-ranging exploration of the ways that children are central figures— and actors—in contemporary contests over definitions of culture, its boundaries and significance.

The aim of our session "Children and the Politics of Culture" was to bring together a small group of researchers from different parts of the world to explore various aspects of the current global politics of culture, in relation to the everyday lives of children, historically changing notions of childhood, and international children's rights discourses. The challenge for session participants was to produce a volume of papers of interest to scholars, policymakers, and a general audience concerned with issues of children and cultural identity.

Session participants shared a sense of frustration and outrage in our discussions of the high price children must pay when their bodies and minds become the terrain for adult battles. But we also came away from the conference both heartened and inspired by the opportunity to learn from one another and by the challenge to do scholarly work that facilitates important dialogues between academics and policymakers.

On behalf of all the session participants, I wish to say a special thank you to Per Egil Mjaavatn, Director of the Norwegian Centre for Child Research, for his vision and leadership in organizing this conference and in particular for his thoughtful and gracious support for our session. We also thank Karin Ekberg, conference coordinator, for her outstanding organizational help; Gunnar Lamvik, Berge Solberg, and Sverre Utseth, for technical assistance; and the entire staff of the Norwegian Centre for Child Research, for making our stay in Bergen not only intellectually productive, but also a great pleasure.

In addition, I would like to thank Marianne Gullestad for her help in developing the session focus and agenda and for her insightful criticisms and suggestions in relation to this volume. I also thank Veena Das, Tony Holmes, and Francesca Merlan for participating in our Bergen discussions.

I presented an early version of the introduction to my colleagues at the Norwegian Centre for Child Research, who, as always, provided me with provocative and useful feedback. I am especially grateful to the following people for their comments on the introduction: Ann Anagnost, Marianne Gullestad, Marilyn Ivy, Allison James, Cindi Katz, Per Miljeteig, Per Egil Mjaavatn, and Per Olav Tiller.

Finally, warm thanks go to Mary Murrell at Princeton University Press and to Sherry Ortner, series editor, for their consistant and enthusiastic support for this volume. I also thank Jane Low for her editorial assistance, Richard Isomaki for his illuminating copyediting, and Celeste Newbrough for her careful work on the index.

CHILDREN AND THE POLITICS OF CULTURE

Children and the Politics of Culture in "Late Capitalism"

SHARON STEPHENS

MANY ATTEMPTS have been made in recent years to map the "postmodern/postcolonial" world, characterized by transnational flows of commodities and people; by vast numbers of refugees, migrants, and stateless groups; by state projects to redefine the threatened boundaries of national cultures; and by a proliferation of ethnic groups, subcultures, and multicultural mixtures that challenge notions of stable, homogeneous identities. What emerges at the end of the twentieth century is an international process of production and exchange, together with a multitude of localized groups struggling to define themselves in relation to decentered global forces. The concept of culture has been central to these struggles. States and national elites, minority populations, and new social movements represent themselves as acting to protect traditional culture or to develop new forms of cultural identity.

In light of such debates about the nature of culture, what does it mean to talk about "children's rights to culture," along with rights to food, shelter, and health care? In *The Political Life of Children*, Robert Coles (1986) argues that a nation's politics becomes a child's everyday psychology. How do new forms of international and local politics of culture affect children? And how do children themselves experience, understand, and perhaps resist or reshape the complex, frequently contradictory cultural politics that inform their daily lives?

What sorts of social visions and notions of culture underlie assertions within international-rights discourses that every child has a right to a cultural identity? To what extent is this identity conceived as singular and exclusive, and what sorts of priorities are asserted in cases where various forms of cultural identity—regional, national, ethnic minority, or indigenous—come up against one another?

It is important to ask how international children's cultural-rights claims differ, for example, from the vision of South African state officials who used a language of people's rights to distinct cultures to justify apartheid. We need to examine more critically what it means to talk about a child's right to a cultural identity in a world where more and more children are growing up in complex multicultural settings, demanding that they move in and out of diverse social roles and create identities that bewilder and trouble their parents. What sorts of hybrid cultures might the children of Turkish "guest workers" in Berlin or Mexican migrant laborers in Los Angeles lay claim to? How do children in war-torn areas of the Middle East, Southeast Asia, or American inner cities experience their relation to "traditional cultures" far removed from everyday realities?

While many argue that international cultural-rights discourses further the best interests of children themselves, in some contexts these discourses may be linked to significant risks to the physical, psychological, and social well-being of children. Insofar as we accept the legitimacy of international-rights language, it might be argued that children also have rights not to be constrained within exclusionary cultural identities and not to have their bodies and minds appropriated as the unprotected terrain upon which cultural battles are fought.

The authors of papers in this volume explore various aspects of the current global politics of culture, in relation to changing discourses on childhood and to changing conditions and experiences of children in diverse world regions and social contexts. Especially exciting are the theoretical insights and practical implications that emerge when these papers—each an important work in its own right—are read together. My aim in this introduction is to suggest ways of reading the papers that push us toward new understandings—and even more significantly, toward new questions—about articulations among the ethnographic areas and themes explored by individual authors.

There are good reasons a combined focus on children and the politics of culture, at this moment in the formation and transformation of a new world order, is important for exploring the shape and significance of contemporary global processes. In order to frame my discussions of individual papers, I begin with discussions of childhood as a social and historical construction, culture as a theoretically and politically contested term, and reasons childhood and culture are both being challenged and reconfigured in fundamental ways today. Discussion of the collected papers then provides a foundation for assessing current affirmations of children's rights to cultural identity and international discourses on the rights of the child more generally.

CHILDHOOD AS A CULTURAL CONSTRUCTION

While Philippe Ariès's *Centuries of Childhood* (1962) was not the first social history to suggest a radical critique of universalistic notions of childhood, Ariès's challenge to naturalistic orthodoxies had a major impact on the social sciences. Ariès's work is striking, both for its impressive scholarly documentation and the boldness of its basic assertion: "[I]n medieval society the idea of childhood did not exist" (Ariès 1962:125). Ariès's work quickly became a foundational text for social-constructionist investigations into the profound "variability of human societies, all the more useful because it looked not to the 'exotic' or 'primitive' but to a familiar western European past" (Prout and James 1990:17).

Ariès argued that the modern conception of childhood as a separate life stage emerged in Europe between the fifteenth and eighteenth centuries, together with bourgeois notions of family, home, privacy, and individuality. Basing his argument in part on an extensive analysis of medieval paintings, Ariès asserted that before the fifteenth century, children past the dependent stage of infancy were conceived and depicted simply as miniature adults. By the eighteenth century, however, special conventions in artistic and literary representation clearly marked children as a distinct group and childhood as a separate domain, set apart from the everyday life of adult society. Notions of children's special nature and needs called for special attention to the child's emotional development in the home and for a protracted formal education in the school aimed at preparing children for the transition to an adult world.

Though the luxury of childhood was initially available only to the upper classes, notions and practices characterizing this new domain came to be propagated—not without significant resistance—throughout society. In time, a vast network of institutions—ranging from the nuclear family to school, health, and legal systems—contributed to the generalization of childhood, at least as an ideal, throughout Western society.

Ariès's work inspired a wide range of historical and sociological studies of private life, childhood, and the family, conceived not as naturally given containers for culturally specific content, but as themselves socially constructed domains. Ariès's claims for the uniqueness of childhood as an historically limited Western European creation also generated vigorous debates and critiques (for example, DeMause 1976, Hanawalt 1993).

But even if we modify Ariès's bold thesis and acknowledge that every known society has concepts and practices that in some respects mark off children from adults in order to assure physical care and socialization for biologically immature human beings, the originality and generativity of Ariès's claim remain. The *particular* form of modern childhood is socially and historically specific.

While all cultures have given meaning to physical differences of sex and age, it can be argued that the social worlds in which these physical signs become significant are so profoundly different that we are already doing analytical violence to complex constellations of meanings and practices when we single out notions of male and female or childhood and adulthood and attempt to compare them cross-culturally. These terms already presuppose a world of *Western* cultural assumptions—for example, that sexual or age differences are self-evidently dichotomous and that they define the parameters for exclusive identities.

There is a growing body of literature on Western childhood suggesting that the "hardening" of the modern dichotomy of child/adult, like the modern distinction female/male, was crucial to setting up hierarchical relations between distinct domains of social life—the private and public, consumption and production, objective need and subjective desire—upon which modern capitalism and the modern nation-state depended (see Boyden 1990; Qvortrup 1985).

As Barrett and McIntosh (1982:35) observe, "[T]he ideological construction of the family as the antithesis to the cash-nexus could *only* refer to a capitalist society." Similarly, the ideological construction of childhood as the privileged domain of spontaneity, play, freedom, and emotion could only refer to a society that contained and drew upon this private domain as the ground for public culture, discipline, work, constraint, and rationality.

In recent decades, there has been a proliferation of important works exploring the centrality of historically specific gender constructions within articulated structures of capital, nation-state, urban life, cultural forms, and subjective orientations characterizing modern Western capitalist society.[1] Compared to this extensive literature on gender, explorations of "the child" and its structural role in modern society are still relatively undeveloped.[2] In what respects are children—as foci of gender-specific roles in the family, as objects of regulation and development in the school, and as symbols of the future and of what is at stake in contests over cultural identity—pivotal in the structuring of modernity? How does the temporal move from child to adult correlate with the synchronic relation between female and male, or the construction of other cultures as our innocent, but immature and undeveloped, past? And if we are now witnessing wide-ranging restructurings of modernity, what implications might these changes have for the concept of childhood and the life conditions of children?

Prout and James, representative of a growing number of researchers arguing for culturalist perspectives on diverse childhoods, emphasize over and over again that "the immaturity of children is a biological fact of life, but the ways in which this immaturity is understood and made meaningful is a fact of culture" (1990:7). They celebrate an "emergent paradigm" in the sociology of childhood that is based on the "assumption that a child is socialized by belonging to a particular culture at a certain stage in its history" (15). Thus, comparative work on childhood should aim at "the analysis of how different discursive practices produce different childhoods, each and all of which are 'real' within their own regime of truth" (27).

But how and where are we to locate in the contemporary world distinct cultures, to be analyzed each "in their own terms"? The culturalization of childhood should not be bought at the cost of an awareness of the complexities of cultural definition in a postmodern world. Rather than merely explicating Western constructions of childhood, to be filled out in terms of gender, race, and class differences and to be compared with the childhoods of other cultures, we need also to explore the global processes that are currently transforming gender, race, class, culture—and, by no means least of all, childhood itself.

A CONTEMPORARY CRISIS IN THE STUDY OF CHILDHOOD: WHAT IS A CHILD?

James and Prout (1990:2) note a contemporary crisis in the study of childhood, characterized by a sense of the inadequacy of previous frameworks. While the modern concept of childhood as a distinct stage in the human life cycle crystallized in nineteenth-century Western thought, the twentieth century has been characterized by a great elaboration of that conceptual space. Various technologies of knowledge (psychological experiments, ethnographic descriptions, medicalized analyses) have been applied to children, while ideologies of child-centered society give "the child" and "the interests of the child" a central place in the practices of legal, welfare, medical, and educational institutions. "But despite this rhetoric," James and Prout assert (1990:1), "any complacency about children and their place in society is misplaced, for the very concept of childhood has become problematic during the last decade."

At the heart of current debates, they suggest, lies the question: what is a child? In 1979, the International Year of the Child was launched, accompanied by internationally televised accounts of children whose lives were devastated by famine, war, and poverty. The concept of "the world's children" emerged in official discourses of international agencies such as UNICEF (the United Nations Children's Fund) and the World Health Organization. At the same time, however, affluent groups in Western society confronted a chasm between their idealized concepts of childhood and the realities of many children's lives, both in the Third World and in the heart of First World urban centers.

A decade later, an explosion of media coverage of child abuse, and particularly child sexual abuse, again challenged traditional beliefs about childhood and made public the private lives of children with no access to the mythic "walled garden" of "Happy, Safe, Protected, Innocent Childhood" (Holt 1975:22–23).

Thus, James and Prout argue, it is the past decade's consciousness of profound differences in the realities of children's lives—a consciousness facilitated by the global media—that has precipitated a crisis in the sociology of childhood and spurred the recognition that each culture defines childhood in terms of its own set of meanings and practices. While I agree with the observations of James and Prout, I would like to suggest a more radical explanation for the current crisis in the study of childhood. A historical perspective on "the world's children" suggests complex globalizations of once localized Western constructions of childhood. Current crises—in notions of childhood, the experiences of children, and the sociology of childhood—are related to profound changes in a now globalized modernity in which "the child" was previously located.

There is a rapidly proliferating literature theorizing the changing shape of the world system. Whether this new historical situation is framed as "late capitalism," "disorganized capitalism," "a global regime of flexible capital accumulation," or "postindustrial society" (see, for example, Mandel 1975; Lash and Urry 1987; Harvey 1989; and Bell 1974), analyses of childhood, gender, and the family have been largely neglected in these writings. Many of the authors exploring the world system, I would argue, are still operating in terms of distinctions between political economy and culture, the public and the private, that are themselves in the process of profound transformation. These shifting boundaries need to be theorized if we wish to explore emergent global processes, spaces, and identities.

A focus on childhood—and on other domains previously differentiated from the realm of political economy—is thus important, insofar as it breaks the frame of dominant models of transformations in the world system. It is also crucial for child researchers to rethink their own studies in the light of social and historical macroperspectives if they wish to understand the explosion of concern about children's rights and to anticipate new risks to children and childhood that would otherwise go unrecognized.

CHILDREN AND CHILDHOODS AT RISK

As signs of a growing concern in recent decades with assaults on the space of childhood, consider the following book titles: *Children without Childhood* (Winn 1984), *Stolen Childhood: In Search of the Rights of the Child* (Vittachi 1989), *There Are No Children Here: The Story of Two*

Boys Growing Up in the Other America (Kotlowitz 1991), *The Disappearance of Childhood* (Postman 1982), *Innocent Victims* (Gilmour 1988), *Broken Promise: The World of Endangered Children* (Allsebrook and Swift 1989), *The Rise and Fall of Childhood* (Sommerville 1982), *Pricing the Priceless Child: The Changing Social Value of Children* (Zelizer 1985), and *Children in Danger* (Garbarino et al. 1992—an exploration of the everyday experiences of American children in urban "war zones").

The list could be greatly extended, but the message here is clear. It was amplified at the May 1992 "Children at Risk" conference in Bergen. Discourses of lost, stolen, and disappearing childhoods and of abandoned, abused, exploited, and "disappeared" children run through the papers in this volume.

The dominant theme is of children as innocent and vulnerable victims of adult mistreatment, greed, and neglect. Researchers cite the literal disappearance of children's bodies from the streets of Brazil and the prisons of South Africa and Namibia. The Chinese government's violent response to student demonstrations in Tiananmen Square was deplored in the international media as a nation opening fire on its own children. The Argentinian military regime was responsible for an unknown number of young people abducted by "security forces" and officially proclaimed as "disappeared." International media present child victims of famine disappearing more gradually: we are shown the starving bodies of glassy-eyed children with swollen bellies and emaciated limbs, literally wasting away.

The theme of lost childhoods includes not only physical assaults on and threats to children's bodies, but also the threatened spaces of an ideally safe, innocent, and carefree domain of childhood. Postman argues, for example, in *The Disappearance of Childhood* (1982) that the decline of American childhood as a protected space within the family began in 1950, as an "age of literacy" began to give way to an "electronic revolution." The inculcation of family values in the home and community values in the school gave way to an uncontrolled invasion of children's minds by market-driven media images and globally circulating signs. With this invasion came a loss of childhood innocence, and especially of sexual innocence.

It is, of course, questionable whether this protected space of familial and community harmony and of sexual innocence ever existed in the ways it is imagined. What I wish to draw attention to is a growing concern in recent decades with the domain of childhood as threatened, invaded, and "polluted" by adult worlds. At stake here are notions not only of innocence, but of nature, individual freedom, social values of enduring love and care (as opposed to temporally restricted economic and bureaucratic transactions), the family as basic unit of society, the bounded local community as the site of value definition and transmission, and the possibility of noncommodified social domains outside the realm of the market and market-driven politics.

THE POLITICS OF THE "NONPOLITICAL"

Discourses of vanishing children and disappearing childhoods challenge us to explore the nature of current assaults on modern notions of childhood and on the bodies and minds of children who exist in complexly mediated relations to these ideals. Such assaults, I believe, must be considered in relation to current challenges to and refashionings of other domains previously conceived as largely *outside* the realm of politics and the market. Thus, we observe in recent decades a proliferation of works on the politics of social domains previously regarded as nonpolitical: naturalized spaces such as the self, the body, the family, childhood, and everyday life; a naturalized realm of the physical environment; and the archetypically cultural spaces of "pure" science, art, religion, and culture itself.[3] It is as though the realm of the political, the discursively negotiable and historically transformable, has moved out from its previous position as a sort of historical buffer between nature and culture, to invade the "timeless" realms of natural law and intellectual purity.[4]

Habermas (1987) explores the progressive colonization of the "life-world" by the "systems world" in late modernity, as the taken-for-granted spaces of everyday life are restructured to accord with shifting political and economic demands. A defining characteristic of postmodernity is often said to be the denaturalization of objects, identities, and structures of social classification. Previously essentialized, naturalized categories come to be seen as transparently—and arbitrarily—organized by symbolic discourse.

While some authors celebrate new freedoms opened up by the dissolution of previously naturalized spaces, others take a more critical stance to the postmodern. The erosion and colonization of social domains previously seen as organized by their own distinctive logics can be seen as threatening an emerging new world order with the loss of any socially protected spaces *outside* the realm of globally circulating signs, goods, labor, and capital. The child—as a crucial modern symbol of nature and the object of protection and enculturation—is at risk of being written off as yet another postmodern discursive fiction.

What are the implications for society as a whole, if there are no longer social spaces conceived as at least partially autonomous from the market and market-driven politics? Where are we to find the sites of difference, the terrain of social witness, critical leverage, and utopian vision, insofar as the domain of childhood—or of everyday life or of a semiautonomous realm of culture—is increasingly shot through with the values of the marketplace and the discursive politics of postmodern global culture? And what happens to the bodies and minds of children in the process?[5]

CHILDREN AT RISK—AND AS RISKS

This sense of the disappearance of childhood as a stable, natural foundation for social life is connected not only to laments for the lost innocence of childhood, but also to many examples of a growing fear of and anger at children. Consider, for example, the newly identified sociological phenomenon of *Kinderfeindlichkeit* (hostility to children) in Germany. In a December 1992 article in the *International Herald Tribune*, Marc Fisher comments on a bill proposed to the German parliament barring German parents from "spanking, boxing ears, withholding affection, constant nagging or threatening children with the bogeyman." Aggressive public policies are required, the argument goes, to inject love and affection for children into German society.

> Government analysts and psychologists say that despite wide-spread affluence, the success of postwar democracy and the best efforts of professionals, *kinderfeindlichkeit*, the German term for antipathy to children, has grown roots in a society suffering from excessive angst about the future. "The lost war and total destruction we suffered stripped away our certainty about basic values," said Ingrid Hoffman, spokesman for the German League for the Child. "The relations between generations were poisoned for a time."[6]

In a world of shifting values and challenged boundaries, we also observe an increasing obsession with the guarding of boundaries of the body, sex roles, the family, ethnic purity, and national identity—and, I would argue, increasing anger at children who cannot or will not fulfill their expected roles in the transmission of "traditional values." In an earlier period of modern society, noncompliant children could be categorized as "going through a stage" (as Prout and James [1990:12] note, "a biological explanation for a breakdown in social relationships") or, in more extreme cases, as "juvenile delinquents," in need of social correction and rehabilitation.

But what can we say about social worlds, such as those inhabited by the escalating numbers of "street children," regarded as largely *outside* the normative socializing control of adult society? From certain perspectives, of course, street children can be seen as *integral* parts of an emerging order of global capitalism. Moreover, there is much evidence that children living on the streets develop their own social organizations, relatively stable attachments to territories, and support networks linked to the sharing of food and goods (Boyden 1990:190ff.). Nevertheless, popular conceptions of street children frequently portray them as unsocialized or antisocial dangers to the established order and as primary *causes* of escalating social problems, such as increasing crime rates, drug trafficking, prostitution, and inner-city decay.

Notions of street children as non- or antisocial beings, presumably without families or values of their own, have been used to legitimate radical programs to eliminate the menace of street children in the interests of the general social good. Systematic assaults on Brazilian street children by organized "death squads," funded by the business community, frequently manned by off-duty policemen, and tacitly condoned by at least some government officials (see Henriques 1986; Larmer and Margolis 1992) are a particularly egregious example, but street children are a prime focus of fear and demands for more severe social controls in virtually every major urban center around the world (Boyden 1990:205).

The category of street children is a slippery one, shading into notions of only partially socialized young people living increasingly outside the regulatory spheres of family and school.

> In cities as disparate as Abidjan, Bogota, Cairo, Manila and Seoul, children playing in the streets and other public spaces and young teenagers congregating on street corners, outside cinemas or bars, have become synonymous in the mind of the general public with delinquent gangs. (Boyden 1990:188)

Frequently detained for the nebulous crimes of loitering and vagrancy, these assemblies of young people are most guilty of not conforming to socialization models according to which children are compliant vehicles for the transmission of stable social worlds.

In *Purity and Danger*, Mary Douglas (1985 [1966]) observes that dirt is "matter out of place"—and that objects in the interstices of conceptual structures are often regarded as profoundly dangerous and mysteriously powerful. Children on the streets are "people out of place."[7] They live in spaces people are supposed to pass through in their movements between socially sanctioned nodes of urban life; they are associated with illicit drug use and promiscuous sexuality, all the more reprehensible in children, who are supposed to be non- or presexual; and they represent a dangerous mixing of languages and cultural backgrounds. As children, they are even *more* out of place in the streets than adults. Street children are also endowed with the power to cause major urban disorders. They elicit violent reactions from those in power—far out of proportion, many have argued, to the numbers or strength of these children.[8]

Just as idle bands of youth and street children are seen as the cause of urban crime and decay, so also are hordes of hungry Third World children often seen as a major *cause* of global environmental problems. The cover of the *Economist*'s special issue on the 1992 UN Conference on Environment and Development depicts a mass of black children, whose images fill the cover frame and and blur together in the distance. Inside we learn that uncontrolled Third World population growth and poverty are the root causes of advancing deserts, vanishing forests, failing crops, and disappearing species ("Question Rio Forgets" 1992:11). The solution to global environmental problems, such perspectives suggest, is population control programs aimed at drastically reducing "excess populations"—people filling spaces and making demands on natural resources outside socially legitimated channels of ownership, exchange, and distribution. It is significant that in the popular media, these excess populations are often represented by crowds of hungry *children*, consuming whatever resources are available, but supposedly unable to participate in the global economy as producers (see Stephens 1992).

In the darkest scenarios of the disappearance of childhood, the theme of lost innocence takes on a negative valence. Children on the streets of Rio de Janeiro or in the ghettos of Los Angeles are not only killed. They also kill. Unrestrained and undeveloped by the ameliorating institutions of childhood, the innocence of children is perverted and twisted. In these stories, children are represented as malicious predators, the embodiment of dangerous natural forces, unharnessed to social ends.

There is a growing consciousness of children *at risk*. But the point I want to make here is that there is also a growing sense of children themselves as *the risk*—and thus of some children as people out of place and excess populations to be eliminated, while others must be controlled, reshaped, and harnessed to changing social ends. Hence, the centrality of children, both as symbolic figures and as objects of contested forms of socialization, in the contemporary politics of culture.

Widespread discourses of the loss and disappearance of childhood alert us to social processes that are currently reshaping the institutional and experiential frameworks of modern childhood. As Norma Field notes in her contribution to this volume, the insight that the modern domain of childhood is a social and historical artifact, not a universal biological necessity, "has made possible the conceptualization (rather than the impressionistic bewailing) of the erosion of this institution in our own day."

The crucial task for researchers now, I would argue, is to develop more powerful understandings of the role of the child in the structures of modernity, the historical processes by which these once localized Western constructions have been exported around the world, and the global political, economic, and cultural transformations that are currently rendering children so dangerous, contested, and pivotal in the formation of new sorts of social persons, groups, and institutions. The challenge is to grasp the specificity of childhood and children's experiences in different world regions, national frameworks, and social contexts, while also seeking to illuminate the historical processes that not only link particular social worlds but are also crucially important in shaping and transforming them.

CONCEPTUALIZING THE ROLE OF THE CHILD IN MODERNITY

Modern children are supposed to be segregated from the harsh realities of the adult world and to inhabit a safe, protected world of play, fantasy, and innocence.

> Adult nostalgia for youthful innocence is symbolized by the whimsy of London's Museum of Childhood, with its display cabinets full of mechanical toys, china dolls, hand-painted dolls' houses, tin soldiers, electric train sets and Dinky cars. There is no place in this kind of childhood for labour in the factory or mine. (Boyden 1990:185)

Properly loved children should ideally be protected from the arduous tasks and instrumentalized relationships of the productive sphere. In the modern industrial world, "[T]he instrumental value of children has been largely replaced by their expressive value. Children have become relatively worthless (economically) to their parents, but priceless in terms of their psychological worth" (Scheper-Hughes 1989:12).

Boyden (1990:186) observes that "the norms and values upon which this ideal of a safe, happy and protected childhood are built are culturally and historically bound to the social preoccupations and priorities of the capitalist countries [and bourgeois classes] of Europe and the United States." The "needs of the child" figure prominently as grounds for the bounded and naturalized domestic space of modernity and for a marked sexual division of labor associated with differentiated spheres of reproduction/consumption and production.

Here we need not fall back on a notion of capitalism "calling for" or "bringing into being" a certain type of childhood—an unproductively reflectionist model of objective political economic processes simply calling forth new forms of subjectivity and everyday life. While children (especially males in earlier periods) eventually have to enter the workforce, the relation between the needs of the modern industrial economy and the socialization and education of children in home and school has never been simple. Modern children and childhood have always occupied more complex and critically important positions in the construction of modernity than a model of children simply as the raw materials of the capitalist marketplace would suggest.

David Harvey (1985, 1989) offers a more productive model for the analysis of changing constructions of childhood in the history of capitalist society. Harvey's aim is to theorize the structural and historical foundations for successive eras of capitalism, characterized by what he terms "structured coherences" of capital, political institutions, cultural forms, urban structures, and subjective orientations and punctuated by periods of wide-ranging disorganization and restructuring. Harvey posits an emerging modern period associated with free-market liberal capitalism (from roughly the 1890s to the 1930s); a period of high modernity linked to imperialist, state monopoly forms of capitalism (the 1940s through the 1960s); and an emerging late or postmodernist period linked to globalized structures of capital (from the 1970s to the present).

There is much important historical work to be done in conceptualizing the role of the child in modernity, for example, in relation to the modern nation-state and the development of child-focused institutions, such as the state-supported compulsory school.[9] In his pioneering work on the modern nation-state as a particular kind of "imagined community," Benedict Anderson (1983:16) asserts that "in the modern world everyone can, should, will 'have' a nationality, as he or she 'has' a gender." And, he might have added, as he or she "has" a childhood.

The creation of a modern state and national culture is integrally related to the creation of new sorts of gendered and age-graded subjects and spaces and the establishment of institutions variously engaged in spreading these constructions throughout society. As conceptions of a proper modern childhood developed within the European bourgeoisie, there was also increasing concern about deviant, wayward, and dangerous classes of children and about abnormal and indigent families.[10] In the early periods of industrialization, there was special concern about children on the streets—street traders, newspaper vendors, match and flower sellers, and messengers (Boyden 1990:187–88). Urban street life in northern Europe, especially in working-class districts, became associated in bourgeois consciousness with notions of physical danger, immorality, and social disorder. The appropriate places for children were considered to be the home, the school, and designated play areas, while children were acceptable in public spaces only at restricted times and under adult supervision (for example, watching parades on national holidays). An English commentator on the British school system remarked in 1912, "[T]he whole system of national education has been reared on the foundation of the Ragged Schools, whose avowed object it was to draw children away from the fascinating misery of the streets" (Phillips 1912:206).

Within the provisionally structured coherence of modernity, notions of deviant childhoods have been a way of acknowledging differences in children's lives, while also legitimizing universalized notions of an ideal childhood. "Juvenile offenders" are thus marked for rehabilitation, while poor black children growing up in extended matrifocal families are seen as in need of compensatory social-welfare programs.

THE GLOBALIZATION AND EXPORT OF MODERN CHILDHOOD

And it is not only modern European national citizens who should have a particular sort of childhood, but populations around the world, in need of "civilization" and "development." Colonial projects were dependent not just on the establishment of new political and economic organizations, but also on the formation of social actors able and willing to function in complementary ways within them.

In recent years, historians and anthropologists have given increasing attention to the export of modern European domestic life as a critical site for producing new sorts of colonial laborers and imperial subjects (see Comaroff and Comaroff 1991). The export of modern notions of childhood, socialization, and education is inextricably connected to the export of modern constructions of gender, individuality, and the family.

Mala de Alwis (1991) explores, for example, the central importance that early-nineteenth-century British and American missionaries placed on refashioning Ceylonese women, so that they could in turn reshape the domestic world and provide appropriate socialization for children, before they became enmeshed within traditional structures of belief.

Missionary-sponsored boarding schools were also concerned with creating new identities for children. It was common practice for young girls to receive a new name, often that of a designated benefactress abroad, to mark this radical shift. "Thus Annamah could become Mary Walton overnight." She was taught Christian Scripture and prayer, together with needlework, orderliness, thrift, cleanliness, and accounting—all encompassed under the title of "Domestic Science" (de Alwis 1991:14).

We get a sense of the complexity of global exports of modern child-hood and gender constructions when we consider how early Sri Lankan nationalists both drew upon and selectively refashioned these imported notions to define and protect visions of their nation's essential difference from the West. Late-nineteenth-century nationalists were concerned with asserting a non-Western native spirituality *within* the internationally legitimated framework of the nation. They wanted to appropriate the Western technologies and political strategies that had allowed the West to colonize and dominate the East, while also maintaining and reinforcing Eastern superiority in the spiritual realm.

> Therefore, great effort was taken to protect this distinctive spiritual essence of culture which the nationalists believed could be contained and nurtured within the home by the women, while men waged the battle for Independence on the treacherous terrain of the profane, materialist outer world. (de Alwis 1991:8)

The ideal female was to stand opposed both to the dangerously Europeanized upper-class woman (who wore European dress, drank alcohol, and smoked and was not sufficiently attentive to men and the home) *and* to the traditional native woman (coarse, immoral, and unable to understand the sacrifices necessary to construct a new nation). In constructing the ideal postcolonial woman, Sri Lankan nationalists negotiated a distinctive space between what they regarded as parochial tradition and uncritical modernity.[11]

And it was by means of this complex division between East and West, private and public, female and male that a distinctive boundary and relation between *child and adult* was made possible. The child, primarily socialized within the spiritual female realm and ideally educated in Buddhist schools, could later move out into the compromised adult world and, the proponents of nationalism affirmed, still retain the purity of timeless spiritual essence at the core of being.

Clearly, the social construction of modern forms of gender and childhood in Sri Lanka is different in important ways from gender and childhood in Europe and in other world regions. Clearly, also, the social spaces and subjective experiences of male and female, child and adult in these diverse contexts are related in integral ways.

In "Africa Observed: Discourses of the Imperial Imagination" (1991), Comaroff and Comaroff explore the complex significance that intersecting notions of children, women, animals, and nature had for diverse European colonial visions of Africans—and particularly black South Africans, considered to be among the most primitive groups on the "dark continent." In late-eighteenth-century Europe, "[T]he non-

European was to be made as peripheral to the global axes of reason and production as women had become at home. Both were vital to the material and imaginative order of modern Europe. Yet both were deprived of access to its highest values." This stratified order was to be legitimized in nature, through biological differences between the sexes and races (Comaroff and Comaroff 1991:105). Just as Africans were feminized, in terms of their ostensibly uncontrolled passions and irrationality, so also were they infantilized and viewed in terms of their lack of qualities characterizing adult white European males—a vision that legitimized the civilizing process of issuing African "boys" into "moral manhood."

The Comaroffs also note, however, that "if degenerate nature was the foil to post-Enlightenment self-confidence, idealized nature was the trope of its critics and visionaries" (109). The naturalized differentiation of children, women, and peasants from civilized urban males made the former groups, together with "savage" non-Europeans, critical sites for the indictment of the "jarring and dissonant thing" that civilization had made of man (Coleridge, quoted in Comaroff and Comaroff 1991:110).

For our purposes here, it is important to note that early modern notions of childhood—as well as of gender, race, and nature—were both significant for and profoundly influenced by European colonialist experiences. If Africans were conceived as feminized and childlike, so also were notions of European women and children affected by the symbolic roles they played in both legitimizing and criticizing the European imperial project and civilizing mission.

Early modern notions of childhood were marked by stark tensions and contradictions, inasmuch as childhood was one of the key sites for the production of a newly emerging and widely contested liberal capitalist order. To what extent does a contemporary consciousness of burgeoning deviations from, as well as tensions and contradictions within, modern childhoods represent the transformation of a modern capitalist world in which these childhoods arose?

"DEVIATIONS" FROM MODERN CHILDHOOD: A CHALLENGE TO MODERNITY?

A crucial part of describing the distinctive shape of modernity in different world regions and social contexts is exploration of the pivotal figure of the child and of the relation of this ideal construct to the diverse lives of children. As previously noted, James and Prout (1990:2) link a crisis in the sociology of childhood since the 1970s with increasing international media coverage of children's lives strikingly divergent from idealized Western concepts of childhood. But child researchers certainly recognized differences among the world's children before this time. The point here is that *within* the provisionally structured coherence of high modernity, the "deviant childhoods" of Third World children could be interpreted as local particularities and instances of backwardness and underdevelopment, thus justifying expanded efforts to export modern childhood around the world.

A crucial question is whether contemporary notions of proliferating deviations from modern childhood—differences that are frequently glossed as "loss" and "contamination"—represent significant transformations in the nature of childhood and, more generally, in the social and historical project of modernity. My argument here is that we should at least take very seriously the possibility that we are now witnessing a profound restructuring of the child within the context of a movement from state to global capitalism, modernity to postmodernity.

A comprehensive theoretical discussion of how this global transformation might be framed is obviously far beyond the scope of this introduction.[12] One model I have found useful for thinking about contemporary children and childhoods at risk is the previously mentioned work of David Harvey. Harvey argues that the postwar Fordist-Keynesian order of production/consumption, big business/organized labor, and Keynesian welfare state was only a relatively stable aggregate of diverse practices and perspectives, whose organization became increasingly tenuous as gathering crises of capital overaccumulation transformed existing structures into obstacles to, rather than facilitators of, continued growth. Harvey sees these crises as coming to a head in the early 1970s, precipitating moves to smaller-scale, more flexible systems of production, marketing, and labor organization; geographical mobility of capital; and revivals of entrepeneurialism and political neoconservatism.

A newly emerging globalized "regime of flexible accumulation"—involving the increasing centralization and concentration of capital in multinational firms, as well as the failure of many older businesses and the proliferation of new sorts of local forms of production and marketing—has wide-ranging implications for the nature of local communities, national frameworks, and regional structures. The erosion of "self-evident" identities makes way for proliferating identity claims, from "traditional" ethnic groups challenging the capacity of national cultures to encompass ethnic differences to affirmations of new sorts of regional and global identities, such as the European Union and the Nation of Islam.

Harvey describes how an emerging global regime of flexible accumulation contributes to a widening gap in the First World between the very rich and the swelling ranks of the downwardly mobile middle classes and poor, as well as to increasing conflicts between the North and South.[13] "Leaner," more flexible firms have little use for large numbers of unskilled laborers engaged in large-scale standardized production. Shifts away from mass production and marketing mean that the First World has less use for Third World laborers and that the primary movement of capital occurs between the wealthy nations of the North. Development programs in the Third World are being scaled down, in favor of "structural adjustment programs" to facilitate the repayment of national debts, with disastrous consequences for the everyday lives of Third World populations (see George 1989).

The implications of these changes for children are legion. As the Third World "comes home" to industrial nations, widespread economic uncertainty, unemployment, and decreased public services (such as health care, child care, and unemployment benefits) drastically affect the lives of children. In debt-ridden Third World countries, "austerity adjustments" and export-based national economies mean cuts in social-welfare programs and disruptions in local support networks. Increasing numbers of children live and work in conditions of poverty, while media representations of ideal childhoods sharpen the experience of material poverty as inner deprivation.

The materially privileged are affected too, as the conditions for economic well-being appear ever more tenuous and the future well-being of children ever more uncertain. Radical changes are called for in educational systems, in order to prepare children for participation in a rapidly changing adult world and to insure a sufficiently flexible body of "human capital" to society.

Add to these pressures on children the ethnic, religious, and racial conflicts set free and refashioned by the restructuring of national frameworks, as well as massive disruptions of local social networks associated with escalating numbers of refugees and migrant laborers, and we begin to see why children and the protected space of modern childhood are so profoundly at risk in a newly emerging world order.

RESEARCH ON CHILDHOOD AND CHILDREN: AN IMPORTANT GENERATIVE SITE FOR EXPLORING CONTEMPORARY GLOBAL PROCESSES

Research on childhood and children has much to gain from serious consideration of diverse models of global political economic transformations. I would suggest, moreover, that interdisciplinary work at the crossroads of child research and world systems literatures has profound implications not only for our understandings of the social and historical construction of childhoods, but also for the ways we theorize capitalist society and its historical dynamic.

Models of political and economic transformations leading to corre-

sponding shifts in consciousness, subjective experience, and social relationships do not adequately account for increasingly widespread notions
of the disappearance, contamination, invasion, and colonization of domains such as childhood, previously regarded as relatively noncommodified (Stephens 1993). To grasp the nature of these shifting boundaries,
we need a more powerful notion of capital, not as an objective thing
whose development calls for superstructural changes, but as a particular
kind of social relation. The social construction of capital involves a far
from natural relationship between objects and subjects and an historical
dynamic according to which the objective realm of "nature" is periodically restructured in the interests of profit (see Postone 1993).

To make sense of the history of a once localized, now globally penetrating capitalist order, we need to explore the ways certain objects and
processes come to be invested with natural boundaries, objective solid-
ity, and material force and the charged moments of historical transition,
when the naturalized structures of social life break open and "flexible,"
"deviant," and frequently contradictory processes emerge, before a new
structured coherence begins to take shape.

From this perspective, what is happening now to children and childhoods—in their locally unique, globally articulated forms—is less a re-
flex of political and economic changes than a crucial part of the puzzle,
an important generative site for exploring and theorizing capitalist society and its historical dynamic.

The point here is that there is no completely adequate theory at hand
to grasp the nature of the current crisis in the sociology of childhood—
or the lived experience of children. But there is much to be gained by
trying to make sense of particular case studies in terms of macrohistori-
cal perspectives on contemporary global changes, *and* by returning from
particular ethnographic explorations with new questions and problems
for theory to illuminate. The papers in this volume, representing diverse
perspectives on vanishing childhoods, disappearing children, negotiated
and newly emerging identities, present important challenges to social
theorists that should not be isolated within a narrowly defined field of
"child research."[14]

THE POLITICS OF CULTURE

If a crucial dimension of late capitalism is a shift in the location and nature of boundaries between the material and the symbolic, nature and
culture, then we should be surprised neither by current challenges to the
naturalized domain of the modern child, nor by challenges to reigning
notions of culture, the privileged realm of the symbolic.

In a review article on anthropological approaches to national and transnational cultures, Robert Foster argues that what is at stake in theorizing the emergent global order is not only "the prospects for conceptualizing cultural differences in world historical terms," but also "the concept of culture itself." There have been fundamental shifts over the past two decades in the ways anthropologists—and, of course, many others—formulate the concept of culture.

> Questions about social agents and agencies, rather than about the structural logic or functional coherence of normative and symbolic systems, now orient cultural inquiry. More and more often culture is treated as the changing outcome of "practice"—interested activity not reducible to rational calculation. (Foster 1991:235)

More and more often, the work of "making culture"—of producing and reproducing collectively held dispositions and understandings—is taken to be problematic. Culture is conceived as "the site of multiple contests informed by a diversity of historically specific actions and intentions" (Foster 1991:235).

In an article entitled "Invoking Culture: The Messy Side of Cultural Politics" (1992), Virginia Dominguez argues that we should be asking much more contextually specific questions about what is being accomplished socially, politically, and discursively when different notions of culture are invoked by different groups—nation builders, minority populations, local communities, academics—to describe, analyze, argue, justify, and theorize.

Like the modern notion of childhood, culture is an "historically situated discursive object with a particular European origin and Eurocentric history" (Dominguez 1992:22). Dominguez recounts a history of the anthropological concept of culture, wrested from elitist Euro-American culture in the late nineteenth and early twentieth centuries and transformed into pluralized, relativist, organically integrated cultures. In important respects, however, these two notions of culture have persisted side by side, with minority or peripheral populations described holistically and organically, while elite populations retain the term *culture*—as opposed to *politics* or *economy*—to refer to refined, aesthetic, intellectual pursuits, such as literature, dance, theater, and the visual arts.

Western culturalist discourses have come to occupy an increasingly global space. In order to make internationally legitimated claims to political autonomy, subject peoples must frame their resistance in national cultural terms. To be a nation means to have a distinctive cultural identity *and* to have the capacity to produce culture in the aesthetic and intellectual sense. Postcolonial populations are concerned with setting up their own museums, writing their own histories, and celebrating their own cultural traditions. Thus, Dominguez asserts, even when non-European peoples seek to resist Eurocentric constructions of their social worlds and to affirm their own distinctive identities, they must now do so at least partially in terms of a world system language of cultural identity and nationhood.

The past several decades have been marked by an increasing concern, both in anthropology and other disciplines and in state agencies, with "the politics of culture"—almost a catchphrase now, suggesting widespread challenges to the self-evident referentiality of the term culture. Within anthropology, for example, there is increasing concern about the ways a relativist, holistic concept of culture has been bought at the cost of a complex awareness of historical negotiation and conflict at the social frontiers within and between designated cultures.[15]

National ministries of culture are concerned with defining official cultural policies. Although the modernist notion of art (and culture more generally) stresses innovation and a certain degree of deviance, discussions of national cultural policies frequently revolve around what sorts of deviance can be accepted within state-funded cultural projects. Should state funds be given to artists whose work offends general public morality? More generally, what is deemed worthy of social reproduction by national cultural policies aimed at orienting cultural activities in schools and other public arenas?

As representatives of the contested future and subjects of cultural policies, children stand at the crossroads of divergent cultural projects. Their minds and bodies are at stake in debates about the transmission of fundamental cultural values in the schools. The very nature of their senses, language, social networks, worldviews, and material futures are at stake in debates about ethnic purity, national identity, minority self-expression, and self-rule.

In recent years, researchers have "discovered" that children are not empty vessels, waiting to be filled with adult values, but rather active, creative participants in society (see Gullestad 1991). The phrase "children's own culture" is meant to foreground children's agency, as well as to emphasize the importance of other children in the process of socialization.

In some of its manifestations, a notion of children's culture is grounded in a universalizing vision of children as naturally creative, playful, and spontaneous. This perspective is often combined with an archival approach to children's culture: the project for researchers becomes one of collecting children's games, rhymes, and songs—of documenting the manifold content of children's common cultural proclivities.

But the notion of children's culture is also important within less universalizing approaches to the study of young people as social actors in their own right, engaged in making sense of and recreating the social worlds they inherit. As several of the papers in this volume strikingly illustrate, children creatively live from the inside complex mixtures of languages and social domains that are external structures for many adults.

THE PAPERS: ARTICULATIONS AND IMPLICATIONS

In "Recovering Childhood: Children in South African National Reconstruction," Njabulo Ndebele identifies the Soweto riots of 1976 as a decisive historical moment in the erosion of childhood in South Africa. As a final act of protest against the imposition of the Afrikaans language in the schools, large numbers of children took to the streets. For the first time, military representatives of the South African government purposefully pointed their guns at children and fired. This was the beginning of waves of arrests, torture, and "disappearances" of black young people. As level after level of the black political leadership was killed, imprisoned, or driven into exile, younger and younger political activists stepped in to fill the vacuum. Ultimately, the targets of systematic government action were as young as eight years old.

Ndebele describes a society so devastated that it has passed the "threshhold of violence" against children and a state so desperate that "it would not allow even children to take refuge behind their childhood." The devastation of a culture has gone so far, he asserts, that children themselves have become the means of violence against other children. Many of the white soldiers responsible for random killings of black children and bombings of schools and churches are young conscripts, sent to kill their black peers. And black youth and children are killing one another, conflicts that the state represents as timeless ethnic rivalries, but that Ndebele sees as integrally connected to the apartheid system itself.

Ndebele's paper does not address the questions of how a modern notion of the protected space of innocent childhood is related to the colonial legacy or to precolonial notions of childhood.[16] He does suggest an important historical tradition of tales of mistreated and neglected children, who stand as powerful witnesses against society and call for its redemption.[17]

Ndebele takes as given the notion of a protected space of childhood and asks, what are the implications for a society when this space is systematically assaulted and gradually destroyed? "Where can we locate the metaphors of hope? No longer in children, for not only do we kill them, they themselves have killed." The "loss of childhood" means not only the terrible loss of life and widespread suffering of actual children, but also the loss of a social vision of a different mode of human relationship—one represented by an ideal image of childhood as the focus of structured adult protection and compassionate nurturing.

Genuine culture for Ndebele is connected to a "national community," an "all-encompassing nationhood."[18] It demands the recognition and protection of a protected space of childhood and a space for moral reflection, outside the dictates of the market, the realm of politics and struggle, and a global "technological culture."

Ndebele concludes that the most important project for South Africa today, in the throes of transforming a rigid apartheid system, is "the recovery of childhood and innocence," followed by the "recovery" and fundamental "redefinition" of the family, neighborhood, and nation.

Note here the *language* of Ndebele's argument: the notion of a brutal end of childhood and the call for a rediscovery, recovery, and redefinition of childhood—and thus of adulthood and the broader social order as well. While Field's study of children in contemporary Japan seems at first sight far from the world of random killings, brutal violence, and imprisonment of children described by Ndebele, the language used by both authors is strikingly similar. In "The Child as Laborer and Consumer: The Disappearance of Childhood in Contemporary Japan," Field asserts that Japanese children are "losing their childhood" and suffering from the "soft violence of endless labor" as they perform their socially defined tasks in Japanese schools and homes.

Field argues that Japanese childhood is being colonized by a logic of ceaseless production, taking over the school system and extending down to very young children, already being educated to take their place in the world of ceaselessly laboring adults. Many young children regularly attend "cram schools" after regular school. Some stay on for private lessons late into the night, returning home at midnight to do homework, perhaps play an electronic video game (the epitome of "efficient, solitary play"), fall asleep around 2 A.M., and awake early to start over again the next day.

The majority of Japanese children, Field argues, are "pampered hostages," and the violence is taking its toll on their bodies. They are increasingly subject to "adult diseases," such as elevated blood cholesterol levels, ulcers, and high blood pressure.

And not only are children the subjects of this ceaseless "soft violence." They also participate in the discipline and control of other children. Being the victim of bullying is said to be a major factor in "school-refusal syndrome": one morning children awake, seemingly paralyzed and unable to rise to begin another day of childhood labor. This is a children's culture far from the romantic vision emphasized by some child researchers.

Field argues that Japanese children are now bodily at risk in a society far removed from war, hunger, and disease. The state, particularly in the form of a state-controlled education system, plays a crucial mediating role in the relation between children and national and world markets. Respect for traditional Japanese culture ideally motivates people's compliance with the severe demands a centralized, nationalized education system places on children and more generally on families. While fathers are out in the adult marketplace, the burden of making sure children perform their allotted tasks falls to mothers, who, together with their children, constitute what Field calls the "mother-child laboring team." While much in this system is radically new, Field argues that the focus in schools on the presentation of Japanese history and traditions, on the flag and the national anthem, provides seemingly natural (because allegedly traditional) foundations for new forms of control.

Significant for my own argument here is Field's explicit articulation of the form taken by the loss of childhood in Japan with other modes of the late capitalist disintegration of childhood in other contexts. She argues that war and poverty in the Third World are expressions of conflicts engendered by capitalism, while the "normalized war situations" in which poor children live in First World inner cities are another. The suffering of children in prosperous societies like Japan is yet another, integrally related, manifestation of capitalist contradictions.

According to Field, it is a logic of global capitalism, mediated by the nation-state, implemented by the schools, articulated with certain historical values and practices, and legitimized by notions of traditional Japanese culture that propels the contemporary loss of childhood in Japan, a nation presently at the forefront of capitalist expansion. Demands for flexibly specialized workers and compliant national citizens require a complex mix of technical creativity and social conformity, that, Field argues, is the antithesis of the creative, exploratory play associated with modern childhood. While Field is clearly critical of the global dynamic propelling the contemporary loss of childhood in Japan, she also regards as worthy of protection certain dimensions of modern Western, now globalized, childhood.

In "Have You Seen Me? Recovering the Inner Child in Late-Twentieth-Century America," Marilyn Ivy links a growing American concern with missing children and child abuse (preeminently child sexual abuse) to increasingly popular "inner-child" therapies. These therapies are directed toward people suffering from various addictions, because their "inner child" (produced by abusive or neglectful "dysfunctional families") has gone into hiding and is "missing" from everyday adult consciousness. While Ivy is careful not to downplay the seriousness of actual cases of child abduction and abuse, she explores why discourses on missing and abused children have exploded into the national media since the 1970s, roughly the period of the rapid growth of inner-child therapies.

Ivy argues that the proliferation of these discourses signals a sense of threat to older categories of identity, including that of the protected child. Changing formations of capitalist consumer culture are reaching into subjectivity and private life in new ways, and media spectacles and new therapeutic orientations mark these changes, even if in sensationalized and depoliticized ways.

Inner-child therapies speak of the "contamination" of children's worlds by the actions of irresponsible adults and of the "toxic shame" that dysfunctional families generate in children. We might interpret these images of contamination, toxicity, and transgressed boundaries as a sign of an increasing colonization of areas previously marked off as outside the realm of market structures and consumer compulsions. Ivy suggests that one important dimension of late capitalism in middle-class America is a sense of being "missing" in one's everyday life—an incentive to perpetual consumption and addictions (to work, gambling, shopping, drugs) in a futile attempt to recover what is missing within.

Ivy's discussion of inner-child discourses—describing the inner child as lost, missing, abused, abandoned, and in need of recovery, healing, reparenting, and reclaiming—resonates in interesting ways with both Ndebele's and Field's papers. It is fascinating to note that some proponents of inner-child therapies posit that the vast *majority* of Americans now come from dysfunctional families and are living lives of toxic shame. Field writes of the "normalization of dysfunction" of Japanese schoolchildren, while Ndebele describes a South African society in which violence to and by children has become commonplace. I repeat here a question raised earlier: when do deviations from the ideal form of modern childhood come to represent not just differences *within* the structured coherence of a globalized modernity, but signs of the dissolution and reshaping of this system?

I have discussed the papers of Ndebele, Field, and Ivy in some detail to show a striking convergence of themes and language in papers concerned with three very different regions. My concern here is not just to identify convergent discourses, but to suggest that these discourses are linked to articulated changes in children's conditions and experiences around the world.

In "Children's Rights in a Free-Market Culture," Mary John observes, following Ingleby (1985), that whereas in the late nineteenth century, the danger to social order was seen as coming from criminals, mental defectives, and vagabonds, the "new dangerous classes" in Britain now seem to be children. In times of profound social change, state-controlled socialization of the young becomes especially important—and contested. Concerns about improperly socialized and educated children legitimize new state-supported interventions into families and new state-controlled programs in schools—billed as "back-to-basics education" and attacks on "discovery learning." It is possible to read these state interventions as attempts to reform the human capital of children, in the tightened circumstances of a British economy peripheral to European political and economic reorganizations. In such a context, debates about children's rights—for example, to self-expression and children's own cultures—become highly polemical.

Hae-joang Cho's paper, "Children in the Examination War in South Korea," explores the great strains on parents and children occasioned by an examination-oriented education system meant to sort children into stratified slots in adult job and marriage markets. She notes that the current competitive education system has deep roots in Korean, and more generally East Asian, cultural history. Present-day attempts to consolidate state power and modernize the Korean economy draw upon tradition to provide the forms and emotional commitment of devoted mothers and educators involved in what some see as a "holy war" and others describe as "examination hell." Cho describes how Korean mothers have transformed Buddhist rituals in their fervent prayers for their children's success.

Cho notes the centrality of the Korean "mother-child laboring team," described in its Japanese and Indonesian variants by Field and Shiraishi. Changes in childhood occur in relation to restructured women's roles, as the state and the market transform the domestic sphere. The affective force of "traditional family values" is called upon to motivate and legitimize the construction of new sorts of national citizens and capitalist workers.

Saya Shiraishi explores "Children's Stories and the State in New-Order Indonesia." She provides another angle on the ways contemporary nation-states use notions of "traditional culture" in the production of new sorts of national citizens in schools. While Ivy argues that public awareness of current risks to children is depoliticized in the American context by shifting awareness away from the public sphere to the privatized scene of the family and individual in need of therapy, Shiraishi suggests that in Indonesia (and more broadly the Asian region), what happens to children is depoliticized because state-controlled education systems present their programs as the socialization of children into timeless, traditional cultures.

In the Indonesian case, this is an especially formidable project, inasmuch as the new Indonesian nation included over three hundred different ethnic groups and over two hundred and fifty languages. Shiraishi suggests that Indonesian, a commercial lingua franca that is no one's "mother tongue," is a particularly effective language for the mass-produced, state-supported children's stories aimed at creating a homogeneous Indonesian national citizenry. Through stories about "traditional Indonesian families," children are supposed to learn important political lessons about the proper boundaries and relations between desire and duty, the leader and the people, national identity and ethnic difference—without explicitly raising these topics for open discussion. An important part of learning the language of Indonesian nationalism, Shiraishi suggests, is learning cultural values and understandings that must remain embedded in narratives not open to critical discussion, but nevertheless crucial to orienting oneself in relation to the job market, the state bureaucracy, and the censorship system.

In "Children, Population Policy, and the State in Singapore," Vivienne Wee shows how state cultural policies not only enter into the socialization of children, but in some contexts set parameters for the very existence of some groups of children at the expense of others. As Foster (1991:248) notes, "The regulation of procreation through state activity asserts control over not only the definition of social being, but also the physical preconditions of social being." Notions of national culture and the ways various ethnic cultures fit into this national picture, of what sorts of national citizens the state wants to have, underlie Singapore's stringent population policy. Wee shows how these policies are integrally connected to cultural policies in the schools, in relation to minorities and minority languages.

In "'There's a Time to Act English and a Time to Act Indian': The Politics of Identity among British-Sikh Teenagers," Kathleen Hall explores the complex process of identity formation of second-generation Sikh adolescents in northern England. While these young people verbally frame their situation as "moving between two worlds," the Sikh and the English, Hall's ethnographic study of their everyday lives reveals a much more complex movement through an array of cultural fields that transgress boundaries between these two "objectified forms of culture abstracted from the more fluid, ambiguous, and plural processes of cultural production that occur in daily life."

Hall suggests that many Sikh young people construct for themselves spaces of relative freedom, as they move between diverse sites of home, school, shopping arcade, temple, and disco. Hall's paper shows clearly that for many second-generation British-Sikhs, the right to *a* minority cultural identity would not be experienced as unambiguously positive.

Hall reminds us that the social worlds of these young people are not just put at risk by new structures of global capitalism. Their cultural repertoires are also enriched by the possibilities of playing with their identities by combining fashions and music from different cultural traditions.

Hall cites the example of a British-Sikh band that combines traditional Bengali music with Celtic songs, Moroccan pipes, and Indian sitars.

She also stresses, however, that there are structural limits to this creative play within a broader British society that naturalizes cultural differences as timeless and impermeable. Within contemporary Britain, these young people cannot choose to go beyond being Sikh or "black." Nationalist arguments in support of "pure British culture" increasingly construct this national culture as "frozen in time and projected back to a historical past beyond the genealogical reach of Britain's most recent black citizens."

In "Second-Generation Noncitizens: Children of the Turkish Migrant Diaspora in Germany," Ruth Mandel explores the complexity of cultural identities emerging within the multicultural society of contemporary Berlin. Second-generation Turkish youth have been labeled "the lost generation," able to be neither German nor Turkish. This term, "the lost generation," resonates with the lost generation of young black South Africans described by Ndebele. Mandel describes the special case of "disappeared" Kurdish children in Berlin, assumed to be Turkish. Because they are unable to speak the Turkish language, some of them are labeled and tracked as retarded in the school system. They virtually disappear through the cracks of officially structured relations between minority groups and the German state.

German immigration policy identifies Turks as "foreign cocitizens," without rights to full German citizenship—even in the case of children born within Germany, attending German schools, and more at home in German society than they are in their parents' Turkish homelands, which children may know only through pictures and stories or occasional holiday visits. German immigration policy now asserts that "the boat is full": no more immigrants should cross the seas separating distinct world regions and cultural worlds.

But this image of cultures as land masses, clearly separated by wide seas, is belied by the everyday lives of Turkish youth in Germany. Mandel observes that many young Turks in Germany do not want exclusive German or Turkish citizenship but prefer the fluid freedom of moving between. They characterize Turkish repatriation and exclusive citizenship as "having their passports killed." For these young people, like the British-Sikh youth described by Hall, the "right to a cultural identity" is neither possible nor desirable. More important for them is to maintain their Turkish language and social connections, while also having access to the German language and social world.

The papers of Carneiro da Cunha and Stephens deal with complexities of cultural definition for children in indigenous populations. In "Children, Politics, and Culture: The Case of Brazilian Indians," Carneiro da Cunha provides a historical context for discussion of indigenous rights in contemporary Brazil. She traces a movement from an assimilationist model to a model stressing the importance of cultural diversity. But what *sort* of diversity is seen as desirable and how might the "right to cultural difference" bequeathed by the Brazilian government to indigenous groups be used by a Brazilian state trying to improve its position within a new international arena stressing the importance of cultural and biological diversity?

Carneiro da Cunha describes a commodified Brazilian Indian "museum culture" of traditional rituals, customs, language, and clothing deemed acceptably indigenous by the majority Brazilian population. This objectified notion of culture is not accompanied by a notion that indigenous groups should have political self-rule or control over natural resources. Indeed, very often indigenous groups must become complicit in the packaging of their native culture and vocal in asserting their rights to an indigenous cultural identity, in order to lobby politically for rights to natural resources and land, the material conditions of their lives. And this occurs despite the fact that such cultural objectification is alien to indigenous groups who have traditionally lived their cultures in the realm of everyday life, rather than packaged for external display.

Clearly, international cultural-rights discourses are important to groups like Brazilian Indians, who have been the historical objects of assimilationist and at times genocidal state policies. Carneiro da Cunha alerts us, however, to the dangers of conceiving culture as an object or product, amenable to transfer intact from one generation to another. "What we must guarantee for future generations is not the preservation of cultural products, but the capacity for cultural production." What sorts of cultural-rights discourses might be most useful to achieve these aims?

My own paper, "The 'Cultural Fallout' of Chernobyl Radiation in Norwegian Sami Regions: Implications for Children" describes how radioactive fallout poses threats not only to the health and economic well-being of the Sami (the indigenous population of Scandinavia), but also to a distinctive Sami cultural identity, linked in complex ways to the viability of a Chernobyl-threatened reindeer industry. Diverse groups, from Scandinavian state officials to Sami women's groups, are concerned with defining the nature of the Sami culture put at risk by Chernobyl and other incursions into Sami everyday life.

One consequence of Chernobyl has been an increasing objectification of Sami culture—manifested, for example, in intensified work by Sami concerned with mapping traditional Sami cultural sites. Other groups have struggled in the aftermath of Chernobyl to articulate what is distinctively Sami about *everyday* life—for example, the preparation of food or the emotional life of families. Some Sami are concerned about how an increasing emphasis on the protection of an objectified Sami museum culture might diminish children's sense of Sami culture as a living resource for the future, rather than as a codified body of traditions and historical artifacts.

It might be argued that *both* objectified notions of indigenous culture *and* radical deconstructions of these notions can represent risks to children. On the one hand, children may fall victim to naturalized constructions of tradition that constrain and limit their participation in the cultural worlds they are expected to reproduce and develop. On the other hand, they risk losing a sense of historical continuity, social coherence, and cultural identity that are preconditions for developing their own capacities for cultural production. In the case of indigenous populations, the deconstruction of notions of distinctive indigenous identities constitutes significant political risks at an historical moment when these populations, and the environments they inhabit, are under new and intensified threats from states and multinational corporations.[19]

The figure of the child, as *both* inheritor of a constituted culture *and* as participant in the ongoing process of cultural creation, is a focus of Pamela Reynolds's paper, "Youth and the Politics of Culture in South Africa." Reynolds warns against dubbing black South African youth the "lost generation," a phrase that leads us to lose sight of significant cross-generational continuities spanning the periods of colonialism and apartheid and to lose sight as well of the courage and inventiveness of young people.

While Ndebele emphasizes the deterioration of South African culture, Reynolds is concerned with tracing threads of cultural continuity that lead through fragmented families and communities. Though she quotes Adèle Thomas to the effect that through torture and imprisonment these young people lost "not only their freedom, but years of irrecoverable childhood," they themselves are far from a lost generation.

Like Ndebele, Reynolds identifies the Soweto schoolchildren demonstrations and killings as a turning point in the nature of South African childhood and relations between generations. Soweto marked a new phase in the politicization of the young, concerned with changing the external structures of domination in which they found themselves. Where, Reynolds asks, did children find the resources for this activism? She outlines a complex constellation of influences, including older relatives and other individuals whose stories and memories gave children an understanding of their political disinheritance. Young people went on to criticize what they saw as adult complicity or, phrased less harshly, passive endurance of oppression and created the Black Consciousness Movement.

Reynolds is concerned with communicating a sense of tenuous, disrupted, but persistent cultural continuity in the black South African experience. She also emphasizes the significance of children's own culture, as groups of young people weave the diverse threads of their inheritance into new sorts of identities, in some respects building upon the worlds of previous generations, but also troubling, angering, and bewildering them.

In light of the provocative and suggestive perspectives on the loss and transformation of contemporary childhoods presented by authors in this volume, we must now ask, what possibilities currently exist for the recovery and reconstruction of diverse childhood worlds in an emerging late capitalist era?

RECONSTRUCTING CHILDHOOD: THE SERIOUS BUSINESS OF PLAY

These essays represent a range of approaches to the topic of children and the politics of culture. Some essays (for example, Field, Cho, and Wee) explore the lives of children subject to objectified, externally imposed cultural identities. Others (such as Reynolds, John, and Hall) emphasize children as active participants in the process of making culture. Most of the essays suggest childhood is a site of active negotiation about what is given from the outside and what is developed from within. Several essays (most notably Hall and Mandel) emphasize the importance of marginality: moving through the charged spaces between objectified cultures is not necessarily experienced as unambiguously negative, any more than a distinct cultural identity is unambiguously positive.

A theme that runs through most essays is the notion of childhood as a domain of *play*, made possible by existing structures and carrying with it the possibility of moving beyond these structures. This is one of the things at risk in missing childhoods, in the discipline-saturated lives of Japanese schoolchildren or the lives of imprisoned South African children. Play is celebrated in the music and fashions of Sikh adolescents, creatively combining clothing and musical styles from around the world.

Keeping in mind that there is no universal, ahistorical form of play, any more than there is a single common children's culture, we might ask, what is represented by contemporary laments about the loss of the quality of play in children's lives? Play requires some measure of physical safety, or at least the possibility of dangers selectively and voluntarily undertaken. The imagined boundaries of play worlds should not be subject to sudden, violent disruptions from adult society. Play requires some measure of consistent adult guidelines and protection, increasingly difficult to maintain in the straitened circumstances of children in various sorts of "war zones" around the world. Play also requires a certain open-endedness and possibility of surprise—qualities that one might argue are in short supply in the solitary, efficient electronic play of some materially privileged children.

Much of the critical literature on late capitalism asks where notions of alternative futures and social difference are to come from, once the localized cultural assumptions and historical dynamic of capitalist society take on a global range and penetrate into other cultures and relatively noncapitalized domains within. Where is the horizon of difference, at least partially *outside* the restricted rationality of the market and market-driven politics?

Postmodernism is frequently described in terms of "the play of intertextuality" and "language games" seemingly unhampered by material restrictions—but also without a solid or coherent connection to the past or the future. In such a world, it is difficult for play to be taken seriously and to have significant consequences.

We might see play as active exploration of imagined environments, built up in the spaces of existing social life. In this light, play is the ground of a notion of culture as living resource, rather than objectified product. The challenge for those concerned with formulating cultural-rights discourses is to develop legal structures strong enough to protect childhood and cultural differences as foundations for "deep play," but flexible and subtle enough to guard against the objectification and commodification of these alternative social worlds within an emerging regime of flexible accumulation—for example, in the commodification of children's games and toys and in the marketing of play, in the form of leisure-time goods and activities and exotic cultural experiences, to adults.

This is what I think Ndebele and Field mean when they talk about the need to "recover" or "redefine" childhood, the domain of play, within contemporary society, a project that also requires a reconstruction of adulthood as the domain of responsible frames for this play.[20] At stake here is a vision of a society concerned with protecting possibilities within itself for significant challenges to a system that takes complex and heavy tolls on the lives of both children and adults.[21]

The project of reconstructing modern childhood and adulthood should not be confused with a backward-looking recovery or return to bounded modern childhoods and bounded, exclusive cultural identities. Recall, for example, that Ariès (1962:407) lamented the advent of modern childhood as a sign of a rupture in the fabric of medieval social life, insofar as modern childhood is integrally connected to the modern reign of individualism, the isolation of nuclear families, and the fragmentation of local communities.

While an uncritical vision of the self-evident value of modern child-hood or of distinctive, exclusive cultural identities should be challenged, it is also important to create a political and legal framework for protecting certain dimensions of childhood and cultural difference in an era of global capitalism. The question to be explored now is the place of international rights discourses in this project.

RIGHTS AND RISKS

In the 1948 United Nations Declaration of Human Rights, there is no specific reference to children (or to women). The foundation for a global standard for children's rights was laid down in 1959, when the UN General Assembly adopted the Declaration of the Rights of the Child. The Declaration specified a series of rights for children, separate from and in addition to the rights of adults, that were phrased largely as general moral entitlements, for example, the "right to love and understanding." Child welfare was identified with protection of the family, with no sense of the dangers to children that modern family life itself might pose. The Declaration was aimed at protecting and nurturing childhood, as defined by adults within the framework of Western modernity. It did not recognize that there might be cultural differences in what constitutes children's "best interests," or that children themselves might have something important to say about the nature of these interests (Boyden 1990).

The debate on children's rights will be dominated in the foreseeable future by the UN Convention on the Rights of the Child, adopted by the General Assembly in 1989 (and reprinted as an appendix to this volume). While the family is still privileged as the ideal protective frame for children's well-being, the Convention also acknowledges that many children live outside families in situations of war and abandonment, and that children should also be protected against abuse and neglect *within* families. Unlike the 1959 Declaration, the Convention is not just a general statement of good intent but is considered legally binding for ratifying states. An independent Committee on the Rights of the Child has been set up by the UN to make periodic assessments of states' compliance with the Convention.

One of the qualitatively new aspects of the Convention is an emphasis on the capacity of children to act at least partially independently of adults. Thus, the Convention lays down rights, such as children's rights to freedom of expression and association, that are not just protective, but also enabling (Cantwell 1989).

The Convention has elicited tremendous international interest and support, as evidenced by the unprecedented rate at which states have become parties to it. (With respect to papers in this volume, it is significant that the United States and Singapore are among the states that have not signed or ratified the Convention.) The Convention has been hailed by children's advocacy groups, elicited policy commitments from UNICEF and other international agencies, and prompted numerous conferences dedicated to implementing the Convention's objectives.

In light of the above argument about new sorts of risks to children and the domain of childhood associated with an historical transition to late capitalism/postmodernism, we might well ask, why the intense concern with a legally binding, universal declaration of children's rights just *now*? A possible answer is that rights are articulated with risks. As domains of "nature" previously taken for granted, such as children, animals, and the physical environment, come under increasingly visible threats from society, there are corresponding moves to assert their rights.[22] Spaces threatened with dissolution in everyday life must be protected by codified bodies of law.

This is an all-too-familiar story in relation to "primitive" societies. The colonial argument can be phrased in the following way: we take away and colonize your primordial spaces and then give you in return goods and rights, including the right to remake yourselves in our image. Some critics of the Convention argue, along similar lines, that its declaration of universal children's rights gives children the right to be remade in the image of adults and non-Western childhoods the right to be remade in Western forms.

Boyden (1990:208) asks whether the "move to set global standards for childhood and common policies for child welfare may be far from the enlightened step anticipated by its proponents." Fyfe (1989) claims that the majority of countries in the South voiced criticisms of the predominantly Western notions of normal childhood and child development underlying the Convention. This led, for example, to proposals for an African charter of children's rights to address social and cultural circumstances specific to the region, such as apartheid, violence and the family, and armed conflict (Newman-Black 1989).

To what extent does the UN Convention, in the name of universal children's rights, actually assert *one* dominant cultural historical framework as the matrix for subordinate "cultural minorities"? Consider, for example, the language of the rights of *the child*, rather than the rights of *children*. The Convention phrasing suggests a universal, free-standing, individual child. This is a child, moreover, on a particular developmental trajectory. Article 29 asserts the child's right to education furthering "the development of the child's personality, talents and mental and physical abilities to their fullest potential."

Just as the Convention relies on a naturalized and individualized vision of the child, so also does it imply that biologically based relations between parents and children are more fundamental and natural than other sorts of family relations. The preamble describes the family as "the fundamental group of society and the natural environment for the growth and well-being of all its members." As Ivy notes in her paper, such a notion constitutes as deviant many other family forms, such as extended, mobile African American kin networks and communities, single-parent households, lesbian and gay families, multigenerational families, and non-kinship-based households.[23]

One aim of the Convention is to limit and regulate child labor, while also promoting education. Article 28 affirms the child's right to free education, with a view to eliminating "ignorance and illiteracy throughout the world and facilitating access to scientific and technical knowledge and modern teaching methods"—an affirmation that calls into question the value of orally transmitted local values.

The Convention also implicitly calls into question the value of social worlds in which children's lives are not clearly separated from adult spheres of work. One important motivation behind the Convention's aim to limit and regulate child labor is recognition of the exploitative and dangerous work conditions of many children in a global era of flexible accumulation and unequal geopolitical development. The Convention calls attention to the special needs of developing countries for child labor laws and national education systems. Several papers in this volume—most dramatically those of Cho and Field—warn us of the ways nationally controlled compulsory-education systems may constitute a new and taxing form of hidden labor for children. In this light, we might well ask critical questions about the sort of modern futures that the UN Convention holds out as natural rights to children in developing countries.

THE CHILD'S RIGHT TO A CULTURAL IDENTITY

If we turn now to an explicit discussion of the child's right to a cultural identity, we find that a primary aim of the Convention is to promote the child's ability "to live an individual life in society . . . taking due account of the importance of the traditions and cultural values of each people for the protection and harmonious development of the child" (preamble). It might be argued, then, that the culture to which the child has *primary* rights is the international culture of modernity, the unmarked, taken-for-granted background to more specialized cultural rights.

It is interesting to note the phrasing of Article 8, which asserts the "right of the child to preserve his or her identity, including nationality, name and family relations as recognized by law." Note here that culture—as a meaningful framework for personal identity, family relations and a sense of belonging to a larger collectivity—is not even mentioned as a central "element of identity" for most children.[24]

The term *culture* is used in several different ways in the Convention. Insofar as it applies to *all* children, it refers to a domain of aesthetic, expressive, symbolic activity. Article 31 affirms: "States Parties recognize the right of the child to rest and leisure, to engage in play and recreational activities appropriate to the age of the child and to participate freely in cultural life and the arts." Article 23, asserting the special rights of handicapped children, states that States Parties should aim to develop the child's "fullest possible social integration and individual development, including his or her cultural and spiritual development."

It is only with regard to children in recognized "indigenous and minority cultures" that the term culture is used holistically to describe an alternative social world. Article 30 asserts: "In those States in which ethnic, religious or linguistic minorities or persons of indigenous origin exist, a child belonging to such a minority or who is indigenous shall not be denied the right, in community with other members of his or her group, to enjoy his or her own culture, to profess and practise his or her own religion, or to use his or her own language."

It is important to note what this notion of culture has in common with the universal notion of culture as a special symbolic domain. Both emphasize culture as the realm of symbols, language, values, and beliefs. Thus, a child's right to a cultural identity is built on liberal democratic principles of tolerance for diverse views and freedom of self-expression. Such principles are far from antithetical to, and may indeed support, certain kinds of national-culture programs and forms of capitalist expansion. Both Carneiro da Cunha and Stephens suggest that there are important senses in which protection of a child's right to an indigenous cultural identity may require radical and extensive political and economic changes that extend far beyond the domain of culture, conceived as a realm of symbols, rituals, and markers of identity. For example, such changes may include resource development and environmental policies that do not threaten an indigenous population's means of livelihood and the grounds of a distinctive cultural vision of the relation between nature and human beings.

Article 20 affirms that when states are considering alternatives to parental care, "due regard shall be paid to the desirability of continuity in a child's upbringing and to the child's ethnic, religious, cultural and linguistic background." This article has been used to argue against the widespread practice of international adoption. It is significant, however, that the Convention does not address the global political economic inequalities that lead to intercountry adoptions (as well as demographic shifts associated with international movements of labor), though these inequalities threaten children's rights to cultural identities in cases that include, but are not limited to, designated "indigenous and minority cultures."

The primacy of an implicit international modernist vision, legislatively framed within a national context, is, of course, not surprising in a United Nations document. Boyden (1990:194) observes that the UN is "the supreme mediator of the principle of liberal democratic rule globally," with a "strong interest in spreading to the poor countries of the South the values and codes of practice devised in the public sector of the industrialized North." Insofar as the contractual obligation to uphold children's rights lies with the state as signatory to international treaties, it is to be expected that states would not endorse a document that calls for radical political and economic transformations in relation to minority and indigenous groups or to dominant geopolitical structures.

The Convention argues that the child has first and foremost a right to international modernist culture (unmarked, but implicit in the document's framing principles), then to identity (conceived in individual, familial, and national terms), and finally, in special cases, to minority and indigenous cultures. A few passages make explicit the claim that when conflicts between these different constructions of identity arise, the universal modern form shall prevail. Thus, Article 24 argues that "States Parties shall take all effective and appropriate measures with a view to abolishing traditional practices prejudicial to the health of children"—as assessed from a Western biomedical perspective. In connection with a child's right to free access to information, the mass media should be encouraged "to have particular regard to the linguistic needs of the child who belongs to a minority group or who is indigenous"—that is, the child's native language should be used to promote modern education and the unrestricted global transmission of "information."

RETHINKING THE NATURE OF
CHILDREN'S RIGHTS CLAIMS

As Veena Das noted in our Bergen discussions, there are important senses in which "the technology of universal human rights may become a means of sanctioning cultural authoritarianism." Lejeune (quoted in Boyden 1990:197) voices an especially strong form of this criticism, arguing that the UN Convention on the Rights of the Child "can only apply to a geo-political area in which the same attitudes to law, the same political system and compatible cultural traditions are firmly rooted."

But in light of the cultural and historical perspective elaborated in this introduction, we might call into question the assumption that there exist clearly distinct cultural regions, each constructing childhood and conditions for the lives of children in their own right. Where, we might ask, do we find regions free of influence from global modernity and the processes of global capitalism or regions free from the processes that are currently reshaping these constructions? This is not to argue that there are not profoundly important regional and local cultural differences, but we must also not lose sight of the ways that these are—and will likely increasingly come to be—globally articulated.

The choice here, it seems to me, is not between cultural relativism and universalism, or between a wholesale rejection and an uncritical celebration of international-rights discourses. Despite the important criticisms that can be made of universal children's rights discourses, there are certainly situations where legally binding international agreements can be seen to be in children's and, more broadly, in society's best interests. This is most clear in situations where children are in immediate physical danger, for example, as objects of official genocidal policies, torture, and imprisonment. It is also important in cases where states conspire in the oppression of ethnic or religious groups or stand behind radical assimilationist policies that would deny children the stable social environments and coherent linguistic and symbolic contexts that, I would argue, should be the preconditions of childhood everywhere.

As the essays in this volume make abundantly clear, there are many other situations where universalizing modernist discourses on children's rights are more problematic and may actually be brought into service to legitimate situations that constitute new sorts of risks to children. The aim of this introduction is not to undermine international-rights discourses, but to make them both more powerful and more flexible. This requires using documents like the UN Convention on the Rights of the Child critically and strategically. It requires rethinking the nature of children's rights claims; disabusing them of their aura of timelessness, absoluteness, universality, and naturalness; and developing these claims as legal tools in the project of protecting and reconstructing spaces of childhood and adulthood in a time of far-reaching local and global change and uncertainty.

In focusing on children and the politics of culture in diverse ethnographic situations, the authors in this volume have made an important contribution to the ongoing development of children's rights discourses, aimed not at inflexible definitions of "the child's cultural identity" or of "children's own culture," but at the provision of material and social environments and legal frameworks for children's "deep play" and cultural invention. In so doing, these authors have also contributed to an understanding of current challenges to the structured coherence, or articulated coherences, of modernity, and to an expanded vision of the risks—and social possibilities—these challenges imply.

NOTES

1. Important insights into modern gender constructions can be found in Mosse 1985; Enloe 1989; Parker et al. 1992; and Butler and Scott 1992.

2. Crucial foundations for this work include Donzelot 1979; Kessel and Siegel 1983; Steedman et al. 1985; Richards and Light 1986; and James and Prout 1990.

3. In "The End of the Body," for example, Emily Martin (1992) asks why the body has become the focus of such intense social and cultural attention today. Following Lévi-Strauss (1973 [1955]), Martin suggests that phenomena become the focus of attention in the academy when they are in the process of ending. While Lévi-Strauss was speaking of "the primitive," a world disappearing with the development of global modernity, Martin suggests that one of the reasons so many researchers are energetically studying the body today is because "we are undergoing fundamental changes in how our bodies are organized and experienced" (121). Some have claimed that under the impact of commodification and social fragmentation we are witnessing the end of the body as a coherently bounded social entity. Martin argues that "we are seeing not the end of the body, but rather the end of one kind of body and the beginning of another kind": "people in the United States (and perhaps elsewhere) are now experiencing a dramatic transition in body percept and practice, from bodies suited for and conceived in the terms of the era of Fordist mass production to bodies suited for and conceived in the terms of the era of flexible accumulation." My own perspectives on the current "end of modern childhood" have been profoundly influenced by Martin's important work. (See also Martin 1994.)

4. There is, of course, a long history of social scientific research exploring interpenetrations between domains of the market economy, artistic practices, religious beliefs, the family and everyday life, in contrast to popular conceptions of "art for art's sake" or of the family as a bounded "haven in a heartless world." I would argue, however, that in the past several decades an explosion of works on the politics of virtually every social domain represents a more radical perspective on the constructedness of social domains than was evident in mainstream social scientific writing in the 1950s and 1960s.

5. Per Olav Tiller has suggested to me that the tendency in academic circles, following Ariès, to see childhood as a historically unique discursive phenomenon, existing only within its own socially and historically limited regime of truth, can itself be interpreted as a new sort of risk to children and to society as a whole. This claim can be used to dismiss or undermine the legitimacy of per-

spectives and values critical of dominant market-driven and politically instrumental practices and beliefs. Children's bodies and minds are thus laid bare as flexible "national resources" and "human capital" to be reshaped, without resistance, as changing economic and political circumstances dictate.

6. It might be argued that hostility to children begins even before their birth. The March of Dimes, an American national foundation focusing on maternal- and child-health issues, has concluded that battering of women during pregnancy causes more birth defects than all the diseases put together for which children are usually immunized (Gibbs 1993b:42).

7. I am grateful to Marianne Gullestad for suggesting the relevance of Douglas's work for the understanding of popular notions of street children.

8. Darcy Ribeiro, a Brazilian senator and anthropologist (cited in Larmer and Margolis 1992:17), observes that ten years of economic crisis and two decades of dictatorship are insufficient grounds for explaining how so many Brazilians have come to accept the idea that large groups of young people are to be treated as disposable goods, or for explaining the nature and level of violence against street children. Such violence and neglect need to be understood in the broader context of systemic violence to children. "While 1,000 children were murdered in 1991 [the official number of murdered street children—the actual number is certainly much higher], more than 150,000 Brazilian infants died before their first birthday from lack of proper nutrition, sanitation and health care."

9. In May 1994, the Norwegian Centre for Child Research hosted an international, interdisciplinary conference on the topic "Children and Nationalism" in Trondheim, Norway, which will eventually result in an edited collection of articles (Stephens, ed.).

10. Foucault's *Discipline and Punish* (1977) has already become a classic exploration of the links between the development of the modern school, the juvenile-welfare system, and the modern penal system.

11. See Partha Chatterjee (1989) for an important discussion of "colonialism, nationalism and colonized women" in the case of India.

12. A discussion of various perspectives on the theoretical framing of late capitalism or postmodernism and of contributions to this project that might come out of the ethnographically grounded field of social-cultural anthropology are the subject of my manuscript in progress, provisionally entitled *Postmodern Anthropology: A Question of Difference* (n.d.).

13. The designations First and Third World, North and South are, of course, only rough markers of geopolitical inequalities and are themselves increasingly problematic in an era of global capitalism, involving fundamental shifts and reconfigurations in national and world regional structures.

14. Katz's research (1991, 1994) focuses on processes of global economic restructuring and other forces of globalization that have drastically changed the everyday environments and future possibilities of children in settings as different as New York City and rural Sudan (as "locals" of the First and Third Worlds), creating rents and tears in what she terms the "ecologies of childhood" that are in many respects strikingly similar. Katz's work is a good example of how child research informed by political-economic perspectives challenges dominant assumptions in both these fields. Her research illuminates incommensurable mi-

crosituations of children's everyday lives, as well as structured, global connections among these particular sites.

15. See Clifford 1988; Appadurai 1990; Gilroy 1987; Hannerz 1989; and Moore 1989.

16. Ndebele's intended audience and aims are important to mention here. His paper is a revised version of a plenary address presented at the "Children at Risk" conference (with over six hundred international participants), where he was appealing to a largely Western audience in a Western context using a Western concept of childhood. Participants in the invited session "Children and the Politics of Culture" agreed that Ndebele's paper resonated in such powerful ways with our own discussions that we invited him to include his paper in this volume.

17. These stories suggest biblical motifs of wronged innocence and redemption and might be usefully considered in relation to Jean Comaroff's study (1985) of the ways black Christian churches in South Africa represent *both* the colonial legacy *and* a powerful source of metaphors and rituals for criticizing and resisting oppression.

18. It is interesting, in light of the earlier discussion on the contemporary politics of culture, that Ndebele has chosen a national idiom for his reflections on "genuine culture."

19. Note here the parallel to Tiller's misgivings (described in note 5) about radical deconstructions of childhood.

20. It is perhaps worth noting here that there are many different ways in which papers in this volume might be read, both singly and in relation to one another. My aim in this introduction has been to draw several threads through the papers and to explore the patterns that emerge.

21. Two stories have recently taken center stage in international news. I would interpret the massive public concern and media attention surrounding these cases as signs of wide-ranging concern about the nature of childhood and adulthood today, and about what encroachments on these domains mean for society as a whole.

First, the story of a Chicago couple who left two children, ages four and nine, home alone while the parents went to Mexico for a two-week Christmas vacation has triggered a proliferation of stories, many with tragic endings, about children left unattended. "The rash of deaths underscores once more that an increasing number of parents in the U.S., through economic hardship or simple irresponsibility, are unable or unwilling to get reliable child care. In December the police were conducting an investigation into whether the parents [of 7 unattended children, the oldest 9 years old, who died in a house fire in Detroit] should be charged with neglect or involuntary manslaughter" (Gibbs 1993a:11).

Second, in Britain, a two-year-old child was picked up in a shopping center and brutally murdered, apparently by two young boys. "The case offers horrific proof that Britain's restless and rootless youth, said former Home Secretary Kenneth Baker, live in a 'moral vacuum.' At week's end police charged two ten-year-old boys with abduction and murder" ("In a 'Moral Vacuum'" 1993:13).

22. See, for example, Singer 1975; Regan 1983; Jasper and Nelkin 1992; and

Nash 1989. I am grateful to Seung-Hoon Song for these useful references on animal rights and rights of nature.

23. Article 5 tempers the nuclear family emphasis of the preamble: "States Parties shall respect the responsibilities, rights and duties of parents or, where applicable, the members of the extended family or community as provided for by local custom, legal guardians or other persons legally responsible for the child."

24. In our Bergen discussions, Pamela Reynolds questioned the Convention's assertion that "the child . . . shall have the right from birth to a name." In Tongan society, she noted, individuals acquire a series of names to mark important changes in social status as they move through their life course. The use of different names in particular contexts foregrounds different sorts of relations between human beings. The assertion that the child has a right to a (singular) name strikes at the heart of this social order, just as the assertion of the child's right to a (singular) national identity undermines the emerging culture of German-Turkish young people who fear "having their passports killed" and being restricted to a single national identity.

REFERENCES

Allsebrook, A. and A. Swift, 1989, *Broken Promise: The World of Endangered Children*, London, Hodder and Stoughton.

Anderson, Benedict, 1983, *Imagined Communities: Reflections on the Origin and Spread of Nationalism*, London, Verso.

Appadurai, Arjun, 1990, "Disjuncture and Difference in the Global Cultural Economy," *Public Culture* 2(2):1–24.

Ariès, Philippe, 1962, *Centuries of Childhood*, trans. Robert Baldick, London, Jonathan Cape.

Barrett, Michele and Mary McIntosh, 1982, *The Anti-Social Family*, London, Verso.

Bell, Daniel, 1974, *The Coming of Post-Industrial Society: A Venture in Social Forecasting*, London, Heinemann.

Boyden, Jo, 1990, "Childhood and the Policy Makers: A Comparative Perspective on the Globalization of Childhood," in Allison James and Alan Prout, eds., *Constructing and Reconstructing Childhood*, London, Falmer Press, 184–216.

Butler, Judith and Joan W. Scott, eds., 1992, *Feminists Theorize the Political*, Routledge, New York.

Cantwell, N., 1989, "A Tool for the Implementation of the UN Convention," in Radda Barnen, ed., *Making Reality of Children's Rights*, International Conference on the Rights of the Child, 36–41.

Chatterjee, Partha, 1989, "Colonialism, Nationalism, and Colonialized Women: The Contest in India," *American Ethnologist* 16 (4): 622–633.

Clifford, James, 1988, *The Predicament of Culture: Twentieth Century Ethnography, Literature, and Art*, Cambridge, Mass., Harvard University Press.

Coles, Robert, 1986, *The Political Life of Children*, Boston, Atlantic Monthly Press.

Comaroff, Jean, 1985, *Body of Power, Spirit of Resistance: The Culture and History of a South African People*, Chicago, University of Chicago Press.

Comaroff, Jean and John Comaroff, 1991, "Africa Observed: Discourses of the Imperial Imagination," in Comaroff and Comaroff, eds., *Of Revelation and Revolution: Christianity, Colonialism, and Consciousness in South Africa*, vol. 1, Chicago, University of Chicago Press, 86–126.

de Alwis, Mala, 1991, "Seductive Scripts and Subversive Practices: 'Motherhood,' Nationalism, and the State in Sri Lanka," proposal for doctoral dissertation research, Department of Anthropology, University of Chicago.

DeMause, Lloyd, ed., 1976, *The History of Childhood*, London, Souvenir Press.

Dominguez, Virginia R., 1992, "Invoking Culture: The Messy Side of 'Cultural Politics,'" *South Atlantic Quarterly* 91 (1): 20–41.

Donzelot, Jacques, 1980, *The Policing of Families*, London, Hutchinson.

Douglas, Mary, 1985 [1966], *Purity and Danger: An Analysis of the Concepts of Pollution and Taboo*, London, Ark Paperbacks.

Enloe, Cynthia, 1989, *Bananas, Beaches, and Bases: Making Feminist Sense of International Politics*, Berkeley and Los Angeles, University of California Press.

Ennew, Judith, 1986, *The Sexual Exploitation of Children*, Cambridge, Polity Press.

Epstein, Julia and Kristina Straub, 1991, *Body Guards: The Cultural Politics of Gender Ambiguity*, Routledge, New York.

Fisher, Marc, 1992, "If Bonn Spares Rod, Will it Spoil the Child?", International Herald Tribune, December 3, p. 1 (cont. p. 4).

Foster, Robert J., 1991, "Making National Cultures in the Global Ecumene," *Annual Review of Anthropology* 20:235–60.

Foucault, Michel, 1977, *Discipline and Punish*, London, Allen Lane.

Franklin, B., ed., 1986, *The Rights of Children*, Oxford, Basil Blackwell.

Freeman, Michael D.A., 1983, *The Rights and Wrongs of Children*, London, Francis Pinter Publishers.

Fyfe, Alec, 1989, *Child Labour*, Cambridge, Polity Press.

George, Susan, 1989, *A Fate Worse Than Debt*, Harmondsworth, Penguin Books.

Garbarino, James, Nancy Dubrow, Kathleen Kostelny, and Carole Pardo, 1992, *Children in Danger: Coping with the Consequences of Community Violence*, San Francisco, Jossey-Bass Publishers.

Gibbs, Nancy, 1993a, "Home Alone, Dead: As Two Tragedies Testify, Unattended Children Are a National Problem," *Time*, 1 March, 11.

———, 1993b, "'Til Death Do Us Part," *Time* January 25, 42–44.

Gilmour, A., 1988, *Innocent Victims*, Michael Joseph.

Gilroy, Paul, 1987, *There Ain't No Black in the Union Jack*, London, Unwin Hyman.

Gullestad, Marianne, 1991, "Barnas egen kultur—finnes den? Tanker om barns aktive samfunnsdeltakelse" (Children's own culture—can it be found? Thoughts about children's active participation in society) *Samtiden* 4:41–49.

Habermas, Jürgen, 1987, *The Theory of Communicative Action*, trans. Thomas McCarthy, vol. 2, London, Heinemann.

Hanawalt, Barbara A., 1993, *Growing Up in Medieval London: The Experience of Childhood in History*, Oxford, Oxford University Press.

Hannerz, Ulf, 1989, "Notes on the Global Ecumene," *Public Culture* 1(2):66–75.

Harvey, David, 1985, *Consciousness and the Urban Experience*, Baltimore, Johns Hopkins University Press.

————1989, *The Condition of Postmodernity: An Enquiry into the Origins of Cultural Change*, Oxford, Basil Blackwell.

Henriques, J., 1986, "Where Little Children Suffer," *Observer Colour Supplement Special Report*, 24 June.

Holt, John, 1975, *Escape from Childhood*, Harmondsworth, Penguin.

"In a 'Moral Vacuum': Britain Agonizes over the Murder of a Child—Perhaps by Other Children," 1993, *Time*, 1 March, 13.

Ingleby, D., 1985, "Professionals as Socializers: The 'Psy Complex,'" in S. Spitzer and A. T. Scull, eds., *Research in the Law, Deviance, and Social Control: A Research Annual*, vol. 7, London, JAI Press.

James, Allison and Alan Prout, eds., 1990, *Constructing and Reconstructing Childhood: Contemporary Issues in the Sociological Study of Childhood*, London, Falmer Press.

Jasper, James M. and Dorothy Nelkin, 1992, *The Animal Rights Crusade: The Growth of a Moral Protest*, New York, Free Press.

Katz, Cindi, 1994, "The Textures of Global Change: Eroding Ecologies of Childhood in New York and Sudan," in Sharon Stephens, ed., *Children and Environment: Local Worlds and Global Connections*, special issue of *Childhood*, vol. 1, No. 1–2, 103–110.

————, 1991, "Sow What You Know: The Struggle for Social Reproduction in Rural Sudan," *Annals of American Geographers* 81(3): 488–514.

Kessel, F. S. and A. W. Siegel, eds., 1983, *The Child and Other Cultural Inventions*, New York, Praeger.

Kotlowitz, Alex, 1991, *There Are No Children Here: The Story of Two Boys Growing Up in the Other America*, New York, Doubleday.

Larmer, Brook and Mac Margolis, 1992, "The Dead End Kids: Who Is Killing Brazil's Street Children?" *Newsweek*, 25 May, 12–19.

Lash, Scott and John Urry, 1987, *The End of Organised Capitalism*, London, Oxford University Press.

Lévi-Strauss, Claude 1973 [1955], New York, Atheneum. *Tristes Tropiques*, trans. John Weightman and Doreen Weightman.

Mandel, Ernest, 1975, *Late Capitalism*, Verso, London.

Martin, Emily, 1992, "The End of the Body?" *American Ethnologist* 19(1):121–41.

————, 1994, *Flexible Bodies: Tracking Immunity in American Culture—from the Days of Polio to the Age of AIDS*, Boston, Beacon Press.

Moore, Sally Falk, 1989, "The Production of Cultural Pluralism as a Process," *Public Culture* 1(2):26–48.

Mosse, George L., 1985, *Nationalism and Sexuality: Respectability and Abnormal Sexuality in Modern Europe*, New York, Howard Freitag.

Nash, Roderick F., 1989, *The Rights of Nature: A History of Environmental Ethics*, Madison, University of Wisconsin Press.

Newman-Black, M., 1989, "How Can the Convention Be Implemented in Developing Countries?" in Report from Radda Barnen, UNICEF seminar on the UN Draft Convention on the Rights of the Child, Stockholm, October, 36–41.

Parker, Andrew, Mary Russo, Doris Sommer, and Patricia Yaeger, eds., 1992, *Nationalisms and Sexualities*, New York, Routledge.

Phillips, M., 1912, "The School as a Means of Social Betterment," in Whitehouse, J. H., ed., *The Problems of Boy Life*, London, King, 206–27.

Postman, Neil, 1982, *The Disappearance of Childhood*, New York, Delacorte Press.

Postone, Moishe, 1993, *Time, Labor, and Social Domination: A Reinterpretation of Marx's Critical Theory*, Cambridge, Cambridge University Press.

Prout, Alan and Allison James, 1990, "A New Paradigm for the Sociology of Childhood? Provenance, Promise, and Problems," in James and Prout, eds., 1990, *Constructing and Reconstructing Childhood*, London, Falmer Press, 7–35.

"The Question Rio Forgets," 1992, *Economist*, May 30, 11–12.

Qvortrup, Jens, 1985, "Placing Children in the Division of Labour," in Paul Close and Rosemary Collins, eds., *Family and Economy in Modern Society*, London, Macmillan, 129–45.

Regan, Tom, 1983, *The Case for Animal Rights*, Berkeley and Los Angeles, University of California Press.

Richards, Martin and Light, Paul, eds., 1986, *Children of Social Worlds: Development in a Social Context*, Cambridge, Polity Press.

Scheper-Hughes, Nancy, 1989, *Child Survival: Anthropological Perspectives on the Treatment and Maltreatment of Children*, Dordrecht, Reidel.

Singer, Peter, 1990 [1975], *Animal Liberation*, New York, Avon Books.

Sommerville, C. John, 1982, *The Rise and Fall of Childhood*, Beverly Hills, Calif., Sage Publications.

Steedman, Carolyn, Cathy Urwin and Valerie Walkerdine, eds., 1985, *Language, Gender, and Childhood*, London, Routledge and Kegan Paul.

Stephens, Sharon, 1992, "Children and the UN Conference on Environment and Development: Participants and Media Symbols," *Barn/Research on Children in Norway* 2–3:44–52.

———, 1993, "Children at Risk: Constructing Social Problems and Policies," *Childhood* 1(4):246–51.

———, 1994, "Children and Environment: Local Worlds and Global Connections," in Stephens, Sharon, ed., special issue of *Childhood* on "Children and Environment," 1(1–2):1–21.

Stephens, Sharon, n.d., *Postmodern Anthropology: A Question of Difference*, book manuscript.

Vittachi, Anuradha, 1989, *Stolen Childhood: In Search of the Rights of the Child*, Cambridge, Polity Press.

Winn, Marie, 1984, *Children without Childhood*, Harmondsworth, Penguin.

Zelizer, Viviana A., 1985, *Pricing the Priceless Child: The Changing Social Value of Children*, New York, Basic Books.

Part One

CHILDREN AND CHILDHOODS AT RISK IN
THE "NEW WORLD ORDER"

CHAPTER 1

The Child as Laborer and Consumer: The Disappearance of Childhood in Contemporary Japan

NORMA FIELD

> When my mother died I was very young,
> And my father sold me while yet my tongue
> Could scarcely cry " 'weep! 'weep! 'weep! 'weep!"
> So your chimneys I sweep, and in soot I sleep.
> (*William Blake, "The Chimney Sweeper"*)

> Didn't get enough sleep last night,
> same as every other night;
> I'm gonna getta a headache. . . .
> Sleep, sleep, sleep, sleep, sleep
> not enough sleep
> (*"Not Enough Sleep"*)[1]

IN HIS MAGISTERIALLY DOCUMENTED STUDY (1962), Philippe Ariès showed childhood to be a historically specific institution and located its secure establishment in Europe in the seventeenth century. The consequent insight that "childhood is a social artifact, not a biological necessity" (Postman 1982:143), with all due qualifications about the biological aspects of psychological as well as physical development, has made possible the conceptualization (beyond the impressionistic bewailing) of the erosion of this institution in our own day. Two influential works of the past decade diagnosed this process in the United States: Marie Winn's *Children without Childhood* (1981) and Neil Postman's *The Disappearance of Childhood* (1982). More recently, Alex Kotlowitz's stark report in *There Are No Children Here: The Story of Two Boys Growing Up in the Other America* (1991), precisely by not purporting to account for American childhood in general, both complements and critiques Winn's and Postman's analyses. My paper is about the ongoing disappearance of childhood in Japan, a society seemingly having little in common with either the suburban domain implicitly constituting the America of

Winn's and Postman's analyses or the Chicago public-housing ghetto in Kotlowitz, but one that is necessarily driven by some of the same global forces. I will begin by situating my sense of the disappearance of childhood in Japan in relation to these works.

"There are no children" in the world Kotlowitz observed with sensitive integrity because children inhabiting the ghettos of major American cities today are *normally* faced with life-threatening psychological as well as physical forces. It makes grim sense that the mother on welfare in Kotlowitz's book should invest in funeral insurance for two of her sons just on the brink of adolescence and that the boys themselves should be skeptical as to whether they will live to see eighteen. This form of eroded childhood bears the burdens of the Third World as well as of the American suburb and the surviving urban middle class.

Marie Winn's chapter titles, such as "Out-of-Control Parents," "The New Equality," "The End of Secrecy," "The End of Marriage," and "The End of Repression," suggest her explanations for the destruction of the classical American childhood. Many of the conditions—the prominence of television and video games, the loss of sexual innocence, marital discord—describe both the American ghetto and urban Japan, but schooling is conspicuous by its absence in Winn's account.

By contrast, the educational process is prominent in Postman's, which shares much of the thrust and the details of Winn's analysis, but is freer of its moralizing, voluntaristic tone precisely to the degree that it is more historically and politically lucid. For Postman, the "maintenance of childhood depended on the principles of managed information and sequential learning" characteristic of a literate society (1982:72). The slow and demanding process of becoming literate guaranteed distinctions between children and adults, guaranteed that the latter would have kinds of knowledge that we call secrets—the *sine qua non* of childhood—revealed to the former only as they were deemed able to assimilate such knowledge. For the institution of childhood, this is as critical a form of protection as the physical protection of the small and the weak that the young in Kotlowitz's world and in other places and times of danger and deprivation are robbed of. The form of protection embodied in the slowness, the sequentiality, the gradations of knowing and not knowing characterizing the technologies of literacy was eroded by successive electric and electronic revolutions beginning with the telegraph and culminating in that most egalitarian of instruments, the television. For this reason, Postman pegs at 1950 both the apex of childhood in America and the unequivocal beginning of its decline.

I find Postman's account enormously persuasive and useful, not least because its unwitting technological determinism allows me to see that in Japan, it is precisely the technologies of literacy that have served as the instrument, not of the maintenance of childhood, but of its destruction.[2] Of course, the electronic revolution has permeated Japanese life at least as thoroughly as it has American. Japanese children, too, have few secrets they can look forward to partaking (their cartoons being both violent and, to American sensibilities, pornographic) when they grow up. It is also still the case, however, that drugs and divorce are, relatively speaking, negligible factors in Japanese childhood and adolescence, even though in fact fathers when transferred often move by themselves, and in any event, regardless of where they live, are unavailable to their families. (Marital discord leads not so much to legal severance as to "domestic divorce," wherein the partners continue to occupy the same dwelling after abandoning all pretense of conjugality.) The father is chained to his workplace, just as his wife and child are chained to the latter's studies so that she, but more likely he, can aspire to the same condition upon attaining adulthood. On the other hand, Japanese children for the past quarter-century or so have been predominantly free of the sorts of risks and privations facing children in the Chicago public-housing projects and the Third World.[3] Nevertheless, as I hope to be showing, Japanese children are suffering and risking the loss of childhood itself precisely by performing the socially defined tasks of childhood. What does this sort of suffering mean in a safe, orderly, and prosperous society?

EDUCATION AS ENDLESS LABOR

For some two decades now, the Japanese media have reported the rising incidence of so-called adult diseases among school-aged children in Japan. A 1990 survey of grammar school children nationwide showed that 63.2 percent were suffering from high levels of blood cholesterol, 36.2 percent from ulcers, 22.1 percent from high blood pressure, and 21.4 percent from diabetes (Arita and Yamaoka 1992:14).[4] While these percentages are high, the symptoms themselves have become too familiar to shock. More freshly startling are the comments of a spokesperson for Aderansu, the leading artificial hair transplant manufacturers, that wigs are finding new customers among schoolchildren suffering from stress-related baldness attributable to the pressures of cram school attendance or bullying in their regular schools.[5] Such reports, added to others detailing a new pervasiveness of eczema and chronic constipation, added to years of stories on school violence (I refer to *ijime*, tamely rendered as "bullying" in English) and school refusal (*tōkōkyohi*), are part of what lead me to believe that childhood itself is at risk in Japan today, and not because of war, disease, or malnutrition.[6]

In thinking about the texture of the lives of children who suffer in these ways, I am led to the example of sports prodigies. We are all vaguely familiar with the texture of the lives led by sports prodigies and would-be sports prodigies in societies around the world, whether in Euroamerica, East Asia, or the former Eastern bloc: of how they relinquish the experience of childhood and adolescence, and of how their families willingly endure prolonged separation and financial hardship, no sacrifice being too great for the possibility of an Olympic medal or a touring contract. The early lives of musical prodigies suggest comparable structures of narrowly channeled self-expression and unremitting demands for discipline and performance.[7] No child labor laws protect these young from the extractive industry for which they are the raw material, to be refined into spectacular commodities of however brief duration. Nor, presumably, do they need such laws, given that it is their "choice" to dedicate themselves to these worthy goals.

There are no child labor laws to protect ordinary (at least, not yet demonstrably prodigious) Japanese two-year-olds from having to trace a path through countless mazes to acquire small-motor coordination, to match the same banal image—of strawberry, ball, shoe—in columns 1–4 with the one in column 5, from having to curb their sensibilities within the regime of the workbook before they can ride swings or wash their own faces—for of course, the point is neither merely to perfect small-motor coordination nor to increase vocabulary per se, but to produce adults tolerant of joyless, repetitive tasks—in other words, disciplined workers.

There are also no child labor laws to protect the 50 percent of fourth through sixth graders in the capital region who attend cram schools from a routine of rushing home after school, grabbing dinners packed by their mothers, exchanging schoolbooks for cram school books, spending from 5 to 9 P.M. at the cram school (or going to more than one extra school if their mothers have chosen to have them specialize), perhaps staying on for private lessons until 11, and, when entrance exams are around the corner, getting home after midnight to tackle school homework, topped off with a touch of video game playing before going to sleep around 2 A.M. (Arita and Yamaoka 1992:12). This, too, can be construed to be their choice, since these children know full well what it takes to get ahead and know, moreover, that the only way they will ever see friends is to go to cram school. The ideology of choice, nestled at the heart of liberalism, necessarily plays a complicated role in most societies. Its promise is compromised, if not altogether canceled, by refusal to acknowledge class, race, gender, and other forms of inequity on the one hand; on the other, it stunts social imagination by short-circuiting the impulse to question the proffered terms of choice. Whenever I hear that children like going to cram schools, or at least, that they do not mind it, I am reminded of the tactful caution with which it is necessary to treat statements that, to an outsider at least, seem to be affirmations by the oppressed of their conditions of oppression. At any rate, the recent statistics are suggestive of how the bodies of children speak even when their tongues do not.[8]

The prevailing motifs in the march of Japanese educational progress are conveniently displayed in the writings of the prolific Ibuka Masaru, former chief executive officer and now honorary head of Sony Corporation and chair of the Conference on Culture and Education, a private group convened in the mid-1980s to advise then prime minister Nakasone. Ibuka's books bear such titles as *Why Age Zero? Life Is Decided at Age Zero* (1989) or *The Fetus Is a Genius: Education Begins before Birth* (1992). Ibuka insists that he is promoting techniques for the advancement of human character rather than recipes for smarter children. (In fact, he observes, in a flourish of opportunistic nationalism characteristic of mainstream views on education, it is among Westerners that one finds a tendency to cling to heredity, in other words, class and racial prejudice [1989:8].) His disclaimers notwithstanding, his books are filled with profiles of model mothers whose children have IQs above 160 and exhortations to exploit not only the right-brain hemisphere of children under the age of seven but also the memory capacity of infants for the absorption of Chinese characters. Current Sony head Morita Akio's efforts in collaboration with parliamentarian Ishihara Shintarō to promote a Japan that can say no (for translation, see Ishihara 1991) fade in significance before the Ibuka infant education industry. *Why Age Zero?* focuses on the role of the mother, with a glancing acknowledgment that the father must be "someone who is respected" and an ostensibly cosmopolitan nod toward Jews and of course Jewish mothers, who are surely responsible for the enviable statistic that 70 percent of New York doctors and a "sizable portion" of its lawyers and other "intellectual" professionals are Jews (1992:179). The spirit of capitalist progress is not only literally evident in the inclusion of advertisements for such devices as the "Athleticot" (the crib that promotes infant development by providing monthly age-appropriate challenges), developed at the Organization for Child Development (headed by Ibuka), but in such chapter headings in the 1992 book as "Even Age Zero Is Too Late," which cancel the hope advanced but six years earlier that education might begin after a woman had actually seen her child ex utero.

The narrative of the progressively arduous journey of schooling can be clarified by referring to the model of the child prodigy once again.

The prodigy is subjected to a punishing regimen where her marketable skills are concerned, but otherwise lavishly pampered. The children of averagely ambitious parents are handsomely rewarded to keep their noses to the bookish grindstone; they are at the least, especially the boys, outfitted with state-of-the-art video games. Indeed, a tongue-in-cheek exchange between two writers analogizes the child-parent relationship today to that of the bourgeoisie and the proletariat, with the absent, laboring fathers placed lower even than the mothers (Nakano and Hashimoto 1991:174–75). This analogy, of course, forgets what is extracted from the children in exchange for their privilege, just as it leaves inexplicit the link between the parents' labor and the child's. Parents and children are suffering conspirators in the education race.[9]

Now, it is crucial to keep in mind that these pampered creatures are not prodigies but ordinary children to be found here, there, everywhere in Japan. (Indeed, health problems of the sort mentioned above and others are found evenly distributed in urban and rural areas.) It is the ordinary Japanese child who has become the raw material for the insatiable schooling industry, the ordinary child who at once toils and consumes, toils at consuming the products of this industry—cram schools, reference books, study guides, and above all, tests, tests, and more tests. To acknowledge the potential implied by, then abused, in this investment in the ordinary is a chilling exercise. For the prodigy model and the Japanese educational model should, and to some extent, do, have antithetical goals: for the former, the production of a relatively small number of individuals with remarkable, visible skills, who generate profit for a few others and themselves through the performance of those skills; for the latter, the production of an exceptionally competent society whose members work remarkably well but do not, should not, produce spectacle as individuals. In postwar Japanese education, the extraordinary investment in the ordinary has ended up generalizing the exploitative procedures designed to produce prodigies.

EDUCATION AS ABUSE

This process of generalization surely accounts in part for the increasingly common reports of violence in the schools, with both children and teachers as perpetrators. One of the best-known cases of bullying illustrates the tangled relationships of the children and their teachers. In 1986 a junior-high-school boy committed suicide after months of bullying by a group of his classmates. His suicide note pleaded that he hadn't wanted to die yet, but that life had become unbearable. The last straw was evidently a mock funeral in which four of his teachers had participated along with the bullies. One of them was his homeroom teacher, who was not, apparently, indifferent to his plight. Indeed, on the boy's last day at school, the teacher had fished out the boy's sneaker from a toilet, washed it for him, and told him that that was the most he could do, that he had to ask his parents to go to the police or to change schools.[10] How are we to understand the teacher's sense of helplessness, the deadening of sensitivity that allowed him and three of his colleagues to join in the torment of a child in their charge?

Before proceeding with this question, let us look at several more examples to get a sense of the texture of school violence in contemporary Japan. On June 7, 1990, a junior-high-school girl was crushed to death by a teacher closing a steel gate in an effort to prevent tardy students from entering. Here are some reactions to the incident from teenagers calling in to a message machine operated by a network called Talking Kids:

> I'm a high-school senior, and I'm on the Morals Committee. One morning, I was checking on who was tardy when a junior girl came running incredibly fast to get to school, but she didn't make it. The teachers shut the gate on her. There was a loud bang, and the kid's hand was hurt. "Ouch," she screamed, but the teacher just said, "It's your fault for being late." I wanted to start a protest and started collecting signatures, but people said they were scared of that teacher or that they weren't tardy, so it had nothing to do with them. I only got a few signatures. It was a shock.

> It gave me the chills to hear that five or six students just rushed past Ryōko's bleeding body without paying any attention to her because they didn't want to be marked late.

> Who do they think they are to say, "If she had been ten minutes earlier, this wouldn't have happened"? They're murderers. What's school supposed to be about? What are school rules for? They say, "They're [the rules are] there for you," but they're really just to make things easier for them. School should be fun, interesting. [But] it's like a robot factory or a concentration camp.

> When I started high school, something really scary happened. One of my friends came to school looking kind of like a hood. He got into a fight with a man teacher. The teacher struck the kid once, then started waving a stick. It got into the kid's eye, and he lost his sight in that eye. I started feeling scared again when I heard about this new event. School is a scary place.

> My hair has always been a little brown, and teachers used to say to me, "I bet you dyed your hair," and they would beat and kick me. I kept on going to school because I wanted to graduate, but one day, I had to get three

stitches above my right eyebrow. The teacher had hit me with a desk. Do these gentlemen have the right to go that far? What's the big deal about being late? Shouldn't high school be a safe place for kids to go to? (Saitō 1990)

In addition to tardiness, some common areas of regulation are hairstyle, clothing, and extramural conduct. Here are sample rules:

"Maiden cut," pageboy, braids, or standard razor cuts are acceptable; two-layered cuts, "wolf cuts" are forbidden. Bangs can extend to the eyebrow. The rest of the hair should not brush against the uniform collar. [For junior-high girls]

Pants should be straight legged without cuffs. Sneakers should be plain and laced, with at least eight holes. Socks should be white for both girls and boys. [Junior high]

After school is dismissed, don't go to stores for food, loiter, or visit each other's homes when our mothers aren't around. From April through September, get home by 6 P.M., from October through March, by 5 P.M. It is preferable to see movies accompanied by a parent. If that is not possible, note it in the student notebook and secure parental seal to indicate permission. It is preferable to wear the school uniform when going out. [High school, in this case "composed" by the students themselves] (Murakami 1990:24)[11]

Teachers, in other words, are expected to monitor ever more minute rules of clothing and conduct as well as to ensure that ever higher levels of mathematical competence are attained and more science and social-studies information ingested. All of this, we must remember, comes in addition to the massive effort required to achieve basic literacy. (Students in the first nine years of school must master nearly two thousand Chinese characters with multiple readings per character.) Perhaps even more important than training students in specific skills is ensuring the formation of an attitude that will tolerate a lifetime of arduous and/or dull tasks. Hence, the significance of establishing a horizon of desire and a range of sensibility in early childhood that will be compatible with such a life course.

The prescribed method of student evaluation encourages both teachers and students to think of the latter abstractly and hierarchically. In order to produce the normal-distribution (Gauss) curve, the teacher *must* assign, on a 5-point system, a 5 (highest) or a 1 (lowest) to 7 percent of the students, a 2 or a 4 to 24 percent, and a 3 to 38 percent (Horio 1986:11), with no flexibility allowed for rewarding exceptional improvement or for recognizing a class with a high proportion of achieving students.[12] As for students, the routine of constant testing habituates children from an early age to their insinuation in a hierarchical world, where their place is "objectively" determined by their standard-deviation score (*hensachi*, a household word), which for upper-level grade school students, junior-high students, and high-school students becomes an identifier more substantive than their names since it denotes the rank of school they can next aspire to.

Teachers, for their part, are subject to constant scrutiny in the form of "efficiency" rating, aptitude testing, in-service training—to name just some of the formal mechanisms. There is little room for even modest deviation from the nationally prescribed curriculum and modes of instruction. Dress and comportment, political beliefs, willingness to participate in supposedly noncompulsory socializing—these are all areas where conformity is advisable.[13] There are, of course, dedicated, sensitive teachers who persist within these confines. But the temptation to dissipate frustration and resolve problems with force is great:

> Corporal punishment works instantly. The classroom's noisy. You can't get ahead with the lesson. Then you do it—bam! It's like pouring oil over troubled waters. The classroom falls silent. It feels great. You get a taste of that, you're addicted. But there's a knack to it. Don't pick on the popular ones, the leaders. You'll stir up bad feeling, and it'll be counterproductive. Knowing how to choose the ones to hit is part of a teacher's wisdom. (Murakami 1990:22)

These are the words of a forty-two-year-old male junior-high-school teacher, a former beater. He stopped beating his students when he noticed how some of them were always flattering him, how that was an expression of fear, and then, how the entire class was obedient to his face but contemptuous behind his back. He has yet to find an alternative to beating. A fifty-four-year-old woman teacher, also a former beater who says she always chose the weaker children, recalls scenes that she witnessed:

> [There's the] teacher who makes the kids sit formally on the floor and then beats them. There are bloody noses. The floor is stained with blood. The girl who wipes her blood with toilet paper and sits silently, lips pursed. A young woman teacher who screams hysterically as she strikes her students. A male teacher who almost always joins in the beating if he sees a colleague doing it.

This teacher thinks that virtually 100 percent of schoolteachers engage in corporal punishment. It is, incidentally, forbidden by law in Japan (Murakami 1990:23–24).

Teachers beat children out of frustration, singling out the ones who are in some way marked as inferior; children curry favor with irascible teachers, report on their classmates, inventively torment the weak. Many parents continue to favor teachers who are strict "disciplinarians": how else can their offspring learn enough to secure a place in a frantically competitive society? Even those who do not favor physical discipline are disinclined to complain to schools, for fear of negatively affecting the confidential report (the *naishinsho*, as much a household word as the *hensachi*, thanks to the common threat: "If you do that, it'll go into your *naishinsho*") that goes from school to school (Saitō 1990: 23; Horio 1988: 279–94).[14] The dyad of parents and children as suffering conspirators is in fact a triad, with teachers as the third term. As Horio (1988:280) puts it, the "*naishinsho* has proven its usefulness as a tool for controlling Japanese students largely because it has been skillfully manipulated to control the activities of teachers as well." It is now difficult for parents and teachers to remember that as adults they have the obligation to protect children, one of the fundamental principles necessary to sustaining the institution of childhood. Parents and teachers, in that sense, must be different from children. Instead, they have locked themselves in the same cage of chronic fatigue, stress, violence, and fear. There, children are stripped of their innocence and adults of their authority.

One increasingly apparent consequence has been, not surprisingly, the normalization of dysfunction. Also not surprisingly, such dysfunction has usually been attributed to individual deficiencies, whether on the part of the family (especially the mother) or the child him/herself. There are signs, however, that the dysfunction has reached such proportions that even the central educational bureaucracy is having to give heed, especially to its somewhat measurable form, school refusal (in contrast to bullying, which is more resistant to statistical control). Thus, the March 13, 1992, report of an advisory committee for the education ministry acknowledged that any child is susceptible to school refusal, technically defined as absence exceeding fifty days per school year. This is tantamount to admitting that more and more children are finding it impossible to attend school. (According to the education ministry, there were eight thousand such children in grade school and forty thousand in junior high in 1990, up four times since 1978.)[15] In the fall of 1992, for the first time in all the years since *tōkōkyohi* (school refusal) became a household word, the ministry has decided that the children who fall prey to this syndrome should be interviewed along with the teachers and administrators, who had always been consulted.

The normalization of dysfunction among Japanese children is striking precisely because, as I have emphasized, it is taking place in an orderly, prosperous society. It is likely, therefore, that had the children's bodies not begun to register (made visible, like prodigious spectacle) their suffering, it would have continued to be officially ignored. In this sense, the costs exacted by the Japanese educational process are perhaps paradigmatic of the price paid silently by so many successful participants in the global regime of advanced capitalism.

EDUCATION, LABOR, AND SOCIETY

Education theorist and children's rights advocate Horio Teruhisa suggests that in Japan school has taken over the whole of society rather than serving one of its needs (1990:100).[16] Another way of looking at it would be to see labor, or the instrumentalizing logic of production, as having taken over all of society, including early childhood and schooling. The normal-distribution curve was itself imported into the classroom from the workplace.[17] Indeed, Japanese education might be generally characterized as Taylorist. Frederick W. Taylor's three principles of scientific management sought

> (1) the dissociation of the labor process from the skills of the workers; (2) the separation of conception from execution; (3) the use of th[e] monopoly over knowledge to control each step of the labor process and its mode of execution. (Braverman 1974:112–21)[18]

This spirit is perhaps most literally represented in a popular series of supplementary beginner math lessons, in which the child must systematically proceed from 1 + 1 to 1 + 2 to 1 + 3, and so on, to 2 + 1, 2 + 2, 2 + 3, and so on, but the atomized, mechanistic mode is crucial to the regime of tests throughout the course of schooling, the apotheosis of which is the university entrance exam.[19] This last is both a procedure consistent with the positivistic mode prevailing up to that point and the final important site of intersection between the national education bureaucracy and the private education industry. Questions for the standardized first round, used by all national universities and a sizable number of private universities, are set by a national board consisting of prestigious academics. But the examination system cannot function without the intervention of powerful computers owned by the leading cram schools. After taking the test, students can calculate their own scores (answers are published in the newspapers) and feed them into the computers, which identify the schools to which they should apply. Students abide by such "advice," so that the rate of competition is much lower than it was in the fifties and sixties (which were also the days of suicides over examination failure).[20]

In other words, students who have grown up identifying themselves by their standard-deviation scores convert themselves one more time into a statistic legible to the schooling industry and sort themselves into the appropriate institutions leading to commensurate workplaces—sort themselves into a future as determined by the guiding hand of computerized data.[21] Whatever that future is, they will most likely live it as the disciplined worker and dedicated consumer necessary for maintaining the economy.

School and work are becoming increasingly continuous, such that the goals of education fail to suggest even a modicum of autonomy from the goals of the economy. One might point to the college years as a stunningly free period for all but those pursuing medical and technical studies. College is the noninstrumental hiatus in the educational trajectory. More accurately, it is instrumentally noninstrumental, insofar as the college years are meant to cancel out the brutal competition of the twelve preceding years and effect the transformation of these young adults into harmonious, consensus-prone workers.[22]

I should add that I am including mothers in the category of disciplined, consensus-prone workers. After a stint of office work following high school or (with increasing frequency) college, the most significant site of labor for most women is the home, where they will supervise the training of the next generation of workers. The coincidence of stress-related baldness in women and children suggests at least two possibilities: (*a*) the *parallel* trajectories of stressful labor for children and women working outside the home; and (*b*) the stress of schooling inducing baldness in the mother-child laboring *team*. In any case, one of the most common reasons for mothers of school-age children to seek part-time work, typically as supermarket cashiers, is to pay for cram schools and tutors.

Needless to say, schooling in all societies not only affects future employment possibilities but is more or less designed to serve that role. But that "more or less" is crucial to the quality of life of the child and to the safeguarding of childhood itself. In Japan (and other East Asian societies) the seamless fit between academic vita and employment opportunity has produced suffocating conditions over the past several decades. The spread of "adult" diseases within the grade school population attests to the commonality of suffering emerging between adult and child laborers—the creation of a national noncommunity of isolated, inconspicuous victims.

STATE CENSORSHIP AND CAPITALIST DISCIPLINE

The conflation of the school and work models of life in Japanese education is both symbiotic with and inscribed by the conflation of state and corporation in the educational system. Prewar Japanese education was entirely dedicated to the needs of a late-industrializing state driven to imperialistic adventurism. The costs were enormous for an earlier version of the mother-child team. To understand the latter, it is useful to know the reception of the work of Swedish feminist Ellen Key (1849–1926). Key's *Century of the Child* (1909), with such striking chapters as "The Right of the Child to Choose His Parents" or "Soul Murder in the Schools," underscored the importance of the maternal function in the context of industrial capitalism and argued for the development of a nonpatriarchal family. In the Japanese feminist debate of 1918–19, Key's works bolstered the assertion of maternal rights over women's rights (Miyake 1991). The proponents of maternal rights sought not only to win public recognition but to earn benefits from the state for women as mothers. Although some of them were not insensitive to the range of needs newly experienced by Japanese women and were mindful both of the desperate conditions of young women and children in the textile mills and responsive to the inchoate desires of women confronting the headiness and terror of cosmopolitan modernity, their choice of mother rights over women's rights had enormous consequences in the subsequent decades. The culturalist strain in that choice, which proclaimed an authentically Japanese course for Japanese women, lent itself to the increasingly strident nationalism of the age and fatally accommodated the instrumental mobilization of mothers and children by the state during the prewar and wartime years. As the family became conflated with the patriarchal, indeed, fascistic, family state, the only role left for the child was that of miniature instrument to be molded in the service of that state.

After surrender and occupation in 1945, education was one of the most vigorously democratized domains, and there were several years of promising activity directed at developing a rights-centered, antimilitarist education for all Japanese. Before such efforts could be consolidated, however, education, too, fell victim to the "reverse course" whereby reforms were undone in the interests of economic growth and alliance with the United States at the onset of the Cold War.[23]

Here, I propose to look briefly at the role of state and capital in the educational system today. The state continues to be omnipresent in Japanese education, exercising a more or less intimate supervisory capacity over private as well as public schools. Indeed, in the course of the postwar decades, control over education has become increasingly centralized (and therefore nationalized) as membership in local education committees became appointive rather than elective, teacher evaluation was instated, and moral education, redolent of prewar ideological practices, entered the curriculum. Textbook screening is a powerful instrument in the hands of the Education Ministry. One category of ministry interest in screening is predictable: historical events with current political implications, having mostly to do with Japan's (until recently) unacknowledged responsibility for bringing about devastation in Asia during World War II. Thus, in the early 1980s, there was heated exchange between Japan and its East Asian neighbors over Japanese textbooks' softening of such episodes as the "Rape" of Nanking. A number of such historical issues are at stake in the ongoing, decades-old legal battles with eminent historian Ienaga Saburō as plaintiff. Related to the censorship of historical materials evidently deemed sensitive by the ministry is the recent mandate (with penalties) compelling schools to observe the rising-sun flag and to sing the anthem dedicated to the emperor at all official gatherings. Both symbols are deeply offensive to some Japanese for their associations with the prewar state (Yamazumi 1989; Field 1991).

There is, however, another, less predictable form of interference by the state. When physicist Tomonaga Shin'ichirō, a Nobel laureate, wrote a high-school physics textbook that offered students a multiplicity of ways to think about given problems (rather than a single correct way), the examiner criticized it for its nontextbook, that is, speculative, style. Tomonaga decided to withdraw from textbook writing. In another case, a poem written by children called "The River" was included in a sixth-grade reader. This poem had an untranslatable line that read, "Sara saruru piruporu doburu pon pochan" (the line following it may be translated "The river says many things as it flows"). The examiner insisted that the correct onomatopoeia for rivers was *sara sara* and demanded that the children's rendition of the river's sounds be rewritten as *sara sara*. In still another instance, a writer's (as opposed to textbook producer's) onomatopoeia and monologue-filled description of a locomotive was reduced to flat paraphrase by the time it was permitted to appear in a second-grade reader (Horio 1986:150–53). Perhaps some of this is attributable simply to the irredeemably dull spirits of education bureaucrats. Nevertheless, the attempt to establish correctness where there had been none, to regulate even the represention of nonhuman sounds, has the effect of squeezing out the lingering drops of play left in Japanese schooling. Performed by the state, the act becomes more ponderous, not to say preposterous, since such surveillance in the context of "national-language" classes has the effect of "nationalizing" the monologue of an engine and the murmurings of a river. What is the relationship between these two forms of censorship, and how do they reflect the relationship evolving between state and capital in postwar Japan?

The Education Ministry continues to play a vigilant supervisory role in the context of increasing privatization, a trend that may be traced back to the "low" economic growth beginning in the mid-1970s following the first oil crisis. Recently, much educational rhetoric has proclaimed the desirability of "liberalization" and "respect for individuality," especially in the reports issuing from the influential Ad Hoc Council on Education (Rinkyōshin), established by then prime minister Nakasone in 1984. Does such rhetoric, suggestively resonant of the calls for freedom and democratization from the immediate postwar years, now issuing from a group including prominent corporate leaders as well as professional educators, signal a loosening of the bureaucratic grip? In fact, it is difficult to discern any content to liberalization other than privatization, difficult to construe individualization as anything more than the diversification of the end product of intensified competition; for, far from promoting the development of individual imagination and aptitude, competition can at most produce only more measurable *kinds* of human being, resulting in a fine-tuned supply of elite and nonelite workers suited for meeting diverse corporate needs.[24] It seems reasonable to suppose that these corporate goals no longer require the heavy-handed ideological control of the education ministry. Indeed, at one point, some of the corporate members of the Extraordinary Council suggested that there was no longer need for ministry censorship of textbooks. Such liberalism seems to have issued from confidence that an education governed by the spirit of free enterprise would eliminate the impulse to produce leftist texts (Horio 1986:193). Yet textbook screening not only continues but since 1989 has been reduced from a three-step to a single-stage process, eliminating the possibility of negotiation between ministry and publisher, with the effect of promoting self-censorship on the part of the latter. Add to this the regressive policies regarding anthem and flag that went into effect in 1990. Such developments seem to fly in the face of the logic of advanced capitalism, which presumably has no interest in such primitive practices, negatively speaking, and requires flexible minds, positively speaking. Yet, in a document targeted to the ad hoc council's deliberations entitled *Toward an Education for the Twenty-First Century*, the Japan Economics Research Council, pointing to the need for the "recovery of humanity" from the ills of rapid technologization, preached the importance of "establishing a Japanese identity" and for developing "consciousness of the state and of oneself as Japanese," and of "introducing Japanese culture [to foreigners] and having it understood correctly" (Kyoto Kyōiku Centā 1987:77). Whatever the tensions underlying corporate and state interests in the arena of national education, they are reconciled in a call to valorize the unchanging elements of tradition.

The growing strength of corporate Japan relative to the state since the era of High Growth Economics in the 1960s seems to be producing a mutual accommodation whereby the state provides the mechanisms of control that contribute to the production of the workers desired by capital. The focus on the presentation of history and the imposition of the flag and anthem provide natural (because allegedly traditional) content for this control (while also satisfying right-wing parliamentarians and the conservative ideologues in the Education Ministry). The other strand of ministry control, which might be characterized as the principle of a single right answer for every question, seems designed to instill discipline as acceptance of the arbitrary, which is thoroughly commensurate with the standardization enforced by competitive modernity. There is a mechanism of mutual reinforcement operating here: the positivistic spirit of brute competition finds a pleasing antidote in the rhetoric of recovering humanity in terms, as it happens, of the rhetoric of recovering Japanese identity. It may be that textbook screening continues because the corporate members of the ad hoc council were persuaded that there were still too many left-wing teachers in the system (Horio 1988:373), but the more fundamental issue may be rather that capitalism, whose only logic is one of perpetual expansion, needs to borrow content for both negative and positive forms of control.

THE DISCOURSE OF RIGHTS

In postwar Japan, not only explicit resistance to these forms of control but the very definition of the institution of childhood has taken the form of a discourse of rights. Most of the progressive measures date back to the early years of the American occupation, before the reverse course driven by American interests not only halted democratization but rehabilitated the architects of the prewar imperial state. These early postwar measures were dedicated to undoing the tenets of the Imperial Rescript on Education (1890), which defined learning as the exercise of hierarchical loyalty culminating in the emperor, and to undoing the notion of state as family with all the people as the children—an obliteration of childhood through its universalization. Several key articles in the Constitution (1947) illustrate both the principles that needed to be legally established and, given the developments discussed above, the fragility of rights discourse in Japan: the elimination of censorship and the protection of privacy (Article 21); the guarantee of academic freedom (Article 23); the right to "maintain the minimum standards of wholesome and cultured living" (Article 25); free, universal education (Article 27); and "the right and obligation to work," coupled with the provision that "children shall not be exploited" (Article 27).[25] These provisions became the basis of several other legal formulations pertaining to children, such as the Fundamental Law of Education (1947), which set out the goals of education and the principles underlying education for a new Japan, and the Children's Charter (Jidō Kenshō) of 1951. The significance of the latter may be gauged by the fact that it covers almost the same range of provisions as the Declaration of the Rights of the Child adopted by the United Nations General Assembly in 1959, itself an elaboration focused on the child of the Universal Declaration of Human Rights adopted by the UN in 1948. Although these principles are more fully spelled out in the UN Declaration, the Japanese Children's Charter refers to the obligation to provide facilities for play (Article 9) and reiterates the prohibition of exploitation (Article 10).

Why, then, does Japanese education look the way it does today? One literal answer is the forty-odd years of one-party rule by the Liberal Democrats, who have been consistently opposed to the principles embodied in these documents.[26] Specifically, it has been the goal of generations of education ministers to do away with the Fundamental Law of Education. A more subtle technique was developed by Prime Minister Nakasone when he announced that it was possible to interpret this law from the perspective of "living law" and to find, in effect, that it was consistent with the spirit of the Imperial Rescript on Education (Horio 1988:372–73).[27] Now, the government is preparing to become a signatory to the UN Convention on the Rights of the Child (1989), which spells out, for instance, "the right of the child to rest and leisure, to engage in play and recreational activities appropriate to the age of the child and to participate freely in cultural life and the arts" (Article 31). Given the tradition of flexible enforcement of the law, there is little reason to expect that the Education Ministry will feel any pressure to translate this into specific measures.[28]

In order to understand the disheartening results of the rights struggle, we would need to consider, beyond the brute fact of conservative rule, the prewar history of the discourse of rights and the social and cultural factors that affect the possibility of dissent. Among the latter, one should be singled out: the spectacular success of the Japanese economy, especially as it impressed itself on the population at large beginning in the 1970s. Economic success began to stand for success in general and dissipate the impetus to contest.[29] If the great majority of Japanese did not feel they were benefiting from the national economy, would they have blunted themselves to the costs of success to this degree?

Does this mean that the struggle to pursue children's rights should be abandoned? It does seem more difficult to use the notion of rights to fight the discipline of sensibility than the censorship of history, or the denial of basic needs. Yet, as I hope my discussion of the Japanese example has shown, the two come together and reinforce each other. And if capitalism borrows from the repertory of conservative positions to give its discipline the semblance of principle, then it is reasonable for the struggle against the discipline of sensibility to borrow from the struggle against censorship and deprivation. It is, to be sure, a daunting, and even diffuse, task. But laws come alive, indeed, take on a content, only when they become the subject of struggle. Now more than ever, as the dysfunction of Japanese schooling becomes increasingly apparent, and the fabulous economy shows signs of faltering, it is imperative to hold on to the only progressive social principles available, so that when the moment comes, they can come to life. This is the responsiblity of adults.

PLAY, CHILDHOOD, AND ADULTHOOD

I have meant by the "disappearance of childhood in contemporary Japan" the emergence of a new continuity between childhood and adulthood through technocratically ordered labor. The negative emphasis on labor in my discussion has obscured the affirmative role of play, which in itself and for what it represents has conventionally given childhood its allure. Before we explore these associations, we should recall the disapproval with which Ariès, standing deep in the twentieth century, saw the entrenchment of childhood in the context of the new concept of the family (and with it, of the home and of privacy), since these came at the cost of "the activity of social relations" (1962: 407). This would not have been quite the view of the multiple contributors to the "cult of childhood" (Boas 1966). The discourse of childhood, with the idealized thematics of play (including freedom, creativity, nature, art, innocence, primitivism/exoticism), was launched by the writings of Rousseau and Schiller, embraced by the English Romantics, and transported across the Atlantic. As it entered the twentieth century, it was elaborated by the legion discontents of Weberian disenchantment and Marcusian repressive desublimation and more recently, its legacy can be said to have animated deconstruction and postmodernism. Jean-François Lyotard, for example, observes that "thought may have more childhood available to it at thirty-six than at eighteen" and that "the thought that would instruct" must "seek its childhood no matter where, even beyond childhood" (1986:166).[30] If we see this migration in space and time as a trajectory of resistance to the constricted instrumentality of bourgeois modernity, then Ariès belongs in it as well, thus demonstrating the commonalities of premodern and postmodern romanticizations, which in turn are not antithetical to romanticism itself, always partly critical of modernity.

Leaping back to Japan: Romanticism in Japanese letters, coming in several waves in the late nineteenth and early twentieth centuries, failed to yield anything comparable to a "cult of the child" in spite of the importance of Rousseau, Schiller, and Goethe. (It did, however, precipitate the not altogether unrelated cult of youth.) Signs of a utopian interest in children crystallized briefly in the publication of a magazine called *Akai Tori* (The red bird; 1922–36 with some interruptions), which attracted some of the most talented writers, poets, and artists of the day; but as the dates show, this impulse was crushed, like so many others, by the forces of emperor-state fascism. In the larger perspective of the sixty-odd years preceding World War II, it may well be that in a Japan in the throes of forced rapid modernization, there was little inclination to seek a redemptive noble savage, and no impetus to find him in the native child. That child, together with his father and mother, had to be transformed into the productive subjects of a nation-state (ideologically cast as the devoted children of the emperor-father), while Asia had to be repudiated as contaminating sign of backwardness. The desire to contest Westernization, when it emerged, took the form of the exoticization of the mature (though pure, bright, and presumably simple) native tradition. Somewhere in this process, the child of so-called folk society vanished, and a discourse of childhood came into its own shortly after the war (Iijima 1987; Horio 1984:52–60).

Any argument about the disappearance of childhood should not be taken to mean that childhood and adulthood ever existed in absolute distinction in Japan or anywhere else except, perhaps, in societies where life was defined by ritual passage from one stage to another. After all, it is adults who invest in a cult of childhood.[31] Play itself, constituted in opposition to work and/or need, can never free itself of these defining others. A glance at the toys of our own past should swiftly remind us of how mimetic they are of the adult world.[32] Even where they are not, they are harnessed to the imperative to make the child creative—"of a life, not property," as the Roland Barthes of *Mythologies* proclaimed, waxing rhapsodic over the virtues of the wooden toy, "of substance familiar and poetic, which leaves the child in contact with the tree, the table, the floor" (1959:60). Play is fated to contribute to the production of a better adult qua adult or qua perpetual child (i.e., creator/genius/artist).

In this rapid sketch I have focused on the discourse of childhood rather than on actual children and the importance of play for modern adults rather than for children, but these are not unconnected. To risk banality and tautology, childhood and adulthood are crucially linked, and because of this, if the discourse of childhood is important for adults, then childhood is important for children. Childhood must be a protected space, and children must be protected, not only from material deprivation and danger, but from bondage to an overdetermined future. The grimness of Japanese childhood today stems not only from the appalling physical and psychic costs extracted from children, but from its constriction of horizon. To be harnessed from childhood to the logic of acceleration and expansion is to be confined to a known yet abstract future. Adults need not only to protect children but to help them acquire the tools with which to transcend the instrumental confines of the present. To preserve, no, recover, the utopian dimension of the future, the future as utopia, we need to help the child father the man, so to speak. In this sense, too, to return to an earlier discussion, society cannot afford to give up the discourse of rights; for, as Horio (1986: 49–57) argues, children's rights constitute the basis of human rights generally.[33]

Japanese children, in suffering from the same ills that afflict adults, make newly visible the increasingly ordinary deaths that come too early to exhausted adults—indeed, make concrete the abstract domination that is the hallmark of advanced capitalism itelf. Can this human condition be unique to Japan? Clearly, historical factors have shaped the forms that schooling and labor now take, and miracles have befallen the Japanese economy within specific global circumstances. I still believe, however, that the emerging human condition in Japan is a logical possibility (if one that will appear with varying predominance) for every society saturated with the mechanisms of advanced capitalism. If war is one expression of the conflicts engendered by capitalism, the normalized physical suffering of children in peace is a different display of capitalist contradictions. To return to the models at the beginning of this paper, it is tempting to see in (a) the American ghetto, (b) the American suburb, and (c) Japan generally, three modes of disintegration of childhood for our historical moment. The first has elements of Third World perils, and the last shares values with American yuppiedom as the latter becomes entrenched in parenthood. Is it possible to see these as representations of different stages of capitalism and to see in their simultaneity and mutual overdetermination specificities of our own moment in capitalism? It is easy, no doubt too much so, to see the American ghetto as suffering the effects of exploitation (including abandonment) by the suburb and Japan (as representative of the global economy), but what is the relationship between the latter? The minimization of school as site of discipline in the American suburb, contrasted to its continued centrality in Japan, suggests two responses to postindustrialism: in the first, the waning of the productivist ethos altogether (without anything affirmative to take its place), in the second, its continued robustness with corresponding forms of oppression.

But these speculations take us too far into a vast and general order that can only thicken the despair that leaves us passive. The protection of children and the reconstruction of childhood are tangible places to direct our attention. Otherwise, historical children grow wizened and adults die young in safe societies, and both die too soon elsewhere.

POSTSCRIPT

The long post-postwar of absolute political stability and constant economic growth in Japan seems finally to have come to an end since this essay was written. It is too soon to predict the educational and general social implications of the chaotic shifts in government following the fall of the Liberal Democratic Party. The Tokyo High Court gave partial victory to historian Ienaga Saburō in October of 1993 by acknowledging Education Ministry excesses in its review of certain textbook passages concerning episodes in Japan's wartime history. The legitimacy of ministry review (in effect, censorship) remains unquestioned, however, and the education minister in then prime minister Hosokawa's "reformist" government even regretted the court-ordered payment of a symbolically minuscule sum to Ienaga. In a different vein, the move to abolish the use of tests manufactured by the education industry as part of an effort to ease pressures on middle-school students was generally viewed as imposing additional burdens on teachers. Such tinkering with specific practices without a reconsideration of larger structures cannot be counted upon to have a positive effect.

The greatest incalculable, however, is the impact of a long-term economic slowdown. It takes some ingenuity, not to say perversity, to imagine that intensified tracking, with the channeling of greater numbers of students toward lesser careers, will be emancipatory insofar as they are banished from the realm of relentless expectation. At the same time, the decline of employment opportunity pushes the more privileged young to pursue further advanced education.

In the meanwhile Japan became a signatory to the Convention on the Rights of the Child on April 22, 1994. The Education Ministry has shown little interest in promoting public awareness of the Convention or in opposing school regulations that violate its terms. Bullying-related tragedies show no sign of abating. All the more reason to cheer grassroots efforts to familarize *children* with the Convention's provisions through cartoons—and rap.[34]

NOTES

It was an exceptional privilege to participate in the panel "Children and the Politics of Culture" as part of the international conference "Children at Risk," held in Bergen in May 1992. I am fundamentally indebted to the dialogue generated by that occasion, and not just in the writing of this essay. It continues to inspire me as a model of imaginative, unnarcissistic (collectively as well as individually) intellectual endeavor. I am profoundly grateful to Per Egil Mjaavatn and Sharon Stephens for having produced such conditions of possibility.

1. Title of the theme song to *Kiteretsu Hyakka* (Weirdness encyclopedia), a children's cartoon show, quoted in Arita and Yamaoka (1992:12). All translations are my own unless otherwise indicated.

2. Thanks to Jim Chandler for discussion on this point.

3. It would be very wrong to suggest that there are no problems of class and discrimination that beset children, notably, but not exclusively, the handicapped and those of Korean or outcaste background. Japan is currently acquiring a sizable minority population for the first time in the postwar period, consisting of East and Southeast Asians and even Middle Easterners, willing and eager to perform tasks that Japanese have become reluctant to take on. These laborers, often illegal aliens, are now producing children who pose challenges for health care and schooling that Japan has not previously had to encounter.

4. Their article is entitled "'Karōji' Shōkōgun" (The 'overworking child' syndrome) with *karōji* punning on the recently familiarized term *karōshi*, meaning "death from overwork," applied to adults who seem to literally drop dead from overwork at any point between their midtwenties and their midfifties.

5. "Hirogaru Enkei Datsumōshō" (Circular baldness on the rise), *Tokyo Shimbun*, March 27, 1992, 2, and an hour-long documentary on NHK's education channel (March 25, 1992) on stress-related baldness in women. The Aderansu spokesperson coyly attributed the dramatic increase of circular baldness in women to the enactment of the Equal Employment Opportunity Law in 1986. The law is notorious for its lack of enforcement provisions, and, in any event, promises "opportunity," not results. What the law seems to have managed thus far is to "accelerate the development of a new type of job segregation between men and women" and therefore the "formation of a flexible labor market" responsive to the requirements of "new technology and the service-oriented economy" (Takenaka 1992:11).

6. For a discussion in English of school refusal, see Lock 1992.

7. Marilyn Ivy and Vivienne Wee, two former pianists among the contributors to this volume, encouraged me to include the musical example. Wee trenchantly described her childhood training as a process of "being prodigized."

8. It would be comforting to say, with Henri Lefebvre, "The body, at the very heart of space and of the discourse of Power is irreducible. It rejects the reproduction of relations which deprive it and crush it" (1976:89). At what point does the body's flexibility, or adaptability, give way to irreducibility? Marx's observation from 150 years ago remains pertinent to the postindustrial

world in general and singularly fitting in describing the cram-school-formed Japanese child: "[I]f a crooked spine, twisted limbs, a one-sided development of certain muscles, etc., makes you more capable of working (more productive), then your crooked spine, your twisted limbs, your one-sided muscular movement are a productive force. If your intellectual vacuity is more productive than your abundant intellectual activity, then your intellectual vacuity is a productive force" (cited in Sayer 1991:285). I am indebted to Bill Brown for the citation from Lefebvre as well as for generous comments on this paper.

9. A vivid account of the horrors of such a partnership is provided by a physician mother who describes her transformation into a *mamagon* (mama dragon) in order to get her amiable son into a reputable senior high school (Murasaki 1987). This book went through nineteen printings within one year of publication.

10. There are numerous accounts in newspapers and magazines of this incident that took place on February 3, 1986. I have drawn on Horio (1986:3–5) because it takes the trouble to emphasize the teacher's concern rather than exploit a Manichaean view of evil teacher and helpless victim. An account in English can be found in Mihashi 1987. While useful, this analysis emphasizes "the symbolism of social discrimination" with invocations of ritual practice, which has the effect of blunting the critique of bullying as a consequence of a specific political-economic-social order. Hope apparently lies in a utopian notion of "the body" as site of chaos (24).

11. Also see Murakami 1988a, 1988b, 1988c, 1989 for a compelling series on bullying, school rules, and school refusal. Another celebrated case occurred in the dead heat of July 1991, when a fourteen-year-old boy and a sixteen-year-old girl suffocated in the cargo container in which a teacher had confined them for smoking (Hosaka 1991). The weekly journal in which these informative pieces have appeared—one of the very few places where the public had access to information and analysis going beyond the sensationalist, commodified presentations marketed by the rest of the media—began publishing in the 1960s, as a characteristic expression of the political activism of the times. The parent company of the journal, the powerful daily *Asahi Shimbun*, let it fold in the spring of 1992.

12. Or, as Horio (1988:292) puts it, the "laws upon which the normal distribution (Gauss curve) of the five-stage relative evaluation system is based are for the most part used for determining probability in the world of natural phenomena. It is only possible to view this as corresponding to the distribution of human talents and competencies if these are grasped as genetically determined; and of course this way of thinking is incompatible with the approach to human competencies that sees them as the outcome of development through education and learning."

13. See Fujii 1989, Ishida 1989, and Inoue 1991 for a range of constraints placed on teachers. It is possible that there is somewhat more maneuvering space in nonelite schools and neighborhoods (personal communication from David Slater, a University of Chicago graduate student in anthropology currently engaged in fieldwork in Tokyo, as well as conversation with my daughter's first-grade teacher when she moved from a white-collar school district to a shopkeep-

ing one). Byung-ho Chung's presentation at the "Children at Risk" conference (1992b), titled "Experiments for Social Change: Day Care Movements and Ideological Strategies in Japan," provided a tantalizing account of flexible, creative preschool care provided especially in minority (such as Korean and Burakumin, once outcaste) communities. See his dissertation (1992a) for details.

14. As one mother with a junior-high-aged daughter told me, she is reluctant to call the school even when her daughter is late coming home from a school-sponsored athletic event because she thinks such a gesture would mark her as a complainer and be held against her daughter.

15. "Tozashita mado e 'yōkō' sasui Tōkōkyohi mittsu no kīwādo" (sunlight shines into a closed window: three keywords for solving school refusal), *Tokyo Shimbun*, March 13, 1992, evening edition, 10.

16. There are obvious resonances of Illich 1970.

17. Personal communication, labor journalist Nakazawa Takao.

18. My thanks to Moishe Postone for directing me to this passage and for sharing his thoughts on the conceptualization of production and consumption in the work of the mature Marx. See Postone 1993.

19. The math program is that of Kumon, a leading extraschool education company. It works on a franchise, or more accurately, a cottage-industry basis whereby the teachers (usually housewives) are licensed to provide a space where children come several times a week to work through vast numbers of specially developed worksheets, primarily in math and language, for improvement of speed and accuracy. The children are given worksheets to take home as well. Caustic fictional depiction of the culture of technocratic schooling may be found in English translation in Shimizu 1991 and Takeno 1991. My thanks to Matthew Mizenko.

20. But see Hae-joang Cho's paper in this volume for the frequency of suicides in Korea, which has been Japan's shadow twin in so many aspects of capitalist development, and which may yet outstrip it. Cho's, Wee's, and my paper together suggest that education might be a fruitful focus for studying the notion of an East Asian capitalism. Francis Fukuyama allows that his "end of history" (and triumph of liberal democracy) thesis is most challenged by the "success of an illiberal, Confucian capitalism in the Far East" (Halliday 1992:90). To characterize this capitalism as underdeveloped in its cultural relative to its economic dimension, as Two Jaw-yann, a Taiwanese economist working in Japan, suggests in his otherwise interesting analysis of "Oriental capitalism," is inadequate (Two 1990:229–37).

21. The implications of the computer's critical role must be built into the Taylorist model invoked above. The "monopoly of knowledge" is no longer in the hands of a foreman, teacher, or section chief, but in computer chips. This is surely part of an answer to the difficult question, who/what is the subject of capitalism? As early as 1952, an American corporate consultant observed that computer-aided automation would result in "emancipation from human workers" (cited in Rifkin 1994:184). It is grimly fascinating to speculate on appropriate forms of schooling for such an emancipated world. The increasing abandonment of education as a public obligation in the United States may be one unwitting response. How will the current recession reshape Japanese schooling?

22. It therefore becomes tempting to view the unimpressive quality of Japanese higher education as intentional rather than otherwise. A new genre of tourism known as "the graduation trip" suggests the amorphous foreboding with which students regard their imminent transformation. The graduation trip, usually financed by parents, typically takes the form of overseas group travel. The young people who embark on this journey during the month or so between graduation in March and the first day on the job in April talk of this as "the last chance" to be free for the rest of their lives.

23. Thoughtful discussions of modern Japanese educational history may be found in Horio 1988. My overall indebtedness to the painstaking, courageous work of Horio should be evident from my citations. I am also indebted to conversation with Steven Platzer on his unpublished manuscript detailing the revival of the prewar ideologues of "total war" in the postwar Education Ministry.

24. It is probably wise not to exaggerate the flexibility of the flexible workforce. Highly skilled workers capable of innovation and adaptation are flexible to a large degree insofar as they are transportable like modules. And we should not forget the flexibility of the reserve industrial army, such as that constituted by women part-timers in Japan. See note 8, above.

25. From the official translation.

26. That the end of the Liberal-Democratic regime in 1993 has not (yet) necessitated the rewriting of this sentence suggests that (*a*) the recent political changes in Japan have meant the generalization of conservatism, with promises of reform signifying rationalization and restructuring that can hardly be construed as progressive and (*b*) education is driven first and foremost by corporate needs.

27. Article 9, the "no-war" clause of the Constitution, has been handled similarly to allow for the maintenance of sizable armed forces under the name of self-defense and now for their deployment overseas under the aegis of the UN. For a detailed discussion of the trials and administrative and legislative measures whereby the postwar reforms were hollowed out, see chapters 4–11 in Horio 1988.

28. It is interesting to note, however, that the government is willing to be explicit about reserving the right to interpret Article 9, section 1 about not separating children from their parents against their will as not applying when parents are deported as illegal aliens (a pressing issue, as mentioned in n. 3, above; "Jidō kenri jōyaku hijune: Seifu, kokkai no shōnin motomeru" (Toward ratification of the Convention on the Rights of the Child: Government seeks parliamentary approval), *Tokyo Shimbun*, March 13, 1992, evening edition, 2). Does this suggest that the government feels little pressure to deal with contradictions between abstractly exhortatory provisions and its own practice, or does it only attend to those provisions that are specifically sensitive today?

29. In speculating as to why high-school students did not rise up in protest over the girl whose skull was crushed, Saitō (1990:28) writes, "College students, labor unions, citizens' groups—no one's doing anything noticeable these days. People have forgotten the dynamism of demonstrations, strikes, collective bargaining, and what's left is ritualized and washed out."

30. My thanks to René Arcilla for sharing this essay with me.

31. The inner-child therapies discussed in Marilyn Ivy's paper in this collection are a reified testimony to and politically disabling expression of the importance of childhood to adults in advanced capitalist societies.

32. This discussion is much indebted to chapter 4, "Stephen Crane's Toys," in Brown (forthcoming). Sutton-Smith and Kelly-Byrne (1984) presents a useful survey of play.

33. As Fraser (1989:182–83) adjudicates between the progressive critics and proponents of rights claims, the translation of "justified needs claims into social rights" is an important tool for opposing paternalism, and "to treat justified needs claims as the bases for new social rights is to begin to overcome obstacles to the effective exercise of some existing rights." To press for the freedom of children to develop their sensibility as a right overlaps with aspects of the feminist, gay and lesbian, and minority ethnic movements.

34. "'Kodomo no kenri' uta ya manga de" (the 'rights of the child' through songs and cartoons), *Asahi Shimbun*, July 18, 1994, 11.

REFERENCES

Ariès, Philippe, 1962, *Centuries of Childhood*, trans. Robert Baldick, London, Jonathan Cape.

Arita Michio and Yamaoka Shunsuke, 1992, "'Karōji' Shōkōgun" (The 'Overworthy Child' Syndrome), *Asahi Journal*, March 20, 11–16.

Barthes, Roland, 1957, *Mythologies*, Paris, Éditions du Seuil.

Boas, George, 1966, *The Cult of Childhood*, London, Warburg Institute.

Braverman, Harry, 1974, *Labor and Monopoly Capital: The Degradation of Work in the Twentieth Century*, New York, Monthly Review Press.

Brown, Bill, forthcoming, The *Material Unconscious*. Cambridge, Harvard University Press.

Chung, Byung-ho, 1992a, *Childcare Politics: Life and Power in Japanese Day Care Centers*, Ph.D. diss., University of Illinois at Urbana-Champaign.

————, 1992b, "Experiments for Social Change: Day Care Movements and Ideological Strategies in Japan," presented at the conference "Children at Risk," Bergen, Norway, May.

Field, Norma, 1991, *In the Realm of a Dying Emperor*, New York, Pantheon.

Fraser, Nancy, 1989, "Struggle over Needs: Outline of a Socialist-Feminist Critical Theory of Late Capitalist Political Culture," in *Unruly Practices: Power, Discourse, and Gender in Contemporary Social Theory*, Minneapolis, University of Minnesota Press, 161–87.

Fujii Seiji, 1989, "Mono iu shinjin kyōshi wa gakkō kara deteike?" (New teachers who speak up should get out of the schools?), *Asahi Journal*, January 27, 37–41.

Halliday, Fred, 1992, "An Encounter with Fukuyama," *New Left Review* 193:89–95.

Horio Teruhisa, 1984, *Kodomo o minaosu: Kodomokan no rekishi to genzai* (Reconsidering children: The past and present of our perspectives on children), Tokyo, Iwanami Shoten.

———, 1986, *Kyōiku kihonhō wa doko e* [The Fate of the Fundamental Law of Education], Tokyo, Yūhikaku.

———, 1988, *Educational Thought and Ideology in Modern Japan: State Authority and Intellectual Freedom*, ed. and trans. Steven Platzer, Tokyo, University of Tokyo Press.

———, 1990, "Gendai shakai to kyōiku: 'Nōryokushugi' no mondaisei" (Contemporary society and education: The problems with "meritocracy"), *Kyōiku no kadai* (Topics for education), ed. Horio, Tokyo, Iwanami Shoten.

Hosaka Nobuhito, 1991, "Manatsu no akumu: kontena kankin" (Midsummer nightmare: Imprisonment in a container), *Asahi Journal*, August 16, 102.

Ibuka Masaru, 1989, *Naze zerosai na no ka: Jinsei wa zerosai de kimarimasu* (Why age zero? Life is decided at age zero), Tokyo, Yōjikaihatsu Kyōkai.

———, 1992, *Taiji wa tensai da* (The fetus is a genius), Tokyo, Yōjikaihatsu Kyōkai.

Iijima, Yoshiharu, 1987, "Folk Culture and the Liminality of Children," *Current Anthropology* 28(4):41–48.

Illich, Ivan, 1970, *Deschooling Society*, New York, Harper and Row.

Inoue Ryūichirō, 1991, *Gerunika jiken: Dochira ga hontō no kyōikuka* (The *Guernica* incident: Which is the truer education?), Tokyo, Komichi Shobō.

Ishida Hiroki, 1989, "'Hi no maru' o kyōsei suru shin shidō yōryō" (The new course of Study that imposes the rising sun), *Asahi Journal*, March 24, 20–23.

Ishihara, Shintaro, 1991, *The Japan That Can Say No*, trans. by Frank Baldwin, New York, Simon and Schuster.

Key, Ellen, 1909, *The Century of the Child*, London, G. P. Putnam's Sons.

Kotlowitz, Alex, 1991, *There Are No Children Here: The Story of Two Boys Growing Up in the Other America*, New York, Doubleday.

Kyoto Kyōiku Centā, ed., 1987, *"Nihon bunkaron" hihan to Rinkyōshin* (Critique of Japanese cultural theory and the ad Hoc Council on Education), Tokyo, Azumino Shobō.

Lefebvre, Henri, 1973, *The Survival of Capitalism: Reproduction of the Relations of Production*, trans. Frank Bryant, New York, St. Martin's Press.

Lock, Margaret, 1990, "Flawed Jewels and National Dis/Order: Narratives on Adolescent Dissent in Japan," *Journal of Psychohistory* 18(4):507–31.

Lyotard, Jean-François, 1986, *Le postmoderne expliqué aux enfants: Correspondance 1982–1985*, Paris, Éditions Galilée.

Mihashi, Osamu, 1987, "The Symbolism of Social Discrimination: Decoding of Discriminatory Language," *Current Anthropology* 28(4):19–29.

Miyake, Yoshiko, 1991, *Women, Work, Family, and the State in Japan, 1868–1990: Rewriting Modern Japanese Social History from a Feminist Perspective*, Ph.D. diss., University of California at Santa Cruz.

Murakami Yoshio, 1988a, "Tōkōkyohi wa byōki de wa nai" (School refusal is not a disease), *Asahi Journal*, November 4, 24–28.

———, 1988b, "Isha mo kusuri mo nakutemo chan to tachinaoreru" (You can get back on your feet without doctors or medication), *Asahi Journal*, November 25, 92–96.

―――, 1988c, "Kita no kuni no aru oyako ga sukashite miseta yosōgai ni moroi kazoku no shōzō" (The unexpectedly frail family portrait revealed by a parent-child pair in the North Country), *Asahi Journal*, December 16, 23–27.

―――, 1989, "Tōkōkyohi: Mō hitotsu no dasshutsuro; sugu mijika ni aru no de wa" (School refusal—another escape route that might be right near you), *Asahi Journal*, February 2, 19–23.

―――, 1990, "Taibatsu to iu mayaku ni hisomu fukusayo" (The hidden side effects of the drug known as corporal punishment), *Asahi Journal*, August 24, 22–24.

Murasaki Fuyoko, 1987, *Kaiwarezoku no hensachi nikki* (The standard-deviation diary of the radish-sprout kids), Tokyo, Kamakura Shobō.

Nakano Midori and Hashimoto Osamu, 1991, *Futari no Heisei* (Our Heisei era), Tokyo, Shufu no Tomosha.

Postman, Neil, 1982, *The Disappearance of Childhood*, New York, Delacorte Press.

Postone, Moishe, 1993, *Time, Labor, and Social Domination: A Reinterpretation of Marx's Critical Theory*, Cambridge, Cambridge University Press.

Rifkin, Jeremy, 1994, "Laid Off! Computer Technologies and the Re-engineered Workplace." *Ecologist* 24(5) (September–October):182–89.

Saitō Jirō, 1990, "Gakkō o norikoeru ni wa" (To overcome the schools), *Asahi Journal*, August 24, 27–29.

Sayer, Derek, 1991, *Capitalism and Modernity: An Excursus on Marx and Weber*, London, Routledge.

Shimizu, Yoshinori, 1991, "Japanese Entrance Exams for Young Men," trans. Jeffrey Hunter, *Monkey Brain Sushi*, ed. Alfred Birnbaum, New York, Kodansha International, 239–59.

Sutton-Smith, Brian and Diana Kelly-Byrne, 1984, "The Idealization of Play," in *Play in Animals and Humans*, ed. Peter Smith, Oxford, Basil Blackwell, 305–21.

Takenaka, Emiko, 1992, "The Restructuring of the Female Labor Force in Japan in the 1980s," *U.S.-Japan Women's Journal*, English supplement, 2:3–15.

Takeno, Masato, 1991, "The Yamada Diary," trans. Alfred Birnbaum, *Monkey Brain Sushi*, ed. Alfred Birnbaum, Tokyo, Kodansha International, 279–304.

Two Jaw-yann, 1990, *Tōyō shihonshugi* (Oriental capitalism), Tokyo, Kodansha.

Winn, Marie, 1981, *Children without Childhood*, New York, Pantheon.

Yamazumi Masami, 1989, *Gakushū shidō yōryō to kyōkasho* (The course of study and textbooks) Iwanami booklet no. 140, Tokyo, Iwanami Shoten.

CHAPTER 2

Have You Seen Me? Recovering the Inner Child in Late Twentieth-Century America

MARILYN IVY

OCCASIONALLY the unnoticed repetitions of everyday American capitalism break the surface of consciousness, emerging into the light of consumer awareness. One such break occurred to me in 1991, when I rented a new apartment in Ann Arbor and started receiving a different set of consumer mailings. Somehow I began to notice the benumbingly regular arrival of a weekly packet of coupons, flyers, and advertisements that came together with a card addressed to RESIDENT. Perhaps it was also my changed circumstances that inspired me to a brief flurry of consumer activism, when I tried to halt these unsolicited mailings (feeling that they were indeed an unconscionable waste of paper). To stop the mailings proved remarkably difficult, although I eventually succeeded.

The familiar cards and their associated packets are sent by a corporation called ADVO, a national advertisement enterprise based in Hartford, Connecticut; they consolidate ads from local businesses and national chains and send them in a weekly junk mailing that RESIDENTs get. The ADVO card *must* accompany the packet of advertisements in order for the post office to deliver it.[1] Since I had become preoccupied with stopping ADVO's mailings (which I normally would have just tossed in the trash), I started looking more closely at the addressee cards that accompanied the packets. On the front of each weekly card, in large, boldface type is printed this: "ADVO asks—HAVE YOU SEEN ME?" Below that question is the two-tone photograph and vital statistics of a child. Although we are never told directly that the child is missing, anyone in America today almost instinctively registers what a photograph of a child and its vital statistics indicate when publicly displayed. We know from milk cartons, grocery bags, and gum machines. And we know from ADVO and its ads. Below the statistics is an imperative: "CALL 1–800–843–5678" (an easy-to-remember 800 number, the ubiquitous requirement for any serious claim to public response). And then in small type below: "National Center for Missing and Exploited Children—Over 50 children featured have been recovered."[2]

ADVO ASKS...
HAVE YOU SEEN ME?

Age at Disappearance	Age Progression

NAME: TYLER JENNINGS INMAN   DOB: 05/27/79 AGE: 12
HT 2'8" (at age 3) EYES: Blue HAIR: Blonde WT 32 lbs. (at age 3)
SEX:M   DATE MISSING: 12/21/82   FROM: Aberdeen, WA

CALL 1-800-843-5678
1-800-826-7653 (TDD * for Hearing Impaired)
National Center for Missing and Exploited Children
Over 50 children featured have been recovered.

ADVO
ADVO, Inc.
231 West Service Road
Hartford, CT 06120

CAR RT SORT
Bulk Rate
US Postage
PAID
ADVO, inc.

511689
RESIDENT   XXWSCR19
111.5 CATHERINE ST
ANN ARBOR MI   48104

Postal Service Regulations require that this address card be delivered together with its accompanying postage paid mail advertisements. If you should receive this card without its accompanying mail, please notify your local postmaster.

The structure of interpellation used in this message is revealing in its disclosure of how a generalized residential addressee (RESIDENT) is put into relation with advertising discourses. It is also revealing for how the concern with "missing (and exploited) children" works to locate this addressee in a mutually reinforcing position of guilt and consumer desire.

First of all, the framing question: "ADVO asks." Advo puts itself in the position of the interrogator, that of a concerned public entity. ADVO wants to know, and you should want to tell ADVO if you know something. It would have been easy to delete that framing condition—merely to print "Have you seen me?" above the photograph. But ADVO (most people have absolutely no idea who or what ADVO is) asks, and therefore ADVO places itself in the position of wanting to know. But it does so by referring to itself in the third person. ADVO (the corporation) does not refer to itself as "We"—a self-identified, corporate first person—but rather as "ADVO," a detached yet interested third-person questioner.

"ADVO asks . . . HAVE YOU SEEN ME?" The question evidently refers the "me" to the photograph of the child on the card. Yet there is a double meaning here, one that repeats the function of the card itself as the necessary accompaniment to the ad mailing. When I pick up the card and read it, I realize that the "you" of the question is addressed to "me"—the nameless "RESIDENT" that is, literally, the addressee of the card in a double sense. Yet what is the status of the "me" in "HAVE YOU SEEN ME?" The "me" obviously indicates the (missing) child, who has now been positioned as the speaker, the speaking subject. The missing child is the one presumed to ask "Have you seen me?" and "me" refers to the absent child. The use of "see" indicates as well the visual referent printed on the card, the photograph that replaces the missing child. But what a strange conjunction: "*ADVO* asks" "Have you seen *me*?" ADVO here is the subject of speech—the discursively located subject, the grammatical subject—yet the speaking subject, the person presumed to ask the question "HAVE YOU SEEN ME?" is the missing child. "Me" is the photographic and statistical missing child, yet there is a confusion of speaking positions between ADVO and this child. ADVO puts itself in place of the missing child, speaking for it and on behalf of it, backing up the query that could only come from the child. Yet there is another slippage, for "me" also refers to ADVO. Another meaning of the question "Have you seen me?" is: Have you seen this card? Did you get your consumer mailing, of which this card is the signifier and harbinger? Have you seen your ads? The child as ADVO and "me."[3]

Yet it is not just any child. The child is, of course, *missing*. The child's bodily whereabouts are unknown; we don't know where the subject is who could ask "Have you seen me?" It's a question whose place of locution is absent. ADVO puts itself in that place; it arrogates the generalized position of the missing child to itself in order to replace it with the lure of the commodity, as the desire to recover the missing child is profitably linked with the desire to find the missing commodity thing. ADVO as a corporate name has an insidiously doubled resonance: ADVO is clearly related to "*ad*vertising" but equally linked to "*ad*vocacy." Advertising is coterminous with the advocacy of (missing) children: ADVO.

How does the ADVO effect work? Part of the answer lies in the guilt, fear, and attendant fascination that many of us feel over the sensationalized fate of missing children. ADVO presumes that the edge of these affects will compel the resident to look at the card, creating the momentary opening necessary for the advertising to insinuate itself. In seeing the indistinctly printed photo, one immediately knows the child is missing—a chillingly effective way to rivet the eye, at least momentarily, to the ADVO card one was about to toss—and, it is hoped, to the ad on the back of the card and to the packet. Yet there is a further implication to this guilt and fear, and like the entire ADVO ad it concerns the question of identity. Remember that the card is addressed to RESIDENT, the not-homeless, abstract, consuming subject. If a child is missing, then I (for example) as an abstract consuming resident must be "here" at home. The absence of the child is bought by the presence of the consumer, and the representation of the (missing) child announces the presence of this week's shopping deals. But of course the abstract consumer doesn't exist either: she or he remains nameless, no addressee in particular. That a child is missing—not at home—also brings up fears that perhaps we as residents at home are missing something, too; some essential part of our identity. A structure of advocated consumption that would

increasingly demand the abstraction of nameless residency dictates that we are all missing, in a sense. Being abstracted in that way motivates a move toward finding what is missing. Since we probably can't find the missing child (although the tiny photograph is a painful reminder that perhaps we could or should), the packet of ads is there to tell us of what else we might be missing and where to find it: Domino's Pizza, Sterling Optical, Tireman, Hydroflo, Twining's Upholstery and Carpet Cleaning, Jiffy Lube.

What at first might strike one as a simple public-service announcement (indeed, that is how ADVO presents it) turns out to be an intense management of consumer desire and fear, complete with the fantasy bribe of the possible recovery of the missing child and the location of the missing consumer and consumer object. It is an everyday example of the pervasive interest in missing and abused children in the United States and the capitalist articulation of that interest. Discourses on missing and abused children have ramified enormously in the last twenty years, particularly during the Reagan-Bush era, and it is a ramification that is not unrelated to changing formations of capitalist culture and the fluidity of older categories of identity—including that of the child.[4] In the remainder of this essay, I want to link the discourse on missing and abused children and their "recovery" through such publicized strategies of surveillance as ADVO's with two other areas of obsessive interest in the contemporary United States: drug abuse and other kinds of abuse (simultaneously, and popularly, troped as "addiction") and popular therapies that focus on "recovering" the so-called Inner child through "recovering" repressed memories, leading to a subsequent "recovery" from addiction, and thence to a "recovery" from all that ails (see Derrida 1993).[5] The interlinked themes of abuse, addiction, and recovery form a medicalized and desocialized triad of tropes that first shifts public awareness from systemic, society-wide mistreatment of children through

class, race, and gender exploitation to an imaginarily privatized scene of the nuclear family and then moves further into the interior reaches of a bourgeois subject that now consumes (and subsumes) the very possibility of the social.

The figure of the child within the family becomes the site for the crossing of these discourses. I do not want to minimize the practical realities of domestic violence in the United States. Societal abuse and the corresponding burden placed on families (and the concurrent familialization of society) are largely responsible for what is a great amount of violence against children and women. But I am interested in examining the sensationalistic nature of much of this public concern and its segregation (within families or familial surrogates, such as day care centers) in the face of overwhelming societal neglect of poor children in the American class system, for example. Most media reports on missing children focus on the grisly, random, and individualized cases of abduction. According to the statistics available from the National Center for Missing and Exploited Children, in 1988 there were 114,600 "attempted abductions of children by nonfamily members" (one wonders what an "attempted abduction" implies), 4,600 "abductions by nonfamily members reported to police," and 300 "abductions by nonfamily members where the children were gone for long periods of time or were murdered." In fact, however, the great majority of missing children are abducted by so-called family members, usually one of the parents involved in a custody dispute: 354,000 children in 1988.[6] It is clear that the great preponderence of abductions occur, then, around the scene of the family, even as it becomes increasingly difficult to demarcate that scene when the difference between family and nonfamily is precisely at issue (thus the linkage of "broken" homes, divorced spouses—no longer "family"—and kidnapped children).

The concern for missing children is paralleled and probably exceeded

by the related national interest in child abuse. Celebrated court cases focused on day care centers as well as within households would lead the casual reader to think that child abuse had reached epidemic proportions. *Newsweek* devoted a cover article to the "panic over child abuse" in the wake of the Mia Farrow–Woody Allen affair; the reversal of the Kelly Michaels case (a worker at the Wee Care preschool in Maplewood, New Jersey, who was sentenced in 1988 to forty-seven years in prison), and the PBS *Frontline* two-part special on the Edenton, North Carolina, day care case have been prominent reminders of the continuing ethico-legal quandaries surrounding child abuse and the testimony of children (Shapiro 1993).[7] The correlate and lurid explosion of publicity on "satanic ritual abuse" (widely known as SRA), the debates about repression and recovered memories—such that an adult "survivor" remembers a repressed incident of abuse (inevitably referencing sexual abuse) years after the fact—and questions of therapeutic intervention all point to a tight intersection of effects that cross the scene of the family and the figure of the child. In the rhetoric of child abuse and recovery, the child becomes the signifier of the certainty of knowledge, because innocent (and because innocent, therefore truthful: children don't lie); sexuality, in timeworn fashion, becomes the idiom in which dangerous questions about knowledge, identity, and the social are framed within late-industrial contexts corrosive of the bounded stabilities of family, identity, and location (see Nathan 1991).[8]

Again, according to many studies, abuse and domestic violence in general *are* indeed problems of massive proportions. The U.S. Department of Justice reports that three out of one hundred Americans are victims of violent crimes each year. Yet Americans are much more likely to be assaulted or killed in their own homes by a family member than anyone else (Gelles and Straus 1988:18). The family is a violent institution, even when we consider that (according to the First National Survey of Family Violence in 1976) some 4 percent of familes are abusive to children (and according to the second survey, that number *decreased* in 1988). In 1978 only one in ten Americans thought that child abuse was a serious social problem. Yet by 1982, nine out of ten people thought that child abuse was serious (Gelles and Strauss 1988:106–7). Had child abuse increased that dramatically in only four years, or had people's perceptions of its ubiquity increased?

Ian Hacking has traced the genealogy of the notion of child abuse and has shown how its definitional reach has expanded considerably in the last twenty years (the phrase itself—"child abuse"—didn't really even exist before the 1960s); correspondingly, a massive increase in the number of child abuse cases has also occurred. In 1967, there were 7,000 reported cases. Yet by 1981 there were 1.1 million reported cases of child abuse and neglect, and twice that many in 1989 (see Hacking 1991:258). In 1992 almost 3 million cases of suspected child abuse were reported, according to a study by the National Committee for Prevention of Child Abuse (Shapiro 1993:57). Some trace this precipitous increase in reporting (if not actual incidence—fewer than one-half of reported cases in 1992 led to further investigations) to the passage in 1974 of the Child Abuse Prevention and Treatment Act, which made it a legal requirement for health care workers and teachers to report suspected child abuse to authorities. Yet the question that returns is precisely this one: has child abuse really increased that much, or are we now so sensitized to all its ramifications that it appears more and more frequently? Has its discursive construction—its appearance and refinement as a category—enabled instances to become visible in a way that wasn't possible before? To ask these questions is in no way to deny the realities of violence toward children, but it is to think about what *child abuse* references. It now most tellingly evokes *sexual* mistreatment, although originally it meant primarily physical abuse; *incest* was the term invariably used for sexual abuse. Why the particular obsession now with child abuse, either in its mass-mediated spectacular forms (like satanic ritual abuse) or in its more generalized and everyday forms as theorized in the inner-child therapies that have flourished in recent years?[9] And, characteristically, why are its causes (if not its effects) located almost exclusively in the domains of the individual and family (or family surrogates)? The concurrent moral panic over drug abuse that marked, in particular, the Reagan-Bush presidencies also locates a chilling conjuncture with child abuse: conservative critics trace both to the breakdown of family values and loving familial (and most notably, maternal) incorporation and protection of the individual child.[10]

I think that spectacular media attention on sexual abuse as well as drug abuse indicates societal fears about what is imagined as the last remaining site of purity in a world of overtly sexualized consumer products: the child. Yet as we know, children are the most intensely targeted market segment in the United States today, and the entire spectrum of their embodied desires are overtly managed by capitalist enterprises. The realities of late twentieth-century America mean that children must often be kept in day care centers, away from home (their mothers are also away from home, too—working); that the child is overtly sexualized in consumer capitalism; and that consumer capitalism has targeted the child as the ideal model of the impulsive, addicted buyer. Thus it is not suprising that conversely the child must be maintained as sexually innocent, "at home," and as the model of the nonaddicted self in American popular discourses.

Along with ADVO ads about missing children, milk cartons, and tabloid spectaculars on child abuse in day care centers—and along with admonitions to Just Say No—there is another popular and public locus of concern that ties together child abuse, missing children, and addiction—one that seeped into my awareness about the same time that ADVO was insinuating itself into my mail. And that is the stunningly popular self-help literature on the inner child and recovery in the United States today. I first became aware of this entire world of discourse slowly, as references to codependence, twelve-step programs, recovery, dysfunctional families, and recovering the inner child began to repeat themselves in the media. I was puzzled about their relationship. I understood that there was a therapeutic movement focused on recovering the inner child in oneself, that "wounded child," as the rhetoric goes, whose needs were not met earlier on and who still existed within oneself, causing trouble in the adult present. (Grown-ups with such needy inner children are called "adult children" in the literature.) But I didn't exactly understand how this was linked to drug abuse, addiction, recovery, and codependence. My excellent local bookstore, I now suddenly noticed, had an entire wall devoted to Self-help, Addiction and Recovery, where a huge array of books about cognitive addiction, sexual addiction, substance addiction, alcohol addiction, work addiction, exercise addiction, shopping addiction, and (lastly) recovery from addiction were shelved along with book after book about healing the inner child, recovering the inner child, reparenting the inner child, and reclaiming the inner child.[11] There seemed to be two intersecting rhetorics: a medicalized one on addiction and abuse—again, the obsession with drug abuse (and the seeming increase in its incidence) in the United States parallels that with child abuse; and a discourse on recovery—in the sense of *healing*—from addiction that links up with recovery—in the sense of *finding*—the lost inner child of the addicted (which, according to many of these publications, includes the vast majority of the population). In short, being an abused child leads to later substance abuse and addiction and thus the need for recovery from addiction by recovering—finding and healing—the abused inner child. (See Kaminer 1992 for a critical yet popular analysis of therapies of recovery.)

The notion of the inner child has been around for quite some time in American therapy; Hugh Missildine's *Your Inner Child of the Past* was published in 1963 and is generally considered the founding text of inner-child therapies today. Some of those therapies' tenets and objectives are not so distant from other psychoanalytic and psychotherapeutic ones. But through the work of the analyst Alice Miller and others, there have been some distinct shifts. One tenet is that—in contradistinction to a certain reified Freudian interpretation—childhood sexual abuse is considered, almost by definition, as factual—*not* as fantasy, or even imbricated with the possibilities of fantasy (see Miller 1981; Laplanche and Pontalis 1986).[12] Starting from the reality of emotional, physical, and sexual abuse (*abuse* has now expanded considerably), inner-child therapies insist that the recipients of this abuse—most children, they would assert—are stuck at earlier developmental stages when their necessary narcissistic needs were not lovingly met (by caretakers who themselves were abused and deprived and thus were not able to meet those needs). Therefore, these adult children—children who really never grew up— compulsively try to get these needs met by various addictions. They must go back and recover those earlier stages with a strategy of getting in touch with the wounded inner child and reparenting it. Only after having met those developmental needs will the person truly recover from childhood abuse and become free from addictive behavior.

The linkage of the inner child with childhood violence and abuse—whether physical, sexual, or emotional—is foundational for these therapies and popular self-help works. (Although the larger concern with child abuse cuts across advanced industrial Euroamerica, the linkage with addiction and recovery is, I think, a distinctly American development.) The other domain of reference that has become thoroughly implicated with inner-child therapies derives from the initially quite distinct one of Alcoholics Anonymous, which constitutes the model of the many, many recovery groups that base their therapies on AA's Twelve Steps. There are now twelve-step groups, publications, and modalities of all persuasions throughout the United States.

Alcoholics Anonymous is by far the biggest and most powerful self-help group in the world. It was founded in 1935, and more than 58,000 AA groups in 112 countries have been founded. According to the information it disseminates, "AA is a spiritual program based on the Twelve Steps, which form the foundation of AA's recovery program. . . . The focus is on staying sober *today*" (Yoder 1990:46). The basis of the group lies in a conversion experience undergone by its founder—commonly known as Bill W., who was highly influenced by the so-called Oxford Group, an evangelical movement popular in the 1930s. The language of Alcoholics Anonymous relies on a rhetoric of power: the first step in the twelve steps is for the alcoholic to admit that she or he is "powerless over alcohol"—in other words, to admit addiction as a state of infantile dependency. (All the steps are designed to bring the addict into a relationship with a higher "Power." For example, step number 2 states that "We came to believe that a Power greater than ourselves could restore us to sanity.")

Most American self-help literature on the inner child tends to start with the assertion of addiction, and it is that emphasis on addiction—which has now expanded to cover almost any compulsive activity (including reading, working, and studying)—that links it to the Alcoholics Anonymous model of recovery (see Yoder 1990:3).[13] This model states what for many is the obvious: that people look for completion in the external world because they feel inadequate and imperfect. The recovery model takes as a given that most families are "dysfunctional" (John Bradshaw, the guru of recovery and inner-child therapies, says some 95 percent of all families are dysfunctional) and that most children are so shamed in these families that they believe that nothing they can ever do will be sufficient to please their parents. They thus feel inadequate and incomplete, searching for fulfillment outside themselves. This shame is passed down within families from generation to generation. The search for external fulfillment, generated by this "toxic shame," as John Bradshaw terms it, synergistically meshes with others' shame, and relationships are formed that are codependent, the dysfunction that arises when one focuses too selflessly on the needs of others. Codependence originally referred to the coping mechanisms of children or spouses involved with an alcoholic family member, but it has expanded to cover the behavior of people raised in any sort of dysfunctional family. In fact, in the expansion of addiction and codependence to cover society as a whole, the popular self-help author Anne Wilson Schaef asserts that codependence describes the majority of the population in the United States; using statistics developed on alcoholism that state there are between ten and fifteen million alcoholics in the United States (and that each one adversely affects between twenty and thirty persons), she claims that "the number of codependents in the United States exceeds the total population" (Schaef 1987:15).[14] Codependency has indeed become an excessive trope.

It is here that the inner child emerges as the focus and theme of therapies of recovery. Charles Whitfield, author of one of the early classics in the field, *Healing the Child Within*, believes that twelve-step programs alone are not adequate to bring people to total health. Instead, people work through twelve-step programs and then work on healing the inner child, "a process that involves reexperiencing early-life traumas and grieving the nurturing support they never received" (quoted in R. Miller 1992:202). As Whitfield states, "Since up to 95 percent of families are dysfunctional, we're all adult children either doing our work of recovery or in need of it. Even though our Child Within has gone into hiding, it never dies. When we rescue that frightened, wondrous inner being, we reclaim the power, creativity, and vitality to make life a spiritual adventure" (quoted in R. Miller 1992:202). This inner being is sometimes referred to as the "true self"; the "false self" is the socialized, addicted adult child.

John Bradshaw is probably the most prominent national figure of this movement, and his writings give a sense of the normative assumptions about the family, addiction, and the inner child in self-help literature. His book *Bradshaw On: The Family* was a national best-seller and has sold over 500,000 copies; his book *Homecoming: Reclaiming and Championing Your Inner Child* occupied the top position on the *New York Times* bestseller list for weeks.

In his book on the family, Bradshaw gives a "profile of a functional family system." A dysfunctional family is one that, not surprisingly, does not function well. He compares the functional family to a car that works, even though it may have rust spots. It is thus a *mechanical* model of the family. He gives these characteristics:

a. The family is a survival and growth unit.

b. The family is the soil which provides the emotional needs of the various members. These needs include a balance between autonomy and dependency and social and sexual training.

c. A healthy family provides the growth and development of each member including the parents.

d. The family is the place where the attainment of self-esteem takes place.

e. The family is a major unit in socialization and is crucial for a society if it is to endure. (Bradshaw 1988:42)

The proliferation of figures here—the family as unit, soil, place, and mechanism—repeats the proliferation of functions that the family is supposed to carry out. What is troubling in the first instance is the unproblematic assumption of the family as the basic unit of socialization—so much so that Bradshaw asserts that it is "crucial for a society if it is to endure." One wonders on what cross-cultural information Bradshaw bases that prescriptive announcement, as he begs the question of what the family might mean in other contexts. Michèle Barrett and Mary McIntosh in their incisive work *The Anti-Social Family* critique this almost unquestioned assertion of the necessity of the family; as socialists, they recognize the ideological dimension of the family and of familialism. As they state, "The mythological character of 'the family' is part and parcel of its ideologial dominance. . . . [T]he ideological construction of the family as the antithesis to the cash-nexus could *only* refer to a capitalist society" (Barrett and McIntosh 1982:35). As Mark Poster has argued in *Critical Theory of the Family*, the dominant model of the family now current in the United States and in Europe emerged from the nineteenth-century European bourgeoisie (see Poster 1978). It is clear that it is *this* "family" that Bradshaw has in mind: a nuclear family with two parents and one primary caretaker (which he still refers to ubiquitously as the mother). It is this (late-)industrial family—a family inscribed within the productive and consumptive apparatuses of capitalism—that Bradshaw wants to make functional, not critique in any fundamental way. It is also this family—dysfunctional or functional—that produces today's addicted adult children.

In *Homecoming*, Bradshaw's book on recovering the (missing) inner child, the rhetoric of addiction and drug abuse weaves throughout the text. For example, the first chapter is entitled "How Your Wounded Inner Child Contaminates Your Life." One wonders why the image of contamination arises here in discussing a part of oneself that presumably is hurt. As he states, "What I now understand is that when a child's development is arrested, when feelings are repressed, especially the feelings of anger and hurt, a person grows up to be an adult with an angry, hurt child inside of him. This child will spontaneously contaminate the person's adult behavior" (Bradshaw 1990:8). He repeatedly uses the figure of toxicity to describe the shame felt by the wounded inner child. In a poem called "My Name Is Toxic Shame," Bradshaw develops this notion. The first stanza goes like this:

> I was there at your conception
> In the epinephrine of your mother's shame
> You felt me in the fluid of your mother's womb
> I came upon you before you could speak
> Before you understood
> Before you had any way of knowing
> I came upon you when you were learning to walk
> When you were unprotected and exposed
> When you were vulnerable and needy
> Before you had any boundaries
> MY NAME IS TOXIC SHAME.
>
> (Bradshaw 1990:47)

The misogynist implications of this poem, in which shame is biologically transmitted to the preborn child through the mother's fluids (epinephrine?) repeat the common rhetorical moves surrounding crack-addicted mothers and the passing on of their addictions to their (crack) babies.[15] Shame, toxic like crack, is always already addictive, thanks to the mother's addiction. The emphasis on addiction (here Bradshaw asserts that "three-fourths of the population is seriously affected"), on contamination, toxicity, and shame, both mirrors and reinforces a dominant, Christian-inflected discourse in the United States about morality, the law, and family. *Addiction* is a medicalized term that resonates with images of toxicity and contamination (words that of course are also used to describe environmental pollution) and thus works to naturalize compulsions and their effects. To link toxicity and shame is to cross-articulate a scientific rhetoric with a moral-psychological one. Bradshaw makes toxic shame a primordial, naturalized state; it is thus akin in some senses to original sin. To the extent that such ideologies permeate contemporary American society, then, the exposure of its ramifications may be therapeutic to many. But in no sense does Bradshaw undo the premises of an entirely fixed, Christian-inflected, misogynist ideology of the family.

It is through this intergenerational transmission of toxic shame and through all varieties of abuse that the child withdraws and becomes the inner, wounded child (while the outer adult is, again, considered an adult child). Bradshaw's techniques for reclaiming this inner child in order to become a fully functional, nonaddicted adult, are laid out in

Homecoming. Reclaiming the inner child requires that the subject re-
gress to the various developmental stages of childhood and work
through any incomplete "business" from those stages; at each stage the
adult uses fantasy and memory to assist and reclaim the inner child of
that moment. It is crucial, according to these therapies, to express grief
for needs that were not met when they should have been:

> At first, it may seem preposterous that a little child can continue to live
> in an adult body. But that is exactly what I'm suggesting. I believe that this
> neglected, wounded inner child of the past is the major source of human
> misery. Until we reclaim and champion that child, he will continue to act
> out and contaminate our adult lives. (Bradshaw 1990:7)

Bradshaw's book is a self-help manual for this labor, with worksheets,
exercises, questions, and quizzes. Based on an array of ego and developmental psychology theories (he states that he is highly influenced by Erik
Erikson's *Childhood and Society*), Bradshaw's book has the merit of clar-
ity. Enumeration is a favorite device. He states, for example, that there
are "four major developmental stages" in childhood and "four basic ego
strengths," and that when these ego strengths are present there are
"four basic powers." Another device is the use of mnemonic formulas.
"Contaminate"—again, a favored notion—becomes the basis for one of
these formulas:

Co-Dependence
Offender Behaviors
Narcissistic Disorders
Trust Issues
Acting Out/Acting In Behaviors
Magical Beliefs
Intimacy Dysfunctions
Nondisciplined Behaviors
Addictive/Compulsive Behaviors
Thought Distortions
Emptiness (Apathy, Depression)

(Bradshaw 1990:9)

Questionnaires called "Indices of Suspicion" open each chapter of
reclamation, chapters on reclaiming the infant self, the toddler self, the
preschool self, and the school-age self. In each chapter there is a section
on what is normal (for example, "normal infancy"), on "growth disorder," "debriefing" (writing down memories from the period in question), "sharing with a friend," "feeling your feelings," "writing letters,"
"affirmations," and "meditations."

200 pound
3–year–old

140 pound
3–year–old

DAD   YOU   MOM

Fig. 2.6. From John Bradshaw, *Homecoming: Reclaiming and Championing Your Inner Child*, p. 77.

One of the most innovative techniques used in this work is the writing of letters to the inner child. This technique requires that the adult go through a process of imagining herself, first of all, as a "wise and gentle" adult who wants to adopt a child, the adult *as a child* (either an infant, toddler, or older child, depending on the developmental stage that is being addressed). Then the imagined ideal adult writes the inner child a letter. This letter can be short or long, the instructions emphasize, but the point is to assure the child that you (the adult) love and want him or her.[16] The next step requires that the inner child (infant, toddler, or whatever) write a letter to you, the adult. ("I want you to write yourself a letter from your inner infant," Bradshaw's instructions read.) What sets this technique apart from everyday letter writing, however, is this: the letter from the inner child is written with the nondominant hand. Writing and drawing with the nondominant hand allows a species of automatic writing to emerge from the inner child in us all. Childlike scrawls and uncontrolled letters become the marks of a communication with an inner child that is fully present and waiting to be reclaimed. Entire books are devoted to this method of opening up a written dialogue

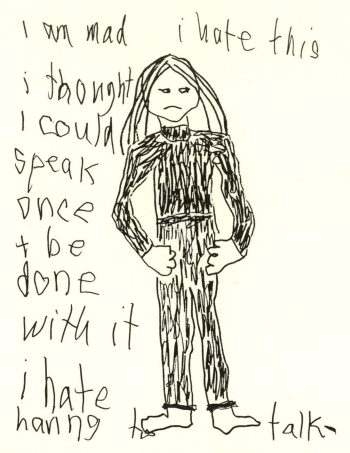

Fig. 2.7. From Lucia Capacchione, *Recovery of Your Inner Child*, p. 96.

with the child within (one is called *The Power of Your Other Hand*; another by the same author is entitled *Recovery of Your Inner Child* [see Capacchione 1991]).

The final step in recovering the inner child at each developmental stage is a series of affirmations, followed by a meditation in which the adult imaginatively regresses to the age of the inner child. In this age regression, the adult moves back and forth between locating herself as the infant (for example, in the crib) and as the wise and gentle adult who is now looking down at the infant with love and is reparenting the child.[17] As with the technique of written dialogue with the inner child, these meditations require a series of splits within the subject. While introjects and split-off parts of the personality are a psychoanalytic staple, inner-child therapy requires that these parts be correlated with the child as a "true self." One takes up a variety of positions—victim and comforter, child and adult, patient and therapist—within oneself. One not only "recreates the self," as the title of another popular manual asserts (see Napier 1990), one subsumes and internalizes within the monadic individual a true self and a false self, a wounded inner child and an addicted adult child, and finally a "wonder child" and a (real) adult. It is as if all the dynamics of human relationships and intergenerational contact are reinscribed within this contained self, and as if the family—itself a certain erasure of the social and of community in the contemporary United States—could now be fully privatized and enclosed within the individual. In the end the child becomes the true guarantor of authenticity and happiness.

From testimonials and therapy reports, we know that inner-child therapies can be remarkably effective in restoring "self-esteem" (another current popular trope) and in healing deep traumas (see Steinem 1992).[18] Spontaneous remissions of serious illnesses have been reported by patients who have done this work. To the extent that Americans are abusive and violent—and to the extent that American society fosters and even encourages this behavior as it puts the burden of socialization and selfhood onto the family—compulsive, so-called addictive behavior and great unhappiness are no doubt common products. These therapies, then, work within the confines of that system in an ameliorative fashion. To the extent American capitalism fosters compulsive gratifications in an all-too-real erasure of childhood, it is understandable that these therapies have arisen to try to understand and mourn this erasure. Their enormous popularity alongside twelve-step groups is undoubtedly an index of widespread pain in the United States.

But the inner-child complex is troubling. These popular therapies talk in sweeping terms about the family as if it were a cross-cultural, eternal verity. They speak of codependency and the need for autonomous selves in ways that would strike many analysts of non-Western societies, for example, as quite Eurocentric. They assume a division between a true self and a false self with a dichotomizing logic that would seem to repeat the pernicious bifurcation of Western thought that recovery writers decry elsewhere. They reduce pain into *solely* the matter of an internalized, familialized self. There are some sharp recognitions of the addictive dimensions of American society in many of these works. But nowhere is this problem of addiction historicized; nowhere is it articulated with the social or economic policies of the American state during the last twenty years, when increasing poverty and the slashing of social services to the poor has kept pace with an hysterical obsession (addiction?) with the problem of drug abuse and child abuse. Although it is clear that the use of drugs has increased in the last twenty years, the criminalization of

Fig. 2.8. From *Homecoming*, p. 155.

that use and the attendant terror surrounding it must be viewed as out of proportion to the increase itself. Similarly, child abuse has emerged as a discursive construct, seemingly in tandem with an actual increase. It has been reconfigured as a medicalized syndrome and it has come, through the reoccurring figure of the abused child, to bear a symbolic burden dependent on the fluidities of advanced capitalist social formations and identities. The tragic prevalence of violence against children in the United States—indeed a sign of something seriously amiss—is not proportional to the hysterical and very narrow concern given to spectacular cases of child abuse by the media and popular discourses. Indeed, the frantic edge to that popular concern discloses a displacement from the more mundane and pervasive abuse of children in late-capitalist America, where one out of five children live in poverty.

Nowhere in this literature is capitalism forwarded as a possible systemic cause for the production of just the kinds of consumptive compulsions these therapies seek to heal within the individual. There is what might be imagined as a certain populist feminist strain in many of these works, with their indictment of patriarchal violence and their recognition of abuse, but antifeminist tendencies usually predominate (particularly in the demonization of mothers); almost no attention is given to race or class. Indeed, the model family in these texts is the idealized white, middle-class, nuclear household—purified of toxins and newly loving, true, but nevertheless fully adapted to the requirements of discipline within an advanced capitalist economy. Extended, mobile African-American kin networks and communities, for example, hardly fit their model of the functional family; neither do single-parent or serial households, lesbian and gay families, multigenerational households, or other, non-American, kinship arrangements or family formations.[19] To the extent that these therapies help people who are embedded in contexts that are based on nuclear families, still the norm if not the dominant reality in the contemporary United States, they are helpful in understanding that context. But nowhere are the narrow familialistic premises of these therapies questioned.

The expansion of the tropes of abuse and addiction (as we have seen, to the extent that codependents exceed the total population of the United States!), as well as the newly installed terms of *recovery*, *inner child*, and *codependency*, speak of a severely circumscribed and normalized discursive world. A friend of mine told me that his brother (who is in therapy and "in recovery" from heroin addiction) now insists that he was abused as a child—emotionally abused. My friend shook his head at this accusation, claiming that his family, although far from perfect, was certainly not abusive. "But," he continued, "if it makes my brother feel better and helps him stay off heroin, then it's fine with me." The pragmatic efficacy of extending the notion of abuse to cover almost any area of childhood disappointment may mask the larger issues involved in such an extension, one that only makes sense when we take into account the enlarged meaning of abuse as including emotional abuse and other types of neglect (see Hacking 1991:271).

The expansion of child abuse parallels, in some respects, a similar trajectory to the category of rape; both categories are similarly fraught in their political and social implications. In no way should the struggles to bring the realities of rape or child abuse to public attention be diminished. Yet even in the comparison of these two prevalent social ills differences emerge, and these differences I take as provocations to think about the ideological configuration of the child, abuse, and addiction in the United States now. Why has ADVO not used rape victims to sell tires and insurance? It is clear that the missing and abused child offers rhetorical assets to consumer capitalism that the rape victim does not. The child can take on the full weight of victimhood in total purity—no one would say that the child asked for its abuse, unlike the sexism that still maintains that women somehow ask to be raped through their sexually provocative behavior. The integrity, purity, and self-sameness of the child—even if missing from the home or hidden in the adult—assures a reserve that is outside the depradations of uncontrolled capitalist desire. At the same time it is a threatened preserve, and it is this possibility of the dissolution of childhood purity (thus the dominant reading of abuse as sexual abuse)—of the effacing of the boundaries between child and adult, private and public—that is intolerable for the upholders of family values.

To assert that virtually all Americans were abused as children, and that we are all thereby virtual addicts and codependents seems to me to collapse differences between forms of oppression. To assert that we can reclaim our inner children is potentially to deny the fragility of a temporally limited childhood in a desperately narcissistic attempt to subsume child, adult, and parent within oneself. And to say that individual self-esteem recovered by reclaiming the inner child is the key to social transformation seems all too convenient for policymakers and politicians unwilling to expend the social resources to fight inequity and poverty; it seems all too close to a serialized "thousand points of light." As the psychotherapist James Hillman (who, strangely enough, is one of the father figures of the men's movement) remarks:

> I believe we now have two ideologies that run the country. One is economics, and the other is therapy. These are basic, bottom-line beliefs that we return to in our private moments. . . . There's been an emphasis on the child archetype in therapy, an archetype that tends to depoliticize the client. Once one is engaged in feeling abused, in feeling victimized, one also feels powerless and seeks to locate blame outside of oneself. The client is concerned with the past, with what happened to him or her, with individual growth. *And the child is not a political being.* (1992:98–99; emphais added)

The child is not a political being: the immense popularity of twelve-step groups and inner-child therapies index the pain that many Americans feel in the late twentieth century; they indicate as well the absence of the political or social networks that could become the places of transformation for that pain. The privatization, familialization, and infantilization of these therapies have accorded well with the dominant American political climate, where the private sector, the individual, and the family are supposed to assume the burdens of the social. (It is not coincidental that the United States is one of the few countries that has not signed the United Nations Convention on the Rights of the Child.)[20] The missing inner child that we are exhorted to recover turns out to have a real connection with the missing child of ADVO: both indicate a displacement from the possibilities of politics and community in late-twentieth-century America into the domains of a privatized imaginary. In both cases, the child becomes the figure of an absent plenitude that can be reclaimed if only the child can be found or recovered from abuse. Out of the three to five million homeless people in the United States, one out of four are children.[21] Not only are these homeless children missing, the very possibility of their ever having been "at home" is erased by the abuses of poverty and racism. Yet they are not featured on ADVO's ads for missing children sent to RESIDENTS. As the title of Alex Kotlowitz's book on childhood in Chicago's housing projects proclaims, *There Are No Children Here*.[22] African-American children are allowed to remain homeless (not even "missing"), abandoned to become the noninnocent objects of a national war on drugs, a noninnocence that in its largest contours buys the unmarked innocence of the generic middle-class white child within the narrative of rescue and recovery.

One of ADVO's recent cards deviated from its usual format with its featuring of a "7th Anniversary Report." At the top in small print is the heading, "A Public Service Provided By," followed by Advo's logo and that of the National Center for Missing and Exploited Children. The next line, "America's Looking for Its Missing Children," preceded a telltale copyright mark. "America's looking for its missing children," in its entirety, is a copyrighted trademark of the ADVO/National Center alliance, a conflation of America with ADVO and company. In the text we are told that over *16 billion* "pictures have been distributed through this public service campaign," a staggering testament to the penetrating power of ADVO's consumer mailings. As the text continues, however, we discover that only *fifty-six* children out of four hundred children "featured" "have been recovered and reunited with their families—approximately one in every seven featured lead [*sic*] to a recovery." The shift from the tallying of past "successes" ("have been recovered") leads to the present-tense generalized assertion of future recovery successes: "one in seven featured lead to a recovery." Yet nowhere is it demonstrated that those fifty-six recoveries can be traced directly back to the ADVO mailings; they may have been recovered by any number of convergent means. Nevertheless, ADVO and the National Center join in a strangely upbeat closing to exhort RESIDENTs: "So join us in celebrating seven great years together. Keep Up The Great Work, America! We couldn't have done it without you!" The great work that America has done to produce the missing and exploited child is now merged with the great work of recovering them and (no doubt) the great work of consuming ADVO's advocated products.[23]

The back of the seventh-anniversary report card was an ad with some discount coupons for Uncle Ed's Oil Shoppe. Meanwhile, ADVO continues to ask HAVE YOU SEEN ME? "No," I think, "not around here." Or more typically, "Of course not," I snap. But such responses really make no difference, for ADVO's all-consuming RESIDENT—the model of the addicted adult child—continues to be found at home, apparently not missing.

NOTES

Thanks to Sharon Stephens, Adela Pinch, John Pemberton, Ann Anagnost, Lauren Berlant, and Philomena Mariani for their comments and suggestions.

1. At the bottom of the card this is printed: "Postal Service Regulations require that this address card be delivered together with its accompanying postage paid mail advertisements. If you should receive this card without its accompanying mail, please notify your local postmaster."

2. This number had increased to sixty, according to the August 1993 ADVO cards.

3. Often in fact the cards ask "Have you seen us?" That is because they often feature photographs of the child in question and her or his known "abductor"—the person the child was seen with last. That person is, not surprisingly, often a relative (usually the mother or father), since the great majority of "abductions" are made by parents in the midst of custody suits.

4. Below the statistics comes the 800 number for identification and recovery, the number for the National Center for Missing and Exploited Children. The ADVO card is produced in such a way that the innocent reader might even think that ADVO *is* the National Center for Missing and Exploited Children. But it is not. I called the center and asked for some information; they sent me a brochure. Although the ADVO ad says that "Over 50 children featured have been recovered," it is not at all clear whether they were recovered via ADVO's ad or by other means. Nor is it clear whether fifty children is a good recovery rate or not (it seems small to me). The center's brochure states that it "has played a role in the recovery of more than 17,000 children" in seven years. It states that "The NCMEC is a national voice, mobilizer, and advocate for those too young to vote or speak up for their own rights—our children. We are working to make America's childhoods safer ones." The organization operates under a congressional mandate and works in cooperation with the U.S. Department of Justice.

5. Addiction was the theme of the spring 1993 issue of the journal *Differences*. An interview with Jacques Derrida entitled "The Rhetoric of Drugs" is particularly relevant to the discussion here, as he both retracks the idea of the *pharmakon* and its significance for any understanding of addiction and thinks seriously about the discursive emergence of the possibility of addiction within modernity itself (what he terms "narcotic modernity").

6. These statistics are printed on the first page of their general information brochure. Various books, brochures, and publication packets concerning miss-

ing, abused, and exploited children can be ordered from the National Center for Missing and Exploited Children. Several of the books concern "sexual exploitation" (it is clear that the "exploitation" the center's name refers to is sexual exploitation): for example, *Child Sex Rings: A Behavioral Analysis* and *Children Traumatized in Sex Rings.*

7. The *Frontline* series was entitled *Innocence Lost*, indicating not only the lost innocence of the children exposed to the aggressive insistences of their therapists that they were abused (playing, of course, on the normative reading that would see "lost innocence" as instead referring to actually sexually abused children) but also the "lost innocence" of the social in Edenton (Eden-town?), which had been forever ruptured by the sexual betrayals, accusations, and denials that marked its deviation from prelapsarian harmony. Innocence stands for the presexual truth of the child, which he or she must speak (when he or she speaks about a sexuality that is not comprehended): the child as the arbiter of knowledge (of good and evil).

8. Debbie Nathan has written some of the most trenchant and clearheaded essays about the panic surrounding child abuse in the United States. See particularly her essays "Sex, The Devil, and Daycare," "The Making of a Modern Witch Trial," and "The Ritual Sex Abuse Hoax" in her book of collected essays *Women and Other Aliens: Essays from the U.S.-Mexico Border* (1991).

9. Stories about satanic ritual abuse (and the question of recovered memories) have become commonplace sensations. Note, for example, the scandalous January-February 1993 issue of *Ms.* with its cover headlines that proclaimed "Believe It! Cult Ritual Abuse Exists: One Woman's Story" (see Rose 1993). Or the skeptical, yet no less sensationalistic reports by Leslie Bennetts, "Nightmares on Main Street," in *Vanity Fair* (1993) and the two-part article by Lawrence Wright, "Remembering Satan" in the *New Yorker* (1993).

10. An article by Barbara Dafoe Whitehead (1993) asserts "Dan Quayle Was Right," echoing pronouncements from all sectors of the political spectrum that, indeed, "the dissolution of intact two-parent families is harmful to large numbers of children" (Whitehead 1993:47). On drug use, *The Recovery Resource Book* claims that the United States has the highest rate of illegal drug use of any industrialized country. Less than 4 percent of the population over twelve had ever used drugs in 1962; by 1985 at least 33 percent had experimented with them and 23 million people were regular users (Yoder 1990:184).

11. Dennis Wholey in the foreword to *The Recovery Resource Book* states that "Hundreds of recovery titles have been published within the past few years. In 1983, when I was putting together *The Courage to Change*, most commercial bookstores couldn't fill half a small shelf with books on alcoholism. In 1990, most of them devote whole sections to alcoholism, other addictions and compulsions, and related problems. There are books for adult children of alcoholics, incest survivors, codependents, sex addicts, food addicts, compulsive gamblers" (Yoder 1990:v).

12. Alice Miller's *The Drama of the Gifted Child* was one of the first therapy books to discount Freud's theories of fantasy. The distinction between Freud's theories of seduction presented in 1896 (in which the realities of incest are rec-

ognized) and his presumed repudiation of the reality of sexual abuse in his later writings on drives and the Oedipus complex is a keystone of Miller's rediscovery of the reality of child abuse. She does, however, oversimplify the distinction in Freud between reality and fantasy. As work on Freud's theories of fantasy has shown, Freud did not completely refute the reality of the sexual seduction of children. But he did develop a theory of fantasy that made the direct, unmediated line between such reality and the elaborations of memory problematic. Jean Laplanche and Jean-Bertrand Pontalis effect a delicate reconsideration of fantasy and psychoanalysis in their "Fantasy and the Origins of Sexuality" (1986).

13. *The Recovery Resource Book* lists the "signs of addiction: 1. You find yourself obsessively thinking about the object or event. 2. A friend or family member has expressed concern over your behavior. 3. Your moods go up and down erratically. 4. You sometimes wonder if you're addicted" (Yoder 1990:3). Even the possibility of addiction ("You wonder if you're addicted") is a sign of addiction.

14. Schaef uses the statistics developed by Earnie Larsen, author of a book entitled *Stage II Recovery*.

15. Lauren Berlant directed my attention to the similarity of Bradshaw's imagery and rhetoric to that surrounding crack babies and their mothers.

16. Bradshaw's letter to his infant self reads this way: "Dear Little John, I'm so glad you were born. I love you and want you to always be with me. I'm very glad you are a boy, and I want to help you grow up. I want a chance to show you how much you matter to me. Love, Big John."

17. One wonders what these "age regressions" signify in relation to the "age progressions" on ADVO cards, wherein a computer-generated photographic projection of the missing child as he or she would look today is printed next to the photograph of the child at the age of disappearance. In both cases, whether retroactive or proactive, there is an attempt to locate and image the missing child. Recent ADVO cards have this printed below the photographs: "Age progression sponsored by JIFFY LUBE INTERNATIONAL, INC."

18. Steinem's recent book *Revolution from Within: A Book of Self-Esteem* uses many of the methods and the rhetoric of inner-child therapies. Steinem speaks of a "true self," of reclaiming the inner child, and of the ubiquity of abuse. For a sharp critique of Steinem's transformation from politicized feminist to a "person in recovery," see Judith Levine (1992).

19. Judith Stacey has uncovered a range of nontraditional, nonnuclear family forms in her *Brave New Families: Stories of Domestic Upheaval in Late Twentieth Century America* (1990).

20. On the question of children's rights within a transnationalizing late capitalism, see Sharon Stephen's introduction to this volume.

21. The ramifications of these statistics and the "feminization of poverty" under Reagan are compellingly addressed in Karin Stallard, Barbara Ehrenreich, and Holly Sklar, *Poverty in the American Dream* (1983).

22. Alex Kotlowitz, *There Are No Children Here: The Story of Two Boys Growing Up in the Other America* (1991). Thanks to Rodger Field for bringing this book to my attention.

23. I want to thank Adela Pinch for showing me this ADVO card.

REFERENCES

Barrett, Michèle and Mary MacIntosh, 1991, *The Anti-Social Family*, 2d ed., London, Verso.

Bennetts, Leslie, 1993, "Nightmares on Main Street," *Vanity Fair*, June, 42–52, 58–62.

Bradshaw, John, 1988, *Bradshaw On: The Family*, Deerfield Beach, Fl., Health Communications.

————, 1990, *Homecoming: Reclaiming and Championing Your Inner Child*, New York, Bantam.

Capacchione, Lucia, 1991, *Recovery of Your Inner Child*, New York, Simon and Schuster.

Derrida, Jacques, 1993, "The Rhetoric of Drugs: An Interview," *Differences* 5(1):1–25.

Gelles, Richard and Murray A. Straus, 1988, *Intimate Violence: The Definitive Study of the Causes and Consequences of Abuse in the American Family*, New York, Simon and Schuster.

Hacking, Ian, 1991, "The Making and Molding of Child Abuse," *Critical Inquiry* 17(2):253–88.

Hillman, James, 1992, "Therapy Keeps Us from Changing the World: An Interview with James Hillman," excerpted from *Sun*, April 1991, in *Utne Reader*, January–February, 98–99.

Kaminer, Wendy, 1992, *I'm Dysfunctional, You're Dysfunctional: The Recovery Movement and Other Self-Help Fashions*, Reading, Mass., Addison-Wesley.

Kotlowitz, Alex, 1991, *There Are No Children Here: The Story of Two Boys Growing Up in the Other America*, New York, Doubleday.

Laplanche, Jean and Jean-Bertrand Pontalis, 1986, "Fantasy and the Origins of Sexuality," in Victor Burgin, James Donald, and Cora Kaplan, eds., *Formations of Fantasy*, London and New York, Methuen, 5–34.

Levine, Judith, 1992, "The Personal is Personal: Little Gloria, Happy at Last," *Village Voice*, 17 March, 65–66.

Miller, Alice, 1981, *The Drama of the Gifted Child*, New York, Basic Books.

Miller, Ronald, ed., 1992, *As Above, So Below*, Los Angeles, Jeremy P. Tarcher.

Napier, Nancy, 1990, *Recreating Your Self: Help for Adult Children of Dysfunctional Families*, New York, Norton.

Nathan, Debbie, 1991, *Women and Other Aliens: Essays from the U.S.-Mexico Border*, El Paso, Cinco Puntos.

Poster, Mark, 1978, *Critical Theory of the Family*, New York, Seabury.

Rose, Elizabeth S., 1993, "Surviving the Unbelievable: A First-Person Account of Cult Ritual Abuse," *Ms.* 2(4):40–45.

Schaef, Anne Wilson, 1987, *When Society Becomes an Addict*, San Francisco, Harper and Row.

Shapiro, Laura, with Debra Rosenberg and John F. Lauerman, 1993, "Rush to Judgment," *Newsweek*, 19 April, 54–60.

Stacey, Judith, 1990, *Brave New Families: Stories of Domestic Upheaval in Late Twentieth Century America*, New York, Basic Books.

Stallard, Karin, Barbara Ehrenreich, and Holly Sklar, 1983, *Poverty in the American Dream: Women and Children First*, Boston, South End Press.

Steinem, Gloria, 1992, *Revolution from Within: A Book of Self-Esteem*, Boston, Little Brown.

Whitehead, Barbara Dafoe, 1993, "Dan Quayle Was Right," *Atlantic Monthly*, April, 47–84.

Wright, Lawrence, 1993, "Remembering Satan," 2 parts, *New Yorker*, 17 May, 60–80, and 24 May, 54–76.

Yoder, Barbara, 1990, *The Recovery Resource Book*, New York, Simon and Schuster.

CHAPTER 3

Children's Rights in a Free-Market Culture

MARY JOHN

> The future is nothing, but the past is myself, my
> own history, the seed of my present thoughts, the
> mould of my disposition.
> *(R. L. Stevenson, "Essays of Travel")*

WHAT PART does childhood experience play in the way we think, the
people we become, the roles we assume as citizens, the political stand-
points we eventually adopt, the ways we read our culture and define for
ourselves our cultural identities? How did we learn about power when
we were dependent and powerless, and how does this affect how we
wield power? How did this learning process influence our views on powerlessness and the powerless? Has our own childhood cast its shadow
over how we treat and think about children now?

A shared international concern about the powerlessness of children
was underlined recently in the production of the United Nations Convention on the Rights of the Child—a concern largely absent from the
Universal Declaration of Human Rights in 1948. The Convention represents decades of careful thought and drafting by the working group of
the Human Rights Commission in establishing a common basis for
agreement on what these rights should be. It establishes a vision of the
kind of life every child should be entitled to. This Convention incorporates civil, economic, social, and cultural rights, exploring what it means
for a child to have a right to cultural identity, and including fundamental
rights such as the right to life; to adequate health care, food, clean water,
and shelter; to protection against sexual abuse, neglect, and exploitation; and to education, privacy, and freedom of association, expression,
and thought.

Yet it is interesting that those responsible for drafting the Convention, while emphasizing in Article 12 the importance of involving children in all matters that concern them, failed to practice what they
preached. Children did not participate in the deliberations or the drafting of the Convention. This indicates how the international community

still implicitly regards children. Verhellen (1992) makes a useful point here in looking particularly at children's rights in education as a reflection of the broader macrosocial dynamic, a point that can be generalized to other rights beyond those concerning education. He talks of the rights *to* education, rights *in* education, and rights *through* education. Many of the rights embodied in the Convention on the Rights of the Child are in fact rights *to*—for example, to many of the privileges of the adult world.

But does the Convention acknowledge the power of children other than in adult-bestowed terms? Returning to our primary focus, what rights are there to be gained *through* a cultural identity and *in* it? Taking Verhellen's point, we might profitably extend our discussion beyond issues of access to issues of the benefits that accrue *through* a cultural identity and the instrumental advantages of being *in* the culture.

The UN Convention on the Rights of the Child was ratified by the British government on December 18, 1991. This was not wholehearted, however, as the maximum permissible number of exemptions was claimed in the areas of child immigration, child labor, and the imprisonment of young offenders in adult jails. Nevertheless, many commentators have suggested that the Convention signals a number of beneficial consequences for children's welfare in the United Kingdom. Franklin (1992) argues that perhaps its most significant feature is not legalistic but symbolic. He suggests that the Convention symbolizes adult society's public declaration to children and young people that they are valued members of the community with shared civic obligations, deserving as well as owing respect. Franklin (1992:105) asserts:

> Documents should not be dismissed because their authority is symbolic rather than statutory. Acknowledging the legitimacy of a group's claim to rights is itself part of a process of empowerment; rights are levers which the empowered group must pick up and put to work. In the mid-70s equal opportunities legislation gave women and black people a set of such levers with which to prise open opportunities in education, at work and in a range of social settings. Moreover, conceding moral claims is undoubtedly a prerequisite for, and might prompt, a firmer statutory guarantee for children's rights. The symbolic significance and desirability of the Convention is difficult to deny.

However, a number of aspects of the Convention remain contentious. One of these is the specific exclusion of political rights. The briefing document (DCI/UNICEF 1988) claimed that "the very status of a child means in principle that the child has no political rights." This is by no means an uncontested view. Secondly, the definition of childhood embraced by the Convention is controversial in that a child is defined as "a human being below the age of eighteen years," even though this includes young people who are parents, workers, in the armed forces, and who occupy positions of responsibility in a variety of fields.

The aspects of the Convention that will exercise us here, however, are some of the principles on which the Convention is based. Possibly one of the most contentious assertions in the Convention is that the rights of young people can best be promoted within the context of a "protective" and "nurturing family." This has been challenged from two quarters. Some feminist theorists have taken extreme exception to this, seeing the family as an institution of patriarchal power, which may not provide a caring environment for children and may indeed be dangerous. They see the family as a conservative vehicle for the transmission of a patriarchal culture that is broadly misogynist. Outside feminist schools of thought children's rights advocates have suggested that "protection" within the family may mean little more than a cover for paternalistic practices that may restrict the child's autonomy and be antithetical to the achievement of rights. It is this latter point about the role of the family that will be expanded below in relation to psychologies of developing individuals.

The present concern with children's rights as embodied in the Convention has assumed particular notions of the self and the processes by which children develop into individuals. Before considering the role of the family in this, it is worth examining these assumptions and their consequences in terms of theories of socialization. It is by this process that the culture, in the sense that the term will be used in this paper, becomes understood by the child as meaningful, significant, and responsive to action. Robert Coles (1986) looks beyond assumptions about development to the politics that feed and reinforce these, claiming that a nation's politics become a child's everyday psychology.

In the UN Convention on the Rights of the Child we have politics on a grand scale. This paper looks at those politics with the eye of a developmental psychologist and hones in on particular regimes in the present political climate of the United Kingdom. Using the United Kingdom in the 1980s and 1990s as a case study, we can explore some of the ways in which politics become translated into developmental processes. The argument here is that implicit assumptions in child rearing mediate political regimes. The origins of those assumptions will also come under scrutiny. The focus of this paper is how a culture gets "inside a child's head," how it comes to have its influence, how indeed the child understands and incorporates that context into his or her own lived realities.

The focus contributes new and useful questions. The word *culture* will be used here, very much in the way anthropologists use culture, to mean a system of social practices, commonly held values, beliefs, and insights into the behavior of others. This is what psychologists commonly call "intersubjectivity"—the system that the child has to grasp in order to become a fully enfranchised participant member of the social world. Let us now look at two important differences of emphasis in the approaches psychologists have taken to the development and enculturation of the self. Such thinking, it must be stressed, relates primarily to European and North American psychologies.

"INDIGENOUS PSYCHOLOGIES"

Marilyn Ivy (this volume) says some provocative things about the way Reaganite America has colored therapeutic psychologies that serve a function of diverting attention away from the plight of actual children toward the child in every adult. Whether it is explicitly acknowledged or not, psychologies are often adopted to serve political purposes. One has only to look at the voluminous literature on the school desegregation debate in the United States to identify examples of this in the relationship between social science research and social policy (Gerard 1983). Gerard (1983:877) asserts, "It seems that whatever rhetoric is in the ascendance at the time determines how we as a nation attempt to solve our social problems."

Sampson (1988) claims that the presidential addresses to the American Psychological Association in the mideighties (Perloff 1987; Spence 1985) offered perspectives on psychology that were generally consistent with the dominant cultural and psychological opinions of that period. He relates this to dominant perspectives on the psychology of the individual and, in reviewing various critiques of American individualism, differentiates between two "indigenous psychologies of individualism." He contrasts these in three principal areas:

1. the placing of the self/non-self boundary;
2. control as a responsibility of the person versus control by forces in the field/context of action (the locus of control); and
3. the conception of individuals in terms of their exclusiveness or inclusiveness.

These three aspects of the psychology of the individual clearly have implications for conceptions of socialization and enculturation processes. Sampson asserts that these contrasting views are of major and pervasive importance to psychological theory, research, and practice, "because questions about individualism fundamentally involve the form of the person-other relationship, where the 'other' includes other persons, society in general, and even nature" (1988:15). Calling on cross-cultural, historical, and intracultural evidence, he suggests a type of individualism that contrasts markedly with prevailing views as promulgated by Perloff and Spence in their presidential addresses and much earlier by Waterman (1981). These ideas are worth exploring in more detail, as they relate significantly to how children's rights are variously conceived and give us some clues as to the links between the political agendas of the state and the socialization of its children.

Looking first at the self/nonself boundary, a comprehensive review of indigenous psychologies of the individual in various cultures (undertaken by Heelas and Lock 1981) suggests that this a universal dimension. They observed, however, that although all cultures differentiate in some way between a region intrinsic to the self and a region extrinsic to the self and thus belonging to "the nonself other," where that line is drawn varies considerably. Sampson's argument is that the indigenous psychology until recently dominant in the Reaganite United States (and arguably presently dominant in the United Kingdom) emphasizes a clear boundary between these regions. The advocates of this view (for example, Perloff and Spence) claim that maintaining a sharp boundary is central to good health and smooth societal functioning. This view, I will argue, is consistent with the politics particularly of the Right and the New Right. Such an emphasis colors approaches to child rearing, how we understand children, the rights we "give" to them, and the role the family is thought to have.

In contrast, there are cultures where the self/nonself boundary is much more fluid, with a much more diffuse boundary marking where the world begins and the person ends. Postman (1983) suggests that the boundary itself has been historically created: with the advent of printing, a medium was created through which musings about the self could be shared and perpetuated, but only among those who could read.

Thus the medium created an exclusivity. It was only by learning to read that the child could become party to the secrets of the adult world and the world of "self" as contained in print.

A second major dimension around which Heelas and Lock (1981) note substantial cross-cultural contrasts is where indigenous psychologies locate power and therefore how autonomous functioning is conceived. They identify indigenous psychologies of high personal control, where mature persons are assumed to be governed internally rather than externally. They characterize such cultures as suspicious toward and even hostile to social institutions, insofar as these are viewed as potential infringements on personal autonomy.

In contrast to this are indigenous psychologies that locate power and control in a field of forces, hence termed by Sampson (1988) "field control" psychologies. These forces include, but go well beyond, the person. Sampson suggests that if the two dimensions of self/nonself and locus of control are treated orthogonally, it is possible to generate theoretical space for indigenous psychologies with varying combinations of the variables of self/nonself and locus of control.

Relevant here is his suggestion that there is a close correspondence between the locus of control and the nature of the self/nonself boundary. This gives rise to two contrasting and identifiable conceptualizations of the psychology of the individual:

1. *Self-contained individualism*: This relates to an indigenous psychology characterized by the combination of firmly drawn self-other boundaries and an emphasis on personal (as opposed to field-determined) control. This formulation and its implications were examined by Sampson some years ago (Sampson 1977). Norma Field's provocative paper (this volume) seems to suggest that Japanese schoolchildren operate within a regime that has a clear emphasis on personal control and possibly a fairly tightly drawn self-other boundary. This may be misleading, as elements of Japanese, Chinese (Confucian), and Islamic indigenous psychologies offer illustrations of a more socially embedded type of individualism. Moreover, Kojima (1984) suggests that the Japanese consider the idea of an individual defined completely apart from the environment to be a very foreign notion. Rather, it is the obligation of the individual to sustain harmony within the social order. Thus the unremitting work by many young children in Japan to keep ahead may have less to do with the competitiveness of the self-seeking individual than with the incorporation into self of a high-achieving society.

2. *Ensembled individualism*: This term was coined by Sampson (1988) to emphasize more fluidly drawn self/ nonself boundaries and field control. An illustration here is Pamela Reynolds's moving account (this volume) of youth and the politics of culture in South Africa. Reynolds shows how the negotiable qualities of "the field," drawing upon both the "incorporated past" and the political forces of the present, combine with a fluid and developing sense of self that is characterized by the struggle for legitimate representation. The individual is not a freestanding entity bounded by a tight personal responsibility but rather emerges out of the social and political processes in which the young person is engaged. In this social context, the peer group is an important force. The working out of culture and the reach for control that Reynolds describes can be seen in terms of "ensembled individualism."

Sampson goes on to characterize these two psychologies of the person in terms of their exclusionary or inclusive properties. Self-contained individualism reflects a view of the person that puts a frame around the person such that others are excluded from the region defined as the self. He contrasts this with the inclusionary properties of "ensembled" individualism, which includes others within the domain of self.

If this broad dichotomy within the psychology of the individual is accepted, it has important implications for how child rearing is practiced and interpreted. Child rearing is about shaping, forming, and educating the emerging self. There is no question that the ideas of ensembled individualism raise anxieties and pose a threat for some people.

There are resonances of this counterpoint in indigenous psychologies of the individual, and of the anxieties it produces, in more recent conceptions emerging from sociological analyses of the self and modernity, particularly when the focus is on children and institutions relevant to them. Giddens (1991:1) suggests:

> Modern institutions differ from all preceding forms of social order in respect of their dynamism, the degree to which they undercut traditional habits and customs and their global impact. However, these are not only extensional transformations: modernity radically alters the nature of our day to day social life and affects the most personal aspects of our experience. Modernity must be understood on an institutional level; yet the transmutations introduced by modern institutions interlace in a direct way with individual life and therefore of the self.

Giddens (1992) asserts that what characterizes self/society relations in the late modern age is a move from prescribed bounded roles in relationships toward an emotional democracy where the self in relationship is not clearly prescribed, but rather negotiated and sensitive to the needs of others. He points out that many have found this fluidity too threatening and have tried to reach for control by putting back the clock, trying to get back to basics and old established family structures and values. This has bred heated controversies about the proper rearing of children.

Further striking evidence of ensembled individualism comes from feminist theory and research. Gilligan (1982), Gilligan, Ward, and Taylor (1988), and Brown and Gilligan (1992) have written convincingly about how girls and women confront the world with the "other voice." The "other voice" is a voice of relationships, connections, and intersubjectivities, rather than the voice of boundaries and separations. Gilligan and her collaborators illustrate a form of ensembled individualism rather than self-contained individualism and also emphasize that the form that individualism takes is a sociohistorical rather than a natural event. Clearly, such a view is not new, having been expounded in various earlier forms such as Mead's symbolic interactionism (1934), Gergen's social constructivism (1985), and Harre's concept of personal being (1983), as well as in the arguments of Vygotsky (1978) and Luria (1979).

Let us move from whether the selves we try to develop or facilitate in our children are bounded or negotiable to a brief discussion of the ways in which political positions have favored one or the other of these models and so have affected the child's "everyday psychology." This is important, as it becomes clear that the model of the individual and of individual development implicit in these political positions determines how children will be treated. I will argue that significant numbers of children are marginalized by the current model implicit in United Kingdom policy.

NEW FORMS OF DEMOCRACY AND CHILDREN'S RIGHTS

Liberal political thought has reached a major turning point in the United Kingdom, as significant challenges to traditional views of individual liberty arise from increasing pressures for state intervention. There has been an enormous impetus to rethink the relation between the economy and the state and between the sphere of private initiative and public regulation. These reconceptualizations have been precipitated by the recession, with high levels of unemployment, inflation, a crisis in the welfare state, and growing demands for a new system of civil government. It is in this context that questions are being asked about the nature of democracy, the individual, and individual liberty.

In Britain politics has frequently been experienced as something distant and remote from everyday life. Held (1984) found that most people were baffled by the affairs of government and national politics. Not surprisingly, Held also found that those closest to both power and privilege were the ones who had most interest in and were most favorable to political life. For most people, if something was recognizably "political," that alone was enough to bring it into disrepute. Politics was linked in the popular consciousness to self-seeking behavior, hypocrisy, and public-relations exercises. Held (1986) concluded: "[S]urveying contemporary politics—including the politics of the protest movements—one is struck by its seemingly contingent, fragmented and 'directionless' nature when taken as a whole." He suggested that anxieties about directionless change have fueled a call for the reestablishment of tradition and the authority of the state. Such anxieties have been the foundation for the appeal by the New Right to the people and the nation.

Let us look at the notions of the individual prominent within the New Right. Sometimes called neoliberalism, the New Right is generally committed to the view that political life, like economic life, ought to be a matter of individual freedom and initiative (Hayek 1960, 1976, 1982). The New Right advocates a free market and a minimal state. In the late 1970s and 1980s Margaret Thatcher (like Ronald Reagan) advocated "rolling back the state" on these grounds (Held 1984). The commitment to the market as a fundamental mechanism for economic and social regulation provided the obverse side of "liberalism." Associated with this commitment was a belief in "strong government" to provide a secure basis upon which business, trade, and family life would prosper. This political vision was predicated on an indigenous psychology of self-contained individualism.

The New Right, however, has not been the only political group using the vocabulary of freedom. The New Left arose as a result of political upheavals in the 1960s and the consequent reexamination of political theory. New Left figures have questioned the extent to which individuals are "free" in contemporary liberal democracies. They argue that the formal existence of rights, while not unimportant, is of little value if rights cannot be exercised in everyday practice. Pateman (1985) suggests that the "free and equal individual" is in practice found much more rarely than liberal theory suggests.

Both classical and contemporary liberal theory assume that the existing relationships among the working, middle, and upper classes, men and women, various ethnic groups, and, more recently, adults and children allow formally recognized rights to be realized. This assumption is the subject of controversy. Critics of liberal and neoliberal views make clear that inequalities of class, sex, race, and age/adult status substantially hinder the extent to which individuals can be legitimately identified as "free and equal." Poulantzas (1980), like other New Left thinkers, has tried to develop a position that moves beyond the usual rigid counterpoint between Marxism and liberalism. He suggests that the whole relationship between socialist thought and democratic institutions needs to be reconceptualized. He argues that social-democratic politics has led to the adulation of "social engineering," leading to policies that make what he regards as relatively minor adjustments in social and economic arrangements, with the result that the state has grown in power and undermined the vision that social-democratic politics once had. This model conceived ensembled individualism as the key to freedom.

It is clear that there are no easy solutions to the dilemmas of either the New Right or New Left in terms of the issues they pose for the future of democracy. Held (1986:6) observes:

> If the new right has posed important questions about the proper form and limits of state action, the new left has succeeded in highlighting severe problems about the extent to which there can be freedom and accountability in a world marked by vast inequalities between races, sexes and economic groupings.

Following Held (1987), two forms of democracy can be broadly identified:

1. Direct or participatory democracy—that is, a system of decision making about public affairs in which citizens are directly involved. This links with indigenous psychologies of self-contained individualism.

2 Liberal or representative democracy—that is, a system of political rule embracing elected "officers" who undertake to "represent" the interests and/or views of citizens. This relates more closely to psychologies of ensembled individualism.

There is of course a huge diversity of forms of democracy, but what is important is that they all attempt either to alter the representative democracy in *scope* or to try to *transform methods* of democratic decision-making.

The relevance of these developments to the UN Convention on the Rights of the Child is that it should have added a new constituency for the representative process—that of young people. The exclusion of political rights from the Convention is significant and controversial. Franklin (1992) suggests that the way to achieve rights for children lies less in the adoption of any specific reforms than in acknowledging and supporting the general principle that wherever possible children should be encouraged to make decisions for themselves and to act on their own behalf. In practical terms Franklin suggests that the way to begin is to introduce democratic and participatory structures in those institutions where children constitute the consumer body for the services provided—for example, in schools. This view rests on a psychology of ensembled individualism and raises questions about what sorts of socialization processes contribute to developing the skills and confidence children need to participate in democratic processes.

DEMOCRACY AND SCHOOLING

The outgoing president of the International School Psychology Association, Stuart Hart, opened the 1992 proceedings of the Fifteenth International School Psychology Colloquium in Istanbul with words about democratic processes as they relate to our activities with children. He suggested that we have four choices in relating to children: to do things to, to do things for, to do things around, or to do things with them (Hart 1993). He emphasized that the knowledge we have gained of children's capabilities encourages us to give them more opportunity for participation and self-determination than in previous generations.

Similarly encouraging messages come from Roger Hart's essay, "Children's Participation" (1992), for the UNICEF International Child Development Centre. Commenting on projects involving street children in Kenya, India, the Philippines, and Brazil, Hart discovered that children's participation is becoming fundamental to the approach to children's rights in a number of countries. While this is encouraging news, his concluding comments are disturbing.

Hart suggests that in looking at where to begin in fostering young people's understanding and experience of democratic participation, the school would seem an obvious place. The school is thought of as an integral part of the community and, of course, many of our great educational philosophers have argued that it is here that the seeds of true democracy should be sown, although in practice this is rare. Hart (1992:43) claims that although in many countries one can find exciting experimental schools, "there is no nation where the practice of democratic participation in schools has been broadly adopted. The most fundamental reason seems to be that, as the primary socializing instrument of the state, schools are concerned with guaranteeing stability; and this is generally understood to mean preserving the very conservative systems of authority." He points out that in the United States, democracy is generally taught in an abstract and largely ahistorical manner.

It is this concern with guaranteeing stability and maintaining authority that has led in recent years to many children with emotional and behavioral problems being excluded from school in the United Kingdom. Lawrence Kohlberg, well known for his work on the problems of moral education in schools, made it clear many years ago that there is a great need to transform the implicit curriculum of authority in schools into a curriculum of justice, in which the reciprocal rights of pupils and teachers are addressed. Kohlberg (1981) essentially advocates ensembled individualism.

THE FREE-MARKET CULTURE AND CHILDREN'S EDUCATION

The Right and indeed the New Right in the United Kingdom have, in contrast, adopted a psychology of self-contained individualism. This has struck at the very core of what should reasonably underpin any policy of equality of opportunity: that all children should be of equal value regardless of their abilities, disabilities, character, or disposition. Within the culture of "self-help" that has arisen within the Right and with the introduction of a National Curriculum in the United Kingdom, a language has built up around entitlements, rights to education for all, rights to a curriculum suitably differentiated to meet individual needs, and the introduction of standards and quality control in the educational process. Yet, within a declared egalitarian approach, activities are taking place that in fact restrict rather than enhance children's opportunities. Since the introduction of the National Curriculum and the free-market approach to education, we have seen a marginalization of children who, in terms of an older vocabulary, would have been described as having "special educational needs." This was not altogether unpredictable. When school budgets, small to begin with, were devolved to be managed locally, when a National Curriculum linked to a public assessment system was introduced, and when schools were required to publish their results and be placed in league tables competing for pupils, it was not altogether surprising that handicapped and disturbed children would not be found to be good public-relations material and would not be welcome additions to a school. Survival of the fittest and discriminatory ideas about individuals are implicitly promoted by this regime.

Shotter (1984:111) points out that "childhood does not exist within the child. It is the niche that a society creates for its newborns to develop into autonomous members." What role is now being created in the social world for children, and, with regard to the educational process, what roles are children being prepared for in adult life? It seems that in the present educational climate in the United Kingdom, we are preparing children to compete, to look after their own interests, to attach differential values to other children in terms of their abilities/disabilities. Children are not being encouraged in the development of participatory democracies. Currently the nation's politics of self-seeking individualism has become children's everyday psychology in school.

Let us look more closely at the psychology implicit in the educational process in the early 1990s. Peter Housden (1992) has presented a detailed and disturbing account of how vulnerable children are currently provided for in the United Kingdom. Forces have built up against a more fully inclusive education system. Since the introduction of the Education Reform Act of 1988, the system is increasingly under the control of market forces. Schools are now in the business of competing with one another for pupils. They are drawn into public-relations exercises and represented by the published results of their pupils' performance, with the quality of their achievements measured against a common and prescriptive curriculum. In such competitive circumstances, schools' reputations for the good conduct of their pupils and the disciplinary atmosphere of the school are zealously guarded. Local committed parents and citizens join with school staff as governors of the school, together managing budgets and deciding on resource priorities. Active parents and local citizens have a large degree of control over staffing, resourcing, and school policy. Managerialism has infiltrated the school, which has effectively become an education market. Teachers have to keep abreast of a new curriculum, meet increasing administrative demands, deal with assessment of their pupils, and monitor their own performance. They have to manage larger classes at the same time that many support services having been cut or restricted. It has been suggested that the incidence and severity of emotional and behavioral problems among pupils is rising sharply, and these too have to be dealt with.

It is through this tight bottleneck that we try to pour some of the poor, disadvantaged, disturbed, noncompliant, environmentally cooped up, restricted, impaired, and sickly children, many of them the casualties of a recession. The political rhetoric is that these children have equal rights of access to the educational system, but the reality is very different. It helps to have some idea of the size of the problem, which tends to be underestimated. In England, the Warnock report (a government report titled "Children with Special Educational Needs" [Warnock 1978]) suggested that about one in five children is likely to have special educational needs in the form of a learning difficulty at some stage. The Warnock committee suggested a move away from classification of children in terms of specific disabilities by using a needs-based approach. Education was to be provided appropriate to individual needs.

On the basis of a cross-cultural study of policies of provision for special educational needs, Fulcher (1989:247) underlines the problems that arise from categorizing children so that they can be provided with additional help. Of the United Kingdom she says, "Whilst the notion of special educational needs was presented as a non-categorical approach to providing special educational services the phrase retains the politics of the traditional discourse on disability and is ultimately defined as disability. . . . It is, of course, an extraordinarily political act to infer that 20% of the school population have an impairment but this is the political logic underlying the notion of special educational needs" (Fulcher 1989:247).

Anderson and Pellicer (1990) indicate that in the United States there have been even more rigorous moves to create new categories of exclusion as a means for claiming further resources for schools. Ysseldyke (1983) asserts that approximately 80 per cent of all schoolchildren in the United States could be classified as learning disabled. Ainscow (1993) makes an important point about the provision of resources for children with such needs. Although we might be unhappy about a system that captures resources by classifying and thereby further marginalizing the child, the alternative might present other problems. Often resources for special needs are simply not available on any formula. If resources are diverted from the general school budget, Ainscow (1993:7) claims, "[W]e are witnessing a procedure whereby the 'victims' of our school systems' failure are provided with extra help by diverting finance in such a way that it becomes likely that more victims will be generated." This becomes a real worry as "integration" policies are invoked to justify the closure of special schools—closed, one suspects, often for economic rather than ideological reasons. As these children are incorporated into normal schools, the chase for resources begins.

Ainscow makes a powerful case for the view that thinking and practice in the special-needs field work to the disadvantage of precisely those pupils who are supposed to be helped. It is probable that this circumstance holds in other free-market economies in the West and considerably affects the child's rights of access to the educational process. Ainscow also claims that not only are the opportunities of children restricted, but attempts to bring about overall improvements in schooling are also inhibited.

Fulcher (1989) has characterized the dominant perspective in recent legislation on special needs as the "individual gaze"—that is, self-contained individualism. Educational difficulties are *in* the child, who is construed as the problem. Thus the problem comes to be defined in terms of pupils' characteristics. Such an individualized perspective is based upon certain assumptions about the nature of the individual and the nature of learning, a process by which the "expert" imparts knowledge to the novice. Schools are organized with this transmission process in mind. If a pupil does not grasp the opportunities offered, the pupil rather than the system or the curriculum is at fault. This identification of the deficit in the pupil has not only held pupils back but has also stood in the way of imaginative breakthroughs in school organization and innovations in mediating the curriculum.

SCHOOL EXCLUSION AND EDUCATIONAL RIGHTS

The full impact of self-contained individualism or the "individual gaze" can be seen within the new educational market operating in the United Kingdom. One aspect has been that schools compete with each other for pupils, who come to the school with a price on their heads—the resources they will bring. Although some disabled and special-needs pupils bring a larger sum to allow for the provision of their needs, sometimes this sum is not sufficient to cover the services and facilities that must be provided. Sometimes special-needs children are not wanted, regardless of the size of the sum, because they may adversely affect the published achievement records of the school—the notorious Standard Attainment Tests (SATs).

Moreover, as schools attract larger and larger numbers of pupils by successful marketing strategies, they may feel that they do not have the time to devote to vulnerable children and that class sizes are not conducive to their incorporation within the class. Although integration of children within mainstream environments has been regarded as a good thing across Europe over the past decade, the reality of this integration may be that individual children experience greater discrimination and diminution of educational opportunities than when they attended special schools. Some pupils with special needs have had difficulties finding schools willing to accept them. Often the schools that they eventually find are ones where few other pupils choose to go. These become the "sink schools," taking all the pupils other, more successful schools do not want.

Even when children with special needs do manage to obtain a place in school, their future is by no means certain. Some schools simply fail to obtain the appropriate resources for the child's needs and therefore have to exclude the child from school, condemning him or her to a home tuition scheme that has already been cut in certain areas of the country from four to three hours a week. Such children cannot be said to be realizing their rights to a full-time education. Moreover, from the perspective of a psychological model of embedded individualism, there are other aspects of this home tuition scheme that are deeply disadvantageous to the child's developing sense of self—most notably, separation from the peer group.

Further problems arise with children who manifest in their behavior at school many of the stresses and uncertainties of their lives outside the school. Such children may be excluded from school either permanently or for a defined period because the school cannot cope with them. If they have parents interested enough to bother, they might then spend considerable time searching for another school.

Many of these children are victims in other ways of the economic crisis and the free-market economy. This crisis has dramatically affected housing in the United Kingdom. Between 1981 and 1991, according to official statistics from the Department of the Environment, the Welsh Office and the Scottish Office (Rose 1993), there was a nearly threefold increase in statutory homelessness as a result of a court order following a mortgage default or rent arrears. In addition to 170,000 households accepted as homeless or threatened with homelessness in 1991, 81,000 households outside the priority need area were given advice and assistance. These are the official statistics. Because of tight official definitions, they do not fully represent the whole picture. At least 164,000 children in the United Kingdom are now estimated to be without homes. This usually means they are living in temporary accommodation. Many of the young people who are squatting here and there or "sleeping rough" are not included in this figure.

A recent report by Her Majesty's Inspectors of Schools, entitled *A Survey of the Education of Children Living in Temporary Accommodation* (1993), concluded—not surprisingly—that living in temporary accommodation disrupts children's schooling and has adverse effects on levels of achievement. This study found that primary-school children showed poor reading, writing, and oral skills and had poor self-images. Secondary-school children were at a disadvantage when it came to choosing options or choosing schools, as they often arrived halfway through a term (having been moved on from one temporary residence or bed and breakfast accommodation to another). The report (1993:3) states: "When these children meet a school system with opportunities and routines which rely on regular and consistent attendance, suitable achievement is often beyond their reach." Furthermore, pupils were often listless from a poor diet and suffered emotional problems that manifested themselves in the child's being withdrawn and tearful or aggressive and difficult. Some of these children may be excluded from school either temporarily or permanently, as teaching personnel have neither the resources nor, sometimes, the will to cope, given the present competitive climate. The present level of school exclusions in the United Kingdom is grave cause for alarm among a variety of professionals who work with children. The aim of "education for all by the year 2000," which was proclaimed at the World Summit for Children (1990), seems unlikely to be met in this relatively wealthy developed country.

In 1991 teachers' organizations and the Association of Educational Psychologists were already expressing alarm about the dramatic increase in the number of children excluded from school since the passing of the Education Reform Act in 1988. Blame has been pinned on competition among schools, including the published examination league tables. In 1991, as the act started to bite, members of the Association of Educational Psychologists reported increasing rates of exclusion from schools around the country; in one county authority more than eight hundred instances had been recorded. The inner London branch of the National Association for Head Teachers found the pattern repeated there. In the same year, concern was expressed by the association's regional officer for London in the *Independent* newspaper, about the number of children with special needs who were excluded from school because no resources were allocated for them in mainstream schools. He indicated that his members could no longer pay for nonteaching help for pupils with behavioral or learning difficulties. In the same newspaper report, Roger Born, the vice president of the Association of Educational Psychologists, asserted that local management of schools, introduced by the Education Reform Act, left individual schools unwilling or unable to cooperate as they had done in the past.

The problems arise from an increase in requests for resources for pupils with special needs at the same time that schools face harsh financial cuts and increased public scrutiny. Many schools are unwilling to accept pupils who have learning or physical difficulties unless they have a statement and the extra resources that this brings in England and Wales.

Queues for statements (assessments of a child's special needs made by an educational psychologist specifying what the child requires) and their attendant extra resources are getting longer. A report by Sheffield Council's Education Department (1991) documents school exclusions at record levels and notes that excluded pupils stay out of the classroom for disturbingly long periods because the authority is "unable to find sufficient placements due to reluctance (and even intransigence) on the part of schools to accept excluded pupils." This is the "freedom" for the individual provided by the right-wing government's practice of the free market in education.

Even the government's own Department of Education became so concerned about this situation that it gathered statistics for school exclusions for the years 1990–91 and 1991–92 and is now actively monitoring exclusions. Figures for the second year were regarded as so unreliable that they have never been published. For the year 1990–91, three thousand children throughout the nation were reported as having been excluded from school. The department expressed doubts about the accuracy of these figures. Other researchers working in the field, notably Margaret Stirling of Warwick University (1993), regard the published figures as a serious underestimate. There are many informal ways of discouraging troublesome children from attending school, including sending them home repeatedly for some trivial inappropriateness of dress, hairstyle, or self-presentation, until they get the message and so do not bother to come anymore. They are then classified as truants, rather than as permanently excluded from school, and therefore do not figure in exclusion statistics. Other means include suggesting to parents that they might like to take their child away rather than face the stigma of a formal permanent exclusion. These children may end up, after a long period of trying to find an alternative school, in a school where there is a very high proportion of "problem children." Some handicapped children recently brought into mainstream schooling from special schools that have closed do not cope well in the hurly-burly of the mainstream classroom. They too may be excluded, as the school cannot provide them the attention they require if it follows the National Curriculum.

It has now been suggested that schools should be forced to keep children and fined for excluding them. This will simply drive the problem further underground, and more of the informal devices for discouraging children from attending schools will be used. During the early periods of compulsory schooling, the local authority must provide something in the way of schooling, even if it is only a very limited and inadequate home tuition scheme. Later on the pressure to keep the child attending school diminishes. Discouragement of various kinds results in the young person not coming to school at all and often means that he or she drifts out of sight altogether. Without a supportive family to ensure that such a young person remains in school the consequences can be very serious. We now see increasing numbers of young people living on the streets with little in the way of financially supportive life skills learned and with no entitlement to state benefits, since they are under the age of eighteen.

This rise in school exclusions, as much as 400 percent over the last five years, was entirely predictable, given the government's insistence on high standards and quality. How were schools to reconcile the needs to undertake marketing to attract pupils, to meet the huge demands of the newly introduced National Curriculum, and to manage their own finances, services, and staffing with the need to educate handicapped children and pupils with severe emotional and behavioral problems? Schools face a dilemma between protecting their standards and their other pupils and making the personally and professionally unpalatable decision to turn away pupils with special needs they cannot meet.

The situation exacerbates problems facing many children whose home lives are shadowed by recession. Many live in families with unstable and shifting arrangements, in difficult housing situations, with adults who are financially and emotionally very stressed. Given the new managerialism and selection processes in the schools, school has ceased to be a stable refuge, the one place that gave a little structure to the lives of such children. Excluded from a school that runs as a business, these young people are denied their rights to opportunities to learn and, most importantly, to develop personal autonomy within a collective school culture.

THE FAMILY AS A POLITICAL DOMAIN

Both Margaret Thatcher and John Major have advocated a return to family values. Similarly, across the Atlantic, the Reagan-Bush presidencies oversaw unprecedented cuts to underprivileged families at the same time as the political rhetoric continued to insist on breakdown of family values as the primary cause of increasing social problems of drug abuse, violence, homelessness, poverty, AIDS, and so on. In 1990, Margaret Thatcher claimed that "children come first because children are our most sacred trust," yet she presided over a steep rise in child poverty and deprivation. The same government that points to the Children Act of 1989 as demonstrating beyond all reasonable doubt its commitment to children "could also boast (though it would prefer the evidence was discreetly veiled) that the number of children living in families with incomes around the supplementary benefit standard (that is subsistence level) increased between 1979 and 1985 by 49 per cent" (Freeman 1992:53).

The Right has always insisted, whatever its practices might have been, on moral discipline and a return to traditional family values and family stability. This might be to shore up defences against any drift toward a psychology of the ensembled individual and what Giddens (1991) terms "emotional democracy." The opposition has, in contrast, pointed to structural and economic factors as the cause of children's problems. The emphasis here, in keeping with an ensembled individualist approach, is on the necessity to address children's problems through appropriate and sensitive government programs. The Right, however, has consistently shown concern about how the family operates not just in its surface forms, but also in its most intimate processes as the ground for socializing children, the citizens of tomorrow.

Ingleby (1985) claims that this concern has involved an infiltration of the socialization process itself as it concerns the formation of the psyche. He makes the provocative claim that children have become the new "dangerous classes." He questions on whose behalf parents and other adults engaged in the socialization process are acting, and whose interests their activities actually serve. To a substantial degree, he argues, the socialization of the child has been taken over by the state and its agencies. There is "a growing army of professionals operating in the psychological sphere" (Ingleby 1985:79). Previous obsessions with medically based psychiatry have given way to a collection of agencies: educational, clinical, and social psychology; social work; and various parts of the legal system (which now, under the guise of new legislative instruments such as the Children Act of 1989, try to coordinate this army).

Ingleby dubs the "psy complex" those whose aims are to apply psychological technology with varying degrees of expertise and success to social problems. He outlines how the state, mediating the psy complex, has infiltrated the very heart of family dynamics. Professionals maintain power *through* the parent by educating the parent about the professional's worldview and turning parents into what Ingleby dubs "proto professionals." The psy complex hones in on the child's primary induction into the culture by trying to guide the construction not only of the child's behavior, but also the child's developing thinking and awareness.

Ingleby believes that the professionals are themselves duped into thinking that the ends are benevolent and the means of achieving them are rational. But are they? The argument suggests that these professionals produce ways of living and thinking consistent with the social order. They exercise social control in the production of individuals who will not threaten government hegemony. The comparisons here with Field's paper (this volume) are striking, as the focus is not only through an increasingly exclusionary state educational system in the United Kingdom, but also on the inner dynamics of the family. Here a particular form of state ideological orthodoxy is seen as the basis for social hegemony, as the Right lashes out against what is seen as the wild liberal legacy of the sixties.

Ingleby suggests how the psy complex achieves its effects. Children, by their very presence, present a challenge to the social order. He argues that the provision of care for children has increasingly become a matter of socializing people, socializing them in prescribed ways that are far removed from personal freedom. It has therefore become "difficult to think of 'help' as separable from 'control'" (Ingleby 1985:101).

> What, then, are the values promoted by the "psy complex"? This is an enormous question, but I shall single out one emerging priority: to guide the construction of the child's psyche itself. . . . No longer can the formation of the infant self be left to the unknowing parents, there is too much danger that this crucial and sensitive process will go awry, resulting in a "failure of socialization." It seems almost as if children were threatening to refuse to join the human race. Whereas in the late nineteenth century the danger to social order was seen as coming from criminals, mental defectives and vagabonds, the "dangerous classes" now seem to be babies. (103–4)

He goes on to stress the huge contradiction on which the psy complex is founded. It sanctifies family relations at the same time that it infiltrates those relations and subjects them to its management. The result of this paradox is that many of the agents of the psy complex are confused, with all the resulting contradictions relating to care and control, libertarianism, welfare, appropriate intervention, and so forth. Ingleby suggests that the only way forward is to demystify these forces.

But has there been progress toward demystification since Ingleby wrote, or have further years of government by the Right merely intensified power over children? Are babies still a "dangerous" class? The argument here is that children have the potential to develop in all sorts of ways, some of which may not be consistent with state orthodoxy as regards the nature of the individual.

A recent correspondence in the United Kingdom press suggests that the psy complex is alive and well behind the new banner of parental rights. Under the guise of giving parents new powers, the state seems to be carving out greater opportunities for control.

> *Sir,*
>
> *The correspondence about stepfamilies raises a worrying myth that is beginning to take hold now that the Children Act is in operation. It is the view (letter, 5 December) that the new Act introduced the notion of parental responsibility in order to improve the behaviour of wayward parents. Such an interpretation being voiced in social work as well as legal arenas, turns intentions behind the Act on their head.*

Parental responsibility was introduced in recognition that parents, by virtue of being parents, have rights and duties that endure throughout childhood and must be recognised by those who provide services for children and their families. The legislators hoped the acknowledgement of this bundle of rights and duties would shift fundamentally the flawed professional practice that research had revealed during the 1980s.

Child-care law had also been exposed as providing an inadequate framework for preventative and child protection work and as failing to facilitate family involvement when children were in care. In seeking to re-align the balance between families and the state, one important intention of the Act was to signal the continuing role for parents when their children were looked after by the local authority.

Given this, it is worrying that a concept introduced with such positive outcomes for children in mind is being overlaid so quickly with negative connotations. Whatever the reason behind it, children and their families will be the losers. If the prevailing view is that workers can and should get court orders in order to spell out how parents should exercise their responsibilities, then voluntary arrangements for looking after children will not be developed as the family support service they were intended to be, and partnership work will be abandoned when care orders are made.

If the spirit of the Act is to breathe through practice, parental responsibility needs to be regarded as a brake against heavy handed state intervention, and a reminder of the continuing importance of both parents after separation or divorce, rather than being used as a stick with which to beat them.
Yours faithfully,
Jo Tunnard,
Director, Family Rights Group (Letter to the *Independent*, December 10, 1991)

Examples of the alleged consequences of poor socialization practices within the family have recently surfaced in lurid media coverage of two ten-year-old boys who abducted and murdered a two-year-old child. It was made clear that, far from being innocents, children are potentially very dangerous indeed if the family has not socialized them properly. Scant regard was given to the socioeconomic conditions of these families, the emphasis being on the failure of the parents.

The potential dangers from children were further emphasized by front-page pictures of the children responsible, captioned "Murderers!!" The fact that in the United Kingdom the ratification of the UN Convention on the Rights of the Child specifically excluded the clause in the Convention that juvenile offenders should not be housed in adult jails perhaps tells us something about how children are regarded—as the dangerous classes that the state must tame, either through the parents or

through the usual treatment of offenders. There are now, in 1994, proposals to spend 30 million pounds on the building of young secure
units, proposals that are being strongly resisted by those who feel such
sums would be better spent on early preventative measures.

What power do children themselves have? Right-wing politics resists
thinking about rights for children. Freeman (1992) indicates that even
those who regard rights as morally important are still inclined to believe
that it is not necessary to extend them to children. One of the arguments
used to support this position assumes that "adults already relate to children in terms of love, care and altruism, so that the case for children's
rights becomes otiose. This idealizes adult-child relations: it emphasises
that adults (and parents in particular) have the best interests of the child
at heart" (Freeman 1992:55). Freeman cites authors arguing that the
only right necessary for children is the child's right to autonomous parents. Minimum coercive intervention by the state would thus accord
with a firm belief in the "individual freedom and human dignity" of national citizens (Goldstein, Freud, and Solnit 1979:12). It is hardly necessary to ask, as Freeman points out, *whose* freedom and dignity these
arguments are aimed at protecting.

The child's induction into the culture has been seen by the political
Right as a matter of proper parenting. This, I have argued, relates to a
psychology of development around a concept of the self that is self-contained and bounded with firmly drawn self-other boundaries and an emphasis on personal control. In the United Kingdom and in the United
States the political right wing has argued that the moral decline of the
nation can be stemmed only by inculcating a firm sense of individual
responsibility through a return to family values and traditional family
structures. The best antipoverty program, the argument goes, is a stable
intact family. Thus the Right presses for policies aimed at sustaining
the two-parent family, slowing down divorce rates, decreasing teenage
pregnancies and illegitimacy, and protecting the children of divorcing
parents.

General assumptions about the socialization process have placed the
parent or major caregiver in a dominant role. This has remained the case
even with suggestions that parenting itself is infiltrated by professionals.
Such approaches have disregarded other powerful influences in the
child's social world and indeed disregarded the role of children themselves. The child is not necessarily a passive recipient of child-rearing
practices, as is often assumed. If we move on to look at the role of the
peer group and of the child him/herself, we approach a much more en-
sembled-individual psychology of child development, one closer to the
political Left's views of the individual and democratic values.

THE ROLE OF THE PEER GROUP IN THE DEVELOPMENT
OF THE INDIVIDUAL

It is instructive to examine ideas about how children come to know the social world in which they live and how they develop skills in interpreting this world. Such ideas reveal significant adult views about the place of the child in the culture and the ways in which that culture is experienced by the child. Interwoven with important questions about how children interpret the world are equally important questions about our interpretations of the child. One assumption commonly made is that it is adults who teach children to understand the world.

Youniss (1981) points to three principal approaches in theories of social development. The first identifies social growth with the acquisition and internalization of adults' views. Adults act as *transmitters*. The second emphasizes growth in the child's own cognitive capacities and skills. The child arrives at adult ideas as a result of the *child's own efforts*. The third is that individuality is constrained early in development through a realization of *relational membership in the social world*. The last view fits most closely Sampson's model (1988) of ensembled individualism in that the emphasis on the child's relational membership in the social world focuses on a self with fluidly drawn self/nonself boundaries and field control.

Youniss elaborates upon the third approach, pointing out that individuality in development undergoes change. The self in this model is dependent upon interpersonal relations. As relationships develop through cooperation with others, they give rise to new constructions of self. This is important as it stresses more than traditional approaches the significance of relationships for the child's developing self, not simply with adults but with other children. We need to look at these relationships to find out more about the world the child inhabits or is excluded from.

If the "relational context" is the basis for a developing sense of personal being and agency, then exclusions from school have a significance beyond educational processes. More fundamentally, the child's banishment from day-to-day relationships with the peer group strikes at the very development of the self.

This goes for handicapped children confined to home tuition schemes, as well as for children excluded from school on the grounds of emotionally and behaviorally disturbed acts. Some of these children live in temporary or uncertain accommodations, with only other children like themselves to consort with throughout the day while their peers are at school. Their developing sense of self is threatened and the growth of their social competence put at risk.

Youniss questions whether adults act as "agents for society" in teaching children how to control themselves. He draws attention to the reciprocity of peer friendships, in contrast to the restricted outcomes of relationships with parents. Relations with adults tend to mystify, whereas peer relations engender mutual understanding. Furthermore, relationships with adults tend to keep people apart, while relations with peers encourage social solidarity. Adults tend to make respect a matter of adhering to external criteria, whereas relations with peers allow respect to be mutual, the establishment of consensus.

How does one come to understand the mind of another, *especially* in relationships between children? An account of the development of social understanding should consider what we can learn from the study of the child in the relational context of his/her peer group.

Interesting work outside the United Kingdom capitalizes upon the significance of the peer group and play within it for the child's sense of self-worth. Ayni is a Lima-based association dedicated to support for integrated child development (see Dawson 1992). Its project focused on children in poor urban communities in Lima and within the Peruvian state school system. In the absence of resources for education of young children, Ayni identified a local resource in the form of secondary-school pupils who were expected by their school to carry out community service. These young people were trained as children's rights promoters who would conduct activities to assist children living in the neighborhood.

A much criticized aspect of Peruvian schools is the authoritarian attitudes of the teachers. Teachers tend to repress creativity, spontaneity, and playfulness among their pupils, instead of recognizing these as essential elements in the development of the child's full potential and powers of expression. Ayni came to see the tendency to negate the importance of play as a denial of the child's right to an individual identity. Ayni defines its main objectives as the promotion of children's rights within the school by means of developing children's identity through play. Secondary-school pupils are trained in drawing, painting, and puppetry techniques for young children. It is hoped this contributes to a more humane society in Peru, a society in which the child would be able to make its own special contribution to improving social relations and to the full development of human potential. Working through play is not using adults as transmitters but enables children to explore important aspects of identity within their own peer group.

The rationale for this project is important here. Ayni asserts that lack of respect for play inhibits the child's possibilities of developing his or her own sense of cultural identity. In support, Dawson (1992:3) quotes from Silva and Lundt (1982): "Children learn much more of the language and customs of their own society by observing others around them, then practicing in play." Dawson points out that many Peruvians consider their lack of a clear sense of identity at national, local, and individual levels a hindrance to development. They ask, how can you develop a country creatively if you have no definite idea of the shape you wish it to take? At the individual level, how can you develop your potential if you have no definite aspirations regarding the kind of person you wish to become?

It is not difficult to see painful similarities between children's diminishing educational opportunities in Peru and in the United Kingdom, with a right-wing government committed to a philosophy of survival of the fittest. What is missing from Ayni's hopes and claims about the importance of play is a recognition of the significance of the peer group in testing out ideas through play and the fact that other young people are the leaders and role models—young people who have only recently left early childhood themselves. Implicit in this whole project is the concept of the individual embedded in the peer group as an extension of self, in the local community and in the nation-state.

EMBEDDED INDIVIDUALISM AND DEVELOP-MENTAL PSYCHOLOGY

The question of peer influences in development requires a more detailed examination of the child's integration into the social world. Unfortunately, only a few studies are useful for this purpose.

The birth of a younger sibling can be a traumatic event for an older child whose world is now invaded by another individual demanding the parents' time and attention. The inner balance of the family is changed, affecting the older child's developing feelings of value and confounding relationships with adults that seemed secure. The importance of siblings in a child's development is obvious, but only in the last decade has anyone tried to observe what happens when a second child is born. A landmark in its time was Dunn and Kendrick's study of sibling relationships (1982). Dunn and Kendrick studied forty families for fourteen months starting shortly before the birth of the second child.

Dunn and Kendrick presented us with a new view of the young child's abilities to understand and relate to others and have enabled us to examine the young child's beliefs about others' states of mind and feelings.

Such understandings arguably operate within the peer group settings as well. "When we observe children with their young siblings, our attention is drawn not to the process of cultural initiation of the child by the adult, but rather *the child's capacity to understand and relate to another human being* as a human being" (Dunn and Kendrick 1982:3; emphasis added). The study revealed that even two-year-olds showed a "pragmatic understanding" of how to comfort and console the baby. They also observed the child being provoking and manipulative. Firstborn children, even at this tender age, could "explain" the baby to the researchers, interpret the baby's emotional expressions, and react sensitively to these interpretations.

Some years after Dunn and Kendrick's study was completed, Stillwell-Barnes (1982) carried out a follow-up study of friendship and family relationships in the same families, talking to the elder children when they reached the age of six. What is remarkable is that the immediate reaction of the firstborn to the new baby sibling is reflected in his/her behavior at six years. Children who had shown friendly interest and concern for the new baby were found to be significantly more likely as six-year-olds to respond with concern if their younger sibling was hurt or distressed. Differences in the quality of the sibling relationship were not linked to the age gap between the siblings. Dunn and Kendrick comment on this consistency, given the major developmental changes both children will have undergone. This constancy of affect demonstrates powerful forces at work in early relationships, affecting later social understanding. The child's initial grasp of the meaning of the event and how to respond to it may be less impulsive and more formative of later attitudes than we might have believed.

This study highlights questions about the relations between social and emotional experience and developmental change. Young children can demonstrate that they are emotionally ready to attend to, respond to, and learn about other people in the world.

In another context, Doise and Mugny (1981) have demonstrated that children can make quite dramatic breakthroughs in their ability to solve Piagetian problems when they try to solve these problems *with another child*. This holds true even when the companion child is less intellectually advanced than the child trying to solve the problem. The Genevan psychologists interpret their findings purely in cognitive terms, whereas Dunn and Kendrick place more stress on the motivating aspect of sibling interaction and the intrinsic interest in helping each other toward an understanding.

Another feature of Dunn and Kendrick's study is the way a mother lays the ground for the child's intersubjective understanding and how this relates to the fluidity of the self/nonself boundary.

Mothers who discussed the motives, intentions and feelings of the baby were much more likely to use justification in control situations, to enter the child's world of pretend, and to use language for complex intellectual purposes. We have emphasized that we should not look for simple links between any one aspect of the mother's speech and later differences in conversational style and their implications for the child's development. It would be particularly worthwhile to investigate, for instance, how much these differences affect the development of children's communication skills and role-taking skills. Light (1979) concluded from his study that the development of these aspects of "social sensitivity" was linked to differences in the symmetry of the relationship between mother and child. (Dunn and Kendrick 1982:216)

The need for another in achieving intersubjective understanding extends beyond childhood. Jean-Paul Sartre, for example, relied on his constant dialogue with Simone de Beauvoir to "give his realities back to him." His experience was not "real" until it had been shared with and reinterpreted by her (see Beauvoir 1983).

How much do we as children and adults rely on another person to "give our realities back to us"? In a recent court case in the United Kingdom alleging the sexual abuse of two young girls by various members of their family during black-magic rituals, one element in the eventual collapse of the case was that "the girl's evidence was so uncertain, inconsistent and improbable." The prosecuting counsel said that "one consideration had been the disclosure that the girl had discussed the matters with her sister before telling her grandmother" (*Times*, 20 November 1991, 20). The implication was that the witness had been contaminated in this way, or that the sisters had cooked up the story between them. These young girls had assumed that they were recounting what happened to everyone, a part of normal experience. They relied on each other for a view of the culture that they took to be every child's experience. This case is interesting not just for the questions it raises about child witnesses in court, but for what it tells us about our culture's view of children and their understandings of the world. If these children had discussed the situation with another adult, would their evidence have been questioned in the same way?

The case highlights commonly held views about the child's power to be manipulative on the one hand and the child's powerlessness on the other. It is taken to reinforce the view that children cannot really know or report on what is/was going on, as such "knowledge" does not stand up under detailed and relentless cross-examination in court. It also shows us the great divide between notions of socially constructed reality in embedded individualism and notions of the responsible self-contained individual responsible for his or her own actions—a cornerstone of the worldview commonly held by the Right and members of the legal profession.

CHILDREN AS AGENTS IN THEIR OWN SOCIALIZATION

In the process of the child's development, language plays a vital role in the construction of the social world. This is not simply a world of spoken language, but also of the written word and, in recent years, of information technology.

Brian Sutton-Smith (1975:85) emphasizes the significance of children's story writing:

> Because . . . children's stories deal in the main part with the normative conflicts that are part and parcel of socialization within this culture, they are also primitive statements of the prevailing mythologies of this culture. According to some authorities, this is where mythologies are born. They develop out of narrative. We like to think, therefore, that in collecting children's stories, we are dealing with the underbelly of living mythology.

A child's growing idea of a social self is not simply provided by the social environment but is also influenced by the way in which the child communicates *with him or herself* about that world. The narratives in children's heads, on paper, or, on occasion, in oral stories, play an important part in the way they experience their social realities and interpret them to themselves. Through these narratives we can get an insight into children's own understandings and detect how the language children hear and the various negotiations and discussions they witness or are party to inform their views.

Carolyn Steedman (1982) offers a remarkable insight into the ways eight-year-old girls understand their social world and their place in the social order. She asked three girls in a class she taught at a school in a fairly poor industrial area of the United Kingdom to write a story. Steedman (1982:1) begins: "In the Summer of 1976, three working-class eight-year-old girls, Melissa, Carla and Lindie, wrote a story about romantic love, marriage and sexual relations, the desire for mothers for children and their resentment of them, and the means by which those children are brought up to inhabit a social world." The study dramatically illustrates what acute observers of the emotional politics of the family young children are.

The "Tidy House" story that Steedman describes is particularly rich since it gives us so many glimpses of the world the child authors experienced, the conversations and manipulations they had shrewdly observed at home, and their dismal but probably realistic views of the future. Their environment had been one of particular sorts of male-female relationships, expectations of adult life, deprivations, and forms of oppression. The dialogue out of which the narrative is mainly constructed casts a cold assessing eye upon this set of emotional and social circumstances. To an extent, the little girls viewed a specific sort of involvement in their own subcultures as inevitable. They themselves participated in their own socialization into the world of working-class, overburdened adults. Through their views of the world, they *indoctrinated* themselves into an acceptance and entry into an adult world that differed little from what they observed as children. It is this that makes the study particularly important.

The argument here is that children have the power to construct their own place in the world. The culture itself, which has many notions of the child but few real notions about children and children's actual lives, treats this power in quite paradoxical ways. Children, as we have already noted, are denied political rights in the UN Convention on the Rights of the Child, yet they are also often given responsibilities beyond their years.

The United Kingdom, for example, has declined to ratify the articles in the Convention that relate to child labor. In recent years increasing emphasis in the United Kingdom has been placed on the responsibility of the "community" in the care of the elderly, the infirm, and the disabled. It appears that this community involves children in such responsibilities, an enormous responsibility placed on many young children's shoulders to care for a sick or handicapped single parent. This is even publicly celebrated, as in the Children of Courage awards given in the United Kingdom, often awarded to quite young children who have cared for ("parented") their sick or handicapped mothers. With the community care policies embodied in the 1993 Community Care Act and rising incidences of single-parent households, it is likely that more and more children will both bring themselves up *and* care for a parent.

The following description of a child responsible for parenting her mother, while taken from the United States, illustrates a situation likely to be ever more common in the United Kingdom in coming years.

> She was just a fact of life when I was growing up: someone to be worried about and cared for; an invalid who lay in bed with eyes closed and lips moving in occasional response to voices only she could hear; a woman to whom I brought an endless stream of toast and coffee, bologna sandwiches and dime pies in a child's version of what meals should be. She was a loving, intelligent, terrorised woman who tried hard to clean our littered house whenever she emerged from her private world, but who could rarely be

counted on to finish one task. In many ways our roles were reversed: I was the mother and she was the child. Yet that didn't help her, for she still worried about me with all the intensity of a frightened mother, plus the special fears of her own world, full of threats and hostile voices. . . . I remember a long Thanksgiving weekend spent hanging on to her one hand and holding my eighth grade assignment of *Tale of Two Cities* in the other, because the war outside our house was so real to my mother that she had plunged her hand through the window, badly cutting her arm in an effort to help us escape. Only when she finally agreed to swallow the medicine could she sleep and only then could I end the terrible calm that comes with crisis and admit to myself how afraid I had been. (Steinem 1983–84:16)

In a recent Stress on Women campaign mounted by Mind (the leading mental-health charity in England and Wales), the following statistics appear: on average, every woman in the United Kingdom receives more than one prescription for psychotropic drugs every year (1992:1). Forty-five million prescriptions for psychotropic drugs are dispensed every year; over 30 million go to women. This gives some substance to dark suspicions that rolling back the welfare state and introducing responsibilities for the community places new burdens on the shoulders of children. While right-wing philosophies espouse a notion of children being socialized by their parents within the family, these same adults are increasingly needy themselves, in an economy that fails to care for its sick, elderly, and mentally ill, as well as its young.

REFERENCES

Ainscow, Mel, 1993, "Towards Effective Schools for All: A Reconsideration of the Special Needs Task," paper presented at the Economic and Social Research Council and Cadbury Trust Project, "Policy Options for Special Educational Needs in the 1990s," Institute of Education, University of London, 1 March 1993.

Anderson, Lorin W. and L. O. Pellicer, 1990, "Synthesis of Research on Compensatory and Remedial Education," *Educational Leadership*, 48(1):10–16.

Beauvoir, Simone de, 1983, *Lettres au Castor et à quelques autres*, Paris, Gallimard.

Brown, Lyn Mikel and Carol Gilligan, 1992, *Meeting at the Crossroads*, Cambridge, Mass., Harvard University Press.

Coles, Robert, 1986, *The Political Life of Children*, Boston, Atlantic Monthly Press.

Dawson, Elsa, 1992, "Ayni, The Association for Integrated Child Development," paper presented at the World Conference on Research and Practice in Children's Rights, University of Exeter, September.

DCI/UNICEF, 1989, *The UN Convention on the Rights of the Child: A Briefing Kit*, London, United Kingdom Committee for UNICEF.

Doise, Walter and Gerard Mugny, 1981, *La Construction sociale de l'intelligence*, Paris, Intereditions.

Dunn, Judy and Carole Kendrick, 1982, *Siblings: Love, Envy, and Understanding*, London, Grant, McIntyre.

Franklin, Bob, 1992, "Children and Decision Making: Developing Empowering Institutions," in Maud Drogveler Fortuyn and Mies de Langen, eds., *Towards the Realization of Human Rights of Children*, Amsterdam, Children's Ombudswork Foundation and Defence for Children Internation, Netherlands, 89–111.

Freeman, Michael D. A., 1992, "Taking Children's Rights More Seriously," *International Journal of Law and the Family* 6:52–71.

Fulcher, G., 1989, *Disabling Policies? A Comparative Approach to Education Policy and Disability*, London, Falmer.

Gerard, Harold Benjamin, 1983, "School Desegregation: The Social Science Role," *American Psychologist* 38:869–77.

Gergen, Kenneth J., 1985, "The Social Constructivist Movement in Modern Psychology," *American Psychologist* 40:266–75.

Giddens, Anthony, 1991, *Modernity and Self-Identity: Self and Society in the Late Modern Age*, Cambridge, Polity Press.

————, 1992, *The Transformation of Intimacy: Sexuality, Love, and Eroticism in Modern Societies*, Cambridge, Polity Press.

Gilligan, Carol, 1982, *In a Different Voice: Psychological Theory and Women's Development*, Cambridge, Mass., Harvard University Press.

Gilligan, Carol, Janie V. Ward, and Jill M. Taylor, 1988, *Mapping the Moral Domain*, Cambridge, Mass, Harvard University Press.

Goldstein, Joseph, Anna Freud, and Albert Solnit, 1979, *Beyond the Best Interests of the Child*, New York, Free Press.

Harré, Rom, 1983, *Personal Being*, Oxford, Basil Blackwell.

Hart, Roger A., 1992, "Children's Participation: From Tokenism to Citizenship," *Innocenti Essays* no. 4, Florence, UNICEF International Child Development Centre.

Hart, S., 1992, Presidential Address, fifteenth International School Psychology Association Colloquium, July, Istanbul.

Hayek, Friedrich August von, 1960, *The Constitution of Liberty*, London, Routledge and Kegan Paul.

————, 1976, *The Road to Serfdom*, London, Routledge and Kegan Paul.

————, 1982, *Law, Legislation, and Liberty*, vol. 3, London, Routledge and Kegan Paul.

Heelas, Paul and Andrew Lock, 1981, *Indigenous Psychologies: The Anthropology of Self*, London, Academic Press.

Held, David, 1984, "Power and Legitimacy in Contemporary Britain," in Greg McLennan, David Held, and Stuart Hall, eds., *State and Society in Contemporary Britain*, Cambridge, Polity Press, 299–369.

Held, David, 1986, "Introduction: New Forms of Democracy?" in David Held and Christopher Pollitt, eds., *New Forms of Democracy*, London, Sage, 1–13.

————,1987, *Models of Democracy*, Cambridge, Polity Press.

Her Majesty's Inspectors of Schools, 1993, *A Survey of Children Living in Temporary Accommodation*, London, Her Majesty's Stationery Office.

Housden, Peter, 1992, "Bucking the Market: Local Education Authorities and Special Needs," paper presented at the Economic and Social Research and Cadbury Trust Project, "Policy Options for Special Educational Needs in the 1990s," Institute of Education, University of London, 1 March.

Ingleby, David, 1985, "Professionals as Socializers: The 'Psy Complex,'" in S. Spitzer and A. T. Scull, eds., *Research in the Law, Deviance and Social Control: A Research Annual*, vol. 7, London, JAI Press, 79–109.

Kohlberg, Lawrence, *The Philosophy of Moral Development: Moral Stages and the Idea of Justice*, vol. 1, San Francisco, Harper and Row.

Kojima, Hideo, 1984, "A Significant Stride towards the Comparative Study of Control," *American Psychologist* 39:972–73.

Luria, Alekscendr Romanovich, 1979, *The Making of Mind*, Cambridge, Mass., Harvard University Press.

Mead, George Herbert, 1934, *The Social Psychology of George Herbert Mead*, Chicago, University of Chicago Press.

MIND, campaign briefing, Stress on Women pack, London, MIND Publications.

Pateman, C., 1985, *The Problem of Political Obligation: A Critique of Liberal Theory*, Cambridge, Polity Press.

Perloff, Robert, 1987, "Self-Interest and Personal Responsibility Redux," *American Psychologist* 42:3–11.

Postman, Neil, 1983, *The Disappearance of Childhood*, London, W. H. Allen.

Poulantzas, Nicos, 1980, *State, Power, Socialism*, London, Verso/New Left Books.

Rose, Philip, ed., 1993, *Social Trends 23*, Central Statistical Office, London, Her Majesty's Stationery Office.

Sampson, Edward E., 1977, "Psychology and the American Ideal," *Journal of Personality and Social Psychology* 35:767–82.

————, 1988, "The Debate on Individualism: Indigenous Psychologies of the Individual and Their Role in Personal and Societal Functioning," *American Psychologist* 43:15–22.

Sheffield Council Education Department, 1991, *School Exclusion in Sheffield*.

Shotter, John, 1984, *Social Accountability and Selfhood*, Oxford, Blackwell.

Silva, Kathy and Ingrid Lundt, 1982, *Child Development: A First Course*, Oxford, Blackwell.

Spence, Janet T., 1985, "Achievement American Style: The Rewards and Costs of Individualism," *American Psychologist* 40:1285–95.

Steedman, Carolyn, 1982, *The Tidy House: Little Girls' Writing*, London, Virago.

Steinem, Gloria, 1983–84, "Ruth's Song (Because She Could Not Sing It)," *Rehabilitation World*, Winter, 14–17.

Stevenson, Robert Louis, 1905, *Essays of Travel*, London, Chatto and Windus.

Stirling, M., 1993, interview, "School Exclusions," *File on Four*, Radio 4, British Broadcasting Corporation 16 February.

Sutton-Smith, B., 1985, "The Importance of the Story Taker," *Urban Review* 8(2):82–95.

Thatcher, Margaret, 1990, George Thomas Society Inaugural Lecture, 17 February.

Verhellen, Eugeen, 1992, "Children's Rights and Education: A Three-track Legally Binding Imperative," keynote address at the fifteenth Annual Colloquium of International School Psychology Association, Istanbul, July.

Vygotsky, Lev Semenovich, 1978, *Mind in Society: The Development of Higher Psychological Processes*, Cambridge, Mass, Harvard University Press.

Warnock, Mary, 1978, *Children with Special Educational Needs*, Department of Education and Science, London, Her Majesty's Stationery Office.

Waterman, Alan S., 1981, "Individualism and Interdependence," *American Psychologist* 36:762–73.

Ysseldyke, James E., Martha L. Thurlow, Janet L. Graden, Caren Wesson, Stanley Deno, and Bob Algozzine, 1983, "Generalisations from Five Years of Research on Assessment and Decision Making," *Exceptional Educational Quarterly* 4(1):75–93.

Youniss, James, 1983, "Piaget and the Self Constituted through Relations," in Willis F. Overton, ed., *The Relationship between Social and Cognitive Development*, Hillsdale, N.J., Erlbaum, 201–28.

Part Two

CHILDREN, CULTURAL IDENTITY, AND THE STATE

CHAPTER 4

Children in the Examination War in South Korea: A Cultural Analysis

HAE-JOANG CHO

PROLOGUE

Before getting into the main part of this essay, I want to warn readers that my writing focuses on negative aspects of Korean education and society. It would not make me feel uncomfortable to present this paper to Korean readers. In fact, I have written several critical papers on the Korean educational system that have aroused stimulating discussions among educators, parents, and students themselves (Cho 1989, 1994a, 1994b). But readers who are not familiar with Korean society in general may read this essay very differently than I intend. To many Koreans, I am overly critical of my own society. What I do here is a cultural critique. I do not attempt to provide a balanced assessment of the strengths and weaknesses of the Korean educational system. I do not intend to show how the Korean educational system functions. My concern is to change the dysfunctional system. Naturally, the negative aspects become more visible. I feel odd about revealing our wounds to outsiders, especially to those who have been controlling us in many ways. However, I submit this paper with a trust in goodwill and competence of Western readers.

EXAMINATION WAR: A CONFUCIAN DRAMA?

My son spent his eighth-grade school life in Palo Alto, California, as he accompanied me during my sabbatical year, 1994–95. He enjoyed school so much as to say that he did not want to have a vacation. He could not understand students who did not enjoy school. Quite a few of them *hated* going to school. When we were about to leave Palo Alto, he remarked, "The educational system of this country has more serious problems than the Korean one. All we should do in Korea is just improve the school life. But here, what could they do?"

It seems that in the 1980s, almost every society began to regard its educational system as in jeopardy. In this crisis atmosphere, advocates often idealized others' educational systems. More notably, Japan's "remarkable achievement of accessible, high quality education" (Segal 1992:13) is widely discussed and envied by Western audiences. An American news reporter speaks for that type of a popular opinion:

> More school seems to be an obvious remedy for the mediocrity that characterizes American education, a mediocrity that hampers America's ability to compete in a global economy. Children in almost every other industrialized nation attend school longer than U.S. kids do—especially the youth of our economic rivals: Japanese kids to 240 days, Germans 210 days. The U.S. school year, by contrast, is just 180 days. Small wonder, advocates say, that foreigners routinely outperform the U.S. especially in math and science. (Segal 1992:93)

The writer concludes, "Eventually, it may prove necessary to extend the academic day or year to accomplish some of these reforms. But quality of time, not quantity of time, should be the underlying motive. American children deserve real changes in the way they're taught—not just more of what isn't working."

While I was in the Bay Area, I often came across stories on homework and school uniforms in the local newspapers. The *San Jose Mercury News* (Melinda Sacks, "The Homework Debate," November 4, 1994, 20–24) quoted a schoolmaster saying, "There's a general tenor in this community and nationwide that schools aren't doing enough." She reported that more schools started giving homework in kindergarten, and by fifth grade, "[T]hey are hitting the books as much as two hours nightly." The *San Francisco Examiner* reported that the San Francisco United School District requires all schools to give homework and that children were stressed by tough requirements (Janet Kornblum, "Time for Homework," October 2, 1994, B1). Of course there are opposing voices. A school board member criticized the policy by saying: "[Y]ou look at the schedule kids are under, there isn't time for family anymore. . . . Where's the time for family values? Where's the time for anything outside of school? I think it's stressing kids out. Bottom line; we forget that kids are kids and they just need time to play." However, the wind does not seem to be blowing in his direction. More schools and school districts are deciding to increase the amount of homework assigned.

There are related news stories that public schools are beginning to require students to wear uniforms (Tanya Schevitz, "Oakland School Promotes Unity through Uniformity." *San Francisco Sunday Examiner and Chronicle*, September 11, 1994, C3). Schevitz interpreted the movement as a measure to promote unity and reduce gang rivalry. It seems clear that many parents and educators want to reform schools in order to have more control over children and discipline them. East Asian models of education are attracting attention because discipline and hard work are emphasized.

This is a rather sudden shift of attitude: we recall that until recently the Japanese educational system was described as inhuman. Japanese education was "the product of an inhuman regime of forced-march study. . . . Childhood as we know it does not exist in Japan: the playgrounds are empty, mothers are homework tyrants; weekends and vacations are devoted to organized study" (White 1987:2). We were also told that the culmination of childhood's toils is examination. Success means entry into a top university and being the ultimate economic animal: failure is shame and leads to the increase in the juvenile suicidal rate. These descriptions are still largely true. What, then, in the Japanese system does the United States want to emulate?

Specialists on Japanese education (Rohlen 1983, White 1987, Stevenson and Stigler 1992) urge American policymakers and parents to learn from the Japanese system. Realizing that the United States has become "a society with a low expectation of the average citizen" in the midst of "the erosion of the family" and "the declining commitment to parenting among the young," Rohlen (1983:4) senses profound contradiction among the many goals of the United States population. Based on an ethnographic study of Japanese high schools, Rohlen (325) suggests setting national standards and acknowledging the value of tracking by ability in secondary education. He further suggests a self-examination by the whole cultural system: "to reverse our retreat from the responsibilities of child rearing, to end our casual, laissez-faire approach to pedagogy, and to enshrine excellence in the academic fundamentals." What Rohlen does through the study of Japanese education is a cultural critique. He wants to see two basic social premises reconfirmed in the United States: that life rests on social interdependence, and that the achievement of human potential is a fundamental social good. He concludes with a critique of Western culture, saying, "Individualism and freedom in any other context are sad illusions, and progress toward social equality that cannot be integrated with the pursuit of general excellence has no long-term viability" (326).

In a similar context Stevenson and Stigler (1992:14) urge Americans to "sit back and examine basic assumptions about the educational process" by tackling difficult questions about motivation, beliefs, attitudes, and practices that underlie American education, while White (1987: 34–49) emphasizes the psychocultural support Japanese children receive from their mothers and society. To White, the cultural emphais on "wise mother" over "good wife" in Japanese society has a profound effect on children's lives in terms of providing them stability, security, and support.

Interestingly, through the cross-cultural study of educational systems, we are challenging our basic assumptions about social life. In fact, what we need in a crisis situation, especially in the age of paradigm shift, is not an impatient search for an easy solution from outside, but a new and critical look at one's own system. The concept of the politics of culture is useful in pursuing this task. Knowing about a drastically different system will help one to gain the necessary distance and a new perspective on one's own system. I hope that this paper will be read by Western readers in that spirit.

The Japanese education system is quite widely known to and discussed by the Western readership, whereas the Korean is not, so let me start with some comparative statements. Between the Japanese and the Korean educational systems there are many similarities. It is nothing to be surprised by, because the Korean public schools of modern style were established by the Japanese colonizers. The hardware of the system established at that time has been maintained without much modification until now.

Let me quote critical statements on the Japanese system, some made by Japanese themselves.

> Bullying, suicides among school children, dropping out of school, increasing delinquency, violence both at home and school, heated entrance exam races, overemphasis on scholastic ratings, and torture of children by some teachers are the result of the pathological mechanisms that have become established in Japan's education system. Without drastic reforms, Japan's education system would not be able to recover to normalcy. (Schoolland 1990:9).

> We have been aware of indications that growing numbers of youngsters are opting out of the education rat race. Are we to exchange the problems of "examination hell" for increased juvenile crime? . . . Actually there has been a constant increase in crimes by jobless minors from 1980 to now. Also, there is a much higher proportion of heinous crimes—especially murders and arson—among this group. (quoted in Schoolland 1990:120)

The educational system of South Korea resembles the Japanese one in its highly centralized bureaucracy, in its extraordinary emphasis on educational accomplishment, in its focus on the university entrance examination, and in its disastrous effects on children's lives. High respect for learning and severe competition in school are common features of East Asian Confucian societies. We know that there are prep schools in the West that have similar problems as schools in East Asia. As a matter of fact, Peter Weir's film *Dead Poets Society*, which dealt with the stressful life in a prep school on the East Coast of the United States, was extremely popular among South Korean children. It stirred empathy among youngsters under examination stress. However, in the West, people go to that type of school by choice. It is, in fact, a choice available only to a small, select group with a certain socioeconomic status. In the case of East Asia, the majority is forced to be engaged in the battle.

The idea of "education as investment" is by no means a novel one in histories of Confucian tradition: education has long been considered the East Asian way of climbing the social ladder. Capitalist development has made good use of this educational zeal, resulting in a warlike situation in school. Of course, there are differences within East Asian societies, differences directly related to the modernization process that each nation has gone through. To be more specific, the Korean case seems to exceed China or Japan in its severity and scale of competition for the school entrance examination. This is related to the cultural definition of social mobility and colonial modernity.

The South Korean phenomenon of rapid economic growth is often discussed as a model for the Third World. One of the major resources underlying this progress is, as Bedeski succinctly sums up, "a talented and resourceful population, able to draw on bonds of familial solidarity and historical memories of a unique national identity" (1994:2). Bedeski further claims that the Confucian heritage has reinforced family values and stressed education both as a means of upward mobility and as an agent of moral improvement. I am rather suspicious of the idea that the Confucian heritage has worked to improve civil morality during industrialization and urbanization, but it surely motivated people for upward mobility through education in a society undergoing drastic socioeconomic transformation.

Under the Confucian patrimonial states, during the last dynasty of feudal Korea (as in China), the ultimate goal of the gentry class was to pass the government examination to become civil servants. By passing the literary examination, one could accomplish everything. Passing the examination compensated for all the toils and brought glory and wealth not only to a man but also to his whole family and lineage. Premodern Japan developed a different system of recruiting bureaucrats, with heavy emphasis on military training and self-discipline. Premodern Korea was much more centrally controlled and tended to neglect other qualities besides the literary ones. Japan has been famous, if not notorious, for its homogeneity, but Korea has been much more homogeneous culturally than Japan. Gregory Henderson (1968:viii) finds homogeneity and centralization to be the keys to Korean society. According to his argument, the unity and homogeneity of Korea acted to produce a "mass society," by which he means a society lacking in the formation of strong institutions or voluntary associations (4). Mass society consists typically of atomized entities, related to each other chiefly through their relations to state power—a society whose elite and masses confront each other rather directly by virtue of the weakness of groups capable of mediation between them.

According to Western sociological theory, as a society is modernized, the importance of the extended family and lineage decreases, whereas other forms of associations and institutions increase. In the case of Korea, however, the functions of the family unit and extended kin network have expanded to an extreme degree without developing any other "modern" forms of associations.

In prolonged unstable and uncertain conditions, Koreans invested all their energy and "capital" for a most secure goal: to send their sons to schools of higher education. Once a son received higher education, the status and economic condition of the whole family improved. By sending him to a university, the family could secure not only a breadwinner, but a new network through his school ties. Having an alumni network was extremely crucial for survival in a society where networking was a major means of accommodating one's needs. Korean society has depended heavily on individual networks rather than on building new institutions or forming voluntary groups. Korean groupism, accordingly, differs from the Japanese form in many ways. This cultural background results in Koreans often being described as independent, spontaneous, and flexible in comparison with Japanese.

What would be the implication of this difference in cultural and social organization for the educational systems of the two societies? To take an example, mothers in both countries are deeply involved in making their children highly achieving persons, but the style of involvement is very different. Since Korean mothers do not have proper public channels through which to participate in children's schooling and are maybe even more eager to see their children's success, they tend to make efforts to improve children's school records by any means, from arranging extra lessons from the schoolteachers, which is prohibited by the government, to "bribing" teachers. The Japanese have a stronger tradition of decentralization and local autonomy, which allows Japanese mothers more chances to participate in local school board committees, and to not interfere in the school life by individual greed. They seem to have more trust in teachers and the school system, while the central government permits room for parent's participation and even for experiments.

There is another dimension that accentuates the sociocultural difference between Japan and Korea: the modernization process. No one can deny that Japan managed to moderize itself successfully. However,

Korea failed in its attempt. The highly centralized Korean kingdom became a Japanese colony in 1910 and was ruled by the Japanese empire for thirty-six years. After liberation from Japanese colonial rule, Korea was torn apart between the two imperial powers and eventually divided into two nations after the Korean War. Colonial occupation shook traditional roots, and the war and division destroyed almost all that was left of a functioning society. Political instability persisted until 1960, when the military regime took over and reigned over South Korea. The military government tried to get popular support by forcefully carrying out economic development projects and was successful in increasing GNP. The 1980s were years of severe confrontation between the military government and the antigovernment activist movement. In 1992, a legitimized civilian government returned.

We can read from this brief political history that there has been little time and energy left for South Koreans to solve their internal contradictions and to build their own internal system. South Korea is still a bureaucratic-authoritarian state in nature, with little experience of democracy. The tradition of civil society for making necessary changes in the infrastructure from the people's side is hardly known, although the tradition of resisting the 'power out there' has been stronger. Educational reform is no exception. Sociocultural instability and the weak basis of civil society have made the Korean educational system extremely rigid. Education has become a dramatic national game easily manipulated by the government and mass media. The government has always tried to maintain total control over its people, particularly through the educational system, and it has been largely successful. It has controlled private and public schools by enforcing severe regulations and even by controlling access by delimiting the tuition. It allows few alternative schools or alternative ways to educate children differently.

Japan has moved into the postindustrial stage. To control youngsters through schooling no longer seems possible in Japan. There are other dimensions to deal with in Japan, such as postmodern alienation and the motivational crisis in the consumer culture of late capitalism (see Norma Field's paper in this volume). Korean youngsters seem, at least until now, to remain under state control. It may be, though, the night before the wild storm.

In the following pages, I present a picture that shows children in the examination war around 1991–92 in Seoul. I describe it as a cultural drama in which most people are deeply involved: a battlefield for the children, a sacred ritual for parents, and a source of major news and scandals for the less-engaged general audience. I ask who gains from this war, and why they do not want to stop it.

THE KOREAN VERSION

Schooling is an all-consuming way of life for students in South Korea. They spend more hours in class than students in the West, and nearly every minute of their lives is organized around school and, in particular, examinations. Children are indoctrinated in their early days to believe that their ultimate goal in life is to enter top-class universities in Seoul.

Graduation from a university is considered a prerequisite to success in society. But university graduation is not enough. People must enter the prestigious universities. It is a shared belief among most parents that the rank of one's university determines one's worth as a social being. Once entering (and graduating, since completion of the degree is virtually automatic) one of the so-called top universities, one can look forward to a secure future—that is, a stable job, good marriage, and respectable social life. Those who fail consider themselves to be second-class citizens. This view is shared by much of the rest of society. In this condition, the values of mainstream culture presuppose that getting on the escalator to academic success should be the top priority in children's lives.

An ambitious mother counts down the days left for her children to take the university extrance examination as soon as her child is born. The game begins at the earliest ages, even as parents choose the baby's toys. Toys that stimulate the baby's left brain are considered the most desirable. It is not uncommon to meet a five-year-old child who goes to a *hakwon* (a private institute for extra schooling) to learn how to read and write before entering primary school. Typically, a child takes classes in piano, painting, mathematics, calligraphy, computers, and English before she goes to middle school.

These lessons are not selected randomly but are systematically chosen to improve classroom performance at each level. In a recent survey administered by a newspaper, out of 1,774 students nationwide from third to sixth grades, 66.7 percent of the children were attending one class, 23.6 percent two classes, 5.9 percent three classes, and 2.4 percent four classes. Those who did not go to *hakwon* comprised only 0.3 percent. Attendance at *hakwon* means five additional hours per class. Children who do not go to the *hakwon* complain that they cannot find friends to play with. From the first grade, most children are complimented and rewarded materially when they get good scores on examinations by their score-conscious mothers. When children get poor grades, they are afraid of going home. The same survey reports that 45 percent of these children answered that they had thought about running away from home, and 47.6 percent said that studying is their most stressful problem.

Basically, middle schools are standardized, and there are no entrance examinations through high school. Except for a few special high schools, such as the high school for science, arts, or foreign languages, students do not have any choice but to enroll in the neighborhood schools assigned by the local education board. In other words, the entrance examination for the university is the only and final battle ground for Korean students. Unlike Japan, where there are entrance examinations as students go to higher levels of schools, Korean students have to place all their bets on one battle. Historically, Korea had the same examination system as Japan, and the competition to enter elite middle and high schools was severe. The Park Chung-hee military regime decided to eliminate the entrance examination at the lower level and began to control the college entrance examination through the nationwide one-day test administered by the governmental agency since 1971. For a while, children enjoyed their freedom.

However, having only one entrance examination does not mean that Korean children are freer during their earlier school years than Japanese children. Parents' anxiety can be even more intense when they have less information with which they can predict their children's performances. It is more like gambling than a fair game. Also, this system sustains fictions of open or upward mobility for a longer period.

Of course, the competition increases with the grade level. Mothers cannot tolerate their children doing anything but studying. Many children become addicted to studying, that is, preparing for the examination. Those children who do not become addicted tend to stay away from their mothers. Up to ninth grade, however, most children can manage to have some time of their own by watching television, reading books, and meeting friends. Middle-school students manage to find time to go to rock concerts and shopping. They manage to express their anxieties and even attempt to challenge school practices: recently, students have demanded that they want coeducational classrooms. (At this moment, most middle schools include both boys and girls but are divided into gender-segregated classes. Most high schools are single-gender schools.) This preliminary period is over by the ninth grade.

Upon entering high school, most students give up their lives to become mechanical functionaries for the examinations. The entrance examination administered by the state is mainly in a multiple-choice format where only one correct answer must be selected. There is a joke about arranged marriages that youngsters these days cannot select a bride unless four candidates are presented. After all, the winners of the university examination race are those who survived three years of multiple-choice tests and thus function too mechanically to digest any liberal-arts issues. Many university professors think that ninth-grade students are better qualified than university freshmen to take various university-level humanities and social science courses, because their minds have not yet been rigidified by intense, test-oriented studying.

Let us look at the daily life of a student in *go-sam*, the last year of high school. Students normally sleep no more than five hours. As in Japan, there is a common phrase among students: "Pass with four, fail with five." Let me share a story of my nephew Chang in his third month as a high-school senior. His grades are in the top 5 percent in his class of fifty students, and he has shown every sign of being engaged in an all-out war since the beginning of the school year. His immediate family, relatives, and neighbors all know that he is under extreme stress and do not dare to take a single minute of his precious time. He gets up at 6:15 A.M. and goes to school at 6:37 with two packed lunches. He eats the second packed lunch around 4:50 P.M., when regular school is over. Then he studies at school again until 9:10 P.M. The extra class, which is called "independent study hour," is done under teachers' supervision. Then he takes a tea break and goes directly to a *doksosil*, a private study hall, a commercialized study room especially for students like him. After reviewing the day's study there, he finally comes home at one in the morning. Very soon, he will change study halls since the study hall he is now attending does not have television facilities. Because extracurricular study programs on the educational TV channel have shown a high rate of success in guessing the content of college entrance exams, many of his competitors watch those programs. He feels that he must study with the TV program, at least for math, his weakest subject.

His mother takes a nap after dinner and wakes herself with the help of an alarm clock before he comes home. She prepares fruit and cookies for him to eat before he takes a shower. She, as any other devoted *kyoiku mama* (Japanese for "education mother"), is tense like her son. She believes that she is to a great extent responsible for her son's academic performance. Therefore, she tries to control and support her son's achievement as best she can. Any extra money is invested in encouraging her son to fight well in the monthly mock exams. Chang's mother is always short of sleep, like her son. She too is fighting the war.

On Saturdays and Sundays, Chang takes private English lessons for two hours, costing $300 a month. His mother feels sorry that the family budget does not allow sending him to a more expensive tutorial class. Many of his competitors take more hours of private lessons under more competent tutors. Fees for private lessons in a normal four-hour-a-week course vary from $200 to $1,000 per month. On weekends, the student may take a nap for about thirty minutes. Otherwise, the schedule is the same as on ordinary days. Mothers of such high-school seniors say that they feel their children are time bombs who can explode at any moment.

Chang is under extreme stress now. Competition is getting severe, and maintaining his score is itself very hard. In his junior year, his grade was within the top five hundred among all students nationwide, according to the national mock examinations, but he can no longer keep up these scores. He feels terrible these days because of his deteriorating grades. Stress is even higher since he cannot count on the opportunity of *jaesu* (spending an extra year or two for the university examination after graduating high school; *ronin* in Japanese). The Ministry of Education has declared that it will change the system of university entrance examinations again next year, which means that he will have less chance to succeed in the new system.

Mothers, especially mothers of the middle class, think of their children's scores as their own. Mothers are extremely cautious and strategic in order to prevent their children from collapsing or falling behind in the war. A mother who succeeded in sending a child to a university last year expressed the change in her son like this: "He was like a very dried fallen leaf, a leaf that when touched, crumbles to pieces at once. Now I see he eats moisture. He is alive now."

Mothers need places to comfort themselves. So they either go to the Christian churches or Buddhist temples. These religious centers have special programs for the *gosam* mothers. For the last hundred days and on the very day of the examination, all mothers go to their religious centers to pray and cry together. It is a moving scene that every television news show displays as the examination date comes near.

Aren't there any students who give up in the middle or explode? In fact, many students do explode: they become criminals, commit suicide, or suffer mental breakdowns. The following news report tells us the story:

Around 8:30 P.M. on the fourteenth of last month in Seoul, Kim (eighteen, senior at Seoul S. High School) was one of two high-school seniors who demanded money from a Miss Y (sixteen, freshman at Seoul E. High School) while choking her in the elevator of the Shin Donga apartments. The attempt was foiled when the elevator doors opened and the girl ran out. Immediately captured by her father and handed over to the police, Kim was arrested and handcuffed the next day on charges of attempted robbery. The person most surprised to learn that Kim was an attempted robber was his mother (forty-six), who had always thought that the only problem was his less-than-outstanding grades and that delinquency was not an issue.

Let us take a look at events leading up to the day that Kim, who turned his back on his mother's trust, committed the crime. Rising at 6 A.M. as usual, Kim left for school before 7. Having ranked forty-sixth in his class on the last monthly exams, Kim had already given up the idea of going to college. Nevertheless, his classes continued to be thoroughly oriented toward preparations for the college entrance exam. Classes ended at 12:30, since it was Saturday. Kim spent the afternoon at the J church, which he often attended. Afterwards, it was time to go home, but, not wanting to hear his mother's nagging to go study, Kim decided to meet a friend. All the money he had on hand, however, was a few one-hundred-won coins. On the way to borrow money from another friend, he met the victim-to-be in the elevator. After covertly planning the crime with eye signals, Kim and his companion rammed into the girl. With that, his behind-iron-bars fate was sealed. At the police station, Kim expressed the agony of non-college-bound high-school seniors who are tossed aside onto education's sidelines when he said, "Although this was committed on impulse, after losing the goal of going to college there wasn't even one bit of meaningful work that I could do." *(Dong-a Daily News,* April 26, 1992, "Weekend" section, 17–18)

In a mass competition where the majority are destined to fail, some active students who are poor in academic performance easily become delinquent youngsters, while passive ones become more passive, merely accepting that they are second-class citizens and failures. Interestingly, there is little active resistance from students in this category. Rather, many of these students and their parents have a lingering attachment to the university even if they know that the chances of being admitted are low.

In other words, most people never completely give up the hope of going to the university. Although they know very well that they cannot go to the colleges, they tend to hang on until the last moment in the atmosphere of "nothing but" studying and without the courage to disappoint their parents. They just kill time by sitting in the classroom dozing or daydreaming.

After graduating from high school, many failed students try one or two more times for the university entrance examination by going to a special cram school. After failing several times, they may finally give up and find themselves with nothing to do. Depending on their family's financial condition, either they get jobs or fool around until they are drafted into the national army. In the case of women, they may get jobs until they find a man to marry and try to be successful *kyoiku mamas.*

What are the major problems caused by this educational system? One is those students, at least two-thirds, who have to play the role of "extras." They are just bystanders in classes and get used to their extra status. Immediately after the announcement of grades in the mock college entrance exam, administered nationwide just like the real one, stragglers crop up. Having received grades too low for college expectations, some students run away from home. The runaway youngsters may engage in robbery, sniffing glue for its hallucinogenic effects, or just fooling around.

However, the majority stay at school rather quietly, merely accepting that they are failures. Those students who give up halfway through the game do not have any choice but to put up with classes that have little use for them. The high school has only one goal: to send as many students as possible to four-year universities. That means that in a senior classroom, more than half of the students are left alone by the teacher no matter what they do, as long as they do not disturb the others. During break, these students may commit minor deviant behavior such as smoking cigarettes in the restroom to relieve the stress accumulated during a class. Even if teachers see it directly, they often turn a blind eye to such actions. Teachers are afraid of students' revenge and do not care as long as students misbehave individually. These students know very well that they have been given up on. It is obvious that the students who do not even receive teacher's guidance in school are even more likely to fall into the temptations of delinquency outside of class. The issue of students who have been marginalized by the education system and loiter on the streets is clearly not only an issue of families or of high-school education at the front line, but also a serious national issue of a society ailing from a pathological overemphasis on school credentials.

The newly formed Korean Teachers and Educational Workers' Union, the Chunkyojo, has mentioned this problem as the first reason for starting their teachers' movement. A booklet introducing their movement says the following:

> Teachers have been faced with the reality of over two hundred suicides per year committed by third-year high-school students under the pressure of preparing for the university entrance exam. In the face of the pained cries/ silence of the students, teachers have been determined to initiate reform of the educational system through Chunkyojo. The need for reform is identified primarily on four grounds: (1) education for the university entrance exam has forced students to engage in inhuman competition; (2) education has become a tool for the will of the successive ruling regimes; (3) the educational environment is extremely poor; (4) the administration has repressed teachers' autonomy to an extreme.

Specifically, the booklet mentions that

> the education system has become merely a gateway to universities, which is the gateway for upward social mobility. In 1988, over 800,000 students competed for some 200,000 university places. . . . The absolute majority of students are unable to enter universities. However, they are socially condi-

tioned to believe that social worth and recognition are granted only if they can go to and graduate from a university. Students who fail to proceed to university education are forced to regard themselves as failures. When they become workers in factories, they are forced to feel ashamed of the fact that they are manual workers. They are forced to feel, "I work in the factory because I failed in my studies."

Moreover, it is difficult to say that the examination game is a fair game. Various kinds of familial support play a crucial part. Aggressive middle-class mothers thrust themselves into the center. Youngsters from the working class have much more difficulty than before in passing the university entrance examination, since middle-class youngsters receive full support from their families—financially, socially, emotionally, and nutritionally. Extra schooling after regular class during middle school has become a normal practice, requiring a high educational fee. It is also said that the mother's managerial skill and information gathering is crucial for children to get into top universities. Many Korean social scientists have maintained that class reproduction is a myth by saying that the school system in Korea has served as a solid ground for fair competition and class mobility. But they might have to reconsider this claim now.

There was, and still is, a strong state ideology that competition in education is equal and open to everyone. This is why the state still administers the college examination, from making the exam sheets to computerized grading. The state has made sure of "justice for all" by controlling the game in class mobility under the principle of fairness. It has been a very powerful popular ideology, which makes people believe that they can elevate their status through their children's schooling and entrusts great power to the state. However, as the role that parent's wealth plays is getting bigger, the situation has changed. Many parents feel pressured to make extra income to support their children, and feelings of relative deprivation prevail among the poor.[1]

What is clear is that all the children in the examination war are stressed and exhausted. Nervous breakdowns, suicides, and increasing delinquency are just small signals of the crisis that children are facing. Another negative result is the distortion of school education at the lower level by the pressure of survival in the examination war. Almost all the high schools became preparatory schools for the examination. All levels of school education are geared to the university exam, which results in extreme distortion of the curriculum.

Students are trapped in a system that calls for intense inhuman competition and rote learning, merely to expand the capacity for summarizing and memorizing a great quantity of piecemeal information. What is certain here is that the students who pass through this ordeal have a great level of self-discipline and endurance for doing something under external pressure. After long years of adjusting to such a learning process, the winners are losers too. In this educational system, flexible and creative innovators cannot survive. The only winners are the mechanical functionaries for Fordist mass-production industries.

Those who have succeeded in entering universities are not all that happy. Most of them are dissatisfied with their universities or departments since they have not chosen them according to their desires, but rather according to their scores. Most of them are not happy with their scores, which in some way determine their social status for the rest of their lives. Moreover, universities are not yet prepared to "deprogram" these exam-oriented students. Students confess that they find university is not what they had dreamed of.

The years of preparing for the examination under extreme tension and stress also make the winners extremely passive and dull. Many of them have difficulties adjusting to university life, which offers them abundant free time. Courses in liberal arts and social sciences that require analytical and critical thinking confuse and frustrate them endlessly. They are particularly annoyed by questions that do not have definite answers. They can be world champions in a game in which one competes with speed to solve well-defined problems. But they are not competent to deal with ill-defined ones. When I asked freshmen to write about themselves in comparison with others, a student protested by saying, "What an irresponsible question that is! You didn't give the criteria for comparison. You must give us clear criteria and the reason why you want this essay from us." Systematically trained to do a special kind of organized memorization, they seem to get lost when they are asked to do a nonspecific task.[2] In the university, many of the students suffer from feelings of inadequacy. They are turned into sheep with no spirit of resistance, by society, adults, and schools. Many university students confess that they miss the good old days of *gosam*, when life was simple and focused.

Until recently, students who became university students considered themselves elites and often turned into angry youth. Most of them showed great interest in the student resistance movement while actively pursuing various activities they had postponed. I think that the social psychological gestalt that the high-school students formed during their preparation for the battle played some role in stirring student political activism. The dogmatic style of the student movement may also be related to the strict and closed way those students were trained or not trained in problem solving during their high-school years.

I regard student activism as a powerful field of experience and discussion for students deprived of these things over a long period. It serves, in a way, as a powerful means for revitalizing youngsters' minds. Unfortunately, the student movement attracts fewer people these days. Drastic changes in the overall political climate have left student activism in disarray. Moreover, the youngsters seem to be too burned out to get involved in such serious tasks while the social competition is getting more severe.

The competition has intensified for the last ten years as more students want to go to colleges. I can report that both winners and losers are getting utterly worn out. It is a recent trend for those students who have succeeded in the examination war to go straight into preparation for another war—that is, job examinations. As one student put it, "exam addicts" feel most comfortable in that condition. This allows students to continue not to think about problems without answers. They can thus avoid culture shock at the university.

The newly emerging generation just wants to play for a while and then prepare for its jobs and/or marriages. Dedication and commitment are the old values. Cultural critics regard this new generation as the beneficiaries of the recent economic growth. They are free from the terrible memories of war, hunger, and military regimes. They are children of abundance and self-indulgence. I would add that they are victims of the fierce university entrance examination war. Like the older generation, they, too, are prematurely aged, both mentally and physically, though for different reasons. (Compare Norma Field's comments in this volume about the prematurely aging bodies of contemporary Japanese children.)

THE EXAMINATION WAR AND THE
POLITICS OF CULTURE

The frame of modern mass education in Korea was built by the Japanese colonialists. Some Koreans blame Japanese colonizers for founding this inhumanly competitive educational system in the early twentieth century. After liberation in 1945, the Korean government tried to liberalize the educational system. However, it has been unable to do so in the face of an already firmly established educational bureaucracy. Attempts to alter the entrance examination system have been made eight times over the last fifty years.

The present format of the nationwide examination system was established in 1969, a time when a strong military state with heavy emphasis on economic development emerged. All the attempts, including standardizing the level of high school by eliminating the entrance examination for prestigious high schools, were closely tied to changes in political

power blocs and image making. Moreover, the prolonged political instability made any genuine educational reform difficult. In a way, education has been instrumentalized by the government as a useful mechanism to instill the dominant ideology and legitimize state power, whose
grounding has always been weak. Textbook production is monopolized,
and schools are run under the tight control of the bureacracy. The textbooks contain explicit government propaganda.[3]

Meanwhile, the sudden economic growth, together with population
growth of the baby-boom era after the Korean War, intensified competition for college entrance. Schools became impoverished by inadequate
educational budgets.[4] Aid to public education by the government is so
limited that parents are obliged to meet some of the major costs of
school maintenance, which in turn invites parents to undermine educational autonomy. Teachers who want to provide "true" education are
thwarted from both sides, the excessively achievement-motivated parents and the government administration.

The Ministry of Education is notorious for its strict hierarchy and
authoritarian structure. Principals of schools are required to follow the
instructions of education authorities, and teachers are expected to obey
their principals. The Education Act provides that teachers must undertake
their educational activities according to the orders of their principals.
Constructive criticism and efforts from teachers to improve educational
conditions are repressed. Many critics consider that this bureaucratic
structure and the principle of militaristic control are legacies of the Japanese colonial era. While there might be some validity to this assertion, I
would rather note several other circumstances to explain the current examination war.

As discussed earlier, all the high schools are equalized, such that the
one short day of the university entrance examination, administered nationwide by the Ministry of the Education, determines the fate of the
students. The military governments, which did not have the basis of legitimacy to rule, tried to gain people's trust by administering the great
event with fairness. In other words, the increased central control and
standardization in education was a means of securing the insecure state.

Family- and kin-based principles of social organization cannot be underestimated in perpetuating the heat of the examination war in Korea.
Unlike Japan, which had a feudal system in the Middle Ages, the Korean
kingdom was a highly centralized patrimonial state. Under the Confucian ideal of rule, the balance of power between the king and the bureaucrats was maintained for several centuries until Korea fell under
Japanese colonial power.[5] The bureaucrats consisted of scholar-politi-
cians who were selected through nationwide examinations called *kwago*.

A heavy emphasis on lineage above locality and on familial success by pushing one of the sons to pass *kwago* is another factor to be taken seriously.

Of course, tradition is not a simple determining force but is constantly revived and activated by actors in changing environments. In the following discussion of specific groups of actors in the panoramic drama, I want to highlight the issues of agency and politics by asking two questions. Which interest groups are most deeply engaged in this drama? Who makes the conspiracy move on? The directors and producers are hidden, but supporting actors are visible: mothers and teachers. Here I describe the active roles played by mothers and teachers that contribute to making the examination war a stable game. The mass media, always searching for the hottest news; the government, which does not have any incentive to change the conservative base of the educational system; and a large portion of the industry depending on the examination war for its survival—all share in the conspiracy.

Let us look at mothers first. The majority of Korean people still agree with the old expression, "The only thing a person can trust is family (blood)."[6] People distrust any kind of social group or institution, such as the company, the school, the nation, and even voluntary associations. This tendency toward exclusive and egocentric familism has been strengthened through recent rapid industrialization. Unlike middle-class housewives in most industrial societies, Korean women have little interest in charitable work or community welfare programs (see Tinker 1980). They invest their time solely in immediate familial interests. Sending children to prestigious universities ranks at the top of the list of familial interests. Mothers can simply ignore or postpone orders from mothers-in-law or services for husbands if they are engaged in activities to improve their children's academic performance. The job of *kyoiku mama* is a respected job for educated mothers and can be a second chance for their own success by pushing their children through.

The majority of middle-class housewives regularly visit their children's school to see teachers. When they visit, they bring an envelope that contains money ($50 to $100 average every couple of months) for the teachers. It is a gesture asking teachers to give special care for their children or at least not to abuse them. It is not legally permitted, but it is widely practiced. When a child runs in an election for class president, where voices of teachers may have significant impact, an aggressive mother may deliver envelope money to the teacher. In addition, she may give a party or presents for all her child's classmates. Delivering the envelope is not limited to the middle class. In the lower grades of primary school, poorer mothers also try to do so, since they fear maltreatment of their children.

There are always teachers who abuse children in the classroom, especially if it is a classroom of fifty students, many of whom do not know how to concentrate. Korea may not be a particularly extreme case, but Korean mothers cannot tolerate the idea that their children might be discouraged or neglected by the teachers. So mothers do their best to protect their children. Delivering the envelope is almost institutionalized in most schools. Some of the money goes into the teacher's pocket, some is passed into the principal's pocket, and some may even pass up to the bureaucrats in the Ministry of Education. There are other occasions for the school to ask for donations from the parents more publicly since the school cannot manage its finances with the current level of support from the government. Parents of children who study well are selected to form a financial committee to assist the school. There is an explicit notion that the students who study well benefit most from the school. Therefore they must pay.

There are many informal meetings for middle-class housewives, such as alumni meetings and meetings of parents whose children are among the top ten students. These meetings are important, as the mothers exchange information on examination schedules or on available competent private teachers in the town. While mothers do discuss how the present system suffocates their children, they say that have little time to participate in any educational-reform movement. Instead, mothers of the middle class are primarily interested in changes in the college entrance examination by the government so that they can prepare their children for any new system. Once the anxious mothers discover that a school does not try hard to raise the level of the students' testing ability but instead spends time on other cultural or athletic activities, they immediately urge the school principal to drop the activities and concentrate only on preparation for the examination. As the main director for the status of the family, middle-class mothers utilize all their time and energy to secure a better chance for their children to win the game.

These middle-class housewives who dedicate themselves to their children's success are in some sense happy. They do not experience the "empty-nest syndrome" or at least experience it mildly. Since there is a sacred role to be played, they are energized. The mothers of the *gosam* are the ones who attract much attention and are pitied by society. Relatives and friends console them and are ready to listen to their stories of suffering. Even bossy husbands are careful not to aggravate their wives when their child is in *gosam*. A male professor told me once that when his wife was a *gosam* mother, she was extremely sensitive and hysterical, just like "a hen trying to hatch an egg."

Being the supporting actors for the examination war can be exciting for middle-class housewives in their forties who do not have any other interests or work to pursue. By displaying her ultimate devotion, a mother can secure her child's filial piety and her husband's and parents-in-law's appreciation. The examination war is intensified by these devoted mothers, who can only see their children's happiness in the context of survival in the war and who do not have anything to do but support the children. These devoted education mamas are often criticized for being antisocial, but they themselves believe deep in their hearts that they are the winners. Scenes of mothers bowing three thousand times a night at a Buddhist temple for their children's success in the exams or praying for a hundred days at Christian churches are still moving for most Koreans. Middle-class mothers may spend less money for the daughter's extracurricular lessons than for the son's, but it is only in degree and not in quality, since educational credentials are as important in the marriage market as they are in the job market.

There are interesting ceremonies for the students who are about to take the exam. On the hundredth day before the university entrance exam, relatives or high-school alumni who are now students of the prestigious universities buy drinks for the high-school seniors. On that night, many students get drunk and fight in the streets, often causing injuries. Just before the date of the entrance examination, relatives and friends bring a small gift of *yot*, a sticky caramel-like candy. People present it to the students with the hope that they will "stick to" or pass the exam for the university they wish to attend, just as *yot* sticks to whatever it touches. Smart businessmen who design new *yot* products with lovely decorations and wrapping paper make good money. On this occasion, the family reinforces its close network of friends and relatives. These rituals indicate how much people are concerned with the university entrance examination and how it has persisted so long that they have ritualized the event.

How do teachers manage to survive in this educational system? Chunkyojo, the Teachers and Educational Workers Union, was established in 1989 by young, socially conscious teachers who realized what they had done to children. But the government banned the union as an illegal organization. A teachers' union of this kind had been formed earlier (in 1960), and over twenty thousand teachers—one-fifth of the total at that time—joined. It lasted less than a year because Park's government harshly suppressed it. In the intervening two decades, there were no visible autonomous teachers' movements or activities. Teachers, as civil servants, are barred from collective action by the constitution, the National Civil Service Act, and the Private School Law (Asia Watch Report 1990:31).

Recently, the *minjung-minjok* (class and national independence struggle) movement inside and outside university campuses and the flowering of the labor movement that followed Roh's June 1987 declaration have stimulated young teachers to form voluntary organizations. In September 1987, an organization was founded advocating reforms in the educational system and improved working conditions for teachers. These teachers wanted more democratic operation of the schools and flexibility in choosing their teaching materials. At a conference in February, participants decided they needed a full-scale union and resolved to establish Chunkyojo. While preparations were under way for Chunkyojo's inauguration, the Ministry of Education announced that it would deal severely with any teachers involved in organizing the union. The government decided to dismiss and arrest the one hundred leading organizers of the union. Despite these threats, Chunkyojo was launched on May 1989 at a rally at Yonsei University. Riot police were mobilized to block the site of the rally, and 1,082 teachers and students of teachers' colleges were arrested. The struggle to legitimize the union is still going on now.

However, this group does not have much popular support due to its movement direction and style. As the organization was born in the midst of political struggle, it adheres to Marxist discourse rather faithfully, claiming their organization as "the workers' union." They tend to emphasize the worker's side rather than the teacher's side, which annoys the parents who believe, in accord with Confucian tradition, that teachers should be different from ordinary laborers. Most Koreans cannot accept the idea that "respectable teachers" try to form a workers' union using the same words that radical student activists use. The organization also tends to rely heavily on organizational power, with agitation and direct confrontation. Since the collapse of the Eastern bloc and after the presidential election in 1992, the tide of the leftist movement is rapidly ebbing. Chunkyojo is in its reorganizing stage.

There are other groups of teachers who wholeheartedly devote themselves to their vocation. Under the given conditions, the "good" teachers are the ones who can upgrade their students' academic scores. "Good teachers" are classified into two types: "capable teachers" who can teach students the skills of doing well on the exams, and "respectable teachers" who encourage students to keep on studying even when the student does not have much chance to go to university.

One critic at a small informal meeting for educational reform by citizens, however, suggested that these respectable teachers are cheating. She thought, and I agree, that if teachers know students have little aptitude for these exams, they should encourage those students to find other ways to develop their potential rather than making them cling to a lost cause. But teachers do not have the courage or means to guide these students. All they do is to pacify them in order not to disturb others who have more chance to go to colleges.

There are bad teachers who are not eager to teach. Especially in rural schools, where only a few students seriously prepare for going to college, teachers tend to be lazy. Many simply ignore the majority of students, feeling burdened by the minority who demand to be taught exam-taking skills. Schools in affluent neighborhoods are in an advantageous position since they can easily collect money from parents—although it is illegal in a strict sense—and scout for "competent" teachers. The so-called good high schools are the ones where the school principals can do this with financial support from the students' parents.[7]

Teachers' performance levels can be easily measured, since each student's academic scores are nationally computerized. The scores are as important to the teachers as they are to the students. If the total score of students in a class is at the bottom of all classes in the school, the teacher supervizing that class is considered to be the "stupid bottom." The teachers are ashamed of their students' performances and often beat them up to make them study harder. An ethnographic study of high school finds that the major cultural themes of the high school are "ability" and "obedience" (Lee 1990:207). The best teacher is the one who is able to encourage his or her students to achieve the best score and at the same time obey the school principal. The best teachers reinforce these survival rules in the teachers' society and sneer at the novice who talks about true education or who staunchly refuses to accept "envelopes" from parents.

Many people find the national grading system convenient. An owner of a small company asked me once to give a lecture to his employees. He said that the level of his employees was around 220 on the nationwide university extrance examination, assuming that the number tells much about his workers. That means they are just below average. Many people think that the score is quite an accurate index for judging a person's ability. We can see here how powerful and convenient a score can be in a homogeneous society where diverse qualifications are not appreciated. The scores provide an easy basis for ranking people. It seems that the highly standardized score comforts those who have gotten used to lining up people in one hierarchical line. The nationwide scoring of the people, in turn, reinforces cultural emphases on hierarchy, uniformity, and order.

CONSERVATIVE FORCES, NEW FORCES

Aren't there groups who want to and can change the education system? Educators and educational bureaucrats are not ready because they want a magical solution that can solve the whole problem at once. Talk about alternative schools makes little progress due to complicated government regulations on founding schools. Parents are split into two groups, the conservative and the reformist, and the conservative voice is much louder. The number of parents who are determined not to let their children be damaged in the education war is increasing, but still the total number is very small. Some of the youngsters of middle-school age are sent abroad to study, for example, to the United States or Australia, but they are severely criticized as "escapists" by the public media. These days some of the students decide to go abroad for themselves, and the number is increasing. The students persuade their parents by saying that they cannot get what they want under this school system. Educational specialists, cultural critics, and some parents do discuss the serious problems in education. However, their movements are too weak to counteract the invisible and pervasive force of devoted mothers and educators in "the holy war."

Although the media try to propose solutions to the examination war with endless special reports and analyses, they ultimately seem to reinforce the situation. The commercialized media know very well that the examination war is a national ritual that excites many people. Thus, the media tend to dramatize the situation in order to draw an audience for their newspaper, news show, or magazine. These exaggerations increase the competitive anxiety of the families and students involved in this year's war, while prompting veterans of past wars to recall their agony and remorse with nostalgia. The emotional response to the examination war, stirred up by the media, often precludes any persistent analytical evaluation of the situation.

The conservative majority considers the liberal education in the West as a failure. The Western educational system may produce a few brilliant people, but it also produces a mass of drug users, sex maniacs, and undermotivated youngsters. The conservative majority also insists that Japan has been able to maintain its economic success due to its competitive educational system.

Moreover, vested institutionalized interests are blocking attempts at reform. A large sector of private industry has already been established on the present educational system of examination-preparatory schools. All kinds of businesses—cram schools, study halls, publishing companies for supplementary reference books, educational firms for producing and distributing the nationwide mock examinations and forecasting the tendency and content of next year's exam, and firms for producing computer-aided or telephone-aided study programs—are flourishing and creating job opportunities for mothers who have decided to work part-time to earn money for their children's cram school tuition. Severe competition in the examination war endlessly inflates fees for private lessons.

According to the Labor Ministry's 1990 statistics, the average wage

for a college graduate and above is 812,167 won, nearly double the average wage of 465,043 won for a high-school graduate. The discrepancy
in income and social status is still so large that the system may persist.
The Ministry of Education is carrying out a plan to strengthen vocational education at the high-school level, but it seems difficult to carry
out. First of all, the expenses are extremely high. Moreover, the cultural
preference for liberal-arts education and college credentials still strongly
resists any reforms.

We have to take another serious look at the historical process if
we want to catch possible clues to break this solid conservativism. Modernization in Korea was driven by Western and Japanese imperialism in
the beginning and then centrally controlled by strong Korean governments in the later stages. In a culture characterized by severe cultural
disruption and social instability, it was quite understandable that great
importance was placed on educational credentials. The credentials have
served as absolute criteria for differentiating and organizing members of
society in the absence of other, more just procedures. So far, this educational system in Korea has worked effectively, at least for rapid economic
expansion.

However, the educational system is no longer as appropriate in the
contemporary era of accelerating global capitalism. Docile, uniform,
standardized students may have suited early-modernist, state-organized
capitalism. But the new social system requires new sorts of flexible and
innovative worker elites. Sooner or later, this lack of fit between the current ritualized examination war and corporate-state needs will produce
conflict and contradictions.

In fact, Japan has publicly recognized the necessity of introducing
greater freedom to the school system in order to supply corporate interests with more creative individuals who will help the nation compete in
computer science and other knowledge-intensive industries. I believe the
media will soon spread this news, which will in turn influence Koreans.

Demographic factors and the job market will have effects on bringing
some changes in the educational system. In 1992, there were 900,000
applicants for the college entrance examination, including 300,000 persons trying to take the exam for the second or third time. The total
number of students who will get admitted to four-year colleges is
250,000. Another 150,000 will be admitted to two-year colleges. This
means that 400,000 students go to colleges, while 500,000 fail. It is
expected that the total number of applicants will be 700,000 in 1996. In
2005, the number of applicants is expected to decrease to 460,000,
which is the number of expected high-school graduates of the year
(Chong et al. 1993:38–39). This change in number indicates that the

competition is likely to lessen in the coming decade, although competition for the top universities may still be very high.

Moreover, in recent years there has been a severe job shortage for college graduates. This is another point that the media use to discourage college aspirations. The strange thing to me is that the industry does not complain about the quality of the college-educated workforce. Is it an indication that Korean society is still in the Fordist stage?

Meanwhile, the demand from outside capitalist forces that Korea open its market to international trade is getting stronger. Once Korea opens the door, educational businesses will be established by foreign enterprises. Private schools and colleges as well as language schools will be introduced. Having different schools will probably cause many problems since Korean society has not had enough time and experience to build an intrastructure for integrating foreign systems. However, the day will come that Korea has to open the door!

Some symptoms of disintegration of the present educational system are visible. In the 1992 college entrance examinations, various frauds were exposed, and the media have taken up the issue very extensively. It was discovered that university administrators and professors have been involved in various unfair admission processes, individually or in groups, while others have committed organized fraud by having university students take the exam for college applicants. In the latter cases, beepers were used to transmit test answers, and many high-school teachers were involved. Some socially respectable men are also suspected of having been involved, although they claim ignorance, saying that their wives did it in secret for their children.

The private universities want to admit students whose parents donate a large sum of money to the university. Presidents of large private universities say that they cannot maintain the high level of educational quality by just depending on tuition revenue. There is a strong opposing voice on the ground that this will seriously damage the popular spirit of equality. But the universities do not seem to give up easily, and the state is not as strong as it was.

Youth who come out of the educational system are also beginning to express themselves. Some of the high-school graduates who decided not to go to colleges became extremely popular singers, as widely reported in the media. The group called So-taiji and Children consists of an intelligent songwriter and two dancers. These three young men have clearly shown the general audience that there are other ways to live happily. Many youngsters, including the academically successful ones, have been stimulated by the news of this brave new generation and seem to be seriously thinking over their life chances. Passive rebellions have been attempted here and there, although they have not yet achieved wide public recognition.

At my daughter's middle-school graduation ceremony, graduating students showed up with supermini skirts, heavy makeup, and strange hairstyles to shock the teachers. They tried their best to do whatever they were prohibited to do. The unpopular teachers did not dare to bring their cars to school for fear of vandalism by angry students. Even at the ceremony closing the regular semester, a small act of resistance was made by the students as they sang a popular song instead of the national anthem or the school song. Interestingly, no such gestures are seen in the high schools. There are high-school students who want to go abroad to study, and they do go abroad much more readily than before. This, again, is a sign of change in the sense that people have become freer from the pressure of nationalistic emotion.

These are small but significant indices for the changes to come. In 1995, Korea is to open its education market to the world. Significant changes may be brought about by this outside stimulus. The educational system will change eventually. Whether these changes will be for the better or worse will ultimately depend on the force of those social agents who are determined to change the system. Critical rethinking and open debates on the politics of culture in the newly emerging world of consumerism and global capitalism are necessary.

The activist side of me wants to say the final word. Politicizing mothers is the key to saving our children at risk. As my feminist group has been advocating, mothers must become "social wives," taking care of a healthy society, not just "housewives" concerned only for their own children's succss (Alternative Culture Group 1990).

NOTES

I am grateful to Sharon Stephens, Nancy Abelmann, Nicole Sault, and Yuh Ji-yeon for reading the draft of this paper and giving valuable suggestions.

1. For further details on the issue of class reproduction through the educational system, see Cho 1994b.

2. Sang-ok Lee, a professor in English literature, analyzed the content of literature education and found that the New Criticism is mainly applied (1992). His interpretation is that a definite answer can be deduced if one applies the method of New Criticism, which in essence imitates "scientific" methods.

3. For a detailed analysis of the education bureaucracy and state ideology in the process of state-monopoly capitalism, see Cho 1989:2.

4. The proportion of the Ministry of Education's budget to GNP was 3.6 percent in 1991 (Bae 1991:73).

5. For historical discussions, see Palais 1976.

6. For further details, see Cho 1987.

7. In Korea, tuition for private schools is regulated by the government. Private schools cannot function properly with this limited budget unless they get donations. This is one of the major reasons Korea does not have good alternative schools.

REFERENCES

Alternative Culture Group, 1990, *Chubu, ku makim hwa ttuim* (Housewives, their confinement and opening), Seoul, Alternative Culture Press.

Asia Watch Report, 1990, *Retreat from Reform: Labor Rights and Freedom of Expression in Korea*, New York.

Bedeski, Robert E., 1994, *The Transformation of South Korea*, New York, Routledge.

Bae, Jong-gun, 1991, "Kyoyuk t'uja ui bin'gon kujo" (The poverty structure of educational investment), in Bommo chong, ed., *Kyoyuk nan'guk ui haebu* (Analysis of the educational predicament), Seoul, Nanam, 67–92.

Cho, Hae-joang, 1987, "Male Dominance and Mother Power: Two Sides of Confucian Patriarchy in Korea," paper presented at the workshop "The Psychocultural Dynamics of the Confucian Family: Past and Present," Seoul.

———, 1989, "Kyoyuk ui sinhwa rul kkeja" (Let's break the myth of education), in Alternative Culture Group, ed., *Nurunun kyoyuk, charanun aidul* (Oppressing education, growing children), Seoul, Alternative Culture Press, 49–62.

———, 1994a, "Kyoyuk kehyok un kwayon kanunghan'ga" (Is educational reform possible?), in *T'alsikminji sidae chisikin ui kuliggi was samiggi* (Reading texts and reading everyday lives in the postcolonial era), Seoul, Alternative Culture Press, 3:79–110.

———, 1994b, "Kajong kwa hakgyo ui yuchak kwan'gye rul t'onghae pon kyoyuk hyonjang" (The educational system and the reproduction of class: School and family in conspiracy), in *T'aksikminji sidae chisikin ui kuliggi wa samiggi* (Reading texts and reading everyday lives in the postcolonial era), Seoul, Alternative Culture Press, 3:111–38.

Chong, B. et al., 1993, *Restoring Korean Education from the Bondage of the Entrance Examination*, Seoul, Nanam.

Henderson, Gregory, 1968, *Korea: The Politics of the Vortex*, Cambridge, Mass., Harvard University Press.

Lee, In-hyo, 1990, *Inmungye kodunghakgyo kyojikmunhwa yon'gu* (An ethnographic study of teaching culture in Korean liberal-arts high schools), Ph.D. diss., Seoul National University.

Lee, Sang-ok, 1992, "Munhak kyoyuk ui munjejom e taehayo" (Problems of literature education), in *Hyondae Pipyong kwa iron* (Contemporary criticism and theory), Seoul, Hansin, 3:95–102.

Palais, James, 1976, *Politics and Policy in Traditional Korea*, Cambridge, Mass., Harvard University Press.

Rohlen, Thomas P., 1983, *Japan's High School*, Berkeley and Los Angeles, University of California Press.

Schoolland, Ken, 1990, *Shogun's Ghost: The Dark Side of Japanese Education*, New York, Bergen and Harvey.

Segal, Troy, 1992, "Better Schools, Not Just More Schools," *Business Week*, March 30, 1993.

Stevenson, Harold W. and James W. Stigler, 1992, *The Learning Gap: Why Our Schools Are Failing and What We Can Learn from Japanese and Chinese Education*, New York, Simon and Schuster.

Tinker, Irene, 1980, *Toward Equity for Women in Korea's Development Plans*, report prepared for the World Bank, UNDP Korea Project ROK/78/002.

White, Merry, 1987, *The Japanese Educational Challenge: A Commitment to Children*, New York, Free Press.

CHAPTER 5

Children's Stories and the State in New Order Indonesia

SAYA S. SHIRAISHI

> The idea that learning to read may enable one
> later to enrich one's life is experienced as an
> empty promise when the stories the child listens
> to, or is reading at the moment, are vacuous. The
> worst feature of these children's books is that
> they cheat the child of what he ought to gain
> from the experience of literature: access to deeper
> meaning, and that which is meaningful to him at
> his stage of development.
> *(Bettelheim 1977:4)*

WHEN PRAMOEDYA ANANTA TOER[1] wrote a story, "What Has Been Lost," and placed the Indonesian conversation, "Mengapa menangis?" [Why are you crying?] "Ibu—bambu itu menangis" [Mama, the bamboo is crying], into the mouths of a mother and her little boy, who could have known no Indonesian but only Javanese, something significant took place both for Javanese and Indonesian (Toer 1963:14). It was not a mere *re*-construction of what had been lost, that is, the childhood world of Java. It was, rather, an innovative literary construction of the Indonesian past, an Indonesian river and landscape, Indonesian childhood, and an Indonesian mother and family, by means of the new national language, Indonesian.

On August 17, 1945, Sukarno and Hatta, two prominent nationalist leaders who were to become the first president and vice president of the young nation-state, declared the independence of the Republic of Indonesia. This meant the beginning of a revolutionary war against the Netherlands and, furthermore, the challenge to transform colonial society into a new Indonesian national society. The new nation consists of over three hundred different ethnic groups. More than two hundred and fifty distinct languages are spoken as mother tongues. Their kinship systems include matrilineal, patrilineal, and bilateral patterns (Geertz 1963:24).

Family and kinship systems in developing countries are often regarded as the core of traditional social structures that resist change. Indonesia is no exception. Indonesia's prevailing "familyism" in economic, political, and social activities appears to prove, in the eyes of Indonesians as well as foreign observers, the force that non-Western society has against modernization. Familyism, therefore, is accepted as a comforting source of national pride and identity even when it functions as an obstacle to social and political justice. What, however, does this familyism actually represent in a country that consists of over three hundred ethnic groups and their distinctive family relations? This essay explores family relations portrayed in contemporary Indonesian children's stories and examines how these notions of the family have developed.

Today, the national language, Indonesian, is still largely a school tongue, and primary-school attendance is essential for young citizens to learn the language, which is a prerequisite for participation in national life. Ninety-seven percent of children aged seven to twelve years old attended school in 1987.[2] School textbooks and other reading materials have been massively printed and distributed.[3] There were far too few literary works to satisfy a rapidly expanding young reading population. The need to produce children's literature is enormous.

Children's literature in Indonesia is characterized by diverse themes such as family life, school activities, national celebrations, friendship, folktales, religious teachings, biographies of national heroes, historical events, policy propaganda, translations of European fairy tales, and new fantasy tales.[4] Each genre reveals intriguing aspects of the imagery of a new nation. Every story and every choice of words enriches or restricts the young national language and literature and contributes to the imagining of national community (Anderson 1983).

The "family life" stories are among the most robust of all the genres. They describe everyday family life by portraying affairs that take place at home. The basic pattern of family relations shows amazing uniformity, considering Indonesia's diverse cultural heritage: the authoritative, all-knowing father; the ever-giving, never-angry, and also all-knowing mother, who is in charge of family life; and obedient children whose mistakes start the stories and are corrected by the parents at the end.

Let us examine the way family relations are constructed in a story entitled "Silence Does Not Mean Approval" (Utami 1991:32–33). The story is from the best-selling children's weekly magazine, *Bobo*, which is published by a newspaper company. The magazine sells between 240,000 and 260,000 copies every week at newsstands on the streets, through schools that receive some commission for it, and through home delivery with the morning paper.[5] *Bobo* is read not only by children, but also by parents, aunts and uncles, household helpers, and occasional visitors.[6] The stories are quite popular and are regarded as highly educational.

This particular story describes a sixth-grade boy, Yoga, who wants to go swimming with his friend.

> As on previous days Mama kept silent. Yoga sighed with relief and finished lunch. After asking permission from Mama, Yoga left for swimming. . . . That evening, Yoga's body felt feverish. He had an awful headache. Yoga closed the book even though his homework was not finished yet. Yoga lay down on his bed. . . .
>
> "Ma, I have an awful headache," moaned Yoga when Mama felt Yoga's forehead with her hand. . . .
>
> "You are too tired, Yo. You have gone swimming almost every day and not taken a nap. Your body has a limit. If we spend too much of our energy without getting enough rest to balance, we will become sick in the end." Mama placed a cold compress on Yoga's forehead.
>
> "But why did Mama keep silent? Doesn't it mean that Mama gave Yo permission to go swimming?" Mama smiled.
>
> "Silence does not mean approval, Yo! Aren't you already grown up now? Mama does not like to treat Yo as a little child who needs to be told everything every time. . . . Yo must know by now what is best to do," said Mama while placing the cold compress on Yoga's forehead. (Utami 1991:32–33)

The story relies heavily on the theory of education that is phrased in Javanese as *tut wuri handayani* (guiding from behind) and is now a state ideology in Indonesia. The autobiography of President Soeharto (published in 1989) carries a two-page-long footnote defining the concept (1989:582–83).

> The principles for the true education of the child were introduced by Ki Hadjar Dewantara, who is considered to be the architect of Indonesia's educational system, known as the *Among* System. This system gives as much opportunity as possible to children to develop genuine self-discipline, through their own experience, their own understanding and their own efforts. The important thing is to watch that this opportunity does not endanger the child himself or pose a threat to others. (Soeharto 1991:498)

The footnote was attached, however, not to his comments on child education, but to his statement clarifying his principle of government. "Guiding from behind" is the principle with which Soeharto's New Order regime rules the adult citizens of the Republic.

Before discussing the story itself, let us examine the political as well as commercial environment in which the story was written. "Silence Does Not Mean Approval" was printed one year after the publication of President Soeharto's autobiography. Soeharto, the silently smiling, "fatherlike" former army general, outlined his political philosophy for the first time by supplying explanations for major historical incidents of political significance. One whole chapter in the book is devoted to recounting the March 1988 General Assembly (held once in five years).

Everyone already knew that Soeharto would be elected president for the fifth five-year term. The main issue of the assembly, therefore, was the selection of the vice president. In the previous cases, Soeharto, in one way or another, had always named a candidate for the vice presidency in the early stage of selection, in order to guide the process in which the vice president, as well as the president, would be chosen unanimously. However, in 1988 Soeharto kept silent, even though one candidate had his unmistakable support.

Soeharto explained that he did not propose a name because he expected that the people must know by then who was the right candidate, without being told this by the president. The political maturity of the nation was, in Soeharto's mind, synonymous with the people's insightful knowledge and acceptance of the president's unspoken intentions.

However, another candidate took advantage of the president's silence and ran for the seat. The assembly attracted more than usual press coverage because the assembly's one thousand representatives might actually have to vote for the first time. A few hours before the vote, "the other candidate" withdrew in tears, under frenzied pressure from party leaders, who had been summoned to the presidential palace.[7] The punishment for his mistake was dire. He is now almost a political and social outcast. Like Yoga, he should have known better.[8]

Let us now go back to the children's story.

> Yoga thought over Mama's words. Ah, Mama is right. Now he is already grown up. He should not expect that Mama will remind him of his duties. He has to know what he should do by himself. (Utami 1991:33)

The decision about whether or not to go swimming is not considered to be a choice for the boy to make for himself. He is not expected to articulate his preference, evaluate the alternatives, and make a judgment. Rather, he is expected to know his duty. The right answer is already there. Mama knows it even if she may keep silent. The child's maturity is measured not by his ability to make decisions according to his own judgment. It is measured by his ability to know the right answer—that is, the answer in Mama's mind, hidden behind Mama's silence.

> "*Terima kashi, Ma!* [Thank you, Ma. Literally, I accept your love]. I am going to make an effort to understand my duties. But if Yo makes a mistake, please, Mama, let me know that. Sometimes I do not know that I have made a mistake. I even believed all this time that if Mama did not forbid me, or said nothing, it meant Mama approved of my conduct."

"Don't be afraid. Mama will always let you know when Mama considers it necessary. Now Yo understands, don't you, that swimming every day is not good for health?" Yo smiled with the feeling of embarrassment. (Utami 1991:33)

The boy was embarrassed because he did not know what he should know. The punishment for his mistake takes the form of sickness, as if to prove that Almighty God is behind Mama—or that they may in fact be interchangeable. Mama's authority is unquestionable.

The lesson that the child learns is not that he should not go swimming every day, but that Mama's silence does not mean that she approves of his conduct. In fact, from the beginning, Yoga was closely watching Mama's countenance, trying to find out what was in her mind. He went swimming mainly because his mother did not say no. He should have known better.

The story makes it easy and understandable for children as well as adult readers to grasp Soeharto's principle of government. This is the reason why the story is regarded as educational. It is beneficial for the readers, who might not have read or understood Soeharto's message, to learn this crucial lesson for survival and success. The "wrong" vice presidential candidate at the 1988 assembly has recently been presented in the magazines in tears, as his political positions and social relations are taken from him one by one. He is just like a little boy crying under parental discipline (for example, *Tempo*, January 6, 1990, 46–47). He used to be photographed with the wise, know-it-all, confident smile of a man who chaired an important religious party with a complex political history.

The theory that the child should be free and learn from his mistakes is thus beautifully turned, in this children's story, into a theory that the child should watch carefully and try to find out what is in Mama's mind, so as to avoid making a mistake and receiving parental/supernatural punishment.

This is the basic principle that any writer has to learn in order to survive in Soeharto's Indonesia. Writers can make considerable profits by voluntarily making their writings effective educational and political tools for the regime. Editors buy the stories and parents buy the magazines because the message in the stories is considered useful. The stories offer vital knowledge people need to know in order to be citizens of the Republic (that is, to know what is in Soeharto's mind). The story becomes politically effective, as well as commercially profitable.

Once this political-educational-commercial value is understood in literary circles, the government does not need to tell each writer what to write or not to write. The government need not be alertly watchful in its censorship. It is the writer, not the censor, who watches carefully and tries to find out what is in Soeharto's mind, just as the boy watches carefully to discover what is in Mama's mind.[9]

Many "educational" children's stories are produced in this manner. Otherwise, parents would not spend their precious money on them. If the Ministry of Education and Culture finds the story sufficiently favorable, it will offer the publisher a subsidy and may buy books to send to school libraries all over Indonesia. Some money from international funds for child education is also used for this purpose.

Let me present another example of a children's story to show how intimately it reflects national politics. Soeharto, who has never presented himself as a candidate who sought the presidency but has always "accepted" the duty upon the request of the people, has been vague on the issue of presidential succession. He would not say what is in his mind.

In late December 1990, under this circumstance, "Crown Prince of the Kingdom of Thessavio" (Suhardi 1990–91) appeared in *Bobo*. Prince Alfonso has to qualify himself as the successor to the kingship by finding the right person for his royal consort. Three women are introduced in the story. At the beginning of the story, the prince falls in love with a flower seller, Nydia. Unlike some fairy tales, which end with the happy love-marriage of a prince and a beautiful young lady, Alfonso's father, the king, declares that Nydia is the wrong answer. In the kingdom, the moon god prescribes certain traditional criteria that must be satisfied by the would-be royal consort. It is the duty of the crown prince to find the right woman and marry her. Nydia's candidacy as his marriage partner is based on Alfonso's personal choice. This is proof, therefore, that Alfonso is neglecting his duty and Nydia is not the right consort. His mistake proves to be fatal, for Nydia kills herself.

Here again the father-king says a fatal "no" only after his son has made the wrong choice. Alfonso suffers over his loss of Nydia because he truly loved her. Now, having experienced his true love, desire, and choice, the young man understands what it is that he must suppress and renounce, and what his duty means. One cannot learn how to suppress desire without ever having it. His true love and subsequent suffering constitute the first step for his qualification, because now it is clear that whoever will be Alfonso's marriage partner will *not* be his personal choice. Alfonso is therefore fulfilling his duty.

Twin sisters, Sosya and Yona, are introduced to the prince as candidates. The prince screams—"Nydia! Oh, you have come back! But why have you become two?"—because they look so perfectly like Nydia after all. Only one woman is the right answer, however, and he has to discover which one. He eventually comes to realize that it is not right for him to choose at all. Instead, he decides to place his fate in the hands of the moon god by jumping into a fire. Sosya, who has come to love him, respects his personal decision. On the other hand, Yona, who knows that it is her duty not to let the crown prince of the kingdom die, guides him from behind out of the way and prepares to jump into the fire herself. The prince declares at this moment that Yona is the right answer. It is Sosya who silently jumps into the fire. The happy nation is now left with the qualified crown prince and his rightful partner.

The story conveys the writer's understanding of Soeharto's mind in the matter of the qualifications of his successor. The would-be successor should have learned to suppress all his personal desires and ambitions. He should know not to choose anything for himself by himself, and he should be prepared to accept his duty. The message is clear enough. If someone makes it apparent that he wishes to gain the presidential seat, he disqualifies himself. The position should come to him as a duty, which the successor resignedly accepts. Furthermore, the one who knows his duty to preserve the would-be king for the nation, as Yona did, may perhaps get the seat next to him.[10]

The two stories appear to follow the theory that the child should be free and learn from his/her mistakes, but in fact this is turned into a theory that the child must know what is the right answer, hidden behind parental silence. Mistakes will invite fatal supernatural punishments. A structure of self-policing is thinly disguised as parental guidance of the child.

These highly political children's stories pose two questions. How has such a close association between representations of family relations and political principles been created and reproduced in Indonesian literature? In other words, why is the description of family relations, especially that between parents and children, so political?[11] Second, how has such a uniform system of imagery of these authoritative family relations been constructed in the children's literature of a nation that consists of over three hundred ethnic groups, each with its own family and kinship systems?

The key to answering these questions lies in the history of the Indonesian language, the language of all the children's stories. Malay, which became Indonesian, was the lingua franca of the archipelago. Kartini once wrote in a letter, dated November 6, 1899, to her Dutch pen friend:

> What do we speak at home? What a question, Stella, dear. Naturally, our language is Javanese. We speak Malay with strange people who are Easterners, either Malays, Moors, Arabs, or Chinese, and Dutch with Europeans. (Kartini 1985:45)

Malay was spoken by the traders, sailors, clerks, missionaries, mercenaries, prostitutes, officials, journalists, union activists, nationalists, and teachers, but it was not spoken by fathers and mothers to their young children at home. The lingua franca did not have any specific family structure of its own. The familial vocabularies of the lingua franca were empty signs.

In the colonial Dutch East Indies, Dutch was the language of power, spoken exclusively by the Dutch and a limited number of privileged "natives" who studied at Dutch schools. For the wider population, whose mother tongues were Javanese, Sundanese, Balinese, Acehnese, and hundreds of other languages, Malay was employed as the administrative language. It subsequently became the political language of resistance and newly found unity of the "awakened natives."

Nationalist leaders, who spoke Dutch among themselves and ethnic languages with their families and neighbors, made their provocative political speeches at mass rallies in Malay. It was often their third language, after their mother tongue and Dutch, but they prided themselves in mastering Malay and used it to create the imagery of a new society. In 1928, Malay was given the new name, Indonesian, by young nationalist youths who adopted their "motherland, Indonesia" and their "national tongue, Indonesian." The new national language of the yet-to-be-born nation was not only a symbol of resistance against the Dutch colonial state and of solidarity among the nationalists, but also a symbol of hope for the new society.[12]

Education of young children was a significant part of the nationalist movement. It became even more important when the colonial police state largely succeeded in suppressing any other political movements by the early 1930s. The network of Taman Siswa (Garden of Pupils) schools led by Ki Hadjar Dewantara expanded from Java to the Outer Islands and became the innovative core of the nationalist educational movement.[13] Jobless, but educated and ambitious, young men and women became the teachers. They debated and experimented with new educational methods and human relationships in the classrooms. They were strongly influenced by European educational theories of the time. Maria Montessori and Rudolf Steiner were their educational heroes, as much as Karl Marx and Gandhi were their political heroes.

Experimental "family-style" instruction was employed in the classrooms. Children addressed their teachers as *Bapak* [Father] and *Ibu* [Mother] in Malay.[14] Teachers let the children, both boys and girls, play and learn freely at their own pace and in their own direction, while the teachers remained in the background.

This family principle, which was named *ke-keluarga-an* (familyism) in Malay, was also adopted as the organizational principle for Taman Siswa schools as the alternative to the colonial bureaucratic organization.[15] Taman Siswa schools, for example, did not have any "employees" other than "family members." They were not bound by regulations or monetary contracts. In principle, they jointly contributed to the organization and shared its resources. They addressed each other as *Bapak* and *Ibu*. Nevertheless, Ki Hadjar Dewantara exercised officially acknowledged dictatorship over the entire Taman Siswa organization and guided its members with his strong personality. He later wrote:

> We used the terms "Bapak" and "Ibu" because we considered that the terms of address currently in use, "Tuan [Malay—Sir]," "Njonjah [Madam]," "Nonah [Miss]," and the corresponding Dutch terms, "Meneer," "Mevrouw," and "Juffrouw," and also the terms in use in Java, such as "Mas Behi," "Den Behi," and "Ndoro," which implied superiority and inferiority of status, should be abolished from Taman Siswa. We introduced the use of the terms, "Bapak" and "Ibu" not only for when pupils spoke to teachers but also for when younger teachers spoke to older ones. We never once spelled this out as a "regulation," but this kind of appellation soon came to be used in educational institutions across Indonesia. Not only that, after the Indonesian Republic became independent, it was even suggested that these terms should be used formally by younger officials in addressing older officials. (Dewantara, quoted in McVey 1967: 114–15)

Through familyism, and with the terms "Bapak" and "Ibu," the young nationalists intended to create a new society based on a new order of human relations, in which complex colonial social hierarchy was simplified into sex distinctions and age distinctions. The empty familial vocabulary of the lingua franca was well suited for the purpose of creating new human relations.

The empty signs of the familyless lingua franca had boundless possibilities. They could absorb modern European concepts and still appear to belong to "the natives." Not to the Javanese, not to the Sundanese, not to any one of three hundred ethnic groups, but to "the natives," which was, in fact, a modern European concept assigned to the diverse colonial population at large. These "natives," the second-class citizens of a colony, transformed themselves into a nation by developing institutional principles and a language with which to express their aspirations for unity.

When the Taman Siswa teachers and graduates manned the new Republic government en masse after independence, the terms *Bapak* and *Ibu*, born in Taman Siswa classrooms, began to grow up in the offices of government ministries.[16] As government regulations and documents were translated from Dutch into Indonesian, the family principle was incorporated wherever possible.[17] As each new national tradition was materialized, that is, the "family style" classroom instruction, "family principle" for organization, or "fatherlike" leadership came into being, the Indonesian family began to assume a form. The Indonesian concept

of family was born in Taman Siswa classrooms, grew up in its organizational meetings and nationalist political rallies, and came to maturity in
the offices of government ministries after independence.

At the beginning of the Guided Democracy period (1959–65), when
parliamentary democracy was considered to have failed in organizing the
nation, familyism provided the alternative model for national politics.[18]
Political leaders and government officials were addressed as *Bapak* and
were defined as fatherlike leaders. *Fatherlike* could only mean, initially,
Ki Hadjar Dewantara–style "dictatorship," and the instructional
method of Taman Siswa teachers who watched the young children from
behind. There was no other actual model of the homemade Indonesian
father.

Sukarno, who was in his sixties and no longer the young, brilliant
student–nationalist leader of the 1920s, became the authoritative
"*Bapak* president" of the nation. In search of an Indonesian, that is,
non-Western, leadership style, Sukarno enthusiastically incorporated the
rich repertoire of Java's theatrical tradition into Indonesian politics.
Bapak, the sign of anticolonial resistance, new experimental education
and social relations, and national unity acquired even newer shades of
Java's antiquity. The young nation began to claim to *have been* an old
people, possessed of sacred old traditions and family relations. The term
Bapak now took on the aura of Java's warrior heroes. This aura was
smoothly incorporated into Sukarno's charismatic leadership style.

Sukarno was a marvelous orator, who could shake the heart of the
nation and affect its course of history with each speech he made and with
each expression he invented or incorporated from a wide range of literary sources into the national language. Indonesian spread across the archipelago. Parents were proud of witnessing their children speak and
sing in Indonesian. Some young parents sang the national anthem as a
lullaby for their babies.

After the abortive coup of 1965,[19] more than five hundred thousand
people were killed in Indonesia's countryside.[20] Villagers killed their
neighbors, youths killed their classmates and teachers, and the army apparently stood behind the killings.[21] The hope of national unity and a
new society for which the people had fought and survived through the
long painful years was undone.[22] In spite of the official statements issued
by the New Order government and subsequent court trials of the coup
members, the most tragic affair in national history has never been openly
discussed and fully analyzed inside Indonesia. Indonesian, which had
once created, spread through, and thus given life to the imagining of a
new nation, kept silent at this crucial hour, refusing to reveal the truth
behind the bloodshed.

Order and stability was restored to the nation by military might.
When the silently smiling army general Soeharto came into power and

assumed the title of the second *Bapak* President in 1967, *Bapak* adopted the silence behind which the unspoken truth of killings was stashed. The New Order stands on this silence of *Bapak* and the silences pervading contemporary use of Indonesian. The New Order stands on suppression of speech. It is as if breaking the silence could fatally, once and for all, destroy the fragile order of the nation that has lost confidence in itself. The nation today is addicted to a national pastime of guessing what is behind the silent smile of the *Bapak* President, who is, in turn, to keep watch on his children, or the citizens, from behind.

Under the New Order, political, social, and economic conditions were stabilized and schools were built in this nation with the fourth largest population in the world. School textbooks and other reading materials have been printed and distributed through the governmental channels. Most of the publication, however, is under direct or indirect governmental censorship. All the works of Pramoedya Ananta Toer are banned, which has effectively discouraged any fresh family portrayals from emerging in Indonesian literature.[23]

Learning Indonesian today implies learning not only its grammar and syntax, but also what has to be kept unsaid and how to know what lies behind the silence. The Indonesian language of today contains within itself the possibility of punishment that may strike without warning. It is safer to accept, memorize, and reproduce what has already been said and has not been condemned. The familyism through which the young nationalists boldly experimented with new social relations has subsided to become the sign of the New Order designed by Soeharto—a society with the right answer.

At this point in history, the rapidly growing field of children's literature is producing and reproducing portrayals of *Bapak* as family father and *Ibu* as mother. The Indonesian "family," which now represents the authoritarian, paternalistic nature of the regime, has penetrated the family home through textbooks and children's stories. *Bapak* and *Ibu* have finally reached the family home. The young boy, Yoga, constantly looks back over his shoulder toward his mother, while the young man, Alfonso, stops exploring his own future.

The lingua franca has largely remained a lingua franca with no one coming forward to own it.[24] The mother portrayed within Indonesian children's stories keeps a distance of silence between herself and her child and remains a lingua franca mother. For the majority of the population, Indonesian is still the school tongue that they learn through uniform textbooks from the teachers, who are still addressed today as *Bapak* and *Ibu*.[25]

People's perceptions of the family are certainly influenced not only by Indonesian books, but by films and TV programs which are also under effective censorship.[26] At present there is little possibility for children's own fathers and mothers to influence the imagery of school literature. Two-way communication between the children's mother tongue (or their life-size parents) and the school tongue (spoken by the all-knowing *Bapak* and *Ibu* in the classroom) appears so far to be negligible.[27]

Children's stories show us not only how the "Indonesian family" is constructed at present, but also how this family is structured in accordance with the design of the present regime.[28] Through constructions of the family, presumably the sphere of people's private life, state politics penetrates and shapes Indonesian society.[29]

NOTES

Research for this article was sponsored by the Toyota Foundation and the Daiwa Bank Foundation. I would like to express my gratitude to these sponsors and to George McT. Kahin, Benedict R. O'G. Anderson, Marilyn Ivy, John Pemberton, Vivienne Wee, and Takashi Shiraishi for their comments, criticisms, and suggestions. I thank the Norwegian Centre for Child Research for the opportunity that the "Children at Risk" conference offered to us. I am indebted to Sharon Stephens for inviting me to participate in the session "Children and the Politics of Culture" and for her extremely close reading and encouragement, without which this paper would not have been completed. Needless to say, neither the sponsors nor the readers mentioned above bear any responsibility for the views expressed in this article.

1. The greatest Indonesian novelist. There is no second, or even third, writer after him because of the political climate I am going to outline in this essay.

2. That is, 24,931,000 out of 25,689,000 (Biro Pusat Statistik 1988; see also Shiraishi 1992:11–12).

3. For comparative analysis of ethnic language textbooks under Dutch colonial rule and in the early days of independence, see Shiraishi 1982:67–86.

4. Children's cartoons have also made an impressive appearance in the last few years. See Shiraishi 1994.

5. These figures are from a telephone interview with an editor of *Bobo*, Jakarta, May 1991.

6. It is still a luxury for the majority of Indonesian households to spend money on books. A weekly television and movie tabloid, *Monitor*, made a record by selling six hundred thousand copies a week in 1989–90. Nationally uniform textbooks, distributed to all schoolchildren, have had tremendous effects in homogenizing the Indonesian language and its literature.

7. For discussion of these events, see articles in the leading newsweekly in Jakarta, *Tempo* (March 5, 1988, 22–29, and March 12, 1988, 34–48).

8. It was, however, a political game in which the opposition group offered the wrong answer, with perfect knowledge of Soeharto's intention.

9. Nevertheless, the chief editor of *Monitor*, Arswendo, made the mistake of not editing the outcome of its popularity poll. The tabloid's publication license

was revoked in October 1990, and the editor is now serving a five-year prison term for his "irresponsibility." See Shiraishi 1992:250–63 and *Tempo* (October 27, 1990, 27–35, and November 3, 1990, 25–34). The printing and publishing licence of *Tempo*, too, was revoked in June 1994.

10. At the 1993 assembly, Soeharto was again "chosen" as president. His former adjutant, who was officially commended by all the parties this time, was "chosen" as vice president unanimously.

11. For discussion of the construction of generation-and-seniority-based categories in contemporary Indonesian, see Shiraishi 1992:124–29.

12. For a brilliant analysis of "political" Indonesian, see Anderson 1990:123–51.

13. For discussion of Ki Hadjar Dewantara, see Scherer 1975.

14. See McVey 1967:128–49 for the significance of Taman Siswa familyism in relation to "bapakism."

15. For the history of Taman Siswa and its family principle, see Tsuchiya's important work (1987).

16. During the revolution, the revolutionaries addressed each other as *Saudara* (Brother/Sister), with no distinctions of serniority or sex, and addressed the leaders as *Bung* (Brother/Comrade) (such as *Bung Karno* for Sukarno). Both of these forms of address are now virtually extinct. (Recently, I have noticed the revival of *saudara* in E-mail correspondence.) The system of address in contemporary Indonesian requires a comprehensive study of its own.

17. For example, see the speech by Wilopo, a former active member of the Taman Siswa movement and prime minister (1970:379).

18. See Feith 1962 for discussion of Indonesian politics prior to the Guided Democracy.

19. In a film made in the early 1980s, the murdered generals are presented as affectionate fathers and husbands, rather than as elite military men. This film is shown to schoolchildren every year.

20. The death of a six-year-old daughter of a general, fatally wounded in the coup raid, was sensationally reported as if to legitimize the subsequent killings.

21. For discussion of the 1965 coup, see Crouch 1978.

22. By this time, Taman Siswa teachers were deeply divided. See Hing 1978.

23. For discussion of reasons for the banning of Pramoedya's works, see Attorney General 1988. Here it is claimed that the following statements by Pramoedya "disparage national moral values": "How happy European children are. They are free to criticise, to declare their disbelief in a policy, without being punished, let alone exiled. Those who are criticised and those who criticise lose nothing, let alone their freedom. Rather, they advance by correcting each other. . . . Try to criticise your Kings. You would have been killed by the sword before uttering your final words."

24. Exceptions may be found among the younger generation of people who were born and raised in Jakarta, where Indonesian has become the language of everyday family life. Their political statements often take the form of literary portrayals of overbearing parents. Their "pop culture" also indicates the emergence of a market in which publishers need not rely on governmental subsidies.

25. An Indonesian friend told me that at the high-school reunion in his

home town in Java, he and his former classmates discussed politics and family in Indonesian, while they conversed about all other topics in Javanese.

26. When an old man was interviewed about his experience during the revolutionary war, his granddaughter, a junior-high-school student, repeatedly interrupted the interview, saying "Grandpa, you are wrong. The textbook does not say so!" I owe this information to Tsuyoshi Kato.

27. Most publication has been in Indonesian, but some intellectuals are now pointing out the need for ethnic-language publications.

28. The other side of the state's familyism may be found in the facts of how the "fathers" with their private interests have camped inside government bureaucracy. See Shiraishi 1992:154–249.

29. For discussion of the dynamism and extent to which this "Indonesian society" manifests itself in the classroom, see Shiraishi 1992:315–53.

REFERENCES

Anderson, Benedict R. O'G., 1983, *Imagined Communities: Reflections on the Origin and Spread of Nationalism*, London, Verso.

———, 1990, "The Languages of Indonesian Politics," in *Language and Power: Exploring Political Cultures in Indonesia*, Ithaca, N.Y., Cornell University Press.

Attorney General of The Republic of Indonesia, 1988, "Considerations Leading to the Banning from Circulation of the Book Titled *Glasshouse* written by Pramoedya Ananta Toer," Decree Attorney General of the Republic of Indonesia Number: KEP-061/J.A./6/1988.

Bettelheim, Bruno, 1977, *The Uses of Enchantment: The Meaning and Importance of Fairy Tales*, New York, Vintage Books.

Biro Pusat Statistik, 1988, *Statistik Indonesia* (statistical yearbook of Indonesia), Jakarta, Biro Pusat Statistik.

Crouch, Harold, 1978, *The Army and Politics in Indonesia*, Ithaca, N.Y., Cornell University Press.

Feith, Herbert, 1962, *The Decline of Constitutional Democracy in Indonesia*, Ithaca, N.Y., Cornell University Press.

Feith, Herbert and Lance Castles, eds., 1970, *Indonesian Political Thinking: 1945–1965*, Ithaca, N.Y., Cornell University Press.

Geertz, Hildred, 1963, "Indonesian Cultures and Communities," in Ruth McVey, ed., *Indonesia*, New Haven, Conn., HRAF Press, 24–96.

Kartini, Raden Adjeng, 1985, *Letters of a Javanese Princess*, trans., Agnes Louise Symmers, New York, University Press of America.

Hing, Lee Kam, 1978, "The Taman Siswa in Postwar Indonesia," *Indonesia 25*, Cornell Southeast Asia Program.

McVey, Ruth, 1967, "Taman Siswa and the Indonesian National Awakening," in *Indonesia 4*, Cornell Southeast Asia Program, 128–49.

Scherer, Savitri Prastiti, 1975, "Harmony and Dissonance: Early Nationalist Thought in Java," Ph.D. diss., Cornell University.

Shiraishi, Saya S., 1982, "Eyeglasses: Some Remarks on Acehnese School Books," *Indonesia 36*, Cornell Southeast Asia Program, 66–86.

————, 1992, "Young Heroes: The Family and School in New Order Indonesia," Ph.D. diss., Cornell University.

————, 1994, "Doraemon Goes Overseas," Paper presented to the workshop "Japan in Asia," Cornell University.

Soeharto, 1989, *Soeharto: Pikiran Ucapan dan Tindakan Saya*, Jakarta, PT Citra Lamtoro Gung Persada.

————, 1991, *Soeharto: My Thoughts, Words, and Deeds*, trans. Sumadi, ed. Mutiah Lestiono Jakarta, PT Citra Lamtoro Gung Persada.

Suhardi, Nana M., 1990–91, "Putra Makota Kerajaan Thessavio" (Crown prince of the kingdom of Thessavio), *Bobo*, nos. 32–41.

Toer, Pramoedya Ananta, 1963, "Yang Sudah Hilang" (What has been lost), in *Tjerita dari Blora* (Tales from Blora), Jakarta, Balai Pustaka.

Tsuchiya, Kenji, 1987, *Democracy and Leadership: The Rise of the Taman Siswa Movement in Indonesia*, trans. Peter Hawkes, Honolulu, University of Hawaii Press.

Utami, Mudjibah, 1991, "Diam Bukan Berarti Setuju" (Silence does not mean approval), *Bobo*, 41:32–33.

Wilopo, 1970, "The Principle of the Family Relationship," in Herbert Feith and Lance Castles, eds., *Indonesian Political Thinking: 1945–1965*, Ithaca, N.Y., Cornell Modern Indonesia Project, 379–81.

CHAPTER 6

Children, Population Policy, and the State in Singapore

VIVIENNE WEE

CONTEXTS OF DISCOURSE

The prevailing scholarly discourse on children is located mainly in four contexts:

1. Socialization/enculturation studies (including studies of child rearing): these focus on the process whereby children learn to be human through the internalization of specific cultures—for example, through language acquisition.

2. Studies of historical constructions of childhood as a particular life phase: these focus on the cultural meanings attributed to the infantile and youthful phases of universal physiopsychological development—for example, the cultural interpretation of biological dependence as "purity" and "innocence."

3. Studies of the sociopolitical constructions of children: these focus on the preconceived molds into which children are born and in which they exist—for example, the "value of children" in the sense of the desirability of children in terms of number, gender, and role.

4. Studies of children as social actors, subjects with social agency: these focus on their strategies of negotiation, interpretation, and adaptation—for example, children's constructions of their social worlds.

What these contexts of discourse have in common is the thematic relationship between children and society, which pertains to the larger theme of the relationship between individuals and society. The various contexts of discourse contain within themselves certain implicit notions of children. The first three contexts of discourse assume that children are prehuman passive objects acted upon by an adult society to which the children do not yet fully belong. In particular, the very term *value of children* expresses the notion of children as objects to which value accrues.

In this paper, I seek to deconstruct the ascription of value to children by parents and by the state as parent. I interpret these "values" as preconceived molds into which children are born and expected to fit. Unlike most value-of-children studies, I will focus on preconceived molds constructed not just by parents, but, more particularly, by the state and its governing agents.

STATE, PARENTS, AND CHILDREN

In deconstructing these preconceived molds for children, we must consider a triangle of relationships:

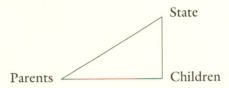

But why should there be a relationship between children and the state? As mentioned above, the relationship between children and society should be understood as pertaining to the relationship between individuals and society. From this perspective, we may compare the two ideal types of social formation. (For the sake of simplicity, I ignore the hierarchical but noncentralized formations known as "chiefdoms.")

1. Society as emergent from population—that is, politically uncentralized society (namely, segmentary tribal societies)

2. Society as an overself imposed on population—that is, politically centralized society (namely, the state)

In politically uncentralized societies, parent-child relations are basically interpersonal relations, with inherent respect for the child as a social person. The ethnographic literature gives ample evidence of this. (See, for example, Benjamin n.d., Endicott 1992, Dentan 1978.) Benjamin (n.d.), for example, notes: "Temiars generally feel that they have no right to command the behaviour of others, even their own children." In such a nonhierarchical society, no one can claim to represent society as a collective overself and, on the basis of this claim, impose themselves on others, including children.

By contrast, in politically centralized societies (that is, states), interpersonal interaction is basically hierarchical. This generates a social space at the top that can be appropriated by certain individuals claiming to represent society as a collective overself and, on that basis, to impose themselves on others, including children. Such claims can be made in various legitimating terms—moral, ideological, medical, legal, scientific, and so on. The "state" in state societies may be understood as a collusion of claims by certain individuals imposed upon all others. Interpersonal relations—for example, parent-child, husband-wife, or, simply, person-person—thereby cease to be purely dyadic. They are transformed instead into mediated relations that are monitored, and ultimately controlled, by a third party in the form of the state as an overself.

It is in this sense that a triangle of relationships exists between parents, children, and the state. This allows the following permutations of the triangle, at least potentially:

State + parents vs. children
State vs. parents + children
State + children vs. parents
State vs. parents vs. children
State + parents + children

This triangle of relationships is often given a particular shape through the cultural interpretation of children's vulnerability. The biosocial relationship between children and society is, after all, an asymmetrical power relationship. Children do not choose to be born. They are or are not born, they live or are not allowed to live, not of their own choice, but through the choice of powerful others, such as parents, religious authorities, government.

In biosocial reality, it is the child who constitutes the newcomer upon whom culture acts, culture being the historical accumulation of the choices and actions of others. Birth is thus an historical moment whereby an apolitical being is caught in an existing political web that has been spun by millennia of preceding others. Socialization-enculturation may thus be thought of as the politicization of this originally apolitical being, whose first political awakening is of its own powerlessness, as it is or is not fed, picked up, cleaned, allowed to live. Children are at risk because of their vulnerability—their lack of choice in being born and, subsequently, in the way they are to live.

This is why it is important to examine the preconceived molds constructed by powerful others (such as parents, religious authorities, governments), for existence itself would be posited on the child's degree of fit into these waiting molds, according to which he or she would be valued or devalued. Convergences and contradictions may arise from the different preconceived molds constructed by various others—in particular, parents versus government. Convergences would increase the pressure for conformity on children, since there would be no given alternatives. Contradictions would lessen the load, since there is a chance of slipping from an ill-fitting mold to a better-fitting one.

The vulnerability of children is a biosocial fact and, as such, is subject to varying cultural interpretations. Continuing for the moment with my ideal-type analysis, the relevant polar opposites would thus be: to exploit this vulnerability, or to protect this vulnerability. Which cultural interpretation prevails is itself the choice of powerful adults, and not of powerless children.

In the exploitative mode of interpretation, adults would assume an unquestioned right to determine the terms of children's vulnerability. ("Be good, do as I say, or else I will not . . .") The adult's power to bestow food, love, or even life upon a child, or to withhold them, could then be regarded, in some cultures, as a taken-for-granted value, part of the natural cosmic order. An historical example of this mode of interpretation is provided by Confucianist China. Confucius said: "If the father says that the son must die, then the son must die. If the emperor says that the subject must die, then the subject must die." Chinese filial piety is thus posited upon a cultural acceptance of the power of life and death wielded by adults—specifically, the father—over vulnerable children.

Jankowiak (1992:347) notes: "China scholars stress that the father-child relationship, throughout much of Chinese history, was organized around an ideology of filial piety that encouraged total obedience, respect, and loyalty toward the father." (See also de Groot 1882—1910 and Freedman 1965.) But whose culture is this anyway? A culture that says that sons must die when fathers command them to must surely be the culture of fathers and not of sons, at least not until sons become fathers in their turn.

The Confucianist social contract was between state and family, between the emperor as superpatriarch and patriarchal families. The Chinese empire was modeled on the patriarchal family, while the Chinese patriarchy was modeled on a centralized state holding a monopoly of violence. In this logical structure, patricide would be tantamount to regicide, which would mean anarchy. Infanticide, on the other hand, would be logically in keeping with the "natural" order of power. Infanticide is not a crime. (In this light, the Tiananmen Massacre of 1990 could perhaps be interpreted as infanticide by the patriarchal state exercising its Confucian right of exterminating its own disobedient children.) In such a context, the child's existence would be construed, not as a basic human right, but as a cultural privilege bestowed by powerful adults—in particular, the father. This is why Chinese expressions of filial piety always articulate gratitude to parents for life itself, for being allowed to live to maturity. In a situation where infanticide is practiced and condoned, every surviving child may feel that, but for the grace of luck, chance, or mercy, he or (especially) she might not have been allowed to survive.

Alternatively, children's vulnerability could be interpreted as purity and innocence, needing the protection of responsible adults. It is this second, protective, mode of interpretation that underlies the very idea of children's rights, needing the protection of a UN charter—hence the UN Convention on the Rights of the Child. While this interpretation of children's vulnerability is child-centered, rather than adult-centered, it nevertheless recognizes, at least implicitly, what *could* happen if children's rights were not protected. The difference is that instead of going with the "natural" tide of power, this child-centered interpretation seeks to control and sublimate it, such that adult power is transmuted as responsibility.

But even this alternative interpretation is not totally benign. It can lead, at least potentially, to collective hypocrisy, as adults pretend to themselves and to the children that all that is done is done for the children's own good. Adult power can be disguised as care, thereby hindering any rebellion with the burden of ungrateful guilt. Thus, we may recognize as the opposing ideal type a pattern I shall label *European*. While Chinese children reared under a Confucianist regime have to reckon with an external "super*alter*," an all-powerful Other, children brought up on this European pattern have to reckon with their internal policing superego. These alternative cultural interpretations of the vulnerability of children would thus generate their own respective political and psychological consequences.

In both these contexts, the state is present. In the Chinese case, the Confucianist state would condone the power and rights of fathers over children, who are theirs to do with as they please, in return for which the state could do with adults as it pleases. The state would thus reign supreme over adult subjects, in return for which the adults qua parents would be given supremacy over their children. In the European case, the interventionist state would restrain parental power and rights over the children, with the state intervening to protect or even remove children from parents who are deemed unfit. The state would thus be supreme over both parents and children and, in some cases, would align itself with children against their parents.

Much of the existing literature on the relationship between children and the state deals precisely with the role of the interventionist state coming between parents and children—for example, in matters of child care, child maintenance, child custody, adoption, juvenile delinquency, and the like, matters that tend to come under the rubric of "welfare," a term that implies the supposedly benign intent of the state. ("All that is done is done for your own good.")

However, not all of the variation can be plotted along this exploitative/protective dimension, for this seems to be most typical only of centralized, state societies. Politically uncentralized, nonhierarchic, nonstate societies have their own cultural interpretations of children's biosocial vulnerability. Such tribal populations tend to subsume childhood vulnerability under human vulnerability. Therefore, children are treated violently in those tribal societies where interpersonal relations are violent, such as the Yanomamös (see Chagnon 1983), or nonviolently in those societies where interpersonal relations are nonviolent, such as the Semais (see Dentan 1978). I would argue that in such societies, children are not treated as a marked category of beings, distinct from other human beings, with whom special relations must be maintained. Our discourse on children, childhood, the value of children, children's rights, and so on belies the context of the state society in which we live. "Parents" and "children" emerge as marked categories through their transformation from dyadic interpersonal relations to mediated relations, monitored and ultimately controlled by a third party, the state.

Singapore is a postcolonial nation-state and, as such, is modeled on the interventionist European nation-state, not on the Chinese empire. However, 77 percent of Singaporeans are of Chinese descent. This implies a certain continuity of ideas, if not of institutions, concerning the relationship between children and society. Singapore thus represents an interesting case of a modern interventionist nation-state, imbued with certain Confucianist notions of relationships between state, parents, and children.

CHILDREN, POPULATION PLANNING, AND THE REPRODUCTION OF SOCIETY

Children are potential and actual members of the population. While there is a tendency to look at population planning as purely a demographic issue, it should be realized that states' population policies have a direct impact on children, indeed on their very existence. By controlling the future through population planning, the state controls the reproduction of society and thereby the structuring of society in the present. Through population planning as an entry point, the state can legitimately intervene in the relevant domains of its citizens' lives—sexual, reproductive, familial, and educational. (Such control would be the inverse of the state's control of the past through the construction of history.)

In terms of population planning, the "value of children" to the state would be constructed in terms of human capital—as investment or consumption. Children would thus be valued as producers of wealth ("hands to work, minds to think") or devalued as consumers of wealth ("bodies to carry, mouths to feed"). Constructions of children in such terms would be in the exploitative mode of interpretation discussed above, and as such, may well come to be shared by parents themselves.

The impact of population policies on children tends to be in the exploitative mode, rather than the protective mode, since the latter tends to protect children who are already born, rather than set the conditions under which they are to be born. This is precisely the area that the UN Convention on the Rights of the Child does not adequately cover—that is, the preconceived molds dictating which children are to be born at all, and for what purpose they are being born.

A nation's politics selects which children are to exist at all. National planning through population planning is particularly important for nation-states in the "developing world," whose governments are actively reinventing their countries in the image of what is deemed a developed society. An example of such reinvention through population planning would be an interventionist Communist China, in contrast to a Confucianist China that left children to the rule of fathers.

> China's current population policy is aimed not only at reducing numbers of people, but at transforming the sorts of persons who are produced. While the official explanation for the one-birth policy is to reduce demands on a dangerously overburdened environment, many people told Anagnost [a social anthropologist who has studied the one-child policy in China] that such a policy was important because it is not possible to nurture more than one child to the level of "quality" necessary to make "progress" in the present world. State policies have led to tremendous parental investments in the one allowable child, often fed special foods believed to raise intelligence and supplied with special toys designed specifically to "open up" the child's mind. (Stephens n.d.)

As in other new nation-states, such as Singapore, the "development agenda" is the ideology shaping the preconceived molds for the number and type of children to be born as "contributions to national progress."

CHILDREN IN THE PLANNED POPULATION
OF SINGAPORE

I will now locate this argument in the context of Singapore by examining the preconceived molds constructed by the government through policies that impinge on the existence of children and the ways they are to live. Singapore is a secular one-party-dominant state, where the ruling People's Action Party has held power since 1959. Such a situation means that the government is the most powerful of powerful others in the making of children's lives, since it is the government that holds the monopoly of violence and the legal legitimacy to govern its nation of citizens. Government policies impinge on the lives of children in at least two significant areas: population planning and educational streaming.

Singapore's population policies may be divided into three historical phases:

Phase 1 (1819–1949): Colonial laissez-faire
Phase 2 (1949–83): "Girl or boy, two is enough"
Phase 3 (1983–present): "Have three or more if you can afford it"

Phase 1 (1819–1949): Colonial Laissez-faire

The British colonial government was concerned primarily with maximizing profits from Singapore, rather than with governing a nation. Labor was a valuable resource for the expanding economic base of the colony. Beginning with the advent of British colonization in 1819, there was an increasing massive influx of immigrants, mostly from China, India, and Nusantara (that is, present-day Malaysia and Indonesia).

This political and economic situation dovetailed nicely with the traditional values of the immigrants' cultural baggage concerning children—that is, the more the merrier. The precolonial Malay population living in fishing villages was rapidly outnumbered by Chinese immigrant settlers whose descendants now form about 77 percent of Singapore's population. In this context, Chinese traditional values concerning children came to be of particular importance. Although the Chinese patrilineage as a corporate kin group was not an exportable unit as such, the principle of patrilineality was nevertheless maintained with some rigor among the overseas Chinese in Singapore. Sons were unquestionably favored over daughters. Under the British colonial government, the Chinese tradition of female infanticide was punishable as a criminal offense of murder, but the disposal of unwanted daughters through sale or adoption continued until a generation ago.

Indian tradition—the other significant immigrant culture—also favored sons, not so much because of patrilineality, but because of the superiority of wife takers over wife givers, who can marry off daughters only if they bring dowries with them. (Singaporeans of South Asian origins now comprise about 6 percent of the population.)

Only in Malay tradition was the daughter valued as much as, and sometimes even more than, the son. This relative gender equality of sons and daughters derived from the bilateral kinship system. Malay kinship, moreover, is skewed toward a preference for married daughters to reside near their mothers, so that local relations tend to have a matrifocal bias. However, Malays are Muslims, and Islam has a male bias, for example, in Muslim laws of inheritance. There is thus some tension between kinship and religion in this regard. (Malays now comprise about 15 percent of Singapore's population.)

All three ethnic traditions placed a positive value on procreation. In the Chinese and Indian cases, there was a gender-specific pronatalism with a distinct male bias: sons were wanted, daughters unwanted. The Malays, however, welcomed both sons and daughters. Given the numerical dominance of the Chinese and Indians combined, their male-biased pronatalism was of greater prevalence than the relative gender equality of Malay pronatalism.

Among the Chinese in particular, sons—born and unborn—were regarded as potential producers of wealth, reproducers of another generation of sons for the patrilineage, and filial nurturers of aged parents. This was the preconceived mold into which all male children were born and in which they were expected to live. Chinese daughters, on the other hand, were regarded as potential consumers of wealth, reproducers of sons for rival patrilineages, and filial nurturers of their parents-in-law in other patrilineages. Hence daughters were said to be "water spilled on the street." This preconceived idea that they were a "useless" burden to their parents was what Chinese female children were born into. Coupled with this was the idea of the female body as polluted and polluting, especially to fathers and brothers.

In the booming colonial economy, children were seen as investment opportunities for the family's upward social mobility, particularly for Chinese and Indian migrants who had come for the express purpose of making their fortune. Such investment was channeled specifically toward education, as the path to middle-class professional status. While sons were given priority, daughters also came to be educated, especially in families with spare surplus. With the greater education and paid employment of females, many parents now say that daughters are "as good as sons," in that they too can be producers of wealth and nurturers of aged parents, as well as being vehicles for the family's upward social mobility. In other words, "good" daughters are seen as honorary males, in that they are capable of filling the preconceived molds hitherto reserved for sons. But still it seems to be the case that sons are loved for what they are, daughters for what they do. The usefulness of sons to parents is an ascribed role, quite apart from its actualization, while the daughter's transition from useless to useful is a matter of individual achievement.

In the Chinese language, "good" children are literally contrasted with "useless" or "unusable" children. Such a linguistic contrast carries implicit structural connotations:

ends	:	means
subject	:	object
user	:	useful/useless tool
parent	:	child.

In one respect, however, Chinese daughters are not regarded as being as useful as sons: that is, as reproducers of patrilineal descendants. In the traditional kinship system, daughters are reproducers for rival patrilineages. But in the absence of patrilineages as corporate groups among Singapore Chinese, and consequently in the absence of any desire to build alliances between such lineages, the role of daughters as reproducers for in-laws has declined in significance. This has contributed to the reshaping of the preconceived mold awaiting female children. Instead of being regarded by parents negatively, as useless burdens being reared as reproducers for rival patrilineages, daughters are instead regarded more positively, as potential producers of wealth, as vehicles of upward social mobility, and as nurturers of aged parents. This also implies a reduction of parental pressure on daughters to marry. From this perspective, an unmarried daughter may well be more useful to her parents than a married daughter. Indeed, some parents are known to tell their university graduate daughters not to get married so quickly, as that would waste the family's investment in their education.

The following figures indicate these currently changing roles of women in Singapore. From 1957 to 1991, the female labor force participation rate rose from 17.5 percent to 50.3 percent. From 1970 to 1980, the female literacy rate rose from 60.1 percent to 76.2 percent. In 1982, 5,563 females were studying at the National University of Singapore, outnumbering the 5,530 males. (See Wee 1987a.) To be born female in Singapore has become less of a liability than it used to be a generation ago.

Nevertheless, it should be pointed out that if the daughter's rise in status is due to her greater usefulness to parents, then this still implies an adult-centered cultural valuation of the child. While such an evaluation may now be less gender specific, to many adults in Singapore it may still be the usefulness of the child to the parent that legitimates the child's existence. Existence still remains a cultural privilege, albeit one that can be achieved.

Phase 2 (1949–83): "Girl or Boy, Two Is Enough"

This theme of the usefulness of the child pervades the population policies of the Singapore government. But it is the state that has now become the supraparental figure deciding which child is useful and therefore wanted, and which child is useless and therefore unwanted. A chronology of events will best indicate the increasing power of the state and the implications of such power for children.

1949

The Singapore Family Planning Association (SFPA), the first such organization in Southeast Asia, was formed. This occurred in the context of the postwar baby boom, coupled with economic depression and unemployment. The SFPA was initially funded by private donations. "The objective of the association was to improve the welfare of the family by preventing unplanned pregnancies" (Bungar 1991:47).

1959

The People's Action Party (PAP) came to power at this time and has formed the government ever since. The newly independent government of Singapore contributed $100,000 to the SPFA, thereby integrating family planning into the wider nation-building program.

1965

After Singapore seceded from Malaysia and became a separate nation-state, the government published a white paper outlining the first Five-Year National Family Planning Programme, targeted at the 60 percent of married women aged fifteen to forty-four. This resulted in the Family Planning and Population Act and the establishment of the Singapore Family Planning and Population Board.

1966

The first Five-Year National Family Planning Programme was launched, with the aim of reducing the rate of population increase from 2.5 percent in 1964 to 2 percent in 1970. A massive public campaign was conducted, marked by slogans that have since become part of Singaporean colloquial discourse:

"Girl or boy, two is enough."

"Stop at two."

"Small families have more to eat."

"Teenage marriage means rushing into problems, a happy marriage is worth waiting for."

I chose the first of these slogans as the heading for this section because it characterizes the government's effort at shifting public consciousness from a male-biased pronatalism to a gender-neutral, but number-specific, pronatalism. (A male-biased pronatalism tends to lead to having more than two children, since those with daughters only will try to produce at least one son and those with one son or two are not averse to having more.)

The second slogan above is a straight command with no attempt to persuade through reason. It indicates clearly that the state is in charge of deciding how many children should be born. It is thus implied that parents have become citizen-parents who should reproduce the politically correct number of citizen-children, as ordained by the state. Stop at two, just as you should stop at the red light.

The third slogan above implies that children are mouths to feed—that is, consumers (rather than as potential producers) of family wealth, and therefore by extension, of national wealth. A nation of small families will also have more to eat.

The fourth slogan above equates marriage with children and implies that children are problems that only mature parents can handle. "It was at this stage that Singaporeans were informed of their responsibilities to the larger unit of which they were a part—the nation. . . . Individuals were asked to think of themselves and their progeny in relation to a larger whole, the citizenry" (Bungar 1991:53).

1969

Abortion was legalized. Arguing for the passing of the abortion bill in Parliament, the then prime minister Lee Kuan Yew (now senior minister) said,

The quality of the population would deteriorate . . . if the present trend of less educated parents . . . producing larger families than better educated . . . parents continued.

We must encourage those who earn less than $200 [approximately US$135] per month and cannot afford to nurture and educate many children, never to have more than two. We will regret the time lost if we do not take the first tentative steps towards correcting a trend which can leave our society with a large number of the physically, intellectually and culturally anaemic. (*Straits Times*, 30 December 1969)

Unlike the situation in other countries, the discourse on abortion in Singapore was not on the "pro-life" versus "pro-choice" debate. Instead it was a class-based discourse, concerning the differential reproductive rights of the middle class versus the working class. Legalized abortion was thus used for a policy of selective breeding to limit the births of the "physically, intellectually and culturally anaemic" who were less educated and poor.

In Lee Kuan Yew's opinion, every population has approximately 5 percent "who are more than ordinarily endowed, physically and mentally and in whom we must expend our slender resources, in order that they will provide that yeast, that ferment, that catalyst, in our society which alone will ensure that Singapore will maintain its pre-eminent place" (quoted in Rodan 1989:89). "Slender resources" thus referred to the state's investment in the mere 5 percent of children who were deemed to have what it takes to keep Singapore on top.

To make the birth of a third child less affordable, especially for poorer families, the accouchement fees for hospital births were progressively pegged to birth order, such that the birth of a first child cost least and the birth of a third child cost most. At the same time, home births were banned by law, so no one could escape the net of the hospitals.

1970

The Termination of Pregnancy Authorisation Board authorized abortions on the basis of certain conditions, including socioeconomic and medical conditions. Fifty percent of the women who underwent abortions that year had no formal education, while 34 percent had only primary-school education. Most of them were married women below thirty years of age.

At the same time, special tax rebates were introduced for mothers who were university graduates; they were allowed to claim an additional 5 percent of their annual earned income for each of their first three children, in addition to the normal tax relief for these children.

The eugenic intent of these measures is quite clear.

1973

Women's maternity leave benefits were used as privileges and penalties to regulate the number of births: paid maternity leave was limited to the births of the first and second children. Paid maternity leave was granted also to civil servants who agreed to be sterilized after the birth of their second or later child.

1976

Priority in school admission, particularly to certain elite schools, was another "carrot" restricted to the firstborn and the secondborn. As a forty-two-year-old mother of two girls said to Bungar (1991:60):

> I had my tubes tied after my second child, another girl. We decided we didn't want to have a third child and make him suffer all the hardship that the third child goes through—can't get into a good school and all that. If I had gone ahead and had another child, I could have had the son we want. But now we're too old.

The first and second children of sterilized parents were accorded even higher priority in school admission. As Bungar (1991:61) reported:

> Most of my informants felt that they had conformed . . . as ultimately, it would have been the children who suffered. This was, however, not a happy compliance born of an absolute belief in the views espoused by the government, but a conformity tinged with resignation and a sense of powerlessness.

The third child thus became a stigmatized child, a blatant manifestation of bad citizen-parents.

Phase 3 (1983—Present): "Have Three or More If You Can Afford It"

The eugenic seeds that had been sown in phase 2 now sprouted explicitly class-biased and ethnicity-biased policies and public statements by the government. The growing institutionalization of such eugenic ideas could best be explicated by a content analysis of an historic National Day speech (with the telling title "Talent for the Future") given in 1983 by the then prime minister Lee Kuan Yew. Numbered excerpts from this speech are presented below for subsequent analysis:

> 1. Researches on identical twins who were given away at birth to different families of different social, economic classes show that their performance is very close although their environments are different. . . . The conclusion the researchers draw is that 80 percent is nature, or inherited, and 20 percent the differences from different environment and upbringing.

2. Even though only 20 percent of the performance of a human being is due to nurture, much more than 20 percent of the performance of human beings as a group depends on training and organisation. . . . So it is crucial to help every Singaporean, whatever his inherited characteristics, to achieve his best through improved training and education.

3. The 1980 Census disclosed that whilst we have brought down the birth rate, we have reduced it most unequally. The better educated the woman is, the less children she has. . . . Adjusted for those women in the group who remain unmarried, the mean figures are: No education—3.5; Primary—2.7; Secondary—1.9; Upper Secondary—2.0; and Tertiary—1.65. We have altered our pattern of procreation producing the next generation, first by educating everyone, second by giving women equal employment opportunities, and third by establishing monogamy since 1960.

4. If we continue to reproduce ourselves in this lop-sided way, we will be unable to maintain our present standards. Levels of competence will decline.

5. Our economy will falter, the administration will suffer, and the society will decline. For how can we avoid lowering performance when for every two graduates (with some exaggeration to make the point), in 25 years' time there will be one graduate, and for every two uneducated workers, there will be three?

6. From data collected by the Ministry of Education on the educational qualifications of the parents of Primary I students for 1981–83, we discover that women marry their educational equals or their educational superiors. In other words, the Singaporean male marries his educational equal or his inferior. Seldom does he marry his educational superior. The result is a considerable loss in well-educated women remaining unmarried at 40 plus and not represented in the next generation: 13½ percent of all tertiary-educated women, 8½ percent of all upper secondary-educated women, and 10½ percent of all secondary-educated women.

7. Most men hope that their children will be as bright as themselves. After all, they carry their father's surname. Many men are ignorant of the fact that biologically and genetically, every mother and father contributes equally to the child's physical and mental attributes.

8. Our projected losses through graduates not reproducing themselves under present patterns will be over 20 percent (based on the mean of 1.65 children born alive per ever-married woman aged 35 to 39) of about 2000 graduates per year or 400 graduates.

9. Our most valuable asset is in the ability of our people. Yet we are frittering away this asset through unintended consequence of changes in our education policy and equal career opportunities for women. This has affected their traditional role as mothers.

10. It is too late for us to reverse our policies and have our women go back to their primary role as mothers, the creators and protectors of the

next generation. Our women will not stand for it. And anyway, they have already become too important a factor in the economy.

11. Therefore, we must further amend our policies, and try to reshape our demographic configuration so that our better-educated women will have more children to be adequately represented.

12. In some way or other, we must ensure that the next generation will not be too depleted of the talented. Government policies have improved the part of nurture in performance. Government policies cannot improve the part nature makes to performance.

13. This only our young men and women can decide upon. All the government can do is to help them and lighten their responsibilities in various ways. (Quoted in Saw 1990:39—45)

Paragraph 1 makes a sociobiological claim on the overwhelming importance of nature over nurture, thereby establishing the supposed scientific truth of the eugenic argument. (Lee and his advisors had clearly misunderstood what geneticists mean by "heritability." The 20/80 figure he cited came from studies that actually had no biological bearing on the nature/nurture issue, either in the test population or in the human species as a whole.) Paragraph 2 concedes that nurture would still be important even if it accounted for only 20 percent of the performance of a human being, because nurture would help every Singaporean to maximize his or her genetic potential. The implication is that since different people are regarded as having different genetic potential, the kind and degree of nurture they will need will also differ. As we shall see below, this idea has serious repercussions for the educational system in Singapore as a rigid hierarchization of children, with their different "inherited characteristics."

Paragraph 3 focuses on "the problem"—namely, that women university graduates have fewer children than women with lower educational qualifications. Paragraph 4 lists the dire consequences that would befall the nation if the "lop-sided reproduction" were to continue, thus explaining why it would constitute a problem. Standards of competence would supposedly decline because fewer people with innate ability would be born.

Paragraph 5 assumes automatic class reproduction: only graduate parents would reproduce graduate children, while uneducated workers would reproduce uneducated children. So according to this logic, to increase the proportion of future graduates, graduate parents must have more children, and uneducated workers must have fewer children. This idea again has serious repercussions for the educational system in terms of how it is supposed to educate children who are innately "able" or "unable" to learn.

Paragraph 6 then moves on to another "problem"—namely, the fact that men marry down and women marry up. As a result, more women at the top are unmarried, because their male peers are busy marrying down. Paragraph 7 shows why this is a problem: the child born of a graduate father and a nongraduate mother would, presumably, be genetically inferior to the child born of graduate parents on both sides. Graduates supposedly reproduce graduates. Paragraph 8 confirms this by giving the number of potential graduates (four hundred per year) that would be "lost" because they were not born when they should have been.

Paragraph 9 expresses regret that the social advancement of women has reduced their reproductive role. Paragraph 10, however, concedes that it is too late to push women back into the home. Paragraph 11 expresses the intention to make policy changes such that the genes of the better-educated women will be perpetuated and not be lost.

Paragraph 12 expresses the hope that Singapore's population will not be depleted of talent, which is believed to come only from nature and not nurture. Paragraph 13 lays the burden of preserving Singapore's talent on the young men and women who should therefore marry and reproduce in a genetically correct way.

The citizen-parent had now evolved into the citizen–gene carrier, reproducing more carriers of genes. What was expressed in Lee Kuan Yew's speech was the aim of promoting the increase of the desired genes (and therefore their carriers) and the concurrent decrease of supposedly talent-depleted genes (and therefore their carriers).

Linked to this class-biased eugenics was also a race-biased eugenics. In 1985, the total fertility rates for Singaporeans of the three major ethnic groups were Chinese—1.50; Indians—1.94; and Malays—2.11. The then prime minister has publicly expressed anxiety, both in Parliament and in the press, about these different fertility rates, because he thinks that the success of Singapore is due to the fact that the population is Chinese dominated. This race bias is, however, more often expressed in class terms, because for certain historical reasons, the native Malays who are numerically fewer have come to be economically dominated by the migrant Chinese. (This is not an unusual relationship between natives and migrants, especially where the latter colluded with the colonizer.)

In 1987, the class-biased eugenics was institutionalized as a basket of policies designed to encourage the largely Chinese middle class to "have three or more if you can afford it." A massive publicity campaign was launched with a number of slogans—for example, the slogan "Children. Life would be empty without them" was always accompanied by pictures of middle-class Chinese families.

The third child born of an appropriate class was now a desired child, a legitimating symbol of compliant citizen-parents. In 1984, priority in school admission was used as an incentive: the third child of a graduate mother was allowed to jump the queue. This measure was rescinded in 1985 because it caused such widespread "animosity and resentment" (to quote the then minister of education).

But the third child born of an inappropriate class was still a stigmatized child, a symbol of bad citizen-parents who had refused to recognize the karma of their lower-class status. To help such self-recognition among the lower classes, the Small Family Incentive Scheme was instituted. According to this scheme, $10,000 (approximately U.S. $6,650) would be awarded to eligible women. Their eligibility was evaluated on the basis of the following conditions:

1. She must have been sterilized on or after 1 June 1984.
2. She must be below thirty years of age.
3. She must not have more than two children.
4. Neither she nor her husband should possess any "O" levels (passes in the General Certificate of Education "Ordinary" Examination).
5. Neither she nor her husband should earn more than $750 (approximately U.S. $500) per month.
6. In the event that the woman has another child, she is obliged to repay the $10,000 plus 10 percent compound interest per year. (Quoted from Saw 1990:10)

Children now came with all sorts of financial strings attached. One such string was, for example, the enhanced income tax deduction of $5,000 per child (approximately U.S. $3,330), available only to mothers with at least five "Ordinary" level examination passes. There was thus a shift in government policy from promoting a universally applicable number-specific pronatalism to a differentiated class-specific pronatalism.

There was also a shift from the previous phase of regarding children as consumers of wealth, whose number should be therefore be kept small, to a new phase of looking at children as producers not just for the family, but for the state. Children of particular class origins were now cast into the mold of becoming producers of the nation's future in quite explicit terms—for example, as future pilots for the Singapore Air Force, as sustainers of economic development, as the "yeast" ensuring "Singapore's pre-eminent place" in the world.

There has thus been a definite historical development of the preconceived molds awaiting children born in Singapore. To some extent, the process of this development is accumulative, such that children in Singapore are now differentiated in terms of gender, birth order, ethnicity, and class (as indicated by the educational qualifications of their parents). The child par excellence, who meets all the criteria of the different preconceived molds, would thus be male, first- or secondborn, Chinese, middle class. In diametrical opposition, the undesired child would be female, fourth or later in birth order, non-Chinese, working class. The thirdborn child's desirability is ambiguous, since it hinges entirely on the parents' educational qualifications, in particular the mother's.

THE EDUCATIONAL IMPLICATIONS OF EUGENICS

The eugenic ideas described above have serious implications for the intent and structure of the educational system. The underlying philosophy informing the educational system may be explicated by analyzing excerpts from an interview on "the prime qualities of leadership," given by the then prime minister Lee Kuan Yew (*Straits Times*, 3 October 1978, 12):

1. A political leader must be able to mobilise and move his people in directions which will take them to security and progress. He must create conditions that make achievements possible.

2. [Question: How early in someone's career can the quality of leadership be identified?] Modern medicine has evidence that most of these characteristics, the emotional make-up of a man—or a woman—his responses, can be observed fairly early in life. I am told by some paediatricians that you can often foretell the kind of person a child is going to grow up to be. I do not know if that is true, but I do know that by the middle twenties a man is complete. However, he may not have disclosed what he is because he has not yet been put under severe stress.

3. [Question: How adequate is the present population to produce the necessary number of leaders required?] It depends on the qualities of the population, the genetic pool we have inherited. We get the leaders we are capable of throwing up.

4. [Question: Do you feel that in learning leadership you have to go through all these various aspects—you have to know the trade unions, government, have to know how to deal with the private sector?] I do not think you learn leadership. You learn about human beings in given cultural, social and economic contexts. You learn to get things done or get people to do things within these contexts. But this attribute called leadership is either in you or it is not.

5. On the average, judging from scholastic records, the capacity to digest and expound knowledge, judging from incipient or nascent qualities of leadership, like sport team captains, and presidents of activity groups, there is about one in a thousand—about 40 a year. For the age group 35 to 45 there will be some 400 potentials. What is difficult to pin down is motivation, the emotional make-up of a man, what makes him tick, what makes him do the things he does, how he feels about people and why he feels the

way he does. These help to determine how he reacts under pressure and that decides whether he is a leader or a follower.

6. I have no doubts that if political leadership is not made up of the best we have got, then we will not achieve the best that we are capable of.

7. We came to a rough figure of one in a thousand and that was the way the top scholarships worked out, based on academic performance, on social and group activities, rugger captain, school cadet, secretary of the chess club and so on. They indicate roughly whether he is an activist.

8. [Question: And this is the new material from which you begin your selection process?] The actual numbers that we give scholarships to is about twice that, just to widen the catchment and take in the borderline cases. The subsequent results in University show one good brain in a thousand. These have more than average intelligence, more than average energy, more than average capacity.

9. [Question: If the leadership is there what is the training period supposed to give the man?] Really to show that he has got it, not that he is hiding the lack thereof behind a show of aplomb and erudition.

10. [Question: It is basically a testing period not a training period? Establishing that the qualities that are apparent are also real and that they can be used in decision-making?] If you want to put it in an unkind way—yes.

Although this interview does not discuss the educational system as such, paragraphs 4–8 explicitly mention the political linkage between scholarships for the top two thousand students each year and the selection out of this number for the "one-in-a-thousand" future leaders of the nation. Paragraphs 1 and 6 articulate the national importance of having "the best" people as political leaders, for without them, there will be no "security," "progress," or "achievement." At the same time, as paragraphs 2–4 make clear, leadership is considered an innate quality: you either have it or you don't. The task then is to track down these innate leaders from among the general population. The opposition between training and testing, as expressed in paragraphs 9–10, is precisely the key tension at the heart of the educational system.

Indeed, the entire educational system in Singapore may be understood as a nationwide searching and testing device for innate leadership. The increasingly stressful streaming process that Singaporean children have to undergo is not a mere historical accident. According to Lee Kuan Yew, "severe stress" is a mechanism for "disclosing" innate leadership qualities. At the age of nine, all schoolchildren have to take a nationwide examination that will stream them into three basic categories, previously named "express," "normal," and "monolingual." (These now have complicated subcategories and code names such as EM1, EM2, and so on.)

Apart from the quality and content of education given in the different streams, these are also differentiated in terms of the number of years of schooling and the qualifications the schoolchildren will end up with. For example, those in the express stream are supposed to finish their primary schooling in six years and eventually have the opportunity to take university-qualifying examinations. But those in the monolingual stream are supposed to take eight years for their primary schooling and then go on to vocational training. (The monolingual stream was so named to indicate the subnormality of schoolchildren who are deemed unable to cope with the normal, bilingual, system of education.)

On top of these three categories is the Gifted Children's Programme, whereby a certain number of handpicked nine-year-olds are invited to sit for a qualifying examination. If they pass this, they may enter one of the four schools in Singapore where the Gifted Children's Programme is offered. This testing procedure is repeated for twelve-year-olds, presumably to catch the late bloomers.

Defining the "catchment" from which to find the "one good brain in a thousand" begins after only three years of schooling—that is, just enough to enable the children to take the test at all. Not surprisingly, the blueprint for the educational system was drawn up by systems engineers—literally so—rather than educationists. Thus, the education system became a filtration plant streaming the genetic pool through a series of progressively smaller catchment areas until in the last catchment, the university, the one-in-a-thousand innate leader is thrown up.

The not-so-hidden agenda of "catching the good brains" may be discerned in the case of mathematics in the 1992 Primary School Leaving Examination (PSLE). There are some significant dates to be noted in the following sequence of events: *20 August 1992*: Senior Minister Lee Kuan Yew launches the Lee Kuan Yew Award for Mathematics and Sciences, made through his donation of U.S. $40,000 to the Ministry of Education. *29 August 1992*: The *Straits Times* publishes an article on "maths whizzes" in primary and lower secondary schools. *17 October 1992*: The *Straits Times* reported that parents had called the Ministry of Education to complain about the difficulty of the PSLE mathematics paper:

> A junior college mathematics teacher said: "They are not straightforward questions. Although not very difficult, the children will need a lot of time to digest them." But a primary school teacher said: "*We need some challenging questions to sieve out the good ones from the rest, naturally.*" (*Straits Times*, 17 October 1992; emphasis added)

However, the disproportionate investment of educational resources in an elite corps of future leaders is still an issue debated in public discourse. This may be illustrated through a series of articles and letters in the main English-language newspaper, *Straits Times.*

On 9 February 1992, it was reported:

> Singaporeans must guard against accepting unthinkingly Western liberal arguments urging for more liberal social and economic policies, Senior Minister Lee Kuan Yew said. "But I advise Singaporeans to exercise care on any proposal that changes policies that have made us successful," he said. "We have succeeded because we adopted policies which made us efficient and competitive."
>
> *Singapore should continue its policy of investing in its ablest to maximise the potential of its people,* he said. . . . He noted that a sociologist [Chua Beng Huat] has recently suggested that children from public housing were under-represented in independent schools since they made up 70 percent of each cohort of students.
>
> "In other words, those going to independent schools must be 85 percent from public housing. Only 11 percent can be from private housing. This is to say that children who are bright, but whose parents are comfortable, must be penalised."
>
> "They say give the good teachers to whose who are not so bright. That's precisely what the British liberal sociologists tried to do. The result was that nobody went far," he said.
>
> Fortunately, however, Singapore had a good education system in place, where students were streamed according to their ability and discipline, and standards were maintained, he said. (emphasis added)

This issue was picked up again on 22 March 1992, when a journalist, Cherian George, wrote an article calling for more attention to be given to the education of poor children. Drawing on government statistics, he repeated the argument that residents of public housing are underrepresented in independent schools and university:

General population:	85% in public housing
	11% in private housing
University students:	73% in public housing
	23% in private housing
Independent school students:	61% in public housing
	38% in private housing.

George wrote:

> Why are poorer Singaporeans less successful in reaching university and independent schools than the better off? Probably . . . children from richer households do better in the examinations that determine whether they get

places. And this could be because such families are generally better able to provide a conducive environment for the education of their young. The child will have his own study table at home, if not his own study room. He will have plenty of books and perhaps his own computer. If his parents are also well-educated, he will receive their guidance in his homework. And if not, he will be given the best private tutors. Certainly, he will not need to take on a part-time job to help make ends meet. . . . There is a flaw in the argument that being blind to differences in wealth is being fair. . . . One would expect the introduction of full-day school and better-trained teachers to give a greater marginal benefit to poorer children than to the richer ones, even though both receive it. (*Straits Times*, 22 March 1992)

The permanent secretary of the Ministry of Education responded rather negatively:

Cherian George's article . . . suggested that a system for higher educational institutions be established in Singapore to equalise opportunities so that their enrolments are more representative of our various socio-economic groups. Can he give examples of such a system in other countries and how successful they have been? In our study of the education systems of Japan, Germany, America and Britain, we did not come across any such schemes. Can he enlighten us? (*Straits Times*, 26 March 1992)

Another response came from Sinnakaruppan, member of parliament and member of an advisory committee on education:

Our highly subsidised and open education system provides equal opportunities for all to go as far as they can. . . . *The playing field [is] level. The problem is perhaps more one of ability than of poverty. . . . People rise by their performance and efforts.* . . . The issue is not, as described in Mr George's article, that children coming from well-to-do homes have a distinct advantage because of their home background. We should not begrudge them their good fortune which comes from the efforts of their parents. (*Straits Times*, 26 March 1992; emphasis added)

Sinnakaruppan's letter is interesting in that it voices a rhetoric of meritocracy based on assumptions of an equal starting point for all ("the playing field is level"). Such assumptions leave innate merit as the sole reason for individual differences in achievement ("People rise by their performance and efforts"). This has the effect of legitimating the status quo, since people are located where they are on the hierarchy, supposedly by virtue of their own merit. The rhetoric of meritocracy and the eugenics discourse thus work in tandem, leading to an acceptance of social inequality as a matter of course, at least on the part of some people in Singapore.

At the same time, the rhetoric of meritocracy does contain a seed of contradiction. Assumptions of an equal starting point for all can be quite easily challenged. This was done implicitly in a study by a government-promoted organization for helping poor Singaporeans of Chinese descent:

> The CDAC's Research Panel noted in its report that 87 percent of students under study came from homes where the monthly household income was between $500 and $1,500 [approximately U.S. $330 and U.S. $1000]. [*The World Development Report 1992* cites Singaporeans as having an average per capita income of U.S. $11,160.]
>
> Many of them had to do "home industrial" work, like sewing garments or helping out at family market stalls, to supplement the household income. When they were old enough to find part-time jobs, they sold newspapers or worked in fast-food restaurants. "This effectively meant that they had less time to study, rest, or engage in intellectually stimulating activities," the report noted. . . .
>
> Other factors which lead to under-performance in schools are: lack of resources, poor home environment, long working hours of parents, and language used at home.
>
> These constraints acted together to create an environment which made it more difficult for children to do well in school, the panel said.
>
> "They can be likened to visible and invisible barriers, which the child has to overcome. It takes a great deal more effort for a child to do well, and it requires a great deal more motivation." (*Straits Times*, 28 October 1992)

This diversity in public discourse indicates a less-than-monolithic political structure, where the eugenicist voice, though dominant, is but one voice among many, even in government-related organizations. The eugenicist voice seeks to persuade with purportedly scientific proof; its discourse is couched in rationalist terms. Eugenicist policies are implemented through incentives and disincentives, which thereby allow their target population a certain degree of choice based on rational motives.

IMPACT, COLLUSION, AND CIRCUMVENTION

But because the eugenicist voice is dominant, it does create a situation of stress for children, especially in the case of colluding parents. What tends to make some parents collude is the pernicious geneticism implicit in the discourse of eugenics: that is, the child's success or failure *is* the parent's success or failure. In this discourse, if the child is evaluated as educationally and hence genetically inferior, then by implication, the parent must be also genetically inferior. Moreover, by geneticist logic, such supposed inferiority cannot be rectified.

The investment of the parent's ego in the child's achievement is evident in the following report:

> Dr Agnes Chang, senior lecturer at the National Institute of Education, said: "Children by nature are competitive, but parents can makes things worse by insisting that the child be the best in the school." She cited cases of parents who set their children unrealistic and unattainable goals, or refused to accept that their children were not brilliant. Some parents went to the extent of telling their children not to play with academically weak pupils, she said. (*Straits Times*, 6 September 1992)

The eugenic molds pronounce on which children, and thereby which parents, are wanted or unwanted. I would argue that this passive state of being judged fit or unfit, wanted or unwanted, leads to a dialectic of arrogance versus shame. Those who fit well into the preconceived molds may feel that they have been ascribed a destiny of superiority; such feelings could be described as arrogance. In diametrical contrast, those who are regarded as misfits may feel ashamed of their very existence. The eugenic molds that outline the shape of wanted (and thereby also unwanted) children thus have the potential of forming a nation of the arrogant few and the self-doubting and shameful many.

Such feelings of existential shame may be akin to the psychological state described by Erikson (1965:244–46):

> Shame supposes that one is completely exposed and conscious of being looked at: in one word, self-conscious. One is visible and not ready to be visible; which is why we dream of shame as a situation in which we are stared at in a condition of incomplete dress, in night attire, "with one's pants down." Shame is early expressed in an impulse to bury one's face, or to sink, right then and there, into the ground. But this . . . is essentially rage turned against the self. He who is ashamed would like to force the world not to look at him, not to notice his exposure. He would like to destroy the eyes of the world. Instead he must wish for his own invisibility. . . .
>
> [But] there is a limit to a child's and an adult's endurance in the face of demands to consider himself, his body, and his wishes as evil and dirty, and to his belief in the infallibility of those who pass such judgement. . . . From a sense of loss of self-control and of foreign overcontrol comes a lasting propensity for doubt and shame.

It was reported that in 1991, 1,211 children sought help at the Ministry of Health's Child Psychiatric Clinic, double the number who had done so in 1980. The head of the clinic said:

The figure would be even higher if children seeing psychiatrists in private practice were included. The clinic saw more patients before and during examinations, including those in the streaming years at Primary 4 and Secondary 2. Other children had adjustment problems when they started school or moved up from primary to secondary school.

The children usually have persistent symptoms associated with stress. These include a change in eating, sleeping and studying habits. Some may develop physical symptoms, like a muscle twitch, or they may even fall ill. Others, who have been doing well in school, suddenly start failing their tests. Some children hide their books, change the marks in their report cards, or lie to their parents about test dates. In extreme cases, the children become violent and may attack their siblings, teachers, or school mates.

One child who was due to take a Primary 6 oral language examination suddenly insisted that she could not see. An eye specialist found nothing wrong, but every time the child was given something to read, she said she could not see. "It was her way of avoiding the test which required her to read a passage and answer questions," said Dr Wong Sze Tai, head of the Child Psychiatric Clinic.

"It becomes a daily battle for them to wake up to go to school. They will fake symptoms and say they have a tummy ache or a headache. One little girl vomited her breakfast every day." (*Straits Times*, 6 September 1992)

Such stresses seem to be built into the educational system itself, as one member of the public wrote in a letter to the newspapers:

All pedagogues must surely be aware of the trauma of streaming. Whatever the good intentions behind this procedure, every child and parent dreads Primary 4 and 6, and, to a lesser extent, Secondary 2. Whatever the official reasons or dialectic polemic, *the psychological scar of being streamed out hangs like the sword of Damocles over our heads*. This, I believe, is the main reason why children are pressured. We, parents and children, are caught in this system of excellence to which we have to conform.

. . . The pressure attributed to class tests, therefore, depends on the measure of importance given to them by teachers, principals and the Ministry of Education. If it is known that these tests are only a diagnostic tool to help remedy weakness, and have no extirpative intentions, such as pushing the less able out of school, the situation takes on a different aspect. The pressure, therefore, does not originate with the parents but in reality has its source in the teaching system. (*Straits Times*, 7 March 1992; emphasis added)

The efforts of parents to enable their children to pass examinations have generated a tuition industry, on which they spent S$260 million (or U.S. $173 million) a year, an amount equivalent to 10 percent of the

Ministry of Education's budget for 1992. Half of all primary school pupils and one-third of secondary school students receive private tuition (*Straits Times*, 4 April 1992).

As another member of the public wrote to the newspapers, "Something must be wrong with a system which drives the students so hard that they have to rely on tutors . . . to pass their examinations. . . . What would the school results show if all students do [*sic*] not have personal tutors?" (*Straits Times*, 1 February 1992).

But untutored school results are precisely what parents do not want to see. Singaporean children are caught in a contradiction between state and parents. Because the educational system of the state has been set up as a filtration plant to differentiate between the superior and the inferior, no parent wants his or her child to be sieved out as inferior. While the state is trying to establish a stable hierarchy, no parent wants his or her child to sink to the base of the pyramid. There is thus a massive push on the parents toward the top of the pyramid, a striving that shows up in ever higher rates of passes and distinctions in school examinations: "The number of students scoring at least five O-level distinctions has increased by more than four times in the past 12 years, according to Education Ministry figures. . . . The percentage of students with at least three A-level distinctions has also tripled over the same period" (*Straits Times*, weekly edition, 17 April 1993).

This "explosion" of passes and distinctions, to use a journalist's term, has led to an increased demand for university places far exceeding those provided by the two existing universities: "For each admission, six are disappointed. You just cannot keep them down" (*Straits Times*, weekly edition, 10 April 1993). This in turn has led to increasing numbers of Singaporean students studying overseas. For example, "Singapore students studying in Australia contributed $136 million [approximately U.S. $91 million] to that country's economy last year in school fees and living expenses" (*Straits Times*, weekly edition, 27 March 1993).

As the base of the pyramid seeks to move upward, pressure also increases for those on top. This destabilizes the state's attempt to hierarchize the children of Singapore, although it is done at some cost to the children themselves. In either case—to be hierarchies or to beat the hierarchy—the children seem to be losers, only relatively more or less so. The irony is that the more persuasive the eugenicist voice is, the more implicated the parents feel. If at one level, parents collude in geneticist values, at another level, they feel impelled to prove their children's, and thereby their own, genetic adequacy. The contradiction that exists between a hierarchizing educational system and parents trying to beat the system is therefore a logical inevitability.

But not all parents collude in sharing geneticist values. There are al-

ternative values from older role models in society—for example, uneducated, monolingual millionaires who migrated from China and rose
from rags to riches. Indeed, there is in some families an intergenerational time lag, because grandparents, most of whose lives were lived
prior to Singapore's independence in 1965, are still around and looking
after grandchildren. In their preindependence frame of reference, education is not the only path of upward mobility; nor is educational
achievement the only means of self-affirmation.

Some parents also actively choose to circumvent the system—for example, by sending their children abroad at an early age, by migrating as
a family, or by arranging for their children to be educated in the private
schools catering to foreign children. Those who cannot afford these ex-
pensive options may simply choose to keep their children at home, give
them private tutoring, train them for a trade. Success can also be redefined in alternative terms: for example, entrepreneurial business, religion, sport, entertainment, crime. The maintenance of sociocultural diversity at an everyday level is therefore strategic in countering the state's
hegemonic definitions of success.

Indeed, the state's monolithic intent is constrained by Singapore's
historical and ethnic heterogeneity, which provides so many different
contexts and constructions of meaning. Moreover, the state depends on
so many intermediaries to carry out its policies that practical constraints
on state control arise almost as a matter of course. An example of this is
the nationally planned school curriculum, which has nevertheless to be
taught by individual teachers with diverse backgrounds and values.
Aware of this contradiction, the National Institute of Education, which
plans the national curriculum, seriously tried to devise what it termed a
"teacher-proof curriculum." (Whether such a phenomenon generates its
own dialectic—curriculum-proof teachers—is an interesting question.)

EXAMINATIONS, EUGENICS, AND
COMPETITION

It should be noted, however, that this kind of "examination hell" is not
unique to Singapore. Nor does it have to be eugenically inspired. It is
not even a phenomenon unique to the modern world. The examination
hell existed as an institution in imperial China. It exists in East Asian
societies such as Hong Kong, Japan, and South Korea. (Compare Field's
and Cho's papers in this volume.) But it is not necessarily limited to
Confucianist regimes: it is also known to exist in such disparate countries as Bangladesh, India, Turkey, Nigeria, and Ghana.

What is the social process at work in these different states? It seems to me that this process is not unlike labor migration: both are fueled by aspirations for upward mobility channeled through paths controlled by the state. In the case of examinations in imperial China, this mechanism served the emperor and his court by unsettling the ensconcement of established bureaucrats, who could always be replaced by new recruits who had passed the state-controlled examinations. At the same time, such examinations provided a path of upward mobility to the masses of peasants, the demand for which enabled the state to ration the scarce supply of elevated positions. This led to fierce competition among families aspiring for upward mobility, a competition further benefiting the state's divide-and-rule strategy. The state-controlled "knowledge economy," based on paper qualifications, was thus a governing tool of great usefulness.

A similar process seems to be at work in the postcolonial nation-states. The bureaucratic vacuum left behind by the former colonial governments made it necessary for the new national governments to draw in fresh recruits on a large scale. This recruiting process can be based either on ascription or achievement. In the former case, recruits would be drawn on the basis of ethnicity, religious identity, place of origin, kinship, and so on. In the latter, recruits would be drawn on the basis of state-controlled examinations.

In this regard, Singapore provides an interesting case of an attempt to combine ascription and achievement. An ideology of eugenics is basically ascriptive: people are believed to be born leaders or followers. Ergo, the child of a leader is believed to have leadership genes. What is interesting in the case of Singapore is that although university graduates are believed to have superior genes, their children still have to take examinations; they still have to prove themselves, to fulfill the eugenic prophecy. There is no lazy aristocracy with an unquestioned birthright to rule. Instead there is a doubting eugenics that needs to test its potential recruits.

But why does the idea of eugenics arise in the first place? Does it emerge at particular historical moments? We may perhaps consider certain historical conditions, such as the social construction of Chinese identity. As I have noted elsewhere (Wee 1988), Chinese identity is an ascriptive category: Chinese think of themselves as born, not made. In contrast, Malay identity is an achieved category, which thereby generates a continuum of varying degrees of Malayness (see Wee 1985, 1987b). This difference may be discerned if we compare the discourse of Lee Kuan Yew with that of Mahathir bin Mohamad, prime minister of Malaysia, who also holds to eugenicist ideas. Whereas Lee is concerned with the genetic purity of graduate mating with graduate, Mahathir is concerned with the hybrid vigor produced by supposedly inferior Malays mating with supposedly superior Chinese (see Mahathir 1970). I should add, however, that the Malaysian category of *bumiputera*, "native sons of the soil," differentiating between indigenes and migrants, is ascribed, not achieved.

I would argue that a discourse of genetic purity tends to arise under the following historical conditions: (1) in an ethnic situation where identity is transmitted through consanguinity, a context in which the idea of geneticism becomes plausible, and/or (2) in a multiethnic situation of pluralist separatism, where ethnic groups keep themselves apart through boundary maintenance (rather than seek assimilation across boundaries), and on the basis of such separatism, lay claim to rights over resources.

Singapore is indeed constructed as a multiethnic state organized as pluralist separatism. This is partly because of its migrant history, partly because of the British colonial policy of divide and rule, and partly because of the government's eugenic ideology. The official ethnic categories are Chinese, Malay, Indian, and Others, which thus constitute a particular array of "races" that all Singaporeans must fit into (see Benjamin 1976). This "CMIO" quadripartite classification is all that is available to Singaporeans for their ethnic labeling. One of these four labels is written on the identity cards that all Singaporeans have to carry, and it will stay with them for life.

For most children in Singapore, their first formal contact with CMIO separatism occurs in school, in the context of bilingualism. While the English language is the national medium of education in Singapore, there is also

> an emphasis . . . laid on the need to supply each individual Singaporean with a "cultural ballast" consisting of his traditional ethnically-defined culture, which is seen as being somehow inherent in his so-called "mother tongue." . . . The strains and contradictions in this situation become immediately apparent when we learn that the conventionally recognised so-called "mother tongues" of Singapore (Mandarin Chinese, Malay, Tamil and—perhaps—English) are often confusedly but erroneously referred to for educational purposes as the "second languages." One's "mother tongue" in other words is not the language spoken with one's mother in childhood, but the language that belongs criterially to the "race" one claims membership of, whether or not one actually speaks that language. . . . Although the formal educational policy with regard to language has been labelled "Bilingualism," the young schoolchild who now has to struggle with two languages from primary school onwards very frequently in practice leads a trilingual existence: his true mother tongue may be Hokkien, for example, while he may be enrolled in an English-stream

school where many subjects are taught in Mandarin. . . . This kind of projection of the Singaporean cultural model into the individual's education is not restricted to the primary level only. A year or so ago, a civil servant whose actual mother tongue was Malay, but whose actual second language was English and whose ethnicity was Chinese, was refused permission to take his qualifying language examination in Malay on the grounds (stated in an official letter of reply to the *Straits Times*) that it was "only natural" that one should be qualified in one's "mother tongue"—in this case defined as Mandarin, a language which the civil servant in question did not know. (Benjamin 1976:1245)

What is more ominous are indications that some schoolchildren have come to internalize this official model of pluralist separatism and to police each other's conformity to it. There are, for example, reports of school violence inflicted by some schoolchildren on others for not learning their supposed mother tongue and for daring to learn the mother tongue of another ethnic group (Nirmala PuruShotam, personal communication).

Another historical condition that favors a discourse of eugenics seems to be the declining fertility of the middle class. A comparative example would be twentieth-century Britain, where eugenics as an idea rose and fell among the middle and upper classes in correlation with the fertility of their own classes. Talk of genetic degeneration came with the middle and upper classes' discovery of their own decreasing fertility, in relation to the sustained or even increasing fertility of the poor but healthy, intelligent, and skilled, though less educated, sector of the population (Soloway 1990). This theme of genetic degeneration through class depletion is certainly evident in Lee Kuan Yew's speech "Talent for the Future" (1983), quoted above.

Moreover, Singapore has a labor situation where migrant workers from neighboring countries form 20 percent of the one-million-strong workforce. Middle-class fears of inundation by the working class could well be exacerbated by fears of foreign contamination. Indeed, migrant workers are given only temporary work permits (two years or less) and are not allowed to marry or have children in Singapore. Female migrant workers are compelled to have a pregnancy and venereal disease test once every three months (see Heyzer and Wee 1992).

In this context then, the discourse of eugenics may be analyzed as a protection of class interests; a protection of the family's ownership of class resources, to be inherited by the children; and a freezing of the social hierarchy through an ideology of geneticism.

Overtly, as stated by Lee Kuan Yew, the purpose of "investing" in those with supposedly genetically superior qualities is to enable

Singapore to retain its "pre-eminent place" in the world; to move toward "security and progress"; to "make achievements possible"; to be "efficient," "competitive," "successful"; and "to maximise the potential of its people."

The discourse of eugenics is thus couched in terms of economic rationality, investment strategy, and human-resource management, and not in terms of the military domination of a master race. This overt aim of competing successfully with other nations in the world economy has made the discourse of eugenics relatively plausible, even to those Singaporeans who would not otherwise hold to eugenicist ideas. A self-avowed liberal once said to me that the former prime minister's eugenic ideas are basically well intentioned, because what he is actually concerned about is the survival and success of the nation. Indeed, economic success seems to be the new nationalism, as the editor-in-chief of the *Straits Times* evidently thought:

> Whether or not Singaporeans can continue to live better depends on how they respond to the competition among nations. To be able to continue to perform with credit against the rest of the world is surely a worthy cause. And to do so knowing that the evidence of history is that performance rises and then falls. With a challenge of this magnitude, do young Singaporeans feel any need to look further for burning causes? (*Straits Times*, weekly overseas edition, 27 March 1993)

CONCLUSION

The saving grace of being a new nation with a relatively uninstitutionalized political structure is the inherent transience of whatever system is being laid down. Singapore is a self-declared society in transition. In deed Singaporeans have become rather cynical about the rate of policy changes, one key example being the overnight shift from "Stop at two" to "Have three or more if you can afford it."

Moreover, as I have mentioned above, whatever the intent may be, the political structure is not monolithic. In fact, the discourse in eugenics has been largely articulated by Senior Minister Lee Kuan Yew. While his role in shaping the Singaporean polity has been immense, he is nevertheless only one person in the political landscape.

In such a situation, the relationship between children and the state is not necessarily a repeating cycle. Instead, what we have is an irreversible, historical succession of generations, with different children, different parents, and different political structures. Indeed, we ourselves are the children of yesteryear, but what our children will undergo will be radically different from what we have undergone, by virtue of the very fact that we precede them. Our lives become their history. We *are* history. While the historical accumulation of lives may initially depress us, on reflection there too lies hope, for what has been and is will in its turn come to pass.

REFERENCES

Benjamin, Geoffrey, 1976, "The Cultural Logic of Singapore's 'Multiracialism,'" in Riaz Hassan, ed., *Singapore: Society in Transition*, Kuala Lumpur, Oxford University Press.

————n.d., "Danger and Dialectic in Temiar childhood," (translated into French) in Jeanine Koubi and Josiane Massard, eds., *Enfants et sociétés d'Asie du Sud-est*, Paris, Harmattan, forthcoming.

Bungar, Joan, 1991, "Sexuality, Fertility, and the Individual in Singapore Society," M.Soc.Sc thesis, National University of Singapore.

Chagnon, Napoleon, 1983, *The Yanomamö*, 3d ed., New York, Holt, Rinehart and Winston.

de Groot, J., 1882—1910, *The Religious System of China*, 6 vol., Leiden, Brill.

Dentan, Robert K., 1978, "Notes on Childhood in a Non-Violent Context: The Semai Case (Malaysia)," in Ashley Montagu, ed., *Learning Non-Aggression: The Experience of Non-Literate Societies*, New York, Oxford University Press.

Endicott, Karen L., 1992, "Fathering in an Egalitarian Society," in Barry S. Hewlett, ed., *Father-Child Relations: Cultural and Biosocial Contexts*, New York, Aldine de Gruyter.

Erikson, Erik H., 1965, *Childhood and Society*, Harmondsworth, Penguin Books.

Freedman, Maurice, 1965, *Lineage Organization in Southeastern China*, London, University of London Press.

Heyzer, Noeleen and Vivienne Wee, 1992, "Domestic Workers in Transient Overseas Employment: Who Benefits, Who Profits?" paper presented at the conference "Regional Policy Dialogue on Foreign Domestic Workers: International Migration, Employment and National Policies," organized by the Asian and Pacific Development Center, Colombo, 10–14 August.

Jankowiak, William, 1992, "Father-Child Relations in Urban China," in Barry S. Hewlett, ed., *Father-Child Relations: Cultural and Biosocial Contexts*, New York, Aldine de Gruyter.

Mahathir bin Mohamad, 1970, *The Malay Dilemma*, Singapore, Donald Moore for Asia Pacific Press.

Rodan, Garry, 1989, "Singapore's Second Industrial Revolution: State Intervention and Foreign Policy," Kuala Lumpur, ASEAN–Australia Joint Research Project.

Saw, Swee Hock, 1990, "Changes in the Fertility Policy of Singapore," Singapore, Institute of Policy Studies, Occasional Paper No. 2.

Soloway, Richard Allen, 1990, *Demography and Degeneration: Eugenics and the*

Declining Birth Rate in Twentieth-Century Britain, Chapel Hill, University of North Carolina Press.

Stephens, Sharon, n.d., "The Politics of Reproduction and Population Control," typescript.

Wee, Vivienne, 1985, "Melayu: Hierarchies of Being in Riau," Ph.D. thesis, Canberra, Australian National University.

Wee, Vivienne, 1987a, "The Ups and Downs of Women's Status in Singapore: A Chronology of Some Landmark Events (1950–1987)," *Commentary: Women's Choices, Women's Lives, Journal of the National University of Singapore Society* 7 (2–3), December.

Wee, Vivienne, 1987b, "Material Dependence and Symbolic Independence: Constructions of Melayu Ethnicity in Island Riau, Indonesia," in A. Terry Rambo, Kathleen Gillogly, and Karl L. Hutterer, eds., *Ethnic Diversity and the Control of Natural Resources in Southeast Asia*, Ann Arbor, Mich., Center for South and Southeast Asian Studies.

Wee, Vivienne, 1988, "What Does 'Chinese' Mean?" National University of Singapore, Department of Sociology Working Paper No. 90.

CHAPTER 7

Youth and the Politics of Culture in South Africa

PAMELA REYNOLDS

Kundera: The same things that happen at the level of high politics happen in private life. . . . Each of us, consciously or unconsciously, rewrites our history. We are constantly rewriting our own biographies, constantly bringing our own sense—the sense we want—to events. We are selecting and shaping—picking out the things that reassure and flatter us, while deleting anything that might possibly detract. To rewrite history, then . . . is not an inhuman activity. On the contrary, it is very human. People always see the political and the personal as different worlds, as if each had its own logic, its own rules, but the very horrors that take place on the big stage of politics resemble, strangely but insistently, the small horrors of our private life.

McEwan: You once said that you thought it was the task of the novel to expose "anthropological scandals." What did you mean by that?

Kundera: I was talking about the situation in totalitarian states. I said that for a writer everything that was going on there was not a political scandal, but an anthropological one. That is, I didn't look at it in terms of what a political regime could do, but in terms of this question: what is man capable of?

(An interview with Milan Kundera by Ian McEwan)

I HAVE A STORY to tell about the lives of young people in South Africa over the last thirty years. Their stories are etched into the plate of the country's politics. It is the individuality, the particularity, of each young person's life that interests me. The particular in a context. Like most stories the beginning is arbitrarily chosen and the end is not an end.[1] The beginning is with Africa, with imperialism, with conflict, with oppression, with apartheid. The end is now, and it is just a beginning. There is, however, a moment in the middle of the story from which we can go back fifteen years and forward another fifteen. That moment occurred on 16 June 1976, when police fired on thousands of children in Soweto who were openly, but peacefully, protesting against the educational system. Five hundred people died. The protests were triggered by the enforced teaching of subjects in Afrikaans, a language that many children identified as belonging to the oppressor. The protests spread to other parts of the country. The children won that particular battle, yet, in the process, many were shot and killed. Behind the cause of this protest lay deep resentment against the Bantu Education System, which was "designed to ensure that the African people of South Africa were not educated beyond their perceived place in an *Apartheid* regime" (Thomas 1990:438). On June 7, 1954 in Parliament Hendrik F. Verwoerd, as Minister of Native Affairs, announced that he would introduce a separate educational system for African children because "there is no place for him [the Bantu] in the European community above certain forms of labour" (see Brittain and Minty 1988:12 for a summary of the impact of "Bantu" education).

Thomas (1990:438–39) sees the protest of 1976 as marking the beginning of a new phase in resistance. She comments:

> The 1976 protest ushered in a new beginning to the opposition to *Apartheid* and structural violence—the birth of a generation of politicized and politically active youth. Schoolchildren now became the leaders in seeking an effective means of changing the structure in which they were trapped. What began as the protest of children against an inadequate and racist education system, in subsequent years broadened to encompass a fight to effect political change that would result in the transformation of South African society.
>
> The impetus from these children, together with the strengthening of the anti-*Apartheid* movement over the following nine years and the introduction of the discriminatory tricameral parliamentary system in September 1984, all led to increased unrest and eventually to the declaration of a partial state of emergency on 21 July 1985 in thirty-six magisterial districts in South Africa. Along with this state of emergency came an increase in detentions without trial, a long-standing . . . feature of the South African legal system.
>
> However, more than in previous times, these detentions now included significant numbers of children who, in the subsequent months and years, were to lose not only their freedom, but years of irrecoverable childhood.

Figures for the detention of children (persons under the age of eighteen years) from 1977 have been released (Human Rights Commission 1988):

1977	259
1978	252
1979	48
1980	127
1981	49

Thomas (1990:439) observes that numbers dropped to eight children in 1982, and nine children in 1984. In 1985, with the imposition of the partial state of emergency, the numbers of detained children rose to 2,016 officially acknowledged as under the age of sixteen years. They represented approximately 25 percent of the detainee population. In November 1986, there were an estimated 4,000 children in detention countrywide; official reports, made on 15 October 1986, stated that 2,677 children, including 254 children aged fifteen years and under, were in detention.

In Parliament in February 1988, the state admitted to holding 234 children in detention. These included 5 fifteen-year-olds; 89 sixteen-year-olds, and 140 seventeen-year-olds. By March 1989 it was estimated that 52 children were in detention despite the dramatic drop in numbers over the previous two years. Webster (quoted in Thomas 1990) stated that, in 1985, 25 percent of detainees were children, a figure that rose to 40 percent between June 1986 and June 1987, the highest percentage recorded.[2]

This paper is a report on a study (still in process) of young peoples' experiences during these years of repression. In April 1991, seven students at the University of Cape Town and I began to explore social means of support that they as political activists have drawn upon in surviving the consequences of political involvement in South Africa. The seven are not a randomly selected sample. Between them they have spent about thirty years in prison and ten in exile. The range is from fifteen months in prison (Nomoya) to nine years (Zolile). Each has been beaten, interrogated, tortured, and kept for months in solitary confinement, except Enoch, who was in exile but not in prison. They do not dwell on their awful experiences but, when asked, recount them in a matter-of-fact way. One of the seven was tortured so severely and so frequently that he attempted suicide. Another was left alone for so long that she yearned for the interrogators to come just to have contact with someone. A third was treated so badly that it took him three years to regain equilibrium while he was on Robben Island. They are linked by a network of friendship and political commitment. Their willingness to participate in this project emerges from the need to heal wounds caused by a system of oppression. We have extended the network to include young people at other educational centers and some older political activists. About twenty-five people are involved so far. We use unstructured interviews that are tape-recorded, basic questionnaires, and group seminars that are also tape-recorded. It is upon reflection, often in groups of peers, that the students give shape to and test out what they have lived in practice. We aim at a "multivocal" representation, but as chief scribe I am responsible for the expression given here to their experiences.

In 1976 the young people about whom this story is told were, on average, fifteen years old, so that 1961 was the year of birth for this cohort. It was in that year that the African National Congress (ANC) formally launched the armed struggle and announced the formation of its military wing Umkhonto we Sizwe (Spear of the nation), known popularly as MK. Most of these young people were to join MK but were then busy with their own births.

So the activists were born alongside MK. One theme in this story is the continuity of the fight against oppression. If we move fifteen years after the 1976 massacre, we reach the time when this project began, 1991, soon after that extraordinary moment on the second day of February 1990 when President F. W. de Klerk began to tell another story. The students, some of whom were released from prison in the amnesty that followed the president's volte-face, began to make new stories for themselves.

The counterpart to the theme of continuity is the transformation of the politics of culture in the forging of individual identity. The antecedents of social and political transformation lie in the reformulation by individual men and women of the nature of self in relation to the body politic.

The story of these thirty years is one of a process of transformation. The young gave the process of change its momentum. They did not initiate it or command it, but they certainly carried the process forward. This story is about how some young people helped to shoulder the revolution. They are not typical because the creative force that makes the character of this kind of revolution decries the appellation of typical. Yet their experiences fall within the range described in a number of studies of their peers, comrades, or prison colleagues. Two recent examples are fine studies by Ractliffe (1990) and Winslow (1991).

In his book on peasant intellectuals in Tanzania, Feierman (1990) details the process of cultural re-creation by ordinary people (whom he calls peasants). He points out the seeming paradox between the re-creation of culture and the endurance of cultural norms in peasant discourse. He sets out to demonstrate that "long-term continuity and active creation are in fact compatible" (1990:3). He believes that in seeking to trace patterns across time historians have ignored short-term fluctuations, and this has led to the mystification of cultural continuities. That is, the continuity of a cultural form is accepted as unexceptional and expected even by the people who use it (Feierman 1990:3). The social analysis of peasant discourse in Feierman's book shows that long-term continuities in political language are the outcome of radical social change and of struggle within peasant society. The approach—seeing patterns in the re-creation of ancient patterns—is one elaborated by a generation of social theorists like Giddens (1979), who writes of "rule-governed creativity," and Bourdieu (1977), who discusses, in Feierman's words, "regulated improvisations" (1990:4).

With the above allusions as backup, this paper intends to show that, in the curious context of political change in South Africa, young people assumed a central role in patterning discourse and in innovating in the repetition of inherited patterns. This forms the first theme: the continuity and transformation of culture as expressed in individual trajectories. In participating in the creation of culture, youth drew upon the "incorporated past" (Bourdieu 1990:178) and the political forces of the moment as agents of change. Change necessitates the acquisition of distance from both the overt and covert order of things by which individuals are introduced to cultural categories.

The second theme analyzes youths' struggle for legitimate representation, expressed in their stand against symbolic domination. Again, we can draw on Feierman's work with peasants to illustrate the theme. Having argued that each moment of new action is patterned and that each bit of patterned discourse continuously undergoes transformation, Feierman then considers the direction of change:

> The overall direction of change in discourse cannot be explained as growing out of thousands of random acts of regulated improvisation. Not all regulated improvisations are created equal; not all have an equal weight in shaping the language that will be in general use in the future. To explain the direction of change it is necessary to introduce power into the equation and explore the relationship between the character of domination by ruling groups and the evolution of discourse. (Feierman 1990:4)

Feierman's study of the social position of intellectuals examines those individuals within peasant society who are best able to shape discourse, their position within the framework of domination, and the relationship between their position and their political language. Given the long-term oppression of people in South Africa and the fragmentation of communities and families, adults who ought to have been best able to shape discourse were variously silenced, so that youth took on the role, at least in some measure. It is their stand against symbolic domination and, in the process, the forging of their identities that is the focus of the second theme—which leads into the third, the negotiation of identity within family and community.

The challenge for ethnographic description is to capture the cultural categories as both continuous and in transformation.

Before tracing the themes, let us examine what we mean by culture and the politics of culture. Williams said that "The working-out of the idea of culture is a slow reach again for control" and that, in its modern meanings, culture "makes the effort at total qualitative assessment, but what it indicates is a process, not a conclusion" (1961:285). Bourdieu (1990:107) talks about culture in terms of symbolic resources and believes that "cultural mastery is always a mastery of forms" (1990:78). Yet he calls for us, especially social scientists, to distance ourselves from "the grip of an incorporated past" (that is, history) that survives into the present. He places his faith in "reflexive analysis" to carry us beyond this surface description of culture. So let us take culture as a process, as discourse, as incorporating symbolic resources, and as representing both continuity with the past and a search for control in the present. The politics of culture has to do with the process of accepting, selecting, inventing, reordering, and mastering. Form is expressed in the present in terms of high politics and of private life.

CONTINUITIES AND TRANSFORMATIONS

The year 1976 is a symbolic divide: it cuts the umbilical cord separating the young people from childhood, and it marks their entry into the maelstrom of adult politics. Part of what interests me is what the young brought from the first half of their lives into the next half: what moral stance, what values, what consciousness of right and wrong, and how these were fertilized by nurturant care. I have written about this elsewhere (Reynolds 1991) and here concentrate on the young persons' fledgling entrée into politics.[3]

One goal of the anthropological enterprise is to account "for the daily individual and collective struggles which aim at transforming or preserving structures" (Bourdieu 1990:124). Bourdieu points out that anthropologists and other social scientists oscillate between two apparently irreconcilable perspectives: objectivism and subjectivism. On the one hand, social scientists can treat social phenomena as "things," in accordance with the old Durkheimian maxim, and thus leave out everything phenomena owe to the fact that they are objects of cognition—or of miscognition—in social existence. On the other hand, social scientists can reduce the social world to the representations that agents make of it. The task of social science then consists in producing an "account of the accounts" produced by social subjects. Bourdieu places these positions in dialectical relation and seeks to account for both in the analysis of social behaviour.

My point is that to understand what role young people in South Africa have played in shaping the politics of culture, we must account for the effect of structures, of social facts, upon the pattern of their lives *and* for their representations of reality. One can easily be seduced by the brute force of oppression in South Africa into offering an analysis of structure while ignoring agents' interpretations—another version of symbolic domination. To avoid the latter, we should trace continuities and transformations in the political struggle. To dub youth, as is often done, as the "lost generation" is to demean their contribution and to deny the inventiveness inherent in processes of inheritance and change.

That there was continuity across the generations in the fight for justice is clear from the histories of political activity in South Africa. It is in relation to these accounts that the life trajectories of the young people with whom I have worked should be set. The intention is to show how their involvement slots into the momentum of the struggle against apartheid (earlier recognizable as colonialism). I am suggesting that we view the young as agents of change, wresting the design of their lives from the premises inherited from the past, exploring the mined field of politics and reshaping the terms upon which each will express his or her membership in the present, that is to say, in culture. Accounts of histories often lend the processes of change an inexorable air—a fiction that is given the lie by individual experiences of pain and loss that involvement inevitably secured.

In telling the stories of their lives, some of the students trace continuity in political consciousness and even action across generations. I shall give three examples. The first is drawn from the life history of an older woman (whom we shall call Anne), whose story supplements those of the young people in our group, as, besides being herself a political activist, she is the mother of three young men who died in the struggle against apartheid. As a schoolgirl aged seventeen, she became involved in political disobedience, and later she actively revolted against the system alongside her children. A sketch of her life follows.

In 1953 the government announced plans for the introduction of Bantu education, and people's resistance caused disruption in the schools. Anne, then seventeen, joined an ANC alternative school in the Eastern Cape that was held in a field. The school was illegal, and police broke it up and beat the students. Some teachers were arrested. The teachers were members of the ANC Women's and Youth Leagues. Classes continued in teachers' homes. Again the teachers were arrested and this time given sentences of three months each. The school continued, but, after police harassment during 1955, classes were held at night. Some of the pupils went on to qualify as nurses.

Anne, however, was married by *ukuthwala*[3] and forced to give up her education. She bore five children, four boys and a girl, and became a clerk at a school for white children in Port Elizabeth. In 1976 her two eldest sons were in standards 8 and 7. Within a year the protest and the government reaction had escalated to such an extent that Anne felt obliged to become active along with the schoolchildren. Her eldest son was arrested in 1976 and given eight lashes; some of his peers were sentenced and imprisoned on Robben Island. He was again arrested in 1977 and held for thirteen days.

Anne and her son attended the funeral of Steve Biko in King William's Town. During the night of their return the police raided Anne's home in search of her son, but he was not there. Their search continued, and fifteen days later Anne was arrested and held for two days. That same night, the police raided her home and, on finding only her eleven-year-old son there, took him into custody and beat him severely on the head and body. They wanted him to point out his brother's girlfriends, kin, and colleagues. He was interrogated and beaten for a day. Upon Anne's release she found that her husband had taken their son to his brother's home in a small town. The police told her that her eldest son had escaped and was in Angola.

With a fresh wave of school boycotts in 1980, Anne's second-eldest child came under police surveillance. The police, in seeking him, tried to take the third eldest boy from home, and Anne struggled to hold on to him, saying, "If you want to arrest A, arrest him, not B," and "I am not going to look for you, you do your dirty work yourselves." That son, too, left for exile. Anne visited him in Lesotho. In 1983 there was a radio announcement about a "terrorist" who had exchanged fire with police on a train and, who, when he had run out of ammunition, had shot himself. This was her second-eldest son. Anne was informed of his death by the ANC but was only told by the police a year later—she identified photographs of his body.

In 1982 her third-born son was arrested in a meeting and so severely beaten that he could neither eat nor sit for some time. He went into exile, to be followed soon after by the last boy. In 1985 Anne was arrested and held in detention for four months. During that time she heard that her eldest child had died in a shoot-out with police and *askari* (turncoats). He, too, it is said, shot himself before being arrested. The police gave her permission to attend his funeral, but she declined, saying, "My comrades will know how to bury him." During the years of school boycotts and police brutality, Anne had counseled the families of students who had been killed and had advised them how to conduct the funerals and how to refuse to countenance police interference and direction in handling the bodies. Even in prison, faced with the loss of another son, she had the courage to refuse to attend his funeral at the behest of the authorities.

In 1989 Anne visited her sons in Tanzania, and in 1990 she was called to collect the body of the youngest boy, who had died in an accident.

Throughout her married life, Anne has belonged to women's and civic organizations. She has spent three years in detention, has been tortured, and still suffers the consequences; her home has been burned a number of times; and she has lost her children—yet she continues to fight.

The lives of Anne and her children (she guarded her daughter from the police and eventually sent her to kin in a quieter town, knowing, she said, what police do to young girls) illustrate dramatically the threads of continuity across generations. The threads between them are unusual in their intensity and accord. The children drew from her strength and spirit. Yet many continuities across generations can be found, and I shall mention just two examples of how the political consciousness of the young was formed by the older generation. The examples are drawn from the histories of the young people with whom I am working.

As a boy, Zolile was befriended by a man in his neighborhood who sold fruit and vegetables. Zolile used to buy newspapers for him and would sit and listen politely to the old man's opinions of the world. It was only once an adolescent that Zolile realized that the man had educated him on national and international issues (see the sketch of Zolile's early involvement in politics later in the paper).

At the age of four Enoch was sent by his parents to live with his father's mother in a city far from home. He lived in a household headed by his father's sister's husband, who is one of the most senior political figures in the country. It was in living with him that Enoch's political consciousness was raised. He carried messages for his uncle, experienced the disturbance of his arrest and imprisonment, of his return and rearrest; he visited him on Robben Island and watched his aunt suffer. At the age of sixteen Enoch was taken by his father from that household to live in another city because his father feared that Enoch was in danger of becoming too politicized. It was some years before Enoch took up an activist role, but his opinions had already been in some measure shaped. Other examples could be given, but let these suffice.

Transformations in action and behavior are more clearly identifiable in most of the young people's lives. None entered political activity at the behest of a parent or guardian. Each became active with peers either at school or university, and each tried to protect their families from the consequences of their actions. What I suggest is that adults imbued children with sets of attitudes and morals that, to some extent, the young adopted as descriptions of reality. Embedded in those descriptions were adults' mature views of their political disinheritance, sometimes overtly expressed in political terms. This is part of the transformation of knowledge across generations out of which communities carve identities. The process does not, however, exclude innovation, and it is a characteristic of the generation that reached adolescence in 1976 that it adopted a position in opposition to that which it saw as adult complicity or, less harshly, passive endurance of state oppression. The black-consciousness movement led by Steve Biko prepared the ground for youths' opposition (see Pityana et al. 1991).

It is the duration of the youth's rebellion that must be emphasized. Political consciousness, commitment, and endurance occurred, for some, over a span of fifteen years. Some reentered the fray at every opportunity despite appalling trauma and despite opportunities to legitimately and honorably pursue directions that would benefit them as individuals and keep them relatively safe. For example, Zolile was released from Robben Island after nine years of imprisonment, and, although he had secured a position as a university student, he resumed clandestine activities and was soon forced to flee into exile, returning four years later to once again begin university as an undergraduate.

It is, it seems to me, no mean task to sustain rebellion before the power of a ruthless state over an extended period of time and to emerge, not unscathed, but well enough, confident enough to become a university student or to resume education at whatever level possible. What are the sources of that endurance? They are impossible to pin down, but there seem to be at least five layers in the support system upon which the students drew. These include the ingredients of each one's individuality; the family; the peer group; political comrades; and prisoner solidarity (see Reynolds 1991, for further discussion). It is worth noting here that the students discuss the difficulties experienced by fellow prisoners who had been sentenced for their involvement in political protest but who had not defined themselves as political activists and had not gone through processes of reflection and commitment in relation to political activity. It took them longer to adjust, to come to terms with their sentences, and to benefit from the influence of senior comrades than it did committed activists. Some of them never adjusted and were unable to take advantage of the possibilities for individual development that incarceration with political leaders in a place such as Robben Island provided.

For many of the young, involvement in political activity began either at school or at demonstrations. Thabo, for example, was a fine athlete, and he enjoyed demonstrations for the chance they gave him of showing off his speed in running from the *casspirs* (armored vehicles). But when his friend was shot and killed beside him at one demonstration, Thabo's play ended, and he was forced to face the reality of protest politics. A common pattern of behavior was an initial participation as part of a crowd, often in the spirit of bravado and the excitement of communal defiance. This was followed by the assumption of leadership in organizing defiance and an escalation in risk taking and responsibility. Often, experience of pain (being teargassed, *sjamboked*, beaten), arrest, and interrogation shocked young people into reassessing their commitment.

The next stage for many was formal alignment with a political group (usually a banned party) and a move into clandestine activity that called for a change in relationships with others, especially kin, and the adoption of new forms of behavior. The students say that they had to learn to be secretive about their movements and contacts; they had to sleep in different places; they had to guard against impulsive behavior and to resist the temptation to share their fears with loved ones because that would implicate them. They became strangers in their own homes and lived with the fear of probable arrest and the possibility that they might not withstand ill treatment stoically.

A major feature of this stage in the transformation of behavior was the conscious decision to disobey authority figures, represented by teachers and parents. For some of the students it was very difficult to disobey parents. Relations between parent and child are ideally founded upon mutual respect, especially that between father and son. It is an ideal that echoes the one recorded in the 1930s among the Xhosa in Pondoland by Hunter (1936:25–26).

> Fathers also are devoted to their children, and make much of them when small, carrying them about in their arms, fondling them, playing with them, and teaching them to dance. Often one sees a child of three or four climbing over his father and mauling him with impunity.
>
> As a child grows older he is taught respect and obedience which are particularly due to his father. Usually a child will carry out any order of his father's much quicker than those of any woman. He fetches and carries for his father, performing whatever tasks he is capable of performing. There is no age at which he is regarded as being free of parental control. In theory his choice in marriage may still be vetoed by his father, although in practice a man usually marries the girl he wants. He still must consult his father in all important matters, even after he has an *umzi*[4] of his own. Old men lament the days when "grey-headed men lived in the *umzi* of their father, obeying him in all things, as if they were children."
>
> A father is responsible for his son's health as long as he remains in his *umzi*, and must make a ritual killing for him when necessary. Even when a son has his own *umzi*, it is obligatory for father and son to consult each other before killing ritually. "Consultation" means discussion until some measure of agreement is reached. Informants did not think that a father could veto a son's actions, or a son, his father's. A good son would listen to his father's advise; a good father should be advised by his sons. It is all of a piece with a general custom in law courts and tribal meetings, that no vote is taken, but the matter thrashed out until some compromise is reached. There is a proverb, *Isala kutyelwa siva ngolophu.* "He who refuses to take advice hears by a hot wind."

In a study in 1983 of migrant men in hostels for "single" men in Cape Town, I found that men subscribed to the same ideal of fatherhood despite the fact that the laws of the country denied them the right to have their children live with them at their place of work, which meant separation of father and child for most of each year that the father worked. It was, under such conditions, almost impossible for a man to live up to such an ideal (Reynolds 1984).

Saul's experience was rather different from the pattern sketched above. In 1984, when he was twelve years old, he was arrested and detained in a small town prison in the western Cape. He was held for two weeks, interrogated, and beaten so severely with *sjamboks* that deep scars remain on his limbs. He was held, he thinks, either because they mistook him for his elder brother, who was a student activist at the local senior school, or because the army commando could not find his brother and Saul was taken in to get at him. He was held in solitary confinement for twelve days and spent the last two with common-law prisoners. Saul says of the experience:

> I was aware of the oppression because I grew up on a farm, and I knew what the suffering there was. And my goal was that, when I grew older, I would follow in my brother's footsteps and become a student leader. It was always my desire, but there was no involvement in organizations. And when they [the army commando] caught me, I was very panicky. I did not know them, and we had no lawyers. They had us; the doctors they sent us to, the state doctors, and the state attorneys. And I mean I had no knowledge of how to behave, because at that time there was no organization except the student bodies, which were not legal at school—the Students' Representative Council.
>
> [In prison] I cried a lot and was very lonely and felt very withdrawn, just wanted to come out. I wanted to see my mother, and they just refused.

By 1986 Saul was a student leader at the primary school. From 1986 to 1991 he was arrested three times a year and spent every Christmas in prison. Of his last arrest in 1990 he says, "And they detained me again last year, but before Christmas. I was really lucky."

Another symptom of disobedience was that many young spurned the high value that the older generation placed on education and resolved to reject it (in the form available to them) or defer concentration upon it. This often led the students into direct confrontation with their parents. Some say they were torn between the desire to obey parents and their conviction that the disruption of education was a necessary political tactic. Few were able to remain at school or university once they had become politically active, and that activity also meant that they found it difficult to secure and keep jobs. Therefore they were unable to meet family expectations of support, and they felt shame in failing to earn money and so release a parent from arduous, unpleasant employment or to help finance younger siblings' education. The students still express feelings of guilt over this sort of failure, and, they say, they continued to fall short of their responsibilities as prisoners or exiles and now as students.

LEGITIMATE REPRESENTATION

The ambition of all ideologies is to ground their arbitrary divisions of the social order in reason, thus providing logical and cosmological solutions to the problem of classifying categories. This description fits the classificatory drive made to justify apartheid. Central to the justification in the 1970s was the imposition of the Afrikaans language as a medium of instruction in black schools. The protest of 1976 was against the real handicap this ruling placed on black children's learning and on the imposition of the symbols of domination. Blacks took up this struggle to wrest, from the state, control over legitimate representation of the social world—that struggle for classification which is a dimension of every kind of struggle between classes, whether of generation, of gender, or of social rank (Bourdieu 1990:180). Bourdieu suggests that the dominated rebel against those who seek a monopoly over the power to judge and to classify and attempt to break out of the grip of legitimate classification and transform their vision of the world by liberating themselves from the internalized limits that are the social categories of perception of the social world. Forms of classification are forms of domination, as experiences in South Africa repeatedly prove. In the current liminal period some of these classifications are being challenged. In challenging the system of symbolic domination, young people contributed to the reformulation of the politics of culture.

I suggested above that some young people had to gird their loins in order to overcome scruples in their learned attitudes of respect and obedience toward elders. Participating in demonstrations with their peers—where the show of strength, the numbers, and cohesion were symbols in themselves—may have helped loosen ties. Fresh self-images were designed, and we await a careful analysis of the clothes, colors, and objects used in presenting these images. There were, too, changes on the subjective level where categories of perception and evaluation of the social world were explored. Words, the names that construct social reality as much as they express it, become the crucial stakes of political struggle. A word like *comrade* instead of *child* implied a universe of difference. Words such as *necklace* and objects such as tires became symbols of a new form of domination that caused widespread fear and horror, just as did the appropriation of ancient metaphors by groups of young people who used them in accusations of witchcraft in their attempts to cleanse and control certain communities (see Niehaus 1991 for a chilling record of such a process). Aberrations and abuse do not, however, negate the effect that changes in collective and individual action had in challenging the state as the holder of the monopoly of legitimate symbolic violence.

As schoolchildren and students, the young demanded legitimate representation on organizing bodies in their immediate areas and at the state level. The following case study records the escalation of political involvement that engulfed one student who, with his schoolmates, demanded representation.

Zolile's early memories of the township in Port Elizabeth in which he grew up are of violence and gangsterism and police vigilance in capturing those without passes. This was in the 1960s. It was, too, a period in which sport was a focus of people's play and passionate interest. Zolile played rugby and represented eastern-province schools (blacks only) in cricket. He says that sport drove him into politics. He was an avid fan of the Springboks and listened to the radio to follow their tours and kept close watch over provincial matches played by whites. He learned to read newspapers starting from the sports page at the back. In his mind was a question as to why there should be "a black ground, a white ground, a colored ground." It was following the 1969 Springbok tour in Britain that Zolile first heard of the antiapartheid movement. He listened with puzzlement to radio accounts of the Springbok players' difficulties in facing demonstrations, in having their sleep disrupted, in being called racists, and he felt sympathetic toward them. He followed, too, the 1972 tour of Australia, which was a violent one. A member of the team had his nose kicked and broken.

His first experience of group defiance was in 1972, when, following a tour by England, black rugby was split. The Kwazakeli Rugby Union (which was affiliated to the South African Rugby Union) followed a nonracial policy, and it gathered a strong following in the eastern Cape. Zolile would join convoys of cars that progressed hooting and giving the Black-power salute en route to the union's matches. Sport brought political awareness to many people.

Another influence on Zolile's early political consciousness was the interest that a man who sold vegetables and fruit at a stall near Zolile's home took in him. Zolile was in standard 6 when the man would see him passing in the morning and would call him over and ask him to buy a newspaper for him. On his way home from school the man would call Zolile over for a talk. He would ask if the boy knew what was happening in, for example, Zimbabwe. And he would tell what he had learned from the newspaper. Zolile came to know and be interested in Nkomo, Muzorewa, Mugabe, and Sithole and relate those names to political demands. "And this was how I learned about black majority."

As student politics began to gather momentum in the early 1970s, Zolile became aware of how much the stall owner was nurturing his understanding. He began to seek out the man's company. There was little political discussion at his home, but his father (a railway worker) told stories of the Second World War that helped to "shed light on the politics of the world." He also told stories of the ANC and of protests in the 1950s and 1960s.

Protests against the use of Afrikaans as a medium of instruction, Zolile says, began in the Cape where some students had to write their Junior Certificate Examination in certain subjects in Afrikaans. A very small student body was formed in 1975—the South African Students' Movement. However, it was only with the Soweto killings of 1976 that widespread revolt began.

The senior students at Zolile's high school used to study at school in the evenings, and, following the Soweto protest, some of them began to read newspaper accounts of their fellow students' activities. An "unusual atmosphere" grew up around the school, and the police made their first blunder in assuming that the students' stirrings of interest represented fully cognizant demonstrations of protest. Police were posted at the school at night. They stood in the corridors with their walkie-talkies and would bustle the students from their study after 9:00 P.M., using their dogs to disperse them. The students protested and drew other students to their cause. The principal was afraid to intervene.

A classroom floor was burned one night. The police arrived and wanted to interrogate some pupils, protested and clashed with the principal (there was no indication that pupils had caused the fire). Pupils began late at night to write slogans against the government on the blackboards. The principal, a black woman, called the police in to see the slogans. The staff room was burned down, and the caretaker accused the students of having done it. Police interrogated the senior students and began to detain students overnight. Schooling came to a stop. A protest march was planned and was held, in September 1976, on a school field. Songs learned from Radio Freedom were sung, and grievances were aired. Riot police surrounded the meeting, township people gathered, and journalists appeared. Security police were there too, although few students knew of their existence. The police gave a five-minute warning calling for dispersal, and the children began to run away. Tear gas was fired. Some regrouped but were again dispersed.

On the following day, the students attempted to demonstrate in a sports stadium, but the police blocked their progress and dispersed them. No plans had been made for such an eventuality, and the students began to burn down liquor bars and stone cars and buses; they were joined by people from the townships. It was the beginning of a spate of uprisings in that area. The students were shocked by the riot and resolved to return to classes, but police continued to harass them, picking pupils up at their houses, so that they began to sleep away from home. Many slept at school and planned to protest police action in the town. Police raided the school, arresting forty-two pupils. They were sent to various police stations, and no one was informed of their whereabouts. They were held for months, then charged with malicious damage to property.

Zolile was one of six students who were singled out by the police as ringleaders. Some of these students were sent to Robben Island, but Zolile was held in detention for another three months. Young people with but the dawning of political consciousness were sentenced to long terms with seasoned political activists on Robben Island.

One more sketch must be added to this sketch of emerging political awareness, and that is the extraordinary violence with which these scholars were treated. Upon their arrest at 3:00 A.M. they were forced into police vans and upon alighting at the police station were beaten, taken to cells, and beaten by policemen with security police in attendance. Interrogation began immediately. Each was taken to a separate room, questioned, and beaten. Cries filled the station all day. Two policeman came into the cells and beat the boys with wire for hours whenever they were on night duty. They did not even ask questions. Complaints were made to the station commander, but he merely expressed his pleasure that they were being beaten.

The students were dispersed to various police stations, some hundreds of kilometers from their homes. Interrogation and torture continued. There was still unrest in the townships, and the pupils were accused of involvement. They would be blindfolded, taken into the bush, and interrogated all night. Sometimes they would be taken to police offices in a high-rise building, and they would be reminded of how a young student activist had died when he fell from the window of the office. The walls were covered with blood. The interrogators threatened the students with instant death. Zolile says, "Yet there was not much for us to confess." They were made to sign confessions drawn up by the police.

Upon release, Zolile returned to school and was quiet for some time but was drawn back into student politics as leaders were detained. There were widespread boycotts, and many young people died. During a school movement meeting in September 1977, Zolile was arrested but later acquitted. It was after this that he joined the underground structures of the ANC.

To reiterate a point already made, the students have been involved in political activity over many years. While some may have entered into the arena by force of circumstance rather than by choice, each has since reaffirmed commitment across time. The acquisition of political consciousness, directed in particular ways within political organizations, has been part of the forging of identity. It is difficult to detail the quantity and quality of their political education because of the turmoil of the period and the clandestine nature of their involvement. Lizo, for instance, underwent prolonged training in other African countries, plus a spell of four months in the USSR, before returning to South Africa to prepare local people for resistance. In contrast, Saul never left the western Cape and received very little political direction outside local school protests and community activities. Exposure to party rhetoric and access to supporting ideologies varied. To stand against the state took courage and fortitude, and, I suggest, many of the students were thrown largely upon their own resources as political activists once they moved beyond the stage of public demonstration.

NEGOTIATING IDENTITIES

Part of the aim of this project is to elicit reflection on the design of self in relation to family and community within a milieu of political activity. Attention has already been drawn to some of these reflections. Two points need emphasis. One is that political activism can increase self-awareness because it is necessary to be vigilant in clarifying one's own motives and emotions as they relate to commitment and the reaffirmation of commitment: without this vigilance one may be a danger to oneself and to others. Besides, self-consciousness is the counterpart to wariness of other people's behavior, in particular, the possibility of treachery.

The other point that needs to be stressed is that the students are articulate about the emergence of their concepts of self as they became more involved in political activities. For example, they note the impact that their activities had on their parents as the disciplinary forces of apartheid entered into their lives in immediate ways; they pinpoint moments of significance in the development of their consciousness, and they trace their increasing awareness of their own potential and possible limits that their asseveration entailed. The constraints of space allow for only one brief excerpt from a student's account. I have highlighted incidents from his prison experience to illustrate the confidence he had acquired in his own integrity.

Lizo was born in 1960, and he grew up in a rural area of northern Zululand. He was the secondborn and first son of seven children. Both of his parents were teachers. His father taught in a number of different schools, and Lizo used to live with him while the other members of the family stayed at home. His father told him that he was privileged in relation to many other children and that he should never assume superiority over others on the grounds of wealth, class, or educational differences. As a boy, Lizo read the books of Charles Dickens, and, he says, the problems of poverty in a rapidly industrializing England impressed his early consciousness.

In 1976, when Lizo was fifteen, he was sent to boarding school. He met pupils from Johannesburg who described the causes and consequences of the protest in Soweto. He took an interest in political discussions, but it was only at university that the full force of oppression became clear to him. He became active in student politics, which made him a target when vigilantes brutally attacked defenceless students in their hostels one night. Lizo was severely beaten and left unconscious, and his friend in the room next to his was beaten and killed. Lizo joined the ANC and resolved to go into exile to train as a soldier. On leaving, he pinned a note on his hostel door saying he had gone home, and it was some time before his parents learned of his disappearance.

Lizo trained as a soldier in Angola, Mozambique, Zambia, and the Soviet Union. He fought against UNITA troops in Angola. Three years later he returned to South Africa as a member of a group whose brief was to politicize people in the countryside and train them in resistance. He and his comrades lived for about seven months in caves in the hills, from where they set about politicizing local people. One member of the group deserted and told the security police of their whereabouts. They were arrested, and a period of intense interrogation and torture followed. Lizo finds it hard to talk of that "terrible time" because of the pain of remembering and because of his fear of the hatred remembering stirs in him. The hatred is "something I don't want."

The four members of the group were placed in separate cells. Lizo was in solitary confinement for seven months. Thirty people from the area in which they had operated were also arrested and held in another prison. Many became state witnesses, but Lizo and his colleagues excuse their behavior because they were untrained and had not had the time to commit themselves consciously to a political program and because they were tricked, threatened, and beaten into compliance with the police. They are, however, bitter about the comrade who sold them out and refer to him as an *askari*.

Even in a state of utter subjection, Lizo tried to act in the light of his principles. For example, interrogation sessions were held by the police in eight-hour shifts. On each shift were white officers and black juniors. The blacks did the actual beating and torturing. When the officers left for a break, Lizo would talk to the black men, pointing out their oppression within the police force and questioning their role in relation to the state and the interests of the people. To gather together the wit and courage to use political persuasion during one's own interrogation takes both strength and self-control. In describing the humiliation of both common-law and political prisoners, Lizo gives glimpses of other incidents that called forth the same directness and refusal to compromise. For example, while standing in the medical section of the prison waiting to see the doctor, he saw a lieutenant use the pocket of a prisoner's uniform as an ashtray. Lizo challenged him as to the meaning of such an act.

In prison Lizo set out to test the relationship between warders and prisoners, a relationship he describes as being founded upon a master-servant, farmer-laborer axis. As a political prisoner he confronted it directly and then challenged the punishment that was a consequence of this action. Lizo says,

> They know that they will get you, . . . but you can't compromise your principles for anything. They had to improve their behavior, or they would have had confrontation day in and day out. For instance, when they switch on the lights at five o'clock in the morning, they would make us wake up (you see that's what they do with the common-law prisoners). . . . I would not do that, just sleep.
>
> They would come, "Hey wake up!"
>
> "Where are you going to? Its five o'clock in the morning. I'm in prison here. Where do you want me to go? I'm doing nothing all day. Must I wake for what?"
>
> "Hey wake up prisoner!" And so on.
>
> I told them, "Until you stop shouting at me, I'm not going to listen to you." I would take a blanket and pull it over again. And the officers feel undermined because you make sure that you do it in the presence of their subordinates so that they cannot scare you about calling a senior officer. I would tell them, "If you are an officer in your army, I am an officer in my army, too, so you can't expect any respect from me unless you pay respect to me." So such things they learned. In fact as time went on, they would just look at me to see if we were still alive and go outside and carry on.

Lizo and his colleagues knew the risks of confrontation. They knew that prisoners could die, and it would be framed as suicide. Lizo commented, "Sure you know of these things, but one thing you say is 'I'm not going to compromise myself for anything.'" Indeed, on his father's first visit to the prison Lizo set out his principles and asked that their relationship take them into account. His father agreed.

Lizo and his three comrades from exile regarded themselves as prisoners of war and refused to be represented in the South African courts. They were expressing their contempt for the country's judicial system. They made a statement about the court's lack of legitimacy and the fact that they owed no allegiance to the state. In refusing representation and in keeping silent the young men had to listen to police lies about their treatment of prisoners and to watch the court officials accept the evidence. The prosecutor called for life sentences, and the advocate representing the locals being charged stood up in their defence even though it was not his role to do so. Lizo thought the judge's sentences were lenient. (Lizo was given a prison term of ten years; the commander of the group received a twelve-year sentence; and the others received eight years each.) The judge acknowledged that they possessed dangerous weapons and were capable of doing a lot of damage but that no one had been killed, and, he said, he preferred to punish people for actual, not intended, offences. It was an enlightened judgment, given the context of the times.

The molding of the self contributes to new constructions of a former reality that may entail the rejection of former descriptions and a reconstruction of the past. It is likely that in South Africa the force of political structures brought some young activists face to face at an early age with the fragility of life and integrity. Williams (1961:320) said,

> A culture, while it is being lived, is always in part unknown, in part unrealised. The making of a community is always an exploration, for consciousness cannot precede creation, and there is no formula for unknown experiences. . . . Wherever we have started from, we need to listen to others who started from a different position. We need to consider every attachment, every value, with our whole attention; for we do not know the future, we can never be certain of what may enrich it; we can only, now, listen to and consider whatever may be offered and take up whatever we can.

We need to listen to the experiences of young people who weathered years of revolution. If their stories are not told, they will not be heard and we will not know how they have enriched the future.

CONCLUSION

History frog-marched youth to the fore of political activism in South Africa. Their role is already being subsumed—as, no doubt, it ought to be—and they are cast in new parts. Only time will tell whether those who were young between 1976 and 1990 will have their stories told and their experiences incorporated into new, healthy constructions of reality. The students upon whose experiences this paper draws represent only a small segment of the young, but their contribution may have been greater than the sum of their numbers—if, that is, we are prepared to accept that even the young contribute to the transformation of culture. In the words of Ben Okri,

> We're very far behind ourselves. We've discovered things in human relations, about love and life, and we live with them as if we haven't made these discoveries.
>
> For me, optimism comes out of patience. It comes out of knowing how hard the facts of the world are, and the refusal to be defined by that. And the belief in the possibility that, as human beings, we do try to redeem ourselves. We might not do it the right way or directly, or even intentionally, but we do try. And if we fail, I think our children, without knowing it, try for us.

NOTES

I am grateful to the University Research Committee of the University of Cape Town for financial support of the project.

1. "Birth, marriage, death, re-birth. They're the only neat endings, traditional culminations for living—for books, even. . . . Living is serial, an unending accretion of alternatives" (Astley, 1990:32).

2. Thomas (1990:440–41) describes the problems that surround the acquisition of statistics on the detention of children. She concludes that there are discrepancies in figures released by official state sources and independent monitoring bodies, but that even the more conservative state-supplied figures confirm that thousands of children in South Africa have been held in detention. Thomas's analysis of violence and the experiences of child detainees is essential reading for all those concerned with children's vulnerability before political forces.

3. *Ukuthwala*: "A man carries off the woman he wishes to marry. She is seized when walking abroad, hustled along with much shouting and some blows, and taken to the groom's kraal" (Hunter 1936:187). If the kinsmen of the two parties agree, then the marriage is ritually acknowledged.

4. *Umzi,* pl. *imi:* local kinship group and the huts in which they live (Hunter 1936:576).

REFERENCES

African National Congress, 1990, *Violence in the Boland,* ANC report, July.
Astley, Thea, 1990, *Hunting the Wild Pineapple,* New York, G. P. Putnam's Sons.

Bourdieu, Pierre, 1977, *Outline of a Theory in Practice,* trans. Richard Nice, Cambridge, Cambridge University Press.

———, 1990, *In Other Words: Essays towards a Reflexive Sociology,* trans. Matthew Adamson, Cambridge, Polity Press.

Brittain, Victoria and Abdul S. Minty, 1988, *Children of Resistance: Statements from the Harare Conference on Children, Repression, and the Law in Apartheid South Africa,* London, Kliptown.

Feierman, Steven, 1990, *Peasant Intellectuals: Anthropology and History in Tanzania,* Madison, University of Wisconsin Press.

Foster, Don, 1987, *Detention and Torture in South Africa: Psychological, Legal, and Historical Studies,* Cape Town, David Philip.

Gerhart, Gail, 1978, *Black Power in South Africa: The Evolution of an Ideology,* Berkeley and Los Angeles, University of California Press.

Giddens, Anthony, 1979, *Central Problems in Social Theory: Action, Structure, and Contradictions in Social Analysis,* Berkeley and Los Angeles, University of California Press.

Human Rights Commission, 1988, fact paper no. 1.

Hunter, Monica, 1936, *Reaction to Conquest: Effects of Contact with Europeans on the Pondo of South Africa,* London, Oxford University Press.

Joyce, Peter, 1990, *The Rise and Fall of Apartheid,* Cape Town, Struik.

Lodge, Tom, 1983, *Black Politics in South Africa since 1945,* Braamfontein, Ravan.

Mager, Anne, 1992, "Girls' Wars, Mission Institutions, and Reproduction of an Educated Elite in the Eastern Cape, 1945–1959," paper presented at the Centre for African Studies, University of Cape Town, 22 April.

McKendrick, Brian and Wilma Hoffman, 1990, *People and Violence in South Africa,* Cape Town, Oxford University Press.

Niehaus, Isak A., 1991, "Witch-Hunting and Political Legitimacy: Continuity and Change in Green Valley, Lebowa (1930–1991)," paper presented at the Anthropological Association of Southern Africa, Rand Afrikaans University, Johannesburg.

Pityana, Barney, Mamphela Ramphele, Malusi Mpumlwana, and Lindy Wilson, eds., 1991, *Bounds of Possibility: The Legacy of Steve Biko and Black Consciousness,* Cape Town, David Philip.

Ractliffe, Tamsin, 1990, "Towards Re-integration: Problems for Ex-Political Prisoners," manuscript, University of Cape Town.

Reynolds, Pamela, 1984, *Men without Children,* Second Carnegie Inquiry into Poverty and Development in Southern Africa, Cape Town, University of Cape Town.

———, 1991, "Youth and Trauma in South Africa: Social Means of Support," paper presented at the International African Institute Conference on Healing the Social Wounds of War, Windhoek, Namibia.

Thomas, Adèle, 1990, "Violence and Child Detainees," in Brais McKendrick and Wilma Hoffman, eds., *People and Violence in South Africa,* Cape Town, Oxford University Press, 436–64.

Westcott, Shaun, 1988, *The Trial of the Thirteen,* Mowbray, Black Sash.

Williams, Raymond, 1961, *Culture and Society 1780–1950,* Harmondsworth, Penguin.

Wilson, Lindy, 1988 *Robben Island: Our University,* film script.

Winslow, Tom J., 1991, "Released into a Prison without Walls: A Preliminary Inquiry into the Socio-Economic Position of Ex-Political Prisoners Living in the Western Cape," Centre for Development Studies, University of the Western Cape.

Part Three

CHILDREN AND THE POLITICS OF
MINORITY CULTURAL IDENTITY

"There's a Time to Act English and a Time to Act Indian": The Politics of Identity among British-Sikh Teenagers

KATHLEEN HALL

> For blacks . . . the battle is not deconstructing
> rights, in a world of no rights; nor of construct-
> ing statements of need, in a world of abundantly
> apparent need. Rather the goal is to find a politi-
> cal mechanism that can confront the denial of
> need. The argument that rights are disutile, even
> harmful, trivializes this aspect of black experience
> specifically, as well as that of any person or group
> whose vulnerability has been protected by rights.
> *(P. Williams 1991:152)*

INALIENABLE RIGHTS, despite their rhetorical packaging, are never self-evident. As a form of political discourse, rights talk marks a site of struggle between the powerful and those whom rights empower. The UN Convention on the Rights of the Child embodies this same ambiguity and potential for political use and abuse.

The assertion of a child's right to a cultural identity raises especially complex questions concerning the issue of power and the politics of culture. Who determines *what* that culture should be? How should it be practiced? When? Where? Vivienne Wee (this volume) and Veena Das (1992) each note how "powerful Others" can "force-feed" culture to children or impose rigid cultural "molds" upon the activities of the child. In contexts such as these, Das argues, "[T]he technology of rights may become a means of sanctioning cultural authoritarianism" (1992:20). With this in mind, Sharon Stephens urges us to consider, "How have cultural rights discourses sometimes been turned against the intention of the Convention and themselves become risks to children?" (1992:n.p.).

As many here have argued, a principal problem with the UN Charter's assertion of a "child's right to a cultural identity" is the notion of culture that these statements seem to suggest—culture as a transferrable object or product. Cultural identity formation, as Manuela Carneiro da Cunha explains (this volume), is an ongoing process, and culture is a process of production. "What we must guarantee for future generations," she concludes, "is not the preservation of cultural products, but the preservation of the capacity for cultural production." Or, as Veena Das reminds us in slightly different terms, "It is not only the right to a cultural identity but also to cultural innovation, play with other identities, availability of the whole repertoire of the culture of man and woman which is the heritage of the child" (1992:20). Accepting this, how is a child's capacity to "play" with multiple cultural identities to be protected? In order to protect this right we must first develop an understanding of processes of cultural production and of identity formation.

The stories recorded in this account portray vividly the multiple dimensions involved in the process of identity formation as experienced within the everyday social interactions of British-Sikhs growing up in Leeds, a city in the north of England. Their experiences are shared by the children of migrant peoples throughout Europe, children raised in social worlds far removed from the homelands of their parents—in this instance both the Indian state of Punjab and East Africa. What becomes clear from the vantage point of their struggles (and the similar conflicts of the Turkish guest workers in Germany discussed by Ruth Mandel) is that cultural-identity formation is not simply a matter of preserving a cultural tradition handed down by one's parents. For ethnic minorities marginalized by the forces of racism and nationalism as well as forms of class and gender inequality, cultural-identity formation, I will argue, is an inherently political process.

In the context of a modern urban environment such as Leeds, the "cultural repertoire" available to these teenagers is greatly increased by the forces of global capitalist commodity production encountered most noticeably in the ideas and influences of popular culture—"fashion" in music, clothing, and style of life that the dominant consumer culture, particularly the media, projects into their daily lives. Second-generation British-Sikhs in the various social contexts in which they live are creatively negotiating these forces of race, class, and gender, as well as the multiple forms of cultural identity available to them in their homes and communities, at school, and within popular culture. As a result of these processes, these young people are constructing alternative ways of being a British-Sikh in modern England. It is to their experiences that I now turn.

In Leeds, in a house on middle-class Street Lane, locally known as "Sikh Lane," I am sitting with Amrit in a small, smartly fitted room, drinking tea in front of an electric fire, an image of a Sikh guru, Guru Gobind

Singh, watching us from his garlanded portrait above the fireplace. The aroma of cumin and coriander filters into the room from the kitchen, where Amrit's mother and sister are preparing the evening meal. Her brother, still suited up from his cricket match, is stretched out on the sofa in the room next door engrossed in an episode of *Dallas* playing on the television. Amrit, at eighteen, wears her hair in a braid that falls half way down her back. Her face is free of makeup, but her look is decidedly "modern," the latest in English fashion: Indian-style pajama pants with a Marks and Spencer's sweater, and an Indian-made scarf to match.

Amrit is a second-generation British-Sikh. Her father came to Britain in the late 1950s from a village in the Punjab where his family, members of the Jat caste, were landowning farmers. Amrit's father and her uncles were part of the first phase of ex-colonial immigration into Britain, at first exclusively men who came to fill a demand for laborers needed to rebuild Britain in the aftermath of World War II. Amrit's mother joined her father in the early sixties, and they have lived in Leeds ever since.

Amrit and her family moved up to the middle-class area of Moortown, both as a sign of their social mobility and in an effort to be nearer to Amrit's high school, Grange Hill High. Before moving here, her family lived in Chapeltown, the infamously stereotyped "inner city," or black working-class neighborhood near the center of Leeds. The boundaries of the school's catchment area cut a pie slice from this middle-class area of Moortown, through a median area called Chapel Allerton, into Chapeltown. This catchment area contains neighborhoods that have served as stepping stones in the path of successive waves of ethnic group mobility. Traversed originally by Jewish families, a substantial number of Sikh families have, over the last fifteen years, moved "up" and north from Chapeltown to Moortown, followed by fewer economically successful West Indian families.

Most of the Sikh youths at Grange Hill High School were either born in England to parents, like Amrit's, who migrated in the 1950s and 1960s from villages in the Indian state of Punjab, or came with their parents from East Africa during the late 1960s or early 1970s at a very young age.[1] They are British citizens. The British Nationality Act of 1948 confirmed that Commonwealth and colonial peoples, many of whom were by then citizens of independent Commonwealth states, were to remain subjects of the British Crown. With this status, all the rights of citizenship—most importantly, the right to enter and settle in Great Britain—were reaffirmed. But as the numbers of black immigrants increased, the legal rights of formerly colonial peoples were taken away in a series of progressively restrictive immigration acts that have redefined British nationality in more narrow, and implicitly racial, terms based on descent and kinship ties.

Families such as Amrit's, who were members of the first phase of immigration, shared with me family photo albums with pictures providing clues to the disjointed stages of cultural adjustment the first generation experienced in coming to terms with British racism and in adapting to English culture. Early photos of Amrit's father with his brothers in Leeds captured a group of very English-looking young men, their short hair slicked back posing in the English version of a James Dean–esque stance. Her father now wears a turban, covering his now unshorn hair, and keeps a neatly trimmed beard, a compromise in keeping the five symbols of the Sikh faith.

Many interrelated factors have led to the recent revitalization of Sikhism and to the production of various reformed versions of the Sikh tradition. Three of the most significant of these include, first, the experience of British racism and the discovery that, as the title of Paul Gilroy's important book states, *There Ain't No Black in the Union Jack;* second, the politics surrounding the fight for a Sikh homeland, Khalistan, in Punjab; and, finally, the arrival of the second group of Sikh immigrants from East Africa. Members of the East African Sikh diaspora, primarily of the Ramgarhia caste, in their segregated communities in British East Africa had created a more conservative approach to Sikh tradition and religion. They had instituted caste associations and had succeeded in tailoring their religious practices to life in an urban and often middle-class context. One gentleman from Kenya, for example, explained that the practice of wearing white, neatly pressed turbans among East African Ramgarhia Sikhs developed in part out of the need to create a style that would "look smart with evening wear." What is forming in Britain is a heterogenous mixture of Sikh communities potentially united and divided according to class, caste, generation, religious belief and practice, educational level, place of origin, residential location, friendship patterns, and style of life.

The topic of this essay, however, takes me back to Amrit and to the concerns and experiences of the children of the Sikh settler generation. What kind of cultural identifications are they forming as a result of their experiences in Britain? In her front room, absorbed in her thoughts about conflicts between second-generation Sikh teenagers and their parents over going out, boys, dress, and Sikh religion and customs, Amrit attempts to describe to me her feelings about growing up in England.

> It's hard for kids at my age, or kids at any age, to be brought up in a place totally different from their parents. I go to school and get Westernized ideas pushed into my brain day in and day out. When I get home, I only get it when my mom and dad shout at me or when there's a lecture given to us all when you go to the *gurdwara* [temple]. . . . I mean . . . you get pulled

between two ways of life. . . . I mean the thing is that really bugs me, you can't be religious and be Westernized. You have to be . . . religious or be Westernized. *You can't have both of two worlds.* And if you do, then it's hard. I mean, I try. I think I've got both of two worlds, and I've done it quite well, in the sense that, you know, I've got friends which are boys. (Emphasis added)

Amrit expresses a feeling commonly shared by young Sikhs that they are being pulled between two ways of life—between two worlds that are separate and mutually exclusive—and that it is hard to "have both of two worlds." I began this account with a description of activities taking place in Amrit's house on a quite ordinary day, one like many I shared with her. My depiction intentionally highlights an obvious point, namely how cultural influences, "English" and "Indian," are interwoven in the taken-for-granted fabric of her daily life. In her choice of clothing, food, in the television programs she watches, and in the styles she and her family select in decorating their home, life in England is permeated with signs and symbols, images and influences demonstrating how cultural boundaries can become blurred due to the forces of advanced Western capitalism, or "modernity."[2]

The complexity of this pattern of cultural mixing is distinctively apparent in the development of popular music styles. As a member of a Bengali band Joi-Bangla explained influences in his music to an interviewer with the British magazine, *The Face:*

At that point we were mixing up James Brown and Bengali music. We're not like our parents. We've lived here, and we've been influenced by things outside our community. The music we make is always going to use traditional sounds with technology in dance styles. But it's not just Bengali sounds, we use music from all over the world, mixing it up to make it sound how we want it to sound. (Allen 1992:108)

The "world sounds" this particular band incorporates into their musical style include "Celtic singers, Moroccan pipes and sitars."

This brings me to the central problem I wish to address in this paper. If the cultural influences within the daily lives of second-generation Sikhs are multiple and varied, what leads them to feel torn between *two* separate worlds? And what does this tell us about the process of cultural production and identity formation?

On the surface, it might seem obvious that Amrit's dichotomous worldview stems from a predicament characterized in innumerable studies on the subject of ethnicity as "culture conflict." Studies such as Roger Ballard's of South Asians in Britain in the 1970s describe how the children of the settler generation are caught between two cultures, two contradictory sets of demands that they encounter at school and at home. As Ballard explains:

> Children of South Asian origin in Britain are certainly exposed to, and participate in, two very different cultural worlds. At home parents expect conformity to the norms of co-operation, respect and familial loyalty. . . . At school, however, children are exposed to a wholly contrary set of values and expectations. . . . As a result of the very fundamental contradictions between these two worlds, many young Asians feel themselves to be faced with acute dilemmas as to how they should organize their lives. However, most have long since learned to cope with these contradictions by switching their modes of behaviour depending on the context in which they find themselves. (Ballard 1982:195–96)

Ballard's analysis is both cogently descriptive and accurate in its representation of a fundamental aspect of the experience of second-generation British-Sikhs. What Amrit's words clearly suggest is her own awareness of these contradictory demands in her life. I propose that these contradictions—and the sets of oppositions such as Indian/English, traditional/modern, black/white to which they conceptually correspond—each exist at the level of ideology as objectified forms of culture abstracted from the more fluid, ambiguous, and plural processes of cultural production that occur in daily life.[3]

What young British-Sikhs encounter are two contrasting ideologies, two sets of dominant ideas or conceptions of the social world; the first I will refer to as the ideology of family honor, and the second, the ideology of British nationalism or British cultural purity. Each of these ideologies in different ways serves to reify a particular cultural order, a set of hierarchical values and standards. Each reflects a commonly shared desire for social wholeness, a desire to impose order and boundaries in the face of everyday encounters in a world of cultural flow and flux—in other words, the desire to preserve and perpetuate a fixed communal identity within communities experiencing a great deal of social and cultural change. As conservative forces—as versions of "invented traditions"—they attempt to halt the forward march of social and cultural change. Cultural forms or traditions, however, do not exist separate from the relations of power they support. To maintain the status quo is to maintain the relations of authority and the distinctions of sameness and difference (or social inequality) by means of which a dominant group strives to control social power.

In the sections that follow I describe the way in which these two ideologies support existing status hierarchies—the relations of class and racial inequality in British society, and the rankings of prestige and honor in the Sikh communities—and how the latter is subsummed by the former, the dominant forces of stratification in British society.

The majority of the Sikhs at Grange Hill High have been in English schools all their lives. They have grown accustomed to the rhythms, restrictions, and rewards of daily life at school. They speak English fluently and comfortably—often with broad Yorkshire accents. They are conversant in important teenage topics such as pop music and the latest episode of *Dallas* or *Dynasty*. They share similar likes and dislikes of popular and despised teachers. And the more ambitious among them (who are in relatively high number) worry obsessively about their performance in exams. Sikhs, like white middle-class English students, are products of the English educational system. But what, in fact, does it mean to be a product of the school?

My analytic framework is founded on the premise that schools as educating institutions (institutions of cultural transmission and socialization) are, in Corrigan's words, "productive—differentially productive—of subjectivities, or social identities" (1937:31; see also Foucault 1979:178).[5] Schools attempt to fix subjectivities, to regulate, normalize, stratify, punish, reward, and thereby marginalize possible forms of human diversity: "to make difference equal disadvantage." Schools subject individuals to what Foucault has termed the normalizing judgment of disciplinary power, in the form of "micropenalities," or implicit control over the basic elements of everyday life: orientations to such things as time, activities, types of behavior, forms of speech, bodily gestures and hygiene, and sexuality (Foucault 1979:178).

At school, British-Sikhs confront the contradictions between the promises of the liberal ideology of meritocracy and the limiting boundaries of race and class differences. The ideology of meritocracy enshrined in official British educational policies asserts that "able" individuals, regardless of their class, gender, or racial status, should be guaranteed the equal opportunity to achieve academic success. In practice, however, British-Sikhs encounter the effects of what Gilroy (1987) and others have defined as the "new cultural racism."[4] This form of cultural racism is implicit in what I have called the ideology of British cultural purity, a form of nationalism that associates legitimate national belonging with the possession of what is defined as the pure and essential British (in fact, English) culture, heritage, and communal identity. This ideology represents a British culture frozen in time and projected back to a historical past beyond the genealogical reach of Britain's most recent black citizens. In this way, according to Gilroy, black cultures and white cultures are assumed to be absolute and "mutually impermeable expressions of racial and national identity" (1987:61). A critical aspect of this ideological formation, however, is that while cultures are viewed as mutually impermeable, individuals are believed to be capable of cultural change and are encouraged to reject their inferior cultures and become absorbed as much as possible in the superior culture of the British. If individuals choose not to assimilate and to assert their cultural difference instead, then, the logic goes, they have only themselves to blame for their inferior status in British society. This rationalization, in the minds of many, serves to justify and legitimate the collective marginalization of those who are defined as Other, or as not authentically British.

At school, British-Sikhs are marginalized collectively as Other in relation to the dominant white middle-class culture and social order in the school. The most significant way "Asians" cross the cultural-racial barrier of "Other" to become accepted in the dominant culture of the school is through academic achievement—by displaying middle-class skills and orientations in their academic work.[5] Mrs. Pound, an English teacher, characterizes academically successful Asian students as those who no longer *seem* Asian.

> This is the other thing, isn't it, that the kids who are in the top set are largely middle class Asian kids and, they've taken on so much of our culture that they think like the rest of the class. And in poetry discussions particularly now, I give them the poem . . . and I put them in groups and I say, I want you to talk about it . . . And the Asian kid in the top sets is exactly like the middle class English kids, it is class rather than ah, culture. And in the top set that I have, well certainly two, Ravinder and Kamaljit, I don't think their culture comes into it. I don't feel that they're in any way Indian kids. They're just kids like everybody else.

Mrs. Pound's analysis underscores a critical dilemma faced by racial-minority (as well as working-class) students. Success in school according to middle-class standards requires that students assimilate to middle-class culture. "Achievement," as Mrs. Pound describes, is marked by how "un-Asian" Asian children seem (or how "un–working class" working-class children seem). Ravinder and Kamaljit blend in with the middle-class students because they are "able"—they possess the ability to choose to give up a part of themselves, their "Asianness," in order to seem more English, and therefore, middle class.

The processes that marginalize difference work in subtle ways. At school certain standards are approved and rewarded over others: those demonstrating independent thinking, confident and assertive self-presentation, self-direction, and individual autonomy are highly regarded. Sikh children are trained at home, however, to subsume individual concerns within the greater needs and interests of the family unit and to show their respect to elders in their silences. The social value of their mother tongue is countered by a school policy that refuses to incorporate exam-level classes in Punjabi into the main timetable and instead ghettoizes these lessons, scheduling them before and after school, or at the margins of the legitimate school day. The emphasis in university applications on participation in extracurricular activities as a sign of student initiative discriminates against the Asian girls who are only allowed to attend such activities when they are related to their course work.

In addition to the contradictory forces British-Sikhs encounter at school, these young people also face conflicting sets of demands in their families and in their communities. As I noted above, these conflicts are related to the ideology of family honor and to the structure of status and prestige that this ideology supports. I turn now to an analysis of these processes of cultural production within the Sikh communities.

Not surprisingly, the most important goals of most Sikh parents in Britain are to see that their children are well educated and to ensure that they marry into the right families. These aspirations, in and of themselves, seem quite typical for parents in general, and especially for a first generation of settlers in a new country offering new opportunities. What is fascinating about their concerns, however, is how these goals are culturally constituted—how the importance of an education takes on particular meanings in the lives of Sikhs in Britain.

An English education signifies a myriad of meanings for members of the settler generation of Sikhs. First, education is seen as a way out of racial discrimination and as a way up the social ladder to a better life, ideally in a professional job that will bring social independence, social status, as well as a lucrative income. Second, as a source for increased income and status, an educational qualification serves as a sort of commodity in Sikh status communities, primarily in the market for marriages. Marriage advertisements found in the "Matrimonial" section of a Punjabi diaspora newspaper distributed internationally illustrate this phenomenon quite explicitly.

> Sought a suitable match for a clean shaven Jat Sikh Doctor 28 yrs. of age, 5'8" tall with fair complexion. He graduated in MB CH.B from Britain and belongs to an educated and well settled family in U.K. The girl must be pretty and most preferably a Pharmacist or Lawyer or a person of that Calibre.

> Educated Jat Sikh parents seek suitable match for their 22 yrs. old, 5'4" tall, British born daughter. She appreciates both Indian and Western cultures and has 'O' levels, 9, a diploma in business studies . . . has taken a Secretarial Course, [and is] now working for the Civil Service. Boy should preferably be clean shaven and suitably qualified.

> Suitable match required for a pretty Jat Sikh girl, Barrister, 5'7" aged 29, has a fine balance of modern and conservative views; very domesticated, kind, loving and faithful; from a very respected and educated family.

How did anthropologists determine social distinctions before the invention of personals? These examples and others share a number of obvious similarities, and do, in fact, reflect markers of social value I also found applied in practices of marriage making. Educational qualifications and job status are important criteria in the marriage market, as are religion, caste membership, age, attractiveness (often qualified as beauty in a woman and whether a man wears the signs of the Sikh faith, the turban, unshorn hair, and beard), whether one is "modern" or "Indian" in one's views and lifestyle, and finally, whether the family is "well settled" or "respectable."

Social status and prestige, within Sikh communities, are based upon distinctions such as wealth, education, and occupation—markers of class position that resonate with class distinctions in British society more generally, yet have a decidedly Punjabi slant, in terms of the professions selectively esteemed, notably medicine, pharmacy, law, and accountancy. But in addition, and sometimes in opposition to these markers of individual achievement, is the supreme concern among Sikhs with family honor, or *izzat*. Family honor is a status possessed collectively. It is "respected" or "ruined" in social transactions, markedly those involving unmarried daughters. Amrit quite eloquently explains her sense of the meaning of family respect and honor:

> The thing is, English girls I know, respect and honor comes to them through earning it through the job they do, through whatever they do, they're not born with it. And if they respect their mom and dad, it's not . . . because they give birth to them, [that] doesn't mean anything to them. It's just human beings, and it just happens that you give birth to them. But with an Asian girl, because it's your mom and dad, you respect them, in the sense that from birth, your mom and dad are everything, honor and respect them. . . . A guy is given it, but it's not shown. He can lose his respect and honor and nothing bother[s] him family-wise. No one will look at the family and say, "Well, that boy does that." But if a girl does it, that's it, bad name for the family, whole life ruined.
>
> For a Sikh woman, she as a person, is the pole of the family . . . in the sense that she holds it up. If the pole breaks, the whole thing breaks. . . . She has been given a gift from God to bear children, which no man can touch. And the fact that they've been given the purity until they're married, that has a lot to do with respect and honor. You respect a woman who hasn't been touched by a man. . . . You know, its sort of like, her virginity is like a gift given, and if a woman can hold that, you know she's strong.

And to give it to her husband, you know, is the utmost thing a woman can do, you know, in our religion. You know, and to break that, there's no point of a woman existing if she does that.

Family honor is central to options for marrying children into good families. Marriage is a joining of families through the children who are married. Sikhs marry ideally within the same caste and with others of the Sikh faith. Caste membership, however, can override religious divisions between Punjabi Hindus and Punjabi Sikhs. It is the ties created through the institution of marriage that serve to perpetuate these boundaries of caste, class, and social status within and between Sikh communities. The ideology of family honor, in this way, is deeply tied to the reproduction of the Sikh family and consequently of Sikh status systems in Britain.

The ideology of family honor together with processes of sociocultural reproduction find their expression as they are embodied, literally, within restrictions and disciplinary judgments and actions focused toward controlling female sexuality—toward protecting the "gift" of female purity and virginity until it can be given away at marriage. The bodies of unmarried women, as I will demonstrate, are the sites upon which the dynamic struggles of sociocultural reproduction within Sikh communities are fought.

Sikh teenagers, in the routines of their daily activities, move through a number of different social contexts. Each of these contexts can be divided analytically into a particular space—a home, a school, a shopping arcade, or a temple—in which are found specific kinds of people, networks of relations, and styles of interacting. I will refer to these socially inhabited spaces as *cultural fields*. Cultural fields exist as "relatively autonomous social microcosms," each composed of constellations of power and authority, cultural competencies and influences that are "specific and irreducible to those that regulate other fields" (Bourdieu and Wacquant 1992:97–98). The regularities of routine practices in a cultural field both reproduce and create cultural expectations for bodily gestures and dress, for appropriate manners and signs of respect between the generations and the sexes, as well as the cultural knowledge people use to interpret social interactions.

The shifts in the relations of power and culture from one cultural field to the next provide varying opportunities for second generations to "play" with cultural identities. In each cultural field, differing forms of cultural production are at work, mediating the effects of the ideological forces of family honor and British cultural purity. As British-Sikhs participate within these different cultural fields, they create, not one unitary cultural identity, but rather multiple cultural identities that acquire situationally specific meanings and forms.[6]

Sikh young people conceive of themselves as neither completely Indian nor English. They possess a fragmented consciousness. As the title of my essay, a quotation, illustrates, second-generation Sikhs believe, with amazing consistency, that there is "a time to act Indian and a time to act English." And, I contend that there is a great deal of time for them to play with identities that lie somewhere in between.

This experience of living in "both of two worlds," or their embodiment of a fragmented consciousness, emerges from their everyday experience in different cultural fields. Together these cultural fields constitute a cultural landscape that becomes inscribed in the consciousness of the young people who move within and between these cultural fields. Sikh teenagers imagine this cultural landscape, or the relation between the various cultural fields, in terms of their perception of the "restrictions" or "freedoms," the opportunities for different types of activities, within each cultural field. Second-generation Sikhs symbolically order or map this cultural landscape both geographically and bodily in correspondence to the way cultural identities are signified and practiced in these fields. These practices are marked to a large degree in the form of restrictions placed on women's bodies and women's movements and on the interactions between unmarried youths.

The bodily and geographical mapping of their cultural landscape, or the fashioning of situational identities, instills in these young people a fragmented consciousness. I use this term to stress that their experiences can not be explained adequately by a simple assessment that these teenagers are bicultural. Certainly it could be argued that they are partially versed in two cultures, as they are partially fluent in two languages, often less so in Punjabi. But I think this way of framing the issue only serves to reify the concept of culture. Models of biculturalism or of cultural conflict tend to underestimate the effects of power and ideology as well as the influences of other forms of culture, leaving open the question of how culture is produced and experienced in everyday practice.

The imagined cultural landscape, shared by Sikh girls and boys alike, encompasses five cultural fields. They conceive of these fields (together with the forms of dress, activities, and modes of gender relations associated with them) as if located on a continuum joining the opposition they construct between things "traditional," "backward," or "Indian," and "modern," "Western," "educated," or "English." In order from "Indian" to "English," these cultural fields include the Sikh *gurdwara* or temple, home, town (or the shopping arcade in Leeds city center), school, and "English nightlife."

The Sikh temple is seen as the place where one is most completely and authentically Indian. Girls always come dressed in their "Indian suits" or *shalwar-kameez*, wear their hair uncut (or looking as uncut as possible) and tied back in a braid, never wear makeup, and never think of talking to boys—who in any case are safely seated in a separate side of the room during the religious ritual. The watchful gaze of cousins, aunts, and others provides a powerful form of social control within this cultural field, and any boundary transgression is immediately noted and entered into the stream of gossip that circulates within the *gurdwara* communities.

It is critical to note, however, that in this as well as other cultural fields, it is the signs and practices, transactions and interactions, that constitute the cultural field, not simply its location in a particular locale, such as the *gurdwara*. The relationship between a space and a cultural field is never natural or preexisting; rather a space becomes a cultural place as it is "habituated or deeply inscribed in everyday routine," as lived in culture (Comaroff and Comaroff 1991:25). A striking example of this relationship is how, in the context of wedding parties, the cultural field most regularly found at the *gurdwara* expands to fill the back room of a local pub, where the same networks of relations and interactions are in play during the wedding dinner and disco, events that are becoming quite extravagant affairs.

Within each of these cultural fields there is room for symbolic play. Some of the more restricted Sikh girls, for instance, express their creativity in playing with possibilities for Westernizing the Indian outfits they make to wear on occasions at the *gurdwara* and especially to weddings. When I asked Jaspir, a Sikh teenager from a less-restricted home, why Asians girls seemed to be continually organizing fashion shows, she explained,

> The thing is, you've got to ask many Asian girls what do they do on an evening. And, they don't do anything, they watch TV, do a bit of cooking, and that's it. And the next best thing they can do is go to temple, or make clothes. And the latest thing, well it's been for a long time, is to get really really fashionable. In the sense of your Indian wear. Make a sort of simple, tight-fitting dress, V neck, you know short sleeved, two massive splits at the sides . . . let's get a bit more Westernized, let's have different styles, you know the back wing, you know the low cut, the back that splits at different places, little buttons here, a bit of flowers here, a bit of bows here and there, and change. Change your colors. Don't have all one-piece suit in the sense of all one color. Change a bit. Or buy a dress and then put a different color pajama on top. Change, that's what it is really. Just make sure your body's covered.

Home is the second cultural field in which young Sikhs are aware of "acting Indian." They speak Punjabi with their parents, particularly with their mothers, who frequently do not speak English (preserving themselves as a model of Indianness until the children leave the home, when they typically enroll in English lessons). Some girls are required to change into their Indian suits, and a very "Indian" code of child-parent interaction is expected and practiced. The forces for cultural production, pressures to pass on ways of being in and understanding the world, create constraints and, in most cases, provide a great deal of family security, closeness, and concern.

Many Sikh girls, and all Sikh boys at Grange Hill High, are allowed to go by bus with a same-sex friend into the city center to shop during daytime hours. The shops lining the maze of market arcades in the Leeds city center offer as many opportunities for "fashioning identities" as the purses of these youngsters will allow them to consume. Here British-Sikhs feel they have the freedom to "act English," but not without caution. For town is frequented by aunts and uncles, Asian taxi drivers and market-stall keepers, all, they believe, on the watch for young and unmarried boundary transgressors. Therefore, to act too English is to risk being seen and found out. So, while girls wear English dress, it usually remains modest, the makeup light, and the meetings with boyfriends, if they occur, are tentative, extremely secretive, and, therefore, all the more exciting.

School is the context where the majority of Sikh young people feel "the most English," for, removed from the gaze of their parents, they feel free to be, as Rabinder phrased it, "what they want to be":

> Well, I think at school you're mostly sort of Westernized or English, but when you're at home you're more like what your parents want you to be. At school it's what you want to be. They can't see what you are here, and they think you are what they see at home. They don't see this side of us.

Their world at school is an English world: they interact with English friends and engage in English activities, but only during schooltime. Some girls have been known to bring along an entirely different outfit to wear in school. Once inside the school walls, the outfit is changed with the cultural context and orientation: on goes the makeup and down, free, goes the hair. And, most importantly, at school, boys become friends. Girls can talk to boys and boys to girls. And things can develop, or not, from there.[7] Harjit and Bobby, two Sikh boys at Grange Hill High, sense that the sudden freedom girls experience at school can overwhelm some Asian girls, distracting them from their studies. In this way, they argue, the restrictions placed on girls at home can work to disadvantage them in coping at school.

> **B:** The parents are not there, just the kids. . . . [Some girls] take advantage of it, and they flirt with anyone. And I think that's over the line. Because they're really just doing it because they happen to suddenly get a lot of freedom, and they don't know what to do with it.
> **H:** I think they have to get out, because they're so deprived of it, they

have to use the freedom that they've been given.

B: They go over the top. . . . If you notice, a lot of these Asian girls when they go into the sixth form find there's so much freedom, than say from when they were doing O-levels, 'cause you get free lessons. You get more chance to talk with other people, you know, other boys, other girls. . . . And they tend to sort of let everything loose all at once. And it's not until later on in the upper sixth when they realize that there other things much more better and they seem to cool down.

H: But sometimes it's too far, it's too late. They've socialized a lot more in school, and when it comes to more socializing than studying, when it comes to the exams, it's too late. I think that's unfair to Asian girls. I mean, to the boys, we are given a certain amount of freedom, and it builds up for us, and it's not as much affected toward our exams.

The final cultural field, "English nightlife," is a cultural world Sikh girls typically hear a lot about but do not experience firsthand. Sikh girls, in most cases, are not allowed out at night—they do not attend social functions at school, nor do they go out on their own, unaccompanied by family members, to parties or to pubs, as white English girls do. The consequences for the girls who do enter this very English field, either with or without parental permission, if "seen," can be serious, both for them and for their family's name and honor. Jaspir, nineteen years old and attending a further-education college while still living at home, describes her experiences of "going out," as well as her parents' reaction:

The issue with my parents is what people think of me if they see me. To my mum, if I'm in a nightclub, she'll say, look, if you're out in an evening at a nightclub and some Indian person sees you, what are they going to think? They're going to think bad, straight away. Or if you walk into a pub, regardless of whether you drink coke or not, as soon as you walk into a pub, it's got a little image of itself for being a pub, you could have been sweet and innocent, you could have stayed there two seconds, it doesn't matter; once you walk in, you're labeled. It does bother my mom a lot, in the sense that she'll say, look, everybody will probably know about you walking out. How am I going to marry you? They'll say, look, she walks around, she's been around all parts of Leeds and everything. She hasn't lived a sheltered life. And another issue is, if you haven't lived a sheltered life about going out, then they think immediately with boys. They'll think you've associated somewhere along the line with boys. And, just one thing leads to another thing, you know.

Within the Sikh communities in Leeds, people watch where unmarried teenagers go and what they do, and they gossip about those whose actions cross the line or go too far, transcending the boundaries of Sikh respectability and honor. Sikh talk about what individuals do can either "respect" or "ruin" a family's honor. When people watch and gossip, they impose a set of moral, physical, and behavioral constraints that serve as a powerful form of social control—a conservative force for social and cultural reproduction—and one that bridges the boundaries of the individual family unit. Sikh teenagers, sounding like typical teenagers while voicing specific frustrations as British-Sikhs, constantly complained, as one young man Jatinder does here, about their parents' participation in this process:

> All Asian parents will say, "We don't really care if you talk to girls or whatever. . . . It's what other parents say." That's what they're worried about is what other people say, but it's like one big circle because everyone else is worried about what their parents will say . . . it's a bit like catch-22, really.

Sikh teenagers manage the cultural conflicts in their lives by mapping their cultural selves onto an imagined cultural landscape, by associating different aspects of their fragmented consciousness with distinctive cultural fields. To end the analysis here, however, would not allow us to understand how British-Sikhs navigate this landscape, or how they interpret and solve their problems and make difficult choices concerning how they will live their lives. Their choices are not directly determined by the cultural forms and forces imposed upon them. Rather, Sikhs act and react, fashioning their identities creatively, within the ambiguous space between their British and Sikh selves.

The choices they make can vary considerably. For the more academically able Sikh students, higher education, particularly at an institution away from home, provides a way out, a context for getting out and enjoying themselves. At university some young people make "love matches" and successfully evade the arranged marriage procedures—provided the potential spouse fits the criteria of caste, family status, and religion. Educational qualifications and economic independence are sources of leverage for young people in negotiating their marital options with their families.

The choice to have sex before marriage, however, is the ultimate boundary transgression, one that can create serious internal conflicts for a girl, causing her to lie, both to herself and to her family. When I asked Jaspir how girls manage if they do have sex before marriage, she said:

> They lie. . . . Internally they're dead. . . . They're dead in the sense that when it comes to actually getting married, they fake it. I know a lot of girls who have said, "Oh, I was a virgin when I got married," since they faked it and pretended it was the first time. And I know a lot, I know a couple of girls who literally blocked it out of their minds. And to this day they think they are virgins, even though we know, and the guys they've done it with know, that they're not. . . . To them to do that, right, is a big thing, and if

it doesn't work out, in the sense of never falling in love, the guy leaves them, the only way they can forget about that, they have to block it out, because if they're faced with it everyday, they won't be able to cope because they've broken a vow, which when they're little, they've been told they can't do. They've got to save it for one person, so they broke it. So they think the only way they can cope is to say, all right, it never happened.

Stories of Asian girls running away to London in search of freedom or independence from despotic parents are favorites with the British media. Familial oppression exists, and Asian girls do run away. But for most Sikh girls, the option of running away is, in the words of Rabinder and Sajdha, "the worst."

> **R:** I think that's the worst. That's the worst.
>
> **S:** You do respect your parents. We do know it's their honor, but that's the last thing you can do is hurt them in that way. I think of writing notes, "I'm running away, but it's not for a boy" (laugh). 'Cause usually girls do run away because they want to marry someone who the parents don't want to. But if I ran away, I wouldn't run away for that. I'd run away to get away from them.
>
> **R:** To get you freedom for yourself.
>
> **S:** But I wouldn't run away.
>
> **R:** You couldn't. I don't think I could, I wouldn't. I couldn't. It's just how I feel for them. I mean, okay, even my relatives all my relations would suddenly be cut. I mean I'd never have any of them again. I'd be looked down on. I would hate that. I couldn't live with it. I mean, okay, I say that they don't understand me, but I couldn't live without my parents. . . . I mean, our parents, even though they don't understand us, but they still mean a lot to us. They are a great deal to us, I mean in their different ways, but they still are our parents.

To successfully have "both of two worlds," young Sikh women must maintain certain boundaries that, if crossed, lead to serious consequences: the severing of family ties. In spite of their personal dreams, fantasies, or desires, most Sikh boys and girls work hard to protect their family honor. While these efforts often involve deceptions of various kinds, the loyalty to one's parents and to one's extended family remains paramount in their hearts and minds. Sikh teenagers consistently told me that they would trust their parents to "assist" their marriages before they would trust an English love match, a form of marriage that seemed, statistically, more apt to lead to divorce.

For the most part, Sikh teenagers do not approach decision making as an individual or personal process requiring them to choose independently from among the options available to them; rather, they make sense of their choices in relation to the consequences their decisions will have for the family as a whole. Sikh young people will routinely suppress their personal desires to protect the family's well-being and to nurture the strong family attachments they cherish. Their fragmented conscious-ness, in other words, has a singularly collective orientation.

Having "both of two worlds," for second-generation Sikhs, means deciding the time (and I might now add the "space") to act "English" and the time to act "Indian." Yet, the choice to embrace an "English" or an "Indian" identity is never a free choice between two equal statuses or identifications. For the boundary between "English" and "Indian" is ultimately immutable. It is a boundary drawn in the relations of dom-ination and subordination in British society and is justified in the minds of many white British by the sentiments and images of cultural racism. Markers of "Asian" racial and cultural inferiority have been translated into signs of class inequality. To choose to remain "too Indian" has con-sequences of its own. To seem "too Indian" (in dress, lifestyle, lan-guage, or manner) is to accept the markers of an inferior status, or to choose to be what the denigrating signs of race and class imply that "Asians" are, namely "immigrants" and "Pakis."

The opposition between modern-educated-English and traditional-backward-Indian reflects the polar extremities of a cultural racism plot-ted along the vertical axis of the British class structure. A large propor-tion of second-generation Sikhs are choosing to pursue upward mobility through their educational achievements. To achieve social mobility, to become members of the British middle class, requires that young Sikhs challenge the barriers of "racialized" class differences and transform themselves—distance themselves from the signs of their Asianness. Yet, to deny one's Sikh identity in an attempt to become English is to at-tempt to become what one never can be. It is this realization that under-lies Devinder's interpretation of what it means to become "too modern" or "too un-Asian" in the process of being educated in Britain. She be-lieves that her fellow Asian classmates at university, like her uncles, are falling into this trap.

> They're all very modern. They've totally lost their religion and their own— you know—they don't think of it the way I do. They're like my uncles, all of them. You see, I've seen the trap my uncles led themselves into, and I can see these kids doing the same. They're trying to be something they're not, without giving in and really being themselves. They're trying to live another life. But then, you see, the problem with my family is rather than standing up to it, they—my uncles definitely—they just took the easy way out and tried to change themselves to fit in. My uncle doesn't look Indian. He looks more English, more Greek, as my friends say. . . . I think if you want to achieve real success in this country, you can't let them bully you. I think they respect you more if you stick to your own.

Caught between two worlds, within the ambivalent space between British self and Asian Other, many Sikhs have told me they feel they live two lives. At home they are comfortable with their British-Sikh selves and the security of family life. But, when they step outside this world, they see their families through the gaze of their assimilated selves, and they are ashamed of the embarrassment they feel. In assimilating, in transforming themselves through education, and consequently, in their identification with the hegemonic British "us," as these final words from Devinder painfully depict, they participate in their own subjugation.

I've got real problems because I'd love my friends to meet my parents and my mum can't speak English. And that I feel they're going to think, you know, she's been here so long, why the hell can't she speak English. . . . I could explain it. I'm sure they'd understand, but I'm almost afraid to explain it. . . . I mean, it's not as if I'm not working with Indian clients. I am. And so are they. And half the time when they can't speak English, it's a real joke with a lot of them. You see what I mean. I'm sure they don't mean it that way. But I feel they'd be embarrassed when an Indian lady comes in, dressed in Indian gear, not being able to speak a word of English. It doesn't look right. It just doesn't—it's an embarrassment. Because, they say if people are living in our country surely they should make the effort to learn the language.

"You see, the thing is," she concludes, "there are too many Indians in this country."

The choices of identity and of cultural identification, for second-generation Sikhs, are crafted out of the constraints and possibilities produced in the ambiguous spaces of power and culture, between the contextually shifting boundaries of class, race, gender, and family honor. British-Sikhs are attempting to create a new culture by negotiating the cultures of school and of home—by attempting to have "both of two worlds." Yet in choosing to become educated, and in challenging the contradictions within the liberal ideology of meritocracy in British schools, young Sikhs are choosing to live their lives at the boundaries of both worlds. Considered from the viewpoint of second-generation British-Sikhs, the right to *a* cultural identity, like all that is solid in modernity, "melts into air."

NOTES

The research for this study was supported by fellowships from the Fulbright and the Spencer Foundations. For their careful reading and useful comments on various drafts of this paper I wish to thank Diane Mines, Bernard Cohn, John Comaroff, Norma Field, Jean Lave, Sharon Stephens, and Terence Turner.

My project benefited greatly from prior research on Sikh communities in Britain, particularly Roger Ballard and Catherine Ballard's studies (1977) of the Sikh communities in Leeds, Parminder Bhachu's ethnography focusing on Ramgarhia Sikhs from East Africa (1985), and Arthur Helweg's work (1986) with Jat Sikhs in Gravesend in Kent.

1. See Roger Ballard (1989) for a general historical account of the stages of Sikh settlement in Britain, as well as Parminder Bhachu (1985) for an analysis of the immigration of East African Ramgarhia Sikhs.

2. Interest in the concepts of modernity and identity, and on the related topic of nationalism and cultural "flows" and boundaries, is stimulating growth in a rapidly expanding body of literature. It is beyond the scope and intent of this essay to discuss the merits of theories associated with these concepts. My analysis, however, incorporates ideas from works that I find important and suggestive, including Appadurai (1990), Berman (1982), Foster (1991), Gilroy (1987), Hannerz (1989), Harvey (1989), Marcus (1992), Moore (1989), B. Williams (1991), and Zukin (1992).

3. My use of the concept of ideology is similar to what the Comaroffs, in part quoting R. Williams (1977:109), have defined as "an articulated system of meanings, values, and beliefs of a kind that can be abstracted as [the] 'worldview' of any social grouping. Borne in explicit manifestos and everyday practices . . . this worldview may be more or less internally systematic, more or less assertively coherent in its outward forms. But, as long as it exists, it provides an organizing scheme for collective symbolic production" (Comaroff and Comaroff 1991:24).

4. The concept of cultural racism was first coined by Barker (1981) to refer to a recent shift in the focus of racist ideologies from biological to cultural differences. As Gilroy (1987:43) explains, the novelty of this form of racism "lies in the capacity to link discourses of patriotism, nationalism, xenophobia, Englishness, Britishness, militarism and gender difference into a complex system which gives 'race' its contemporary meaning. These themes combine to provide a definition of 'race' in terms of culture and identity. . . . 'Race' differences are displayed in culture which is reproduced in educational institutions and, above all, in family life. Families are therefore not only the nation in microcosm, its key components, but act as the means to turn social processes into natural, instinctive ones."

5. "Asian" is a British term that glosses over the differences between groups from the South Asian subcontinent by subsuming these peoples under one category, "Asian." British-Sikhs and others defined as "Asian" have appropriated this category as one aspect of their identities since it reflects their collective experiences in relation to British racism.

6. Lave and Wenger (1991) provide a powerful theoretical formulation of how meaning is produced within a particular field of social interaction. Lave's work has creatively shaped a framework for studying social learning within situated practices, one that continues to influence the focus of my own analyses.

7. For British-Sikhs of high-school age, "friendship" with members of the opposite sex still involves interacting as acquaintances in groups mainly com-

prised of Asians. When dating does occur, Asian girls often become interested in Asian boys (not necessarily of the same religion or caste), and Asian boys fancy either Asian or English girls. English girls, of course, are more accessible for dating since they are allowed the freedom to go out. The dating practices of Asian girls as well as interracial relationships are sensitive subjects of considerable complexity, issues I discuss in more detail in the larger study from which this account is taken.

REFERENCES

Allen, Vaughan, 1992, "Bhangramuffin," *Face* 44 (May):104–8.

Appadurai, Arjun, 1990, "Disjuncture and Difference in the Global Cultural Economy," *Public Culture* 2(2):1–24.

Ballard, Catherine, 1979, "Conflict, Continuity, and Change: Second-Generation South Asians," in Verity Saifullah Khan, ed., *Minority Families in Britain*, London, MacMillan, 108–29.

Ballard, Roger, 1982, "South Asian Families," in: Robert N. Rapoport et al., eds., *Families in Britain*, London, Routledge and Kegan Paul, 179–204.

———, 1989, "Differentiation and Disjunction Amongst the Sikhs in Britain," in N. Gerald Barrier and Verne A. Dusenbery, eds., *The Sikh Diaspora*, Columbia, Mo.: South Asia Publications, 200–34.

Ballard, Roger and Catherine Ballard, 1977, "The Sikhs," in J. L. Watson, ed., *Between Two Cultures*, London, Blackwell, 179–204.

Barker, Martin, 1981, *The New Racism*, London, Junction Books.

Berman, Martin, 1982, *All That's Solid Melts into Air: The Experience of Modernity*. New York, Simon and Schuster.

Bhachu, Parminder, 1985, *Twice Migrants: East African Sikh Settlers in Britain*, London, Tavistock.

Bourdieu, Pierre and Loic J. D. Wacquant, 1992, *An Invitation to Reflexive Sociology*, Chicago, University of Chicago Press.

Comaroff, Jean and John Comaroff, 1991, *Of Revelation and Revolution: Christianity, Colonialism, and Consciousness in South Africa*, vol. 1, Chicago, University of Chicago Press.

Corrigan, Philip, 1987, "In/Forming Schooling," in D. W. Livingstone, ed., *Critical Pedagogy and Cultural Power*, South Hadley, Mass., Bergin and Garvey, 17–40.

Das, Veena, 1992, "Ironic Negation and Satire: Children's Talk on Politics," paper presented at the conference "Children at Risk," Bergen, Norway, May.

Foster, Robert J., 1991, "Making National Cultures in the Global Ecumene," *Annual Review of Anthropology* 20:235–60.

Foucault, Michel, 1979, *Discipline and Punish: The Birth of the Prison*, trans. Alan Sheridan, New York, Vintage Books.

———, 1982, "The Subject and Power," *Critical Inquiry* 8 (summer): 777–95.

Gilroy, Paul, 1987, *There Ain't No Black in the Union Jack,* London, Unwin Hyman.

Hannerz, Ulf, 1989, "Notes on the Global Ecumene," *Public Culture* 1(2):66–75.

Harvey, David, 1989, *The Condition of Postmodernity: An Enquiry into the Origins of Cultural Change,* Oxford, Basil Blackwell.

Helweg, Arthur W., 1986, *Sikhs in England,* 2d. ed., Delhi, Oxford University Press.

Lave, Jean and Etienne Wenger, 1991, *Situated Learning: Legitimate Peripheral Participation,* Cambridge, Cambridge University Press.

Marcus, George, 1992, "Past, Present, and Emergent Identities," in Scott Lash and Jonathan Friedman, eds., *Modernity and Identity,* Oxford, Blackwell, 309–30.

Moore, Sally Falk, 1989, "The Production of Cultural Pluralism as a Process," *Public Culture* 1(2):26–48.

Stephens, Sharon, 1992, introductory statement, session "Children and the Politics of Culture," at the conference "Children at Risk," Bergen, Norway, May.

Williams, Brackette F., 1991, *Stains on My Name, War in My Veins: Guyana and the Politics of Cultural Struggle,* Durham, N.C., Duke University Press.

Williams, Patricia J., 1991, *The Alchemy of Race and Rights,* Cambridge, Mass., Harvard University Press.

Williams, Raymond, 1977, *Marxism and Literature,* London, Oxford University Press.

Zukin, Sharon, 1992, "Postmodern Urban Landscapes: Mapping Culture and Power," in Scott Lash and Jonathan Friedman, eds., *Modernity and Identity,* Oxford, Blackwell, 221–47.

CHAPTER 9

Second-Generation Noncitizens: Children of the Turkish Migrant Diaspora in Germany

RUTH MANDEL

IF NAMING IS POWER, then the young people discussed in this paper might best be seen as victims of their nomenclature. This population has been named with any number of titles: second generation, involuntary migrants, descendants of migrants, Turks, and *Gastarbeiterkinder* (guest worker children) are but a few. Notably, none of these names contain the terms *immigrant* or *ethnic*, as in, for example, "ethnic Turks." This absence, far from accidental or incidental, reflects the macropolitics of the foreigner policy of the Federal Republic of Germany.

The everyday psychology that Turkish children living in Germany internalize derives from the politics and cultures of two nations, Germany and Turkey. As the descendants of migrant workers who were recruited for their cheap labor in the 1960s, they occupy a cultural and political space that relegates them to the social and legal margins of both German and Turkish societies.

In this paper, I endeavor to show how some of the underlying processes that created this situation have come into being. I do this by examining the historical, political, and legal structures that shape the constraints and realities affecting this generation of Turks. In addition, I look at the interplay between these constraints and their encompassing cultural assumptions. In considering these multiple aspects, the paper argues that the children of migrant workers in many ways are victims of a set of systems stacked against them. The interconnected systems—social and cultural, educational, and economic and political systems—are shown actually to reinforce a status quo, serving to ensure that this group remains separate and unequal.

THE DISCOURSE OF RETURN AND THE "SECOND GENERATION"

One area where the interplay of these systems colludes is the discourse surrounding repatriation to Turkey. An analysis of this discourse illuminates the complex dynamics that make up the (psychological) identities of this generation of Turkish youth. During the course of fieldwork in West Germany and Turkey, I heard nearly identical declarations expressing the intention to return, voiced by both migrant adults as well as their children. The latter often were born, and chiefly bred, in Germany. What I came to understand as a master narrative, repeated endlessly by parents and children, helps to situate the dilemma faced by the second generation. Variants went like this:

> "We don't belong here in Germany, it is better to live in one's own country."
>
> "We are foreigners, strangers here."
>
> "In Germany we are not at home; Turkey is our home; we are Turks."
>
> "It's better to be in one's own homeland—we'll be returning there soon."

This paper will attempt to understand this ubiquitous recitation in light of the fact that the youthful narrators seldom if ever have seen this homeland, or, if so, only as a distant, dreamlike vacation land. Often they are far more fluent and literate in German, the language of the host country, than they are in their native Turkish. What does it mean that these children of the so-called second generation share in this master narrative, perpetuate it and consequently remain, in some sense, victims of its paradoxes and contradictions? The living out of the contradictions inherent in their predicament begins to make sense when we examine the role assigned to this group by German society. Especially relevant in this discussion will be German ideologies of citizen and state, of incorporation and of exclusion.

First, let us look at the term *second generation*. The term refers to Turkish citizens living in Germany who are the children of the original labor migrants. The very term marks them—it indicates that they are the second generation of *Turks;* they are not, therefore, Germans, despite the fact that Germany may indeed have been the land of their birth. As Wilpert (1988a:3) has pointed out, "[T]he Federal Republic of Germany does not recognize itself as a country of immigration, and thus there are neither first- nor second-generation immigrants, but strictly speaking either migrants or foreigners." However, two, and now three generations of resident noncitizens, foreign migrants and their descendants, have come of age in the margins of Germany's social fabric. They have carved for themselves a niche of de facto permanence despite the label they inhabit, as "second-generation" offspring of temporary guest workers, Gastarbeiter.

Even those few who have managed to acquire German nationality still are considered second-generation Turks. One such young man, barely out of his teens, but who had secured for himself a German passport, told me:

I want all the rights of everyone else. However, even though I now have a German passport, I am still a Turk. Because of German ideas about nationality, I cannot say that I am a German—I'm not. I'm a Turk, *zweite Generation,* second generation.

Thus the term, like that of Gastarbeiter, serves linguistically to delimit the social space inhabited by this population. And, of course, it is only a "population" by virtue of its being named as such. It includes, for example, the youth of several national origins. Despite the generalizable statements that can be made about certain commonalities, this "population" actually comprises extremely diverse individuals and groups with widely varied experiences, based on class, regions of both origin and present residence, gender, politics, and age.[1]

"THE BOAT IS FULL": THE TURKISH PROBLEM AND CO-CITIZENS

These children are the people who form the focus of Germany's "foreigner problem." And, as Wilpert (1988b:113) has pointed out, "[T]he 'problem' of the second generation is often viewed as a Turkish problem. . . . Slightly more than one-half of the almost one million foreign youths under the age of sixteen are of Turkish nationality." Thus, the "foreigner problem" generally is the euphemistic term for what is perceived as a Turkish problem. The most pressing dimension of this problem is the concern about the future of the youth of the second generation. Frequently called the "lost generation," they are portrayed as the possessors of no culture, as they are caught, or lost, between the two that are depicted as just out of their reach. They are seen as collectively having slipped between the cultural cracks, fallen between the social stools. This perception is reinforced in some of the research that attempts to measure the degrees of integration using quantitative, "objective" tools.

Just as this group of people is seen as a social and political problem by German society, they have become the object of inquiry for writers and researchers. Sometimes the works about them focus on specific traits, practices, or customs deemed by the authors to have either poetic or essential qualities. Often, these objects of study are marked simply as undifferentiated outsiders or foreigners—in German, one word, *Ausländer,* describes both. Some of the titles of social-science and journalistic articles and books on this subject include:

"Foreign Children in German Schools"
"Children without Future"
Oya: Foreign Homeland Turkey

"Respect the Elders, Love the Younger"

"Foreigners or Germans—Integration Problems of Greek, Yugoslav, and Turkish Population Groups"

"Role Conflicts of Foreign-Worker Children between Family and School"

"Factors That Influence School Behavior of Foreign Youth"

"Criminal Foreign-Worker Children? Structural Determinants of Delinquency"

"Turkish Youth—No Vocational Opportunities in Germany?"

"School Problems of Foreign Children"

The Bartered Bride

"Endlessly Disadvantaged? Toward the Social Integration of Foreign Children"

"Education of Foreign Children: Educational Goals and Cultural Outlook of Turkish Worker Families"

"Diseased Integration: Socialization Problems of Guest Workers and Their Children"

The list could go on for scores of pages. It is relevant to reiterate that the "foreigners" to whom many of these titles refer have resided in Germany most, if not all, of their lives. Also germane is the fact that not one of the mentioned, or hundreds of unmentioned titles, contains the word *immigrants*. There are few attempts to deforeignize them; however, it is arguable that until they lose their foreignness, the integration advocated by many of these books and articles will not be achieved.

The unfortunate state of these young people, sometimes referred to as involuntary migrants (since it was their parents' decision to migrate), is considered a result of their bad luck and poor timing, of having been shuttled back and forth throughout their childhoods, and as adolescents, between Turkey and Germany. But sometimes the distance traveled is no further than a few subway stops, a journey that takes a child between the heart of Kreuzberg, Berlin's "Turkish ghetto," and a German public school. The two environments are seen as irreconcilable, and this misfortune is blamed as the cause of their predicament. And it is this predicament that is used as an excuse for their alleged inability to integrate. Their contact with Turkey, or things Turkish, their having spent too much time in Turkic environments, has ill prepared them for successful lives in Germany. Tainted with the stain of what is often portrayed as the romantic *Morgenland*, the land of the morning or the Orient, they are by association identified with preenlightenment backwardness, despotism, Islam, fundamentalism, and more recently, summer holidays. In Germany, as regards migrants from Turkey, Orientalism is alive and well.

An underlying assumption permeating much of German society af-firms a fundamental, ontological difference between the "foreigners" and "us." If ever we/they, or us/them oppositions were germane, they are in this instance. Here, it is explicit not only in the calls for Turks to repatriate by right-wing politicians and neo-Nazis, whose rhetoric serves to separate an "us" from a "them." It is also apparent with the liberal do-gooders, those who see themselves in the forefront of proforeigner, civil-rights groups.

For example, an ecumenical coalition of progressive Protestant groups annually sponsors Intercultural Week (actually lasting over a month; cf. National Brotherhood Week). Oblivious to the inbuilt iro-nies and questionable implications, it is called *Woche der ausländischen Mitbürger*. This translates as "week of foreign co-citizens." The colloca-tion "foreign co-citizen," oxymoronic at best, further marks an already marked population in a way that full, unmarked citizens are not—Ger-man Protestants or Bavarians are not referred to as co-citizens. Thus, a simple prefix, deployed to denote innocent inclusion, instead brings at-tention to the fact that these are not true citizens, only ersatz, and, in effect, serves to further exclude them.[2]

As part of the annual foreign co-citizen week, over two hundred so-cial events, lectures, films, readings, exhibitions, concerts, street fairs, and worship services are held. Some of the events from the 1991 week included an exhibit of paintings by children, entitled "Are You Really So Different?"; a social afternoon, entitled "Tea with Foreigners"; a series of lectures (including "Is the Boat Full?" and "Children with No Fu-ture?"); readings by "foreign" authors (entitled, for example, "How I Feel under the Germans" and "Those Lost between Two Worlds"); an information exhibit about Germans "for foreigners"; a discussion about "War in the Cities: Turkish Youth Gangs in West Berlin"; viewing of a video, called "I Have Nothing against the Foreigners, but . . ."; and a concert called the "Sinti Swing." And, in the spirit of progressive con-troversy, a radio program (broadcast in 1992 on Sender Freies Berlin) dealing with the increased violence against foreigners, was called "Ter-ror, Totschlag, Turkenjagd" (Terror, murder, and Turk hunting). Again, as with the scientific literature, it is notable that the word *immi-grant* is avoided, and the people in question are seen as the "others" among us: the Turks in our midst.

Despite the often well-intentioned efforts on the part of the media, researchers, or the clergy, it sometimes seems as though by the very rhet-oric deployed, an implicitly segregationist discourse is set in place. Fur-thermore, this discourse reflects the official ideology and policy, which repeatedly makes claims that Germany is not an immigration country, that the boat is full. Thus, however well-meaning, these popular efforts barely camouflage the underlying social and legal structures that serve to separate this generation from the encompassing host society.

It is inconceivable to imagine that such immigration politics would not somehow find their way into the psychological lives of the children involved. Perhaps it is oversimplifying the point, but it would seem that by refusing to make the terminological leap, at least in the first instance, from "foreigner" to "immigrant," from the naively hypocritical "foreign co-citizen" to simply "citizen" (for those who are, and to ease the way for those who wish to be), the conceptual categories that now serve only to segregate, discriminate, alienate, and isolate could begin to be questioned.

Such a change is neither easy, nor forthcoming. With reference to voting rights for foreign denizens, two reporters in *Die Zeit* wrote, "It is unimaginable both in Karlsruhe and in Bonn that one can have German citizens of Turkish origin and Muslim religion" (quoted in Buruma 1992:18). And indeed, this is the case. A Turk who is a naturalized German citizen is, socially, still and always a Turk. One such recently naturalized German, a doctoral student who has lived in Germany twenty years, joked that no longer would Germans be able to express their xenophobia to him with the old phrase *Turken raus!* [Turks out!]. Now they would have to amend it: the new expression would be "Germans with Turkish origins out!"

Why are the descendants of persons of Turkish origin now resident in Germany necessarily migrants, not immigrants, and why are they designated co-citizens, not citizens? As mentioned, German politicians take pains to emphasize again and again that "the boat is full"; that "Germany is not an immigration country." This creed guides the shaping of *Ausländerpolitik*, foreigner politics, thus effectively precluding the guest workers from making that conceptual, or legal, quantum leap from being temporary workers to being immigrants.

With reference to citizenship, the answer is contained in the German constitution, which defines Germanness in terms of indigenous beliefs about racial ethnicity. Germanness is based on ancestry and native notions of blood—not birth, residence, or any set of objective criteria adding up to a right of naturalization. Instead, a "natural"—and hence naturalizable—German is one who can prove direct descent from a German who lived in 1937 boundaries defined by the Third Reich.

In practice this means, first, that monolingual Polish speakers from Poland whose proof of their genealogy meets the requirements may claim the automatic right to German citizenship and all the benefits it accrues. Ironically, this proof has sometimes taken the form of claimants' parents' membership papers in the Nazi party. By the same token, the second- and third-generation descendants of migrants from Turkey, born and educated in Germany, have no automatic right to become German citizens.[3] Even these young German-born Turks know full well that the boat is only too full for them—though not for select others. With this double standard, the fragments of the master narrative, quoted at the start of this paper, told to me by young Berliner children of Turkish parentage, begin to take on a deeper meaning. Their invocations of homeland and belonging, echoed in the myth of return, simply reflect the realpolitik of the host nation that refuses to make room for them.

TURKEY AND THE DILEMMAS OF REPATRIATION

As already mentioned, during the course of several years of research in both Germany and Turkey, I heard numerous migrants' stories, narrating their migration to Germany and their anticipated return to Turkey. Though by far most of the migrants and their families remain in Germany (many of them have been there for over a quarter century), the return migration to Turkey is rarely out of their plans. Thus, the return must be considered as part and parcel of the migratory cycle, despite the fact that most migrants have not repatriated. Some observers have called this seeming contradiction—of preparing for a perpetually postponed return—the myth of return. The myth of the final return retains a prominent place in the consciousness of many, if not most, migrants. For many, this "myth" of the future justifies the indignities of the present difficult situation.

Significantly, a sort of rehearsal for the final return unfolds annually, during the summer holiday, when hundreds of thousands of Turks in Europe return to their villages for a month's visit. A great deal of preparation goes into this voyage. First, the journey itself is perilous, and, in addition, the relatives and friends at home have, by now, high expectations of the "rich uncle in Germany." In order for the returning migrants to maintain their newly acquired high status, they must prove to those back home that they are successful. This they do both by conspicuous display, and by distribution of consumer items as gifts.

The vacationing children might treat Turkey as a sort of holiday village. This contrasts sharply with the tensions and alienation experienced by many of the second-generation youth upon permanent repatriation. Here, the problems only increase. First of all, the high expectations of the entire family of a happy homecoming generally are shattered. The returnees are labeled *alamanci*, or *alamanyali*, roughly equivalent to "German-ish," "German-like," "from Germany." After years of living with the stigma of *Ausländer*, foreigner, in Germany, this new appellation can be painful. Children regularly are taunted by their peers and find it difficult to fit in, to be accepted.

A twelve-year-old-boy in a provincial Anatolian town, "returned" the previous year, told me about his troubles. He had done very well in school in Germany, been at the top of his class, excelled especially in mathematics and had found his young "alternative" teachers friendly and supportive. He boasted that he even had used the informal vocative *du* with them. In Turkey, on the other hand, he repeatedly had found himself in trouble with his teachers, who had beaten him for unwitting insubordination (he was not accustomed, for example, to standing at attention in the formal, paramilitary atmosphere of many Turkish public schools). As a result of his ignorance in the ways of Turkish classroom behavior, his teachers had accused him of arrogance ("he thinks he's better than the rest, that he does not have to conform to the same rules") and labeled him a troublemaker. The older brother of a girl in his class to whom he had spoken several times also had given him a thrashing and warned him never to get near his sister again.

Nearby, an eighteen-year-old girl working in a tourist town, returned for two years, told me her story. Though she was very lucky to have found a job due to her fluency in German, at a luxury hotel not far from her village, she was troubled that no one in her village would associate with her. "They all assume that I am a loose woman, that because I lived in Germany I am like the Germans. The think that I am not a virgin, so people won't talk to me. I'll never find a husband, they think I'm a fallen woman—but I'm not," she assured me, sadly.

Returnee families in Istanbul often had problems with their children in schools, in part due to Turkey's woefully inadequate infrastructure to accommodate the needs of returnee children. The handful of special schools cannot begin to deal with the thousands who need language and other help. Many of the returnee children are illiterate in Turkish, and are, therefore, placed in classes with children half their age. Sometimes the school in Turkey never receives the German transcript, and so places the child in an inappropriate class. Desperate parents do not know where to turn and must suffer along with their children. Parents have their own troubles readjusting to life in Turkey after decades away. Financial and social problems are just some of the difficulties they might face. Most importantly, they lack native know-how and networks, essential to accomplish nearly anything. The absence of an organized policy to aid reintegration into Turkey reflects the official governmental policy.

Right from the inception of the guest worker program in the early 1960s, Turkey has found it convenient to export a willing portion of its population to Germany. In return, Turkey has received much-needed remitted hard currency. The Turkish government appears to be uninterested in changing this status quo and has done nothing to encourage its citizens in Germany to come home. This situation, combined with news of countless problems faced by repatriates in Turkey, filters back to the migrants and relatives still in Germany. Implicitly, then, the inadequate assistance to returnees results in a disincentive to return.

TURKEY, GREECE, AND THE EUROPEAN UNION

A stark contrast is offered by Turkey's neighbor to the west, Greece. Greece, with only one-sixth the population of Turkey, unlike its neighbor suffers from a negative population growth, and the government of the Pan Hellenic Socialist Party (PASOK) throughout the 1980s instituted an aggressive pronatalist policy. Part of this was aimed at the Greek workers in Germany, who were offered an attractive package of incentives to repatriate. As well as large financial inducements, the incentives included promises of special reabsorption schools for the children, offering bilingual education. Though this program was quite well organized, to the extent that an Undersecretariat for Greeks Abroad was established at the Foreign Ministry, there still were inadequate numbers of schools and places for the returnee children. And, not unlike the Turkish children taunted with the name *almanyali*, Greek returnee children complained of being called names such as "little German" and "little Hitler." However, despite the problems, the explicit policy of promoting repatriation yielded enormous results, and significant numbers of Greeks in Germany did repatriate in the 1980s.

However, the equation is not quite as simple as it might appear. Certainly, home country inducements do encourage repatriation, but the fact that in 1981 Greece joined the European Community, and by the late 1980s could claim full membership privileges, no doubt played a not insignificant role. Free movement of labor is guaranteed among member states; thus, should a Greek family decide, after repatriating, that they wished to return to Germany, they were legally assured of this possibility. Likewise, a repatriated Greek child who had been schooled in Germany could return there to attend university.

This stands in vivid contrast to Turkey, and the fate of returned Turks, since Turkey is still only marginally affiliated with the EU.[4] Rather than being assured of guaranteed movement within Europe, Turks must, as they call it, "kill" their passports in order to repatriate. This refers to the fact that Germany requires that the returnee workers— and their entire families—have their work and residence permits permanently canceled in order to receive the social-security and pension benefits owed them once back in Turkey. For the most part, this is an irreversible process, and surely not unrelated to the fact that relatively few Turks have repatriated to date. (This is not the sole reason, of course, but it needs to be understood as an important factor in the decision.)

We can assume that the differential status of migrants from Greece and Turkey in Germany certainly plays a part in the political psychology internalized by migrants' children. Turkish children know the phrase "killing passports" very well. Many repatriated children told me sadly that their passports had been killed, and that they felt trapped, unable to return to that northern country to which they felt more suited. Decisions of their parents had irrevocably sealed their fate. For example, a teenaged potential computer programmer in Germany, now newly illiterate in Turkey, told me that he decided to drop out of high school and to apprentice himself to a barber.

Again, as with the situation regulating citizenship and naturalization, a double standard inscribed in law shapes the present realities and future prospects of the offspring of labor migrants. As such, the children's innocent phrase "Turkey is our homeland; we are not at home here in Germany" highlights a predicament about which they may very well feel powerless to transform. Rather than reflecting a realistic assessment, perhaps this should be viewed as a defensive statement, meant to psychologically empower the powerless. It asserts a putative inclusion with this faraway place and counteracts the exclusion these children experience in their daily lives.

STRUCTURAL INEQUALITIES: EDUCATION AND THE FAMILY

The lives of the children of the second generation are marked particularly by the changed parent-child relationship they are compelled to master. A role reversal often has been remarked upon, in that the parents frequently enter into a relationship of partial dependency with their children. (See, for example, Wilpert 1988b:145.) This occurs due to the children's better mastery of the language and ways of Germany. Thus, children are called upon to serve their parents in ways that never would occur in the homeland. The ramifications for familial hierarchies, generally very strict and structured, can be profound. Thus, incidents that in other circumstances would be considered severely disobedient, and threatening of authority, now, in the German context, happen with significantly greater frequency. Young people may convince their parents that their school requires something of them—such as extra afternoon classes—in order to socialize with persons of whom their parents may not approve.

Especially with regard to education, the parents frequently have little control or knowledge. They often cannot and do not communicate with the teachers. Moreover, they sometimes see the teachers as antagonists, the symbolic gatepost separating them from their children. The teachers are perceived as tempting their offspring away from Turkishness, from Islam and Qur'an schools, or whatever the salient value or issue might be.

One controversial issue is the headscarf. German public schools usually ban the headscarves worn by some Turkish girls, but it remains for the teachers to remove them. In donning the headscarf, some girls (and women) are engaged in a form of sartorial resistance against the larger host culture's insistence that they abandon it, and thus with it, abandon their culture. For them, it expresses a very conscious, deliberate, well-thought-out act. It displays pride in Turkish or Muslim identity. In the German context, the most potent non-German—even anti-German—symbol with which they can identify is the loathed headscarf (Mandel 1989).

Interestingly, the headscarf has become more of a fetish for Germans than for Turks. To the former, it symbolizes the intransigence of the latter: either it demonstrates the Turks' arrogant unwillingness to "come halfway" on the road to benevolent "integration," (i.e., assimilation), or, alternatively, it provides evidence that the Turks are incapable of integration. Many Turks are confused by all the attention paid to, and intolerance directed at, the headscarf. Sometimes they compare this with the tolerance shown to the antisocial dress flaunted by German punks, with amply mutilated bodies and colorful, spiked, attention-getting hairstyles. (In Berlin and other cities, it is common for Turks and punks to share the same poor, dilapidated neighborhoods.) Interestingly, some Turkish girls and women explain that they feel that on some level Germans expect them to wear headscarves—that to be defined as a Turkish female in Germany necessarily means to cover one's head. This contrasts with Turkey, where such questions of Turkishness do not arise in this way.

Not all girls wear scarves, wish to wear them, or even keep them on. Some girls, in taking off their scarves in secret, once they are out of sight of their families' homes, might be resisting their parents, who insist that they wear it. Though outwardly it may appear that these girls accommodate the school system's values, in fact, such an act does not ensure success in the system.

Though Turkish students have widely varying experience in the German school system, certain patterns can be isolated. The teachers, who both represent a movement away from the values, practices, and language of the parents, also can stand in the way of the children advancing in the system. For the deeply tracked German school system weeds out at a young age those promising students who will be earmarked for the prestigious university-oriented, academic gymnasium. The others will either attend a *Realschule* and graduate at sixteen with a vocational diploma (such as kindergarten teacher, nurse's aid, medical technician, etc.) or else are guided into the *Hochschule* track and will leave school even earlier, with an all-but-worthless school-leaving certificate.[5]

In order to enter the academic gymnasium track, the child must have the support and recommendation of the teacher. Parents who are aware of the system can play a crucial role in the higher tracking of their children. However, Turkish parents not only often are unaware of the intricacies and pressure that must be levied on the school and teachers, but some do not want their children to enter the university track, thinking instead that a vocation will be much more useful, particularly in light of the family's intention to repatriate. Technical skills are thought to be transposable back to Turkey, whereas higher education might be thought to be of little use. Parents often invoke the proverb "A vocation is like a golden bracelet" (*Meslek bir altin bileziktir*) when explaining this preference.[6]

Fatma, the mother of two children whom she had reared in Germany, related to me the trouble she had had placing her son in the gymnasium track. At the time they were one of the only Turkish families living in a small town in West Germany. She and her husband, a small businessman in Turkey, had moved to Germany in hopes of greater financial success. She felt that education was the most important means of upward mobility, and Fatma was determined that her children would have every chance to achieve that she, herself, had not. Despite the fact that her son was a good student, she had had to fight in order to place him in the gymnasium track. She met with resistance from teachers, who asked, "What good is a gymnasium education to a Turk?" Besides, there had never been a Turk in the local gymnasium. Only with a great deal of persistence did she succeed in winning a place for him. Needless to say, most Turkish parents do not have the know-how required to place their offspring in this track.

Interestingly, it has been shown that "the presence of foreigners in German schools has contributed to an apparent educational mobility among native [German] pupils" (Wilpert 1988:119). As the proportion and numbers of foreigners in schools have increased, it has increased least in the gymnasium, where "foreigners contributed to about 8 per cent of the student body. However, almost one-half (49.8 per cent) of German young people eligible for secondary school attended gymnasium" (Wilpert 1988b:119). The

> Hauptschule, already losing its former importance as the normal prerequisite for obtaining apprenticeships, declined the furthest in its absolute numbers of pupils. Once more, it was the German pupils who profited the

most. Today, only 8 per cent of German pupils but 35 per cent of the Turks in secondary school in Berlin are likely to attend the *Hauptschule*. (Wilpert 1988b:119)

Wilpert cites figures from the mid to late 1980s, which showed that foreign youth comprised a full "40% of pupils in this least favoured type of school," and discusses the controversial role of the newer *Gesamtschule*, the comprehensive school. Though about 30 percent of foreign youth attend these internally tracked comprehensive schools, it is arguable that they are, "with [their] internal streaming . . . in reality, replacing the function of the *Hauptschule*." Wilpert writes that

> currently about one-third of the foreign youngsters leave the *Hauptschule* without a qualifying certificate. In the comprehensive *Gesamtschule*, however, at most about one-half of the children who enrol complete the middle-school certificate, and this is much less for foreigners (14%). (1988b:119)

What can the school leavers look forward to? The postschooling stage provides no relief for the youth of the second generation. This is due in part to an inadequate number of places in apprenticeships, in part to inadequate qualifications, but other reasons crop up as well. Proportionately, the number of young migrants in vocational training has been about one-third that of the corresponding group of Germans (Boos-Nunning and Hohmann 1989:47). In addition, the percentage of out-of-school, unemployed youth between the ages of fifteen and eighteen has risen over the past two decades and has been estimated at 37 percent (Stoltenberg, cited in Boss-Nunning and Hohmann 1989:47). Moreover, for those foreign youth who do complete a vocational-training course, their chances of employment are only half that of the equivalent group of Germans. These statistics show that, in addition to social marginalization, economic marginalization occurs as well. In general, then, beginning from their restricted educational experience, the children of guest workers do not achieve integration into the labor market.

UNIFIED GERMANY IN A GLOBAL SYSTEM

After three decades of this guest worker migration, many details of the social and psychological hardships faced by Turkish migrants have filtered back to the homeland. Despite this, however, the difficult expectations placed on migrants contribute to a vicious circle of self-demands and financial indebtedness, resulting in delayed repatriation. Compounding such problems is the fact that Germany, along with other First

World industrial powers, has changed the rules of the game, and once welcomed "guests" are welcome no longer.

At one time it was thought sensible to import cheap labor from poor, peripheral countries to the economic core on a continually rotating basis. As such, initially the workers from Turkey were welcomed into Germany. As the rotations became unfeasible, due to high transport and training costs, the imported worker population remained longer than intended. For these and other reasons, this is no longer the practice. The nations of the First World core are now having to pay the high social and economic costs of this policy. Instead of importing workers, the formerly labor-importing countries now practice outsourcing. They can thereby avoid the human misfortunes that inevitably result from poorly conceived programs to import populations designed to be kept disenfranchised. Needless to say, outsourcing has its own host of problems, social and economic, manifested both locally and globally; a discussion of these processes exceeds the scope of this paper.

In the years since the revolutions in eastern Europe in 1989, Germany, with postwar Europe's most liberal asylum law, has been the destination of scores of thousands fleeing present difficulties in the former socialist states. Thus, in recent years the situation has become extremely complex, as the nexus of foreigners in the new Germany has changed dramatically. In the changed context the foreigners from Turkey have come to share that appellation with despised Romanian gypsies, tens of thousands of refugees—"economic" and otherwise—from all over eastern Europe and the former Soviet states, and, to some degree, with the *Übersiedler*, the former East Germans now residing in western Germany. Thus, the notion of foreignness is undergoing a major reconfiguration. Accompanying this has been the virtual dismantling of Article 16 of the German constitution, which had guaranteed, at least on paper, certain rights of asylum-seeking refugees. The new asylum law radically alters the legal framework for those wishing to seek asylum, rendering their possibilities almost nil. This can be understood as the political and legal reflection of the perception of many Germans that there has been an uncontrolled deluge of unwanted foreigners.

The larger context of Germany's position in the European Community plays a crucial role as well. Many now refer to the exclusionary tendencies of the EU as constituting a "fortress Europe" in which there are (at least) two distinct classes of persons: citizens with rights of full movement and work, and disenfranchised noncitizens—currently about fourteen million—who lack these rights. The Turks in Germany currently belong to the latter group, despite several generations of residence within the confines of the EU. Germany is often seen as the emergent European superpower, economically and politically. The Bundes-bank's zealous defence and protection of the powerful Deutschmark against inflation, along with the extremely high rate of savings, for ex-ample, have helped to offset the economic pain caused by the ostensibly surprising high cost of unification.

Unified Germany appears to have found a new political will and mus-cle, unseen since World War II. This is evident in a variety of acts, such as Germany's payment of capitation money to Romania to take back gypsies who had fled persecution. Germany's unilateral recognition of Croatia's independence is another instance, particularly given the warn-ings and condemnation of the other EU governments. Some privately speculate whether the tragedy in Bosnia could have been averted had Germany not acted in such a precipitous manner. Moreover, the rise of neo-Nazi groups and the alarming escalation of xenophobic violence, including the murders of dozens of foreigners, must be seen in this con-text. The threatened repeal of the asylum law and restrictions of for-eigner rights foreshadow an even more sinister phase for those already disenfranchised within Germany's borders.

However, the work of the violent xenophobes has been bad for busi-ness, causing some large German corporations to take a financial beat-ing. Due to the bad press resulting from the murders of foreigners, some foreign companies have chosen not to do business with German firms. One consequence has been the emergence of a "philoforeigner" move-ment. "My friend is a foreigner" buttons and posters can be seen and, ever vigilant about customer relations and falling profits, some large cor-porations have taken out advertisements boasting about their employee relations and their valued Turkish workers.

SOME CONCLUDING THOUGHTS

The cards do indeed appear to be stacked against the offspring of the labor migrants from Turkey. After assessing their social, educational, and political situations, we can conclude that, as well as being second generation, they are second-class noncitizens. In Germany, a nation that conceives of citizenship, ethnicity, and race as conflated into one-and-the-same package, the prospect for this group of involuntary migrants looks dim. The prospects appear even more pessimistic when we look at the recent rise in both xenophobic violence and restrictive immigration legislation aimed at many types of foreigners in Germany. German unifi-cation has brought with it many challenges—economic, social, political, educational, to name but a few. It would appear that the foreigners—

once the welcome and much needed manual labor, used to pump the German economic miracle—are the victims, squeezed out of their share in the future of the new Germany.

We have also seen how the myth of return has been invoked to ameliorate the dissatisfaction and social barriers faced by the migrants, both voluntary and involuntary. In a sense, the imagined (mytho-) presence of an idealized future envisioned in Turkey justifies the absence of a tolerable present in Germany. The Turkish children who describe themselves as outsiders in Germany reproduce both the stereotypes they hear about themselves and their parents' visions of futures in Turkey.

The youth of the second generation, far from cultureless, or caught between two cultures and part of neither, instead lack the recognition due them. Oftentimes, powerless to stake a claim in German society, they cling to the only categories available, those stereotypical images just enumerated. Yet few will return to Turkey; most will remain in Germany. Perhaps it will be their children, or their children's children, who finally will win the acknowledgment denied to them. They are forging a new identity, one that in other countries would not be particularly problematic. For example, in the United States, they would be adopted, ideally, into the millions of hyphenated Americans, their ethnicity accepted unquestionably. But in Germany, insistent on its manifest destiny of imagined racial homogeneity, that day, if it comes, will arrive only if difference can be tolerated as legitimate and equal.

I will close with a poem written by a Turkish girl, of the second generation. Though melodramatic in its tone, it sums up the emotions, conflicts, and fears experienced by the young poet and many of her peers.

> They call us "strangers," "foreigners" here;
> They call us "Germans" there.
> Oh, my Anatolia, we were left midway in between—
> Just do not pierce us through the heart.

NOTES

1. One problem that has come up often concerns the special needs of Kurdish-speaking children from Turkey. Kurdish community workers in Berlin told me of incidents in which monolingual, Kurdish-speaking children have been put in Turkish-language classes, due to their Turkish citizenship. Knowing no Turkish, they have been labeled as retarded and placed in special remedial courses. Thus, in some cases, the Kurds, escaping repression and persecution in Turkey, have found Germany to be inhospitable in other ways.

2. *Mitbürger* often is used, quite problematically, to describe the German Jews.

3. Recent (1993) changes in citizenship legislation provide for descendants of migrants who fulfil certain specific conditions of continued residence and school attendance in Germany will open the way for some to acquire citizenship. Many, however, will not be affected by this change, if, for example, their residence in Germany was interrupted at key periods by return stays in Turkey.

4. Turkey has been applying for membership in the European Community for years. To date, the chief objections to its entry have been raised by Greece and Germany, for obvious political and economic reasons. At times, human-rights violations have also been cited as obstacles to membership. Now, with the end of the Cold War, a new group of potential members from eastern Europe are natural candidates and, no doubt, will jump the queue.

5. It is possible that with the growing number of mixed comprehensive schools, some of the most severe tracking will be reduced.

6. *Altin bilezik,* a golden bangle-type bracelet, is the most common wedding gift and an important portion of the bride price among many people from Turkey. Gold, most often in the form of these bangles, is the preferred sort of wealth, in that its value is believed to be quite stable and flexible, as the bangles can be sold and repurchased when needed. A useful vocation also is seen to be transferable, for example, from Germany to Turkey.

REFERENCES

Boos-Nunning, Ursula, and Manfred Hohmann, 1989, "The Educational Situation of Migrant Workers' Children in the Federal Republic of Germany," in Lotty Eldering and J. Kloprogge, eds., *Different Cultures, Same Schools,* Amsterdam, Swets and Zeitlinger, 39–59.

Buruma, Ian, 1992, "outsiders," *New York Review of Books,* April 9, 15–19.

Mandel, Ruth, 1989, "Turkish Headscarves and the 'Foreigner Problem': Constructing Difference through Emblems of Identity," *New German Critique,* 46:27–46.

Wilpert, Czarina, 1988a, "From One Generation to Another: Occupational Position and Social Reproduction," in Wilpert, ed., *Entering the Working World: Following the Descendants of Europe's Immigrant Labour Force,* Aldershot, Gower, 1–23.

————, 1988b, "Work and the Second Generation: The Descendants of Migrant Workers in the Federal Republic of Germany," in Wilpert, ed., *Entering the Working World: Following the Descendants of Europe's Immigrant Labour Force,* Aldershot, Gower, 111–49.

CHAPTER 10

Children, Politics and Culture: The Case of Brazilian Indians

MANUELA CARNEIRO DA CUNHA

IN THE UN Convention on the Rights of the Child, there are clauses to guarantee a child the right to a name, a nationality, and a cultural identity. The topic I would like to address is: what do we mean and what should we mean when we speak of a "right to a cultural identity"? This is not merely an academic issue. The right to cultural identity has been used in very perverse ways, as several of the papers in this collection remind us: it has been used to justify the confining of South African peoples in homelands, and in Singapore to force-feed Malay, Indian, or Chinese descendants into what is supposed to be their culture; and, last but not least, it carries a lingering (but quite contemporary) fascist flavor. Understanding what one calls "cultural identity" entails understanding culture and identity, which is of course too large a task for this paper. But there are some comments one could make that seem to be of relevance here.

To announce my cards, let me put it this way: there are, grossly, two different views about what culture and identity mean. The first sees identity and culture as *things*. Identity is to be identical to a model, with which one identifies oneself. It is therefore to be equal to oneself, somehow unchangeable. As for culture, it is then conceived as a given set of items, rules, values, positions that, in a Durkheimian way, shape cultural identity. We could call this position "Platonic," for convenience.

As against this, one can view identity as simply the awareness of continuity, as a flow, a process. Correspondingly, culture would not be a set of products but instead a process of production.[1] We could call this view after Heraclitus, for well-known reasons. I will try to show that this second position is the one that should be adopted, first because it is based on sound anthropology and second because it avoids the traps I have just referred to.

I will give you, as food for thought, a number of cases to brood upon. Most of my examples will be drawn from the Brazilian Indians' situation, for one thing because this is a topic I have been following for the last fifteen years, but also because in doing so, I will convey some information about a specific country and a specific minority.

Contact was made with the Xavante in 1951. Thirty years later one of them, chief of a traditional village in the state of Mato Grosso, was elected to the Brazilian Congress as a deputy from Rio de Janeiro. His popularity resulted from a successful invention: Mário Juruna carried a tape recorder to his interviews with public administrators and politicians and demanded that the promises he recorded be fulfilled. Juruna's recorder became a symbol of Brazilians' disbelief in election promises and found an immense echo in public opinion. Elected, Juruna was a fiasco. He was also unable to continue personifying the Indians' innocence as the country's moral reserve. He turned out to be just one more politician among many and was not reelected.

In the same decade that Mário Juruna was a deputy, the 1980s, the first indigenous movement with national ambitions was born and gathered strength, a complicated task in this extremely vast country where some 180 indigenous societies are found. With reduced populations, they total no more than 200,000 people. This movement's leaders characteristically had a profile opposite that of Mário Juruna. Almost all of them had been educated outside of their societies of origin. Some, the children of Indians who had migrated to the cities, had never previously considered themselves Indians. Others, born in the villages, had tried for years to hide their indigenous identity, locally disparaged, and had become "assimilated." Theirs was a trajectory very similar to that of Theodor Herzl, the founder of Zionism. Such is often the path of revivalist or nationalist leaders.

Thus, while Mário Juruna was learning Portuguese and how to move about amid national institutions, these leaders were searching for their local roots in order to oppose a national policy. This contemporary episode is not isolated. During the seventeenth and eighteenth centuries the leaders of indigenous revolts in South America were also men whom we would today call "assimilated," educated by priests and, so to speak, re-Indianized.

If we take the reaction of the Tumpinambá and the Guarani of southern Brazil to the presence of settlers and Portuguese missionaries (first Franciscans, later Jesuits) as an example, we can see that a first generation of traditional indigenous leaders confronted the recent arrivals, affirming their worth in their own terms. Let me make this clear. Around 1570 Guarani prophets asserted that they were gods, leaving the Jesuits flabbergasted (Vasconcelos 1658). This was a traditional declaration. A few years later, around 1585, Indians from Bahia were slaughtered for following a leader who declared that he was "pope" and an Indian woman who called herself "mother of God." In the words of the Inquisition, they worshiped a stone they called "Mary" in a house they called "church" (Vasconcelos 1977 [1655]).

The difference between these two moments is clear. In the first, political participation took place in traditional language; it is what we could call political monolingualism. In the second, a language shared with other actors was used, but for two different, new purposes: to assert a difference and to demand power. It was no longer traditional cosmology opposed to Catholic cosmology. Here we are moving within the Christian discourse. The point had become the following: to whom does Christ belong? Is God Indian or Portuguese? To a certain extent, it is as if the conquerors had been able to attract the vanquished to their very own terrain, forcing them to use a new language in order to express themselves politically. The signs of their resistance had to be formulated in a colonized language. And yet this very language was now conveying heterodoxy.

In the earliest areas of colonization, such as the northeast and eastern Brazil, many indigenous societies, discriminated against by their neighbors and having intermarried, had obliterated their indigenous identity. Official policy had encouraged miscegenation since the mid–eighteenth century (Carneiro da Cunha 1987). By the mid–nineteenth century, it had become a pretext to dispossess northeastern Indians of their lands. Nevertheless, various communities persisted, in spite of discrimination, cultivating their indigenous identity around certain exclusive rituals or by keeping the remains of their own language, in a type of ethnic hibernation (Dantas and Dallari 1980; Carneiro da Cunha 1993).

In the 1980s several of these communities began making demands regarding their indigenous identity. In order to understand what took place, we must state some facts about Brazilian legislation and its interpretation.

The essential Indian rights in Brazil are their rights to the land and its natural resources. In 1937 Indian land rights, whose long-standing recognition dates from the sixteenth century, were written into the constitution. In the several Brazilian constitutions that have followed (1946, 1967, and, most recently, 1988), these rights were broadened and consolidated. The Indian Statute, detailing these guarantees, was approved in 1973.

The basis of these Indian land rights is historic in nature since they are, in the words of a 1680 decree, "the first and natural lords of the land." The 1988 constitution included this principal. In it Indian land rights are described as "originary." In other words, they existed before the state itself, and the state can only recognize them, not confer them.

But who are the subjects of these rights? To be Indian in Brazil, unlike some other countries, does not depend upon a proven genealogy. Since 1973, the Indian Statute uses a definition of indigenous groups approaching that of anthropology; that is, it prioritizes the fact that these groups consider themselves and are considered indigenous. But, even so, the judiciary continues to demand "cultural proof," overt and explicit manifestations of being Indian, such as language, dress, way of life, and so on. Furthermore, at least until 1988, either in bad faith or simply because of assimilationist mentalities, many people contended that the condition of being Indian was transitory and that, in the final analysis, Indians' special land rights should be eliminated when culturally they ceased to be "different."

In 1978 the government attempted to proclaim a decree that implicitly would have resulted in the release of lands from Indians who were in what was called an "advanced stage of acculturation." That project caused an unexpectedly large movement in opposition to it and was filed. New avatars, however, reappeared in subsequent years, though none ever succeeded in being decreed. It was in this climate of mobilization that several groups from the northeast and the east demanded recognition of their status as indigenous societies. Thus, they activated available ethnic symbols: rituals, bows and arrows, feather headdresses. In short, they assumed the existing image of a generic Indian and made a parody of themselves.

Since the late 1970s the Pataxó Hã-hã-hãe in southern Bahia, whose land had been delimited in the 1930s, were in conflict with cacao growers who had encroached upon and expelled them from their lands. In addition to instigating attempts on the Pataxó leaders' lives, the landowners had contracted lawyers who asserted that they were no longer Indians but were common peasants. In that period, only one person, an elderly woman, spoke the Pataxó language. The Pataxó asked two anthropologists to make a vocabulary with her and sent two young men to another indigenous group, the Maxakali, to learn their language (Urban 1985, Lopes da Silva n.d.). Thus, in order to demonstrate their indigenous identity, Indians from southern Bahia had to reinvent a culture. And furthermore, they had to invent it in the terms of an external view, or rather, they had to be the Indians they were expected to be, with feathers, bows, and a strange language.

Now, when the very traditional Kayapó Indians lobbied the Constitutional Assembly for Indian rights, they too wore ceremonial feathercaps. Although the caps were "right," the place and the situation were "wrong," inappropriate. Yet they were appropriate, of course, but on a different level, for the symbolic statement they were making. Again, does the question of authenticity have any meaning in this context? Which are more authentic, the Pataxó who reinvent themselves a culture through the white man's eye, or the Kayapó who wear the right feather-cap at the wrong time and the wrong place and therefore stage their own Indianness?

Another case I would like to discuss is that of schools. In the last two decades bilingual education has been initiated in some indigenous schools. Among the innovations introduced was literacy in the native language. Since Brazilian Indian languages are unwritten, that novelty brought about much discussion. Furthermore, as there are around 150 living indigenous languages, they do not serve for communication outside a restricted social circle. Thus, many societies protested that they were interested only in learning to write in Portuguese, since writing was only functional in that language. Nevertheless, the fact that schools considered indigenous languages worthy of being written conferred upon them a status equivalent to that of Portuguese, a dimension that was duly appreciated. That right to bilingual schools was registered in the new 1988 Brazilian constitution.

Questions correlated with that of writing are the books of mythology (at times even written for use in the schools) and the cultural centers that are beginning to be established by Indian leaders and Indian teachers in their own Amazonian groups. No matter how faithful these cultural centers are to the transmission of knowledge, they involve a profound subversion of customs: the modes of passing on traditional knowledge, linked to social status and hierarchies, are just as fundamental as their contents. Wherever writing has been introduced, it has revolutionized the hierarchies based on knowledge.

Within the environment of a state, indigenous groups change: they become minorities, rather than autonomous societies. The point of reference ceases to be solely internal (if ever it was so), and culture acquires a new function in addition to its former ones, as it becomes an element of contrast in a multiethnic whole. This does not necessarily mean that the existence of a state signals the end of those traditional societies, since the dimension of contrast may only constrain rather than destroy these societies' internal dynamic, just as the linking of a carbon molecule to others in order to form a new compound does not necessarily annul its internal structure; it only constrains it in certain directions.

Before anything else, it is worthwhile to dissipate some misunderstandings relative to the idea of culture. In order to do this, I will base myself on a noted Norwegian anthropologist, Fredrik Barth, who published a fundamental book, *Ethnic Groups and Boundaries,* in 1969. That same year Abner Cohen came out with a book containing theses similar to Barth's; its self-explanatory title was *Custom and Politics in Urban Africa*. The point of these two books was that culture is the result of a political situation.

The notion of culture, oddly enough, inherited at first many of the attributes of the concept of race which it intended to replace as a criterion for defining ethnic groups.[2] Our ideas about cultural authenticity closely resemble the "racial purity" of old. For one thing, they assume one can rely on objective, tangible criteria. But, as Barth has pointed out, culture varies in the same group in time and in space: no one speaks the same language or wears the same dress as one's own grandmother; nor do the Pathans dress the same in Pakistan and in Afghanistan. Thus, if tangible criteria are to be retained, there is no possible way to establish cultural authenticity.

Until the fifties, everyone seemed to think that a general assimilation was in course: the global village seemed to be at hand's reach, as all peoples melted in New World melting pots. The sixties were a period of disenchantment: not only did the melting pot turn out to be a fallacy, but all over newly independent African states, where planners had expected modern nations to emerge, so-called tribalism increased. The more the world system expanded, the more it seemed to generate internal diversity.

All this led to the rediscovery of what Max Weber had said long ago, namely that ethnic communities were forms of political organization and that ethnicity was a language that served for communication with other ethnic groups. The original culture of an ethnic group, either in a diaspora or in situations of permanent contact, does not fade away or melt. It acquires a new and essential function that is added to all previous functions: it becomes a contrast culture. This will normally entail that culture will be simplified and reduced to a smaller set of diacritical traits. By the same movement, culture will become more rigid.

Now which diacritical signs will be selected depends on the general multiethnic shared language. If religion or food, for instance, are adequate idioms, insofar as they are understandable by all people involved, then they may be selected as the cultural items that define a particular group. The liberated Yoruba slaves who, from the 1830s on, returned to what is now Nigeria, established themselves in Lagos as a separate trading community. Although in Brazil they were and continued to be Orisa worshipers, in Lagos they established themselves as Catholics. This is readily understandable, since each community in Lagos had its separate and exclusive god(s), and the appropriate language for distinguishing oneself was indeed religion (Carneiro da Cunha 1985).

The point this makes is that ethnic groups cannot be objectively recognized on the basis of their culture. Group identity necessitates culture, but culture, instead of being the prerequisite of an ethnic group, is in many respects the product of its very existence.

As totemism draws on natural categories to express social distinctions, ethnicity uses cultural objects to produce distinctions in multiethnic societies. Thus, ethnicity is a language that uses cultural signs to express social segments.

Natural species are given in the world. I don't mean that species are natural objects, but merely that animals and plants possess an internal coherence, a physiology that animates and coordinates their constituent parts. Yet, it is not in their entirety that they are used by a totemic system; rather, it is their culturally selected differences that entitle them to be organized in a system that now commands their meaning. What happens when we leave the natural species used in totemism and take cultural species used in multiethnic societies? As physiology commands each natural species, so too cultures are systems whose parts are determined by the whole that organizes them. As they become signs in a multiethnic system, they lose their "wholiness" and they become part of a metasystem that will now organize them and bestow upon them their positions and meanings. The move from one reference system to the other is such that, even though nothing tangible has been changed, the significance of cultural items is altered. As it becomes a diacritical sign in a multiethnic system, a cultural trait becomes a figment, a parody of itself. Suspended in time like Dorian Gray, its fidelity is the very sign of its death.

What I am trying to say, by successive approximations, is that culture and policies associated with its "protection" are especially deceptive phenomena; to a certain extent, the more capable of substantive innovations a culture is, the more traditional it is. And, inversely, the more faithful a culture is to its substantive contents (myths, rites, etc.), the more likely it is to have undergone profound changes and have lost its autonomy. If, as Marx said, history repeats itself as a farce, culture repeats itself as folklore. Truly traditional culture is that which invents new myths, new ceremonies, that which preserves its initiative in cultural production. It is a living culture.

What does this imply for a cultural policy among Brazilian Indians? Particularly for children? Brazilian indigenous societies had a high opinion of themselves and of their cultures. Since, as Lévi-Strauss said, ethnocentrism is the most commonly distributed thing in the world, they could be no exception. Almost all simply designate themselves "people," or, in the best of cases, such as the Kaxinauá, Huni-Kuin, "the true people," which leaves no doubts as to how they considered their neighbors. Self-esteem—and to say this, one need not be a psychologist—is fundamental for a child. Pride in being a member of a society with its values, its rules, its mythology, its ceremonies is fundamental.

Contact between indigenous societies and the rest of the world has always been made under the sign of depreciation; administrators, settlers, and missionaries, just as ethnocentric as the Indians, disparaged everything they saw. The garments, houses, systems of marriage, political system, initiation rituals, traditional science, funeral customs, mythology, cosmology, all were dismissed. Examples abound, but I will only cite two. With an extraordinary adroitness for attacking indigenous cultures through their central institutions, missionaries induced the Apinayé (a group from the Gé linguistic family) to abandon their villages' semicircular form and arrange their homes along a single street. Since Gé villages constituted a sociological map of an extremely complex dualistic organization, this urban reform meant the dismantling of the system. In the 1930s, when the noted ethnographer Nimuendaju visited them, the Apinayé still thought in terms of the circular village, but they were disoriented: the new generation no longer knew to which moiety they belonged. Another example from the end of the last century that also illustrates the missionaries' ethnological perspicacity in dismantling cultures is the great auto-da-fé, led by an Italian Capuchin on the upper Rio Negro. This man exposed the Baniwa's ceremonial masks to women—a sacrilege, since women are not supposed to see the masks—and then publicly destroyed them (Wright 1992).

Since the sixteenth century, but particularly in the first half of our century, it was thought that children should be removed from contact with their relatives and educated away from their villages—because the adults were already incorrigible. It was a tremendous period of boarding schools, especially for the Salesians. It was also the period in which a children's version of the Spanish colonial *encomiendas* was created, so they could be "educated" in landowners' homes. In several areas, such as in the Rio Branco valley in Roraima, these landowners had, in addition, encroached upon traditional lands and driven the Indians into a few refuges.

The result of all this was that, in the boarding schools or in the landowners' homes, Indian children learned to disparage their cultures of origin and their native languages, which, significantly, were called "slang." Their only way out was to attempt to suppress their indigenous identity. As I said above, the new indigenous leaders who had to discover or reinvent their roots came from this very group (Santilli 1994).

For a child, having a respected ethnic identity can be a powerful aid in self-affirmation; he or she will have a secure identity, a reference group, and pride in customs and will feel a continuity with a particular history. When his or her group is disparaged, a child can only choose between being ashamed before others or attempting to hide, and therefore renouncing, his or her identity. Both options are extremely difficult. The best of all worlds is, on the contrary, to fully participate in a respected group. Rarely, however, is this the given situation.

Indians' national political action is giving them back their self-esteem. As elsewhere, it is coming about through the reinvention of culture. That reinvention affects both the culture's form of production and the cultural products that, while appearing to be the same, take on a supplementary function, namely that of being diacritical marks. Thus, a headdress may serve equally for a village ritual, for wearing while making a demand in Congress, or even for hanging up in a "cultural center."

What should be done in relation to these ethnic processes? Today, there appears to be a growing consensus on the value of diversity and on the importance of traditional knowledge; we prefer that there be 350 cheeses in France, undoubtedly a sign of regional diversity, and we feel cheated when some of those cheeses are substituted by ersatz products that are merely different from the neighboring one, without being "really traditional," whatever that means.

This international posture is fundamental for preserving the so-called traditional cultures. Yet it runs the risk of imprisoning them in a singular Procustean bed; one that forces them to become equal to themselves (or to a general "indigenous" paradigm), parodying themselves, imprisoned in a sameness that is a paralysis.

Today, the defense of traditional societies and of cultural diversity departs from the epicenter of modernity. But precisely because culture is production and not a product, we must be attentive in order to not be deceived; what we must guarantee for future generations is not the preservation of cultural products, but the preservation of the capacity for cultural production.

NOTES

1. As regards the discussion of "culture," I rely here on the seminal work and formulations of Eunice Durham (1977).

2. In the following paragraphs, I am using relevant passages of my own previous writings, namely Carneiro da Cunha (1985, 1986).

REFERENCES

Barth, Fredrik, 1969, Introduction to *Ethnic Groups and Boundaries*, Bergen-Oslo, Universitets Forlaget.

Cohen, Abner, 1969, *Custom and Politics in Urban Africa*, London, Routledge and Kegan Paul.

Carneiro da Cuñha, Manuela, 1985, *Negros, Estrangeiros: Os escravos libertos e sua volta a Africa*, São Oaulo, Brasiliense.

Carneiro da Cuñha, Manuela, 1986 "Etnicidade: Da cultura, residual mas irredutivel," in *Antropologia do Brasil: Mito, historia, etnicidade*, 97–108. São Paulo, Brasiliense e EDUSP.

Carneiro da Cuñha, Manuela, 1987, *Direitos dos Indios: Ensaios e documentos*, São Paulo, Brasiliense.

Carneiro da Cuñha, Manuela, org. 1993, *Legislaçao indigenista no século XIX*, São Paulo, Editora da Universidade de São Paulo and Comissao Pro-Indio.

Dantas, Beatriz and Dalmo Dallari 1980, *Terras dos Indios Xocó*. São Paulo, Comissao pro-Indio.

Durham, Eunice, 1977, "A dinâmica cultural na sociedade moderna," *Ensaios de Opiniao*, 1:32–35.

Lopes da Silva, Aracy, Eni Orlandi, Greg Urban n.d. *Licoes de Baheta: Sobre a Lingua Pataxó Hã-hã-hãe*. São Paulo, Comissao pro-Indio.

Santilli, Paulo, 1994, *Fronteiras da Republica: Historia e politica entre os Macuxi do Vale do Rio Branco*, São Paulo, Nucleo de Historia Indigena e do indigenismo and FAPESP.

Urban, Greg, 1985, "On Pataxó Hã-hã-hãe," *International Journal of American Linguistics* 51 (4):605–8.

Vasconcelos, Simao de, S.J. 1977, [1655], *Crônica da Companhia de Jesus no Brasil*, 3d ed., 2 vols., Petrópolis.

Vasconcelos, Simao de, S.J. 1658, *Vida do Padre Joao de Almeida da Companhia de Jesus na Provincia do Brasil*. Lisbon, I. da Costa.

Wright, Robin 1992, "Historia Indigena do noroeste da Amazonia: hipoteses, questoes, perspectivas," in M.Carneiro da Cunha, ed., *Historia dos Indios no Brasil*, São Paulo, Cia das Letras e Secretaria Municipal de Cultura, 253–66.

CHAPTER 11

The "Cultural Fallout" of Chernobyl Radiation in Norwegian Sami Regions: Implications for Children

SHARON STEPHENS

ON 28 APRIL 1986, technicians at the Forsmark nuclear reactor north of Stockholm recorded abnormally high levels of radiation during routine measurements. Elevated radiation measurements were soon found in other parts of Scandinavia and the source of radioactive clouds traced to the southeast—to the USSR. But when the governments of Norway, Sweden, and Finland demanded an explanation, they were initially met with evasions from Moscow.

Finally, twelve hours after the Forsmark alert, Moscow TV broadcast a terse statement from the USSR Council of Ministers:

> An accident has taken place at the Chernobyl power station, and one of the reactors was damaged. Measures are being taken to eliminate the consequences of the accident. Those affected by it are being given assistance. A government commission has been set up. (Quoted in May 1989)

Thus began what many regard as the gravest crisis in the troubled thirty-two-year history of nuclear power. Contrary to the Soviet statement, the consequences of this crisis are far from having been "eliminated." Indeed, researchers from many disciplines are still trying to identify and analyze both the causes and the consequences of the Chernobyl nuclear disaster.

This paper begins with a brief discussion of current debates about some of the global consequences of Chernobyl, with special consideration of risks to children. I then focus on the post-Chernobyl situation in Norwegian Sami regions, where radioactive fallout poses threats not only to the health and economic well-being of northern Europe's indigenous population, but also to a distinctive Sami cultural identity, linked in complex ways to the viability of a Chernobyl-threatened reindeer industry.

Many different groups—Scandinavian state officials, health professionals, economic experts, international journalists, environmental activists, and diverse Sami groups—have been concerned with defining the nature and significance of the "invisible event" of Chernobyl in Sami areas. Each group has its own vision of the Sami culture at risk. By focusing on the politics of culture in the post-Chernobyl Sami situation, we can gain insight into some of the ways that notions of culture can constitute both resources and risks for children, in whose names and through whose minds and bodies cultural battles are often fought.

I conclude with a discussion of some of the implications that consideration of post-Chernobyl Sami cultural politics might have for assessing international children's rights discourses, with particular reference to assertions of a child's "right to a cultural identity."

GLOBAL MEDICAL AND SOCIAL RISKS FROM CHERNOBYL FALLOUT

The tragic health consequences of Chernobyl fallout in the immediate vicinity of the accident are beginning to be charted. While some scientists continue to maintain that medical risks from Chernobyl fallout in regions distant from the accident are relatively insignificant, there are profoundly troubling reports from other researchers suggesting that long-term health consequences of Chernobyl, even in areas of Europe and North America receiving relatively low-level fallout, may be more serious than previously expected. (See, for example, Gould and Goldman 1991.)

Previous extrapolations of the effects of low-dose radiation made on the basis of research done on Japanese atomic-bomb victims exposed to high-level radiation may have greatly underestimated the effects of low-radiation doses for the most sensitive members of the population—the elderly, those with impaired immune systems, and especially infants and young children. International "safe" or "acceptable" standards set for exposure of adults to low-level radiation may be thousands of times too high for the developing fetus (Knox et al. 1988).[1]

Some scientists have argued that risks associated with prolonged low-level radiation exposure include not only development of leukemia and cancer, but also a wide range of immune-system problems, contributing to accelerated aging, lowered resistance to disease, and increased likelihood of asthma and allergies. Low-level radiation exposures may also pose much greater reproductive dangers—miscarriages, premature births, and birth defects—than previously thought. In addition, exposure to low-level ionizing radiation may act synergistically to increase dangers from toxic chemicals. (See Bertell 1985; Baverstock and Stather 1989; Gould and Goldman 1991; Jones and Southwood 1987.)

Since the dawn of the nuclear age, atomic-weapons programs, atmospheric bomb tests, uranium mining, and accidents and leaks at nuclear-energy facilities have resulted in a massive increase of radionuclides in the global environment. A recent investigative report by a team of journalists from the Hiroshima-based *Chugoku Newspaper* (1992), based on research in fifteen countries, gives a wide-ranging picture of the global diversity of radiation risks—from the Cold War legacy of nuclear-weapons development in the United States and former USSR, to risks from uranium mining on American Indian reservations and in Namibia, to the "nuclear refugees" resulting from American and French weapons testing in Oceania, to Third World areas used as dumping sites for First World radioactive wastes and as manufacturing sites for products deemed too risky to produce in the First World.

And it is not just health risks that should be of international concern when we consider the global effects of radiation exposure. Ulrick Beck (1987) also notes political risks to democratic societies and social risks to local communities and forms of everyday knowledge occasioned by an "invisible event" that can be known only through its representations by technical experts. What would have happened in Europe during the fallout period, he asks, "if the weather services had failed, if the mass media had remained silent, if the experts had not quarreled with one another? No one would have noticed a thing" (Beck 1987:154).

Beck (1987:55) argues that Chernobyl dramatically brought home to many people what has been true for a long time: "[N]ot just in the nuclear age, but with the industrial universalization of chemical poisons in the air, the water, and foodstuffs as well, our relation to reality has been fundamentally transformed." Our senses are increasingly expropriated from local communities, as the reality of unseen dangers is defined, negotiated, and administered by experts in the weather services, mass media, cabinet offices, radiation commissions, and laboratories.

A "doubling of the world" occurs in the nuclear age between those forms of knowledge adequate for everyday life and those forms required to grasp and respond to radiation dangers. With Chernobyl,

> [T]he global character of the threat and the devaluation of our senses lend to the debate over the degree and dangerousness of the contamination, which now rages in the public and which has strayed into the magical realm of physical formulae, its deep cultural significance. (Beck 1987:154)

Richard Gould, in *Fire in the Rain: The Democratic Consequences of Chernobyl* (1990), writes of how the Chernobyl cloud moved through the atmosphere, descended to earth with local rains, and generated complex chains of consequences as the radiation moved through interconnected chains of the environment and human institutions. Each European state, for example, had its own distinctive political responses to Chernobyl fallout.

France, with a greater dependence on nuclear energy than any other country in the world (generating 65 percent of its electrical energy from nuclear reactors), instituted an "information blockage at the border" (Gould 1990:73). Even as late as May 6, the French Minister of Agriculture publicly stated that France had been spared the fallout, despite the fact that right across the border, German farmers were advised to keep their cows from grazing outside and parents were advised to keep their children indoors. The minister of the German state of Saar (quoted in Gould 1990:73) described a "field divided between France and Germany. At the French end everything was normal. Children were playing and cattle were grazing. At the German end there were no children and no cattle."

The response to Chernobyl in Italy, whose northern alpine area had the highest levels of contaminated milk in western Europe, was marked by uncoordinated and contradictory directives from various government agencies. While the Ministry for Civil Protection announced radiation levels were so low that there was absolutely "no cause for alarm" (though people might want to rinse their lettuce), the Ministry of Health banned radioactive milk from the market and issued warnings about the special dangers contaminated foods pose to pregnant women and children.

Contradictory Italian state actions contributed to a general panic, causing a run in the stores on frozen, canned, and powdered foods and iodine in all forms, in order to counteract the dangers of radioactive iodine. A few people died from self-administered doses. The state response to this public panic was dissimulation and information control, ending with the Atomic Energy Commission's refusal to release any further information about cesium and strontium levels in foods. A spokesman for the Civil Protection Agency (quoted in Gould 1990:70) asked: "What do you want with those figures? By now the damage is done. Whatever cesium there is has been absorbed into our bodies." Clearly, political decisions on radiation policy put children at different sorts of risks within different national boundaries.

According to Gould, the Norwegian government, with no civil or military commitments to nuclear power, rates high on informing the public, though not always so high on the accuracy of reported information. No country in Europe was prepared to deal with Chernobyl, Gould (1990:101) notes, but Norway was particularly unprepared, with only a few radiation monitors in the south associated with two small reactors used for physics research. The first Chernobyl reports from Norwegian health authorities assured the public that there was no reason to panic, and that the very low levels of fallout in Norway did not extend farther north than Tunset (a town between Trondheim and Oslo). This information turned out to be false.

As more accurate fallout maps began to be developed, it became clear that the heaviest fallout had occurred in central Norway, with lesser fallout levels in the north and a few isolated fallout areas in the south. Concern about the special vulnerability of Sami reindeer herders to radioactive threats (already well known from earlier studies of the elevated radioactivity levels in lichen, deer, and Sami populations in the far northern area of Finnmark as a result of Soviet nuclear testing in Novaja Semlja in the 1950s and 1960s) appeared in the press soon after news of Chernobyl broke on the international scene in late April 1986.

Norwegian Sami occupy areas from central Norway to the far north. The uneven fallout pattern, combined with marked linguistic and social/historical differences between South Sami (in central regions) and their North Sami neighbors, has meant that assessing and responding to the risks of Chernobyl—"this peculiar, paradoxical combination of weather and history" (Beck 1987:158)—has involved struggles between Sami and state officials, South and North Sami, Sami reindeer herders and Sami with other occupations, and men and women about the nature and interests of the communities at risk. These struggles, I will argue, have important implications for the sorts of cultural identities to which contemporary Sami children can lay claim.

GENERAL BACKGROUND

The special vulnerability of reindeer herding to radiation is due to the biological characteristics of lichen, the main winter reindeer food. Lichens have no underground root system and must get all their nutrients directly from the air, resulting in relatively high radionuclide concentrations in lichen-pastured deer (known as "biological amplifiers") within areas of heavy fallout. In some areas, radioactivity levels measured in deer after the first autumn slaughters were so high that scientists predicted that it would be twenty to thirty years before contamination levels would fall below legal limits for the public sale of reindeer meat.

Deer meat above the legal limit for market sale was dyed blue to mark it unfit for human consumption and then sold as fodder for northern fur farms or discarded in abandoned mine shafts. Freshwater lakes and inland forests were also contaminated, rendering vast quantities of fish, wild game, and berries—important foods and sources of income for many Sami—unmarketable and well above suggested safe levels for domestic consumption.

In the most seriously contaminated Sami areas, Chernobyl fallout has had important economic consequences, increasing the dependence of Sami herders on state support. The governments of both Norway and Sweden have promised to hold the Sami "economically undamaged" by Chernobyl and have promised monetary compensation for unmarketable deer "for as long as the situation requires." Herders have been advised to continue herding and slaughtering as usual, in order to avoid unbalanced herd growth and pasture depletion. The long-term aim of most Sami herders is to maintain their herds and herding way of life until contamination levels fall to acceptable legal limits for market sale.

Sami have also been advised by government health agencies on "safe" levels of contamination in deer meat marked for domestic consumption. The difficulty of defining these levels is shown by the fact that legal limits for the sale of radioactive foods vary from country to country (300 becquerels/kilo in Sweden, 1,000 in Finland, and, in May 1986, 300 in Norway). Limits also vary over time. In June 1986, market limits in Norway were changed to 370 bq/kg for milk and children's food and 600 bq/kg for other foods. In November, the legal limit for reindeer meat was raised to 6,000 bq/kg, while the limit for other foods remained the same. State officials claimed that the higher limit would not put the average Norwegian consumer of reindeer meat (a luxury and holiday item) at any greater risk and would significantly aid the endangered reindeer industry, at least in northern regions, where the new limit would mean that the majority of deer could be legally sold. Much higher fallout levels in southern regions suggested that South Sami would have to rely on government compensation for many years to come. (In autumn 1986, cesium 137 measurements from the hard-hit area of Snåsa, where my own research has been based, averaged 40,000 bq/kg.)

But if contaminated reindeer meat represents an "insignificant risk" to the average Norwegian consumer, this is not the case in Sami families, many of whom eat deer meat almost daily. State health department advice to these families has changed over time. One Sami man showed me several reports suggesting safe consumption levels broken down into different acceptable levels for healthy adults, pregnant and nursing women, children, and the elderly or sick. "Look," he said, "how the numbers on the charts change from report to report. How can they tell us what to do when they don't know themselves?"

Changing official recommendations reflect heated international scientific debates about what a safe or acceptable level of long-term exposure to low-level radiation might be and about the nature of the risks entailed. Sami families are currently advised that health risks will be relatively insignificant if people consume reindeer meat under 2,000 bq/kg and make efforts to vary their diets to include other foods.

In the first two years after Chernobyl, most of the slaughtered deer from South Sami regions was declared unfit for human consumption. Since 1988, state-sponsored programs to feed deer before the autumn slaughters with "clean" lichen brought in from outside have been successful in bringing radioactivity levels of selected deer below legal limits and allowing more deer onto the market, as well as more local deer onto Sami tables. These programs have introduced significant changes in herding routines, as well as increased Sami dependence on outside expert knowledge and on state subsidies to pay for clean lichen and fences needed to contain herds during the preslaughter feeding period.

Chernobyl has resulted in wide-ranging demands on Sami to change their everyday production and consumption patterns. Official regulations and special medical advice are premised on the assumption that Sami people should make prudent restrictions in their consumption of contaminated foods and appropriate changes in economic practices, in order to maintain their health and the economic foundations for preserving their culture (conceived as ideas about the world, values, language, and ethnic symbols like clothing and handicrafts) for the future.

In contrast, for many South Sami in the most heavily contaminated regions of central Norway and Sweden, cultural identity involves more than just worldviews and marks of ethnicity. For many, everyday practices of food preparation and herding are central to their culture, conceived not just as ideas about the world, but also as the ways people produce themselves as Sami, with certain kinds of bodies, senses, memories, and connections to one another, their deer, and the places where deer are pastured. After Chernobyl, Sami were advised to wait out the period of contamination and continue to herd as usual, without actually eating the deer they raised. In the early post-Chernobyl period, before deer-feeding programs began, the fear was that this waiting period might extend well into the next century.

Such policies resulted in a Sami "doubling of the world"—between the visible world and unseen dangers, between the real and the pretend—that was experienced by many as very painful and dislocating. Sig-Britt Toven, from a reindeer-herding family in Snåsa, observed in January 1987:

> It seems sometimes that things have become strange and make-believe. You see with your eyes the same mountains and lakes, the same herds, but you know there is something dangerous, something invisible, that can harm your children, that you can't see or touch or smell. Your hands keep doing the work, but your head worries about the future.[2]

By calling into question previously taken-for-granted aspects of everyday life, the South Sami experience of Chernobyl has challenged people to articulate in new ways what is distinctively "Sami." What can be changed, and what must be preserved, so that Sami culture can be maintained in the face of Chernobyl's multifaceted dangers to health, economic stability, and forms of local knowledge? In their struggles to deal with the Chernobyl labyrinth, Sami in the most hard-hit areas are also renegotiating their sense of a distinctive cultural identity, in relation to other Sami groups, local Norwegian populations, and "Western culture" (associated with science, technology, models of economic rationality, state bureaucracy, and mass media).

LIVING AND REPRESENTING "SOUTH SAMI CULTURE"

A frequently quoted figure for the Sami population in Scandinavia is 60,000: 30,000 in Norway, 20,000 in Sweden, 8,000 in Finland, and 2,000 in the former USSR. Of these, only about 3,000, located in central Norway and Sweden, are designated as "South Sami." Unlike their North Sami neighbors, who comprise a majority in some northern areas and often live in distinctively Sami towns and villages, South Sami have long lived dispersed throughout the central Norwegian population. Mixed Sami/Norwegian marriages are increasingly common. In the youngest South Sami generation, Swedish and Norwegian have virtually replaced Sami as the first language. The South Sami dialect is so different from North Sami that speakers of South Sami must communicate in either Swedish or Norwegian with their North Sami neighbors. The special linguistic and social situation of South Sami contributes to their sense of being a minority within a minority—a sense dramatically intensified by their experience as the Norwegian group hardest hit by Chernobyl.

Chernobyl fallout in South Sami areas occurred within a society already struggling to maintain a strong sense of ethnic identity. Reindeer-related practices have been centrally important in constructing marked Sami spaces and contexts. By the 1930s and 1940s, most South Sami had made the transition from a nomadic life, in which households migrated annually with their herds, to a more sedentary life, usually with a house in town where women and children live and to which men periodically return when herding activities permit. Summer, when deer graze in the high mountain areas, is a period when many South Sami families live in mountain cabins and tents, away from Norwegian centers. In the first years after Chernobyl, however, many women remained in their winter homes with their children, while men did the summer herding alone, often packing in tinned food from outside rather than living off deer and mountain fish.

Sami winter houses are distinguished from neighboring Norwegian houses by the reindeer hides hung to dry from rafters outside and by the smell and sight of dried reindeer meat hanging above the stoves inside—marks of Sami ethnicity that disappeared from many households in the first years after Chernobyl.

Traditional patterns of using not just the meat, but every part of the deer, were disappearing well before Chernobyl. One of the consequences of Chernobyl, however, was that people experienced, seemingly overnight, a more thoroughgoing commodification of everyday life. Gerd Persson, a Swedish South Sami woman, explained:

> This is not just a matter of economics, but of who we are, how we live, how we are connected to our deer and each other. Now [in the winter of 1986–87] we must buy everything. Thread, material, food, shoes are now all different things, when they used to be parts of one thing.

Consumption of reindeer meat is regarded not just as an ethnic marker, but also as a way of forming substantial links among people and between people and places. People described to me how important it was for them to send dried meat from their own herds to their children away at school, in order to maintain a physical link with them. Children from herding families who have gone into other occupations maintain a link with the places they grew up through gifts of meat from their relatives. South Sami complain of deer meat bought from the north that it "doesn't taste right": "North Sami don't know how to care for the deer as we do. This food does not nourish our bodies."

It is considered particularly important for pregnant women to eat reindeer meat to strengthen both mother and child. The herding knowledge of the man and the food-preparing knowledge of the woman come together to make food that nourishes the unborn child and strengthens the bodies of growing children. In the winter of 1986–87, one woman described her worries about Sami men's morale after Chernobyl:

> It is not just that men are worried about their immediate economic futures, or the more distant future of children as reindeer herders. It is also the frustration of not being able to feed their families from their own herds. We are not going to starve, but we are suffering in ways that compensation payments can't help.

Much research still needs to be done into the ways in which South Sami herding practices, work relations, kinship connections, and ethnic identity have been framed in terms of herding-related activities and substantial connections among people, deer, and places effected through Sami patterns of distributing and consuming reindeer meat. Perhaps enough has been said here to suggest why state-orchestrated programs to get people to buy uncontaminated foods from outside have been only partially successful and even when successful are experienced by many as a literal severing of bonds among people, deer, places, and previous generations.

We can begin to understand why some South Sami chose to eat meat at levels of radiation that would pose "unacceptable risks" to health professionals in Oslo. Some Sami say that after Chernobyl they simply ignored state directives and continued to consume deer meat as before. One family I heard about "hedged its bets" in the first years after Chernobyl by having three freezer compartments: one for meat designated for the children that was bought from outside and was within suggested safe limits; another for meat from the family herd that was close to safe limits and was consumed by the parents; and a third for the most radioactive meat, eaten by the old people.

Robert Paine (1987, 1989) writes of the scepticism he observed among many South Sami herders about the gravity of the fallout situation, "visible" mainly through the reports of government officials and state-employed scientists, with whom Sami had complex, often difficult relations long before Chernobyl. State programs existed well before Chernobyl to rationalize Sami herding practices, to make them more productive and profitable by implementing scientific breeding, herding, and slaughtering practices. In this context, some herders were wary of state policies to deal with Chernobyl that greatly increase Sami dependence on "expert knowledge" from outside.

At stake here are different notions of the relation between culture and reindeer herding. While the dominant vision of state policies is that reindeer herding is an occupation that "carries" a distinctive Sami culture, for many Sami it is a form of experiencing and acting in the world that makes herding, as many people note, "not just an occupation, but a way of life." While the experience of Chernobyl fallout in South Sami areas did not *cause* modern separations between notions of culture and the economy and between the domains of production and consumption, social responses to Chernobyl have certainly intensified these divisions.

The historical connection of reindeer herding with Sami identity is extraordinarily complex. Here I can only note that the development of extensive nomadic reindeer pastoralism—now seen by many as the mark of traditional, authentic Sami culture—was itself associated with the sixteenth-century expansion of Scandinavian states into areas occupied by Sami who lived by hunting, fishing, and small-scale herding. Scandinavian states continue to play a problematic role in maintaining an identification of Sami culture with the practice of reindeer herding, despite the fact that only 10 percent of Scandinavia's approximately sixty thousand Sami (defined as someone who speaks Sami as the native language, or who has a parent or grandparent who did so) make their livings primarily as reindeer herders. In Norway and Sweden, reindeer herding is legally defined as an exclusively Sami occupation to be carried out in specially designated Sami areas.

Sami society today is a result of centuries of intensive contact with the "outside"—and, indeed, the location and nature of boundaries between "inner" and "outer worlds" have changed historically, with significant implications for how people conceive of and prioritize identities defined in terms of ethnicity, occupation, nationality, gender, or political orientation. International press coverage of the Sami situation after Chernobyl, claiming that the fallout might spell the tragic end of an "ancient Sami reindeer-herding culture," precipitated virtually overnight into "the nuclear age" (see, for example, MacKenzie 1986), often revealed more about the authors' preconceptions about indigenous peoples than about the complexities of the Sami situation.

Certainly, reindeer herding today is both economically and symbolically important for many Sami. This is particularly true in South Sami areas, where about 70 percent of the Sami population is tied to reindeer herding as a primary occupation. Nevertheless, Chernobyl-associated threats to this occupation (together with a wide range of other threats, from incursions into Sami areas by mining, hydroelectric, and tourist interests to industrial pollution and legal complaints from neighboring farmers) have led some Sami to question the state-supported identification of reindeer herding with Sami identity. It is partly as a result of state policy that Sami—standing, as people say on the "one leg" of reindeer herding—are so extremely vulnerable to environmental risks like Chernobyl fallout.

In August 1990, Pia Persson Toven observed:

> There is something that makes me uncomfortable about how journalists keep linking Chernobyl dangers to reindeer herding with the "death of Sami culture." I think that even if there were not a single deer left, we would still have Sami culture as long as we had Sami people who see and act in Sami ways.

What these ways might be and how they might be preserved and developed in the modern world are questions that have fueled a wide range of cultural activities since Chernobyl. Paine (1989:14) describes a post-Chernobyl "flurry of re-energizing practical cultural activities" such as crafts courses, South Sami language classes, theatrical presentations, and an emphasis on distinctively Sami food preparation, "lest we lose these things."

Sverre Fjellheim, previous director of the South Sami Cultural Center in Snåsa, describes how the experience of Chernobyl—coming on the heels of a number of other assaults on South Sami life (including losses of pasture areas to military, logging, and agricultural interests and the pollution of pasture areas and mountain lakes by industrial chemicals and acid rain) contributed to intensified cultural work at the center. "We thought of starting a project here on the effects of Chernobyl," he explained, "but our resources are limited and we felt it was better to put our efforts into work that makes people feel proud of their culture and gives them something positive to do." Thus, the center's main project in recent years has been charting the "cultural landscape" of previous generations and registering old "cultural sites," such as living places, herding areas, and offering places.

While many Sami are critical of notions of Sami "museum culture," depicting an unchanging Sami society engaged in ancient reindeer-herding practices, South Sami have also participated in the "museumization" of Sami culture for their own purposes. The cultural center in Snåsa includes a small museum, with examples of traditional handicrafts under glass and with old black-and-white photographs of South Sami ancestors on the walls, A large illustrated wall panel, entitled *Vi og De* (Us and Them), depicts key events in the history of Sami/Scandinavian colonial relations over the centuries.

South Sami have drawn upon such notions of separate Sami identity to articulate the social significance of Chernobyl's wide-ranging threats—even while they also live and act in a world where a collective Sami ethnic identity is often split by national, regional, occupational, political, and gender differences.

Chernobyl radiation in Sami areas foregrounded and intensified differences and tensions between North and South Sami, groups characterized by different histories, as well as different fallout levels. Some South Sami felt that the more numerous and politically influential North Sami were more concerned with marketing their own deer and assuaging consumer fears in the majority population about the safety of reindeer meat than with showing solidarity with South Sami in the most contaminated areas. When an Alaskan Inuit women's group collected caribou meat and berries to send to the South Sami, Swedish and Norwegian governments dissuaded official Sami groups (led by North Sami politicians) from receiving the Alaskan group and provisions, despite assertions from South Sami that they welcomed the gesture of international solidarity—even if they didn't need the food. Scandinavian governments, for their part, did not want to be seen as requiring international assistance to take care of their own minority population.

Consideration of a South Sami women's meeting held in Snåsa 20–23 September 1990 gives us a sense of the complexity of post-Chernobyl identity politics in the South Sami area. Chernobyl-related issues figured prominently on the agenda for discussion, but these issues were incorporated within a broader set of concerns about women's roles in contemporary South Sami life. The central question was, how can women best care for their families and communities in the face of complex modern threats to health and identity like Chernobyl?

The main invited speaker at the meeting was Berit Ås (professor of psychology at the University of Oslo), who has been vocal in her criticisms of official Norwegian information policy after Chernobyl. Ås discussed the work of scientists who have challenged internationally dominant scientific assessments of the risks posed by low-level radiation. She and others have argued that despite the fact that Norway has neither nuclear energy nor weapons, state radiation and health agencies are still staffed with scientists who espouse largely "orthodox" scientific views about low-level radiation that have been formed within an international medical/political/military nexus of interest groups.[3]

South Sami women's explorations of more disquieting scientific views of the potential dangers of Chernobyl led them to draft a letter to the national Sami reindeer-herding organization and to the state health department, in which they assert:

> Until now we have not understood what long-range health problems could affect the whole South Sami people. Until now the focus has been mainly on Chernobyl's effects on the economic situation and whether groups are for or against comprehensive support for reindeer herding. This has meant that women feel they are not taken seriously when they express concern and horror about having to prepare contaminated reindeer meat for their families.

They go on to demand more extensive information and comprehensive health monitoring from health agencies, as well as state support for bringing the becquerel counts in reindeer not just to "acceptable levels," but to zero, so that women can in good conscience prepare reindeer meat in Sami ways for their families.

A dualistic view of Sami traditional knowledge versus Western science is insufficient to do justice to the ways these women have drawn upon alternative forms of scientific knowledge to make demands on a male-dominated Sami reindeer administration and the official scientific community.

The exploratory nature of South Sami responses to Chernobyl (and to other threats to cultural identity, for which Chernobyl serves as a dramatic symbol) can also be seen in the plans of another women's group to develop a South Sami-language child care center, for infants to preschool age children, in order to reinvigorate South Sami as a living language and not just a secondary subject in the Sami School. The model for the proposed child care center is the New Zealand Maori "language nest," aimed at protecting and developing Maori language for the next generation.

South Sami are thus exploring a wide range of responses to Chernobyl. Most of these responses are framed as ways of protecting "South Sami culture," a term that has different meanings for different groups and, indeed, is used in different ways by the same people at different times.

What might it mean, then, to speak of Sami children's right to a cultural identity? The right to instruction in the Sami school and cultural center about Sami language, history, and traditions? The right to safe physical environments in which children can develop more embodied and practice-oriented forms of "Sami culture"? The right of children to create and develop new hybrid cultural forms significantly different from the worlds of their parents?

Confronting these diverse notions of cultural identity, we might ask whether certain constructions work against one another. Are there notions of cultural identity that might be seen more as risks than as resources for future generations?

THE "CULTURAL FALLOUT" OF CHERNOBYL IN SOUTH SAMI REGIONS: IMPLICATIONS FOR CHILDREN

This essay represents research still in progress.[4] One area I would like to explore much more is the experiential world of Sami children themselves, with particular reference to ways they understand and experience notions of cultural identity and risk. During my first visit to Snåsa in December–January 1986–87, I talked mostly with adults, who repeatedly expressed fears for their children in the aftermath of Chernobyl—fears for their children's (and their children's children's) health; fears about the effects on children of having their daily food and environments suddenly become dangerous things; fears about the consequences within families of parental economic worries and feelings of dislocation and uncertainty; and fears that children would come to see their Sami identity as a liability, as something that makes them especially vulnerable, rather than as a strength.

We can get some sense of children's own perspectives on Chernobyl in the first years after the accident from a collection of Sami children's drawings, compiled and published by the Swedish Sami youth organization, Sáminuorra (1988).[5] It is likely that schoolchildren in Sweden, where there has been over a decade of national debate about Sweden's

own nuclear reactors, will have a different consciousness of nuclear issues than Norwegian children, but there is also a sufficiently strong
sense of Sami connections across national borders to justify looking at
these drawings here.

A striking characteristic of many drawings is the lack of distance
between the world of Chernobyl and the Sami world. The Chernobyl
reactor appears right next to a child, or on the near horizon, behind a
reindeer herd (see Fig. 11.1). Beck (1987:158) writes of the "anthropological shock" of Chernobyl, involving a recognition that "our constructions of limits, of protected areas, and of possibilities of withdrawal
collapsed like a house of cards." A sense of Chernobyl as something that
entered directly into children's everyday life experience is dramatically
evident in these drawings.

A number of drawings depict the animals—reindeer, elk, and freshwater fish—that children were no longer supposed to eat (see Fig. 11.2).
Children express their fears of cesium from the reactor accident that
might harm them personally (Fig. 11.3).

Other drawings and accompanying texts depict children's awareness
of economic problems resulting from the fallout. (A picture of a man
lassoing a deer shows the man as saying, "It is sad that I cannot sell this
fine deer.") Some drawings depict trucks taking away slaughtered deer
with radioactivity levels over legal limits for sale (Fig.s 11.4, 11.5). A
number of drawings show children's concern for the contaminated deer
(Figs. 11.4, 11.6; Fig. 11.7 shows a deer crying and saying, "I think it
is a pity").

Figure 11.8 shows a person (standing beside a deer?) and, beside
these two figures, a graph of radioactivity. How might the emphasis
after Chernobyl on external instrumental measurements—of lichen,
grasses, deer, and people—affect children's notions of the world?

One of the most disquieting aspects of Chernobyl fallout for adults
was the fact that it could not be sensed. Many of the children's drawings
give Chernobyl fallout a more concrete form. Some drawings show birds
or fish coughing as rains descend: "Let's get out of here," they say.
"This is dangerous." Figure 11.9 shows a mouse sniffing food cooking
on a stove: "This smells of Chernobyl. It is not good, even though one
can't taste anything." In this drawing, the child combines an awareness
that radiation is beyond the reach of a sense of taste with the claim that
fallout is something that can be smelled.

Several drawings show a sense of something dangerous not just in
food or people, but in all of nature. One drawing, of a Sami tent in the
mountains with smoke rising from it, a herd of deer on a distant hill,
birds in a meadow, sun in the sky, and a horse wandering beside a stream
full of fish, is captioned: "The nature we live in has been hit." Another

Fig 11.1

Fig 11.2. "This has a lot of cesium. This elk can't be eaten.
I am afraid."

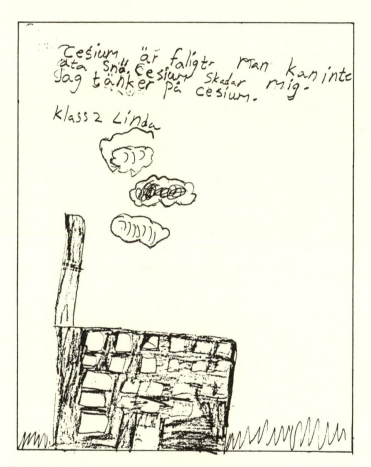

Fig 11.3. "Cesium is dangerous. One cannot eat the snow.
I think about cesium."

Fig 11.4. "It was a very terrible experience. It should not have been allowed to happen. I want my reindeer to be able to eat healthy food."

Fig 11.5

Fig 11.6. "I became shocked and afraid. Then I thought of my reindeer.
What will happen to them?"

Fig 11.7. "I think it is a pity."

Fig 11.8

shows a person in the rain, under the words: "Soon the whole earth will be poisoned." One drawing (Fig. 11.10) links the dangers from nuclear reactors to other forms of pollution and holds all adults responsible.

What consequences might children's experiences of Chernobyl have for their sense of Sami identity—for example, as a site of vulnerability, or as somehow "contaminated," or as built on forms of knowledge insufficient to deal with threats from the modern world? To what degree do children continue to live with the "cultural fallout" of Chernobyl, even if they no longer experience Chernobyl as a significant aspect of their daily lives?

Nora-Marie Bransfjell, principal of the South Sami School in Snåsa, described how the children gradually ceased to speak of Chernobyl:

When the children returned to school in September [1986], they spoke only of becquerels. They asked each other, "Did you eat fish from the lakes before you knew? Did you walk in the rain last spring?" They would open their lunch boxes and say, "I can eat this meat. My father bought it in the north so it has only 300 becquerels." But by December I noticed that hardly anyone spoke anymore of Chernobyl. "Do you think about it?" I asked. A nine-year-old girl replied, "No, it's like war. You know it's real, but far away. You can't see it, and you try not to think of it coming to you and your family."

Fig 11.9. "This smells of Chernobyl. It is not good, even though one can't taste anything."

In April 1992, Bransfjell observed:

> I don't think so many of the younger children today know much about Chernobyl. The older ones remember the times right after the accident, when people around them were so worried, but now that things look OK again economically, and we can eat deer from our own herds again, things seem to be back to normal. Children seem to adjust to such things faster than adults.

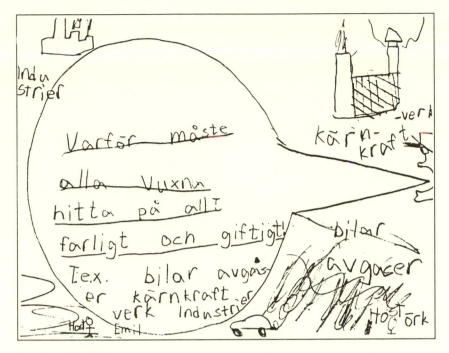

Fig 11.10. "Why must all grown-ups invent everything dangerous and poisonous! For example, car exhaust, nuclear-energy plants, industries."

But what, we might ask, is the "normal" situation now? Though South Sami may now eat deer from their own herds, there may still be risks involved in regular consumption of foods even at "acceptable" radiation levels—still a good deal higher than previously "normal" radiation levels. "Normal" today also means a changed context of herding and household practices, social relations (between Sami and state officials, North and South Sami, South Sami men and women) and definitions of cultural identity. What can we learn from this discussion of the post-Chernobyl politics of culture in South Sami regions that might be relevant to the discussion of international children's right discourses, and in particular, assertions of the child's right to a cultural identity?

THE CHILD'S RIGHT TO A CULTURAL IDENTITY: RESOURCE AND RISK

Sami people themselves worry about what changing constructions of Sami culture and conflicts over its definition will mean for their children's sense of identity and future possibilities. There is a danger, some have observed, that South Sami will respond to staggeringly complex threats like Chernobyl by "routinizing" and "normalizing" them out of awareness and by turning inward, seeking to fortify the boundaries between Sami and the "outside world" and to define, catalog, and regulate what counts as Sami culture, the correct use of language, style of native dress, and so on. (This construction of an authentic, normative Sami culture is, as I have suggested above, at least partly a result of state policies and modernist notions of culture as something outside of and "carried by" everyday life.)

The danger here is that South Sami culture will come to be seen as something that belongs in a museum or textbook, to be brought out for special cultural festivals, marketed in the interests of local tourism, or used as the basis of claims to special state economic benefits. What might this sort of "museum culture" have to offer, some people wonder, to children who watch Norwegian children's TV every night at 6 P.M., listen to international popular music, and play video games with their Norwegian neighbors?

On the other hand, people are also concerned over too easy an accommodation to "multiculturalism" and too uncritical an adoption of outside expert knowledges, technologies, and modes of thought, without critical discussions of what may be at risk, including Sami ways of forming children's bodies and senses and materially producing connections among people, places, and deer. As Pia Persson Toven observes:

> I know I am Sami first, so I can go out from there to Norwegian places and situations and I can have things like television and radio in my home, but I am still a Sami person and our home is a Sami home. It is important for children to have an identity to go out from, and not just be "Sami" in one situation, "Norwegian" in another, a member of a political party when it comes time to vote, a teacher or some other profession when it comes time to be in a labor organization. If you must change who you are whenever you step into a new place, then you just respond to outside definitions that you have no way of criticizing.

"It is important to give children a place to stand," observed Britt-Inger Gustafsson. "Our children are going to have to deal with more 'Chernobyls,' of one sort or another. Where are they going to find the strength and the vision to do this?"

The answers to this question clearly cannot be given from outside but must be developed by people actively engaged in constructing and debating the nature of cultural identities as they live everyday lives and respond to events, such as Chernobyl, that disrupt and call into question things that are usually taken for granted.

A primary aim of the cultural rights discourses articulated in the UN Convention on the Rights of the Child is to hold signatory nations to state policies that provide space, within national and international legal frameworks, for the existence of distinctive "indigenous and minority cultures" as living resources for "the protection and harmonious development of the child." The Convention also seeks, however, to protect children in situations where "cultural tradition" is seen more as a risk than as a resource. Article 24, section 3 asserts, for example, that "States Parties shall take all effective and appropriate measures with a view to abolishing traditional practices prejudicial to the health of children," potentially pitting internationally dominant biomedical constructions against "traditional" ways of producing social persons. Article 29, asserting children's rights to education, includes the potentially explosively contradictory statement that education should aim to develop "respect for the child's parents, his or her own cultural identity, language and values, for the national values of the country in which the child is living, the country from which he or she may originate and for civilizations different from his or her own."[6]

This essay has tried to show, by examining the complexity of modern identity politics within one northern European indigenous community, some of the issues that must be confronted in asserting a child's right to cultural identity. There are cases in which cultural-rights discourses seem clearly to further the "best interests" of children—for example, in protecting children from being uprooted from their families and communities at young ages and sent away to boarding schools, where they are not allowed to speak their own language and are taught to look down on the ways of their parents (as was the case with Sami children during the period of state-sponsored "Norwegianization" lasting into the 1950s).

There are other cases where international cultural-rights discourses are used by states to define, control, and exploit the "different cultures" in their midst—for example, South Africa's legitimation of apartheid "homelands" as sites of cultural preservation, or the Indonesian government's use of notions of traditional village culture to perpetuate the political subordination of villages to centralized state control (see Pemberton 1994).

It is important to recognize that the very existence of "indigenous" and "minority cultures" is bound up with complex histories of colonization and state formation, which have left these groups particularly vulnerable to a wide range of global risks. The case of radiation danger is instructive. Because of the historical conditions of their formation, "indigenous peoples" like the Sami are often identified with primary subsistence, "one-legged" occupations. Thus, they are often the most immediately and intensely affected by global environmental catastrophes like Chernobyl. Moreover, indigenous areas (often sparsely populated peripheral territories) and minority regions have frequently been chosen as nuclear-waste disposal sites, because of the expectation that organized political protests are less likely in these areas.

A powerful argument could be made that the development of more responsible nuclear policies—and more generally, of globally responsible environmental policies—would be one of the most significant contributions signatory nations to the UN Convention could make to promoting children's rights to "indigenous and minority identities."

In critically examining the implications of international-rights discourses for "children at risk," my aim has not been to undermine the UN Convention on the Rights of the Child, but to contribute to debates necessary to clarify and strengthen the Convention's potential for protecting children and promoting political change in the direction of the best interests of present and future generations. Such debates, I argue, must include critical explorations of the intersecting politics of culture at global and local levels, and of the implications of these politics for children's experience, understandings, and future possibilities.

NOTES

Various stages of this research have been funded by Cultural Survival, Inc.; The University of Chicago Social Sciences Research Program and The University of Chicago Anthropology Department Lichtstern Fund; the Wenner-Gren Foundation; the U.S. Education Foundation in Norway (Fulbright Program); and the National Geographic Society. I gratefully acknowledge this support, as well as substantial collegial support from the Norwegian Centre for Child Research.

1. There appear to be significantly different biological processes associated with low- and high-level exposures. In 1972, Petkau showed that low-level radiation generates highly toxic charged oxygen molecules ("free radicals") that destroy cell membranes. These free radicals produce systemic damage to immune systems much more efficiently under prolonged low-dose exposure than at high-intensity exposures—for example, those associated with atomic bombs or special medical treatments. (See Petkau 1972, 1980.) Waldren et al. (1986) have also found that very low levels of ionizing radiation produce mutations in human chromosomes two hundred times more efficiently than single high-dose exposures, such as brief bursts from X-ray machines.

2. All translations from Norwegian are my own.

3. Gould (1990:46) writes of debates concerning safe or acceptable levels of radioactivity between institutionally dominant and alternative scientific communities: "I can think of no area of science today where the prior intellectual commitments and stances so strongly shape the interpretations placed on scientific 'texts.'"

4. This paper is based on research conducted during two trips to the Norwe-

gian South Sami area in December–January 1986–87 and in September 1990, as well as on research done to date as part of a long-term project on the social construction of Chernobyl in Norwegian society. During this study, I have been based at the Norwegian Centre for Child Research, where I have been engaged in library research and periodic visits to Snåsa (about 150 miles north of Trondheim).

5. My interpretations of these drawings are preliminary and are intended to raise questions for further study. Much more information would be needed about these drawings, the circumstances in which they were produced, and the understandings of the child artists themselves before a more anthropologically and psychologically nuanced analysis could be done.

6. Parts of the UN Convention on the Rights of the Child especially relevant to this discussion include the following:

Article 8: "States Parties undertake to respect the right of the child to preserve his or her identity, including nationality, name and family relations as recognized by law without unlawful interference."

Article 17: State policies should encourage "the mass media to have particular regard to the linguistic needs of the child who belongs to a minority group or who is indigenous."

Article 20: In arranging alternative care for children temporarily or permanently deprived of their families, "due regard shall be paid to the desirability of continuity in a child's upbringing and to the child's ethnic, religious, cultural and linguistic background."

Article 30: A child belonging to a minority or indigenous culture has a right, "in community with other members of his or her group, to enjoy his or her own culture, to profess and practise his or her own religion, or to use his or her own language."

REFERENCES

Baverstock, K. F., and J W Stather, eds., 1989, *Low Dose Radiation. Biological Bases of Risk Assessment*, London, New York, Taylor and Francis.

Beck, Ulrich, 1987, "The Anthropological Shock: Chernobyl and the Contours of the Risk Society," *Berkeley Journal of Sociology* 32:153–65.

Bertell, Rosalie, 1985, *No Immediate Danger*, London, Women's Press.

The Chugoku Newspaper, 1992, *Exposure: Victims of Radiation Speak Out*, trans. by Kirsten McIvor, Kodansha International, Tokyo.

Gould, Jay M., and Benjamin A. Goldman, 1991, *Deadly Deceit: Low-Level Radiation, High-Level Cover-Up*, New York, Four Walls Eight Windows.

Gould, Richard, 1990, *Fire in the Rain: The Democratic Consequences of Chernobyl*, Baltimore, Johns Hopkins University Press.

Jones, Robin Russell, and Richard Southwood, 1987, *Radiation and Health: The Biological Effects of Low-Level Exposure to Ionizing Radiation*, Chichester, John Wiley & Sons.

Knox, E. G., A. M. Stewart, E. A. Gilman, and G. W. Kneale, 1988,

"Background Radiation and Childhood Cancer," *Journal of Radiology Protection,* 8(1):9–18.

MacKenzie, Debora, 1986, "The Rad-dosed Reindeer," *New Scientist,* 18 December, 37–40.

May, John, 1989, *The Greenpeace Book of the Nuclear Age: The Hidden History, the Human Cost,* New York, Pantheon Books.

Paine, Robert, 1987, "Accidents, Ideologies, and Routines: 'Chernobyl' over Norway," *Anthropology Today* 3(4):7–10.

————, 1989, "Making the Invisible 'Visible': Coming to Terms with 'Chernobyl' and Its Experts, a Saami Illustration," *International Journal of Moral and Social Studies,* 4(2): 139–62.

Pemberton, John, 1994, *On the Subject of "Java,"* Ithaca, N.Y., Cornell University Press.

Petkau, A., 1972, "Effect of 22 Na+ on a Phospholipid Membrane," *Health Physics* 22:239.

————, 1980, "Radiation Carcinogenesis from a Membrane Perspective," *Acta Physiologica Scandinavia,* supp. vol. 492, 81–90.

Sáminuorra, 1988, *Mina tankar om Tjernobyl: Samebarn berättar om sina tankar efter kärnkraftsolyckan i Tjernobyl* (My thoughts about Chernobyl: Sami children tell about their thoughts after the nuclear plant accident at Chernobyl), Lula, Alltryck AB.

Waldren, Charles, Laura Correll, Marguerite A. Sognier, and Theodore T. Puck, 1986, "Measurement of Low Levels X-ray Mutagenesis in Relation to Human Disease," *Proceedings of the National Academy of Sciences* 83:4839–43.

Part Four

THE RECOVERY AND RECONSTRUCTION
OF CHILDHOOD?

CHAPTER 12

Recovering Childhood: Children in South African National Reconstruction

NJABULO NDEBELE

EARLY THIS CENTURY, Thomas Mofolo, Lesotho's most famous writer, published a book about the life of one of the central figures in Southern African history: *Chaka: The King of the Zulus* (1981). What fascinated me as a young reader of this book, something that has also fascinated many other readers with whom I have spoken, is how Chaka, an illegitimate child cruelly treated in his early years, flees with his mother to seek refuge under a sympathetic chief. Years later he returns with vengeance to claim his right to the throne. I felt that there was something satisfyingly just about his triumphant return. It was marvelous how Chaka proceeded to build one of the most powerful kingdoms in Africa.

Unfortunately, it was not long before the justice of his return was tragically undercut by his excessive ruthlessness, which negates the earlier sense of moral triumph. At the end of the novel, one is left disturbed by how something potentially glorious, in which there was the real possibility that the kind of cruelty shown toward Chaka as a child would be a thing of the past, finally degenerated into physical and moral ruin. One closes the book feeling deep disappointment over the failure of potential.

Stories of this kind, I believe, are many the world over. Taking many various permutations, they all reveal one major strand: how the hero or heroine, highly vulnerable as a child, is ill treated, subjected to all kinds of indignities, and is finally spurned by a society that should have known better. The child protagonist has no means of physical or intellectual self-defense, but depends on the protection of society through its laws and its conscience.

Underscoring the moral thrust of these stories are the many deprivations visited upon the children. The children are denied human contact and become lonely. They are starved; they are spoken to harshly, with never a kind word; they are exposed to illness and disease; they are made to work under extremely dangerous and sometimes slave conditions; they are deprived of education; and they may even be turned away from the gates of churches and hospitals. What we see are the workings and the effects of the invisible hand of an unjust and insensitive society. The travails of children are presented as reminders, prodding the slumbering conscience of society as an indication of some pervasive disorder. The moral logic behind such stories is that should the victims grow up to wreak vengeance upon us, we should understand that we shall certainly be receiving our just rewards. The images of the travails of children are powerful metaphors of indictment, calling for the urgent redemption of society.

However, no matter how compelling the metaphors, there tends to be a threshold that is seldom crossed. We are generally spared the ultimate horror: the sight of the blood of children. Seldom are we shown the dashing of little heads against a wall, or their splitting with *pangas* that are withdrawn dripping with the gore of blood and brains. Seldom, if ever, are little children thrown into burning furnaces. Such images involving children are "too ghastly to contemplate," as the South African prime minister John Voster once said.

But should they appear, they would most likely indicate the ultimate degeneration of society. They would indicate that there were few horrors left in society, for horror that has become the norm profoundly ceases to be horror. If such a point is ever reached, it would surely demand the most far-reaching efforts for a society to rediscover its conscience.

South African literature has generally handled the images of childhood as social criticism in the conventional manner indicated above. Two images in particular became archetypal. The first one is an image of an infant abandoned by its mother. In the February 1955 issue of *Drum* magazine, Ezekiel Mphahlele published a story entitled "The Suitcase," in which a man claims a suitcase left in a bus by a female fellow passenger. As he carries the suitcase away, hoping that it contains things of value, he is stopped by the police and is forced to open the suitcase. Hidden under a cover of clothes is a dead infant. Through a horrible twist of fate, the man had picked up the corpse of an infant apparently abandoned by its mother. At least the story spares us the details of how the death actually occurred. By the time we see the infant, it is already dead. We are left only with the shock of its discovery.

The second image concerns the tragedy of racism. In the late 1950s, Arthur Maimane published a story called "Just Another Tsotsi," in which two boys, one white and the other black, grow up together on a farm, far out in the remote rural areas of South Africa. They become so close that they enter into an oath, committing themselves to lifelong brotherhood. Ritualistically cutting themselves, they join their wounds and mingle their blood in a clasp of brotherhood.

Unfortunately, when they grow up, they part, going their own separate ways, only to be thrown together by fate many years later. One day, the white boy, now a grown man in the police force, chases away a suspected black criminal and shoots him dead, only to notice the ritual mark of his connection to the one he has just killed. The death of a young adult may not be so horrifying: it is common enough. What is horrifying in the context of the story is the tragic breach of a bond made in the innocence of childhood.

The adult world has made it impossible for this bond of friendship to persist. It has denied permanence to a friendship. The adult world breaks up a friendship in a manner that gives one friend rights over the life of the other.

In 1971, sixteen years after Mphahlele published his story, Oswald Mtshali, in a collection entitled *Sounds of a Cowhide Drum*, published the following poem:

An Abandoned Bundle

The morning mist
and chimney smoke
of White City Jabavu
flowed thick yellow
as pus oozing
from a gigantic sore.
It smothered our little houses
like a fish caught in a net.

Scavenging dogs
draped in red bandanas of blood
fought fiercely
for a squirming bundle.

I threw a brick;
they bared fangs
flicked velvet tongues of scarlet
and scurried away,
leaving a mutilated corpse—
an infant dumped on a rubbish heap—
"Oh! Baby in the Manger
sleep well
on human dung."

Its mother
had melted into the rays of the rising sun,
her face glittering with innocence
her heart as pure as untrampled dew.

Here we are shown "a squirming bundle," an infant dumped on a rubbish heap, being set upon by the hungry dogs of the ghetto. The environment in which this takes place is bleak. People are trapped in it, with no avenue of escape. It is hell on earth. In this hell, and in a tremendous daring of the imagination, Mtshali actually shows us the sacrificial blood of a child. However, we are still spared the ultimate horror. It is, after all, dogs that tear apart the child, and not the hand of a human being. Nevertheless, this poet was like a seer, foreseeing the oncoming tragedy of a nation that would soon begin to slaughter its children. The killing began in earnest in June 1976. It is still with us.

On the morning of June 16, 1976, the schoolchildren of Soweto in their school uniforms took to the streets to protest against the imposition of the Afrikaans language as a medium of instruction in black schools. This development, the children reasoned, was the final act in the attempt of the racist government to complete the subjugation of black people. But what the children had not bargained for was a state so determined to have its way that it would not allow even children to take refuge in their childhood. For the first time, the government purposefully pointed its guns at children and opened fire. Many children were killed that day, and from that moment onward, no one, no matter what age, would be spared the wrath of the government: men, women, and children.

And so we began to hear of the arrest, detention, torture, and disappearance of those even as young as eight years old. The military occupation of the black townships became a regular feature of the times. One irony in this occupation is that the soldiers were young white conscripts, sent in to kill their black peers. Of course, you will immediately notice in this drama the replay of one of the archetypal images seen above. These events have found their way into our literature. Mbulelo Mzamane published a book called *The Children of Soweto,* based on those incredible years. And so, the children of South Africa effectively entered national politics as active participants.

This dramatic entrance of young people into national politics should be seen in perspective. When the major political organizations (Nelson Mandela's African National Congress and the Pan-Africanist Congress) were banned in 1961, the entire political leadership of these organizations was either imprisoned or in exile, leaving a political void bound to be filled sooner or later. This void was indeed filled toward the end of the 1960s by the advent of the Black Consciousness Movement that organized mainly university students. It was this movement that drew its inspiration from Steve Biko. The average age of the participants was between twenty-four and twenty-six years.

In 1976, with the banning of all major organizations of the Black Consciousness Movement, the average age of the participants went down to approximately sixteen to eighteen. As many of the student activists in this age group fled into exile, even younger ones filled the vacuum created. And if the targets of the government could be eight years old, then the phenomenon of childhood in my country was dangerously close to an end.

Nowhere was the impact of the entrance of the young into national politics more visible than in education. The children involved in the upheavals of 1976 were products of a system of education designed especially for black people. The system was introduced in 1953 following the passing of the Bantu Education Act. The rationale for a separate system of education for Africans was summed up by the then Minister of Native Affairs, Dr. H. Verwoerd (statement to Senate, June 7, 1954):

> There is no place for him (the African) in the European community above the level of certain forms of labour. Within his community, however, all the doors are open. For that reason it is of no avail for him to receive a training which has as its aim absorption in the European community, where he cannot be absorbed. Until now he has been subjected to a school system which drew him away from his own community and misled him by showing him the green pastures of European society in which he was not allowed to graze.

This legislation legalized and institutionalized inequality in the provision of educational services for blacks and whites. For blacks, this meant systematic deprivation in education: overcrowding and poor educational facilities in available schools; a restricted syllabus and career options; inferior teacher training; authoritarian school discipline where corporal punishment was rife and principals ran schools like army barracks; and a host of other deprivations. This was the situation against which the youth rebelled.

In the determination of the white, racist government to lower the ambition of the black children, and, consequently, to limit the aspirations of the entire black population, the government spawned universal bitterness, which took the form of a generalized struggle for liberation. For the children, particularly after June 1976, this struggle meant targeting the education system for attack. The current crisis in South African education is a culmination of that resistance.

In the heat of that resistance a new slogan was proclaimed by schoolchildren: "Liberation now, education later." This slogan expressed the children's perception that it was impossible to have normal schooling in an abnormal society, that a repressive education system was the product of a repressive politics. They were calling for postponement of the education process. Perhaps an unwise, suicidal demand. Nevertheless, it was not long after the youth entered the political arena that an already discredited education system was finally reduced to dust.

If this is what has happened to education, what is it that will bring about the vital socialization of the young? What is it that will prepare them for creative and responsible citizenship? The decline of educational values and the educational system itself should be seen in perspective. Then perhaps these questions can be answered.

The social well-being of the black community was targeted by the European colonizers for destruction as soon as the conquest was achieved. The indigenous economic system was undermined in the colonial days when men in particular were compelled to abandon their normal social tasks and go to work in the mines and other new industries in order to be able to pay a variety of taxes. The social fabric began to tear apart. A labor force was created that would relieve workers of the responsibilities of making economic decisions for themselves. Henceforth, the official ideal would be workers producing with minimum demands on their thinking capacities.

The African family was further undermined when single-sex living compounds were established, with regulations preventing men from bringing their families along to live with them. Many families broke up as a result. New communities were established in the growing urban areas. It was there that one of the earliest working-class communities in Africa was created.

There developed in our literature a tendency to compare rural and urban life as metaphors for, respectively, good and evil. Life in the cities represented moral degeneration of the worst kind, whereas the rural areas were romantic places of refuge for spiritual and moral regeneration. This easy dichotomy, of course, simplified a very complex phenomenon. In fact, the rural areas progressively ceased to be viable as communities, whereas the new urban communities represented new opportunities for many that could find their way there.

The overall picture that emerges is one of many African communities gradually experiencing a diminishing integrity as organic communities. The members of those communities, politically welded together by their color, became politically marginalized in phenomenally large numbers, being virtual observers in an unfolding historical drama in which they were instruments used to produce the continent's most advanced economy.

It is in the context of this general dislocation that after many decades of the horror of apartheid, South Africa is finally settling down to try to become a nation of people who, at this most challenging moment in our history, find that they know very little about one another. The divisions, purposefully cultivated, have taken their toll. However, the removal of much of the repressive legislation has only made it possible for previously repressed tensions to emerge more fully. Having relatively little experience in managing these tensions without recourse to force and repression, we are only just discovering the full force of the depth and range of human issues with which a new democratic order will have to contend.

At the root of the problem is the near total devastation of the social fabric of the vast majority of the South African population. As we face the reality of the implications of this understanding, we simultaneously also face another problem, further undermining our capability to heal our wounds. I am referring to the current rampant violence in many parts of the country in which even children are not spared. The threshold of tolerable violence against children has been decisively passed. Violence against children as a metaphor for measuring societal degeneration has lost its shock effect. If children are butchered in real life, is there any effect in depicting such butchery in literature as metaphor?

Let me share with you a recent report in the *Weekly Mail*. The report has a general headline: "Children in the War Zone." But specific reference is made to an article entitled "Playing Games among the Ruins." It is about children in a squatter community that was attacked by an unidentified group of people. Such attacks are now common all over the country.

> All that's left alongside the flattened shacks of families wiped out in an attack on Crossroads, a predominantly Zulu squatter camp next to Katlehong in the East Rand are the trampled remnants of once-thriving vegetable gardens. Now, children who survived the onslaught and are on holiday from school, play among the ruins.
>
> At first sight, they appear unaffected by the brutality of the attack—which was an example of children joining their parents as specific targets of township violence. . . .
>
> After the early morning attack last Friday, mothers, fathers and children were left for dead in the smouldering ruins of their corrugated iron shacks. One mother, identified only as "Khampane" by a neighbour, was asleep with her husband and two children when, shortly after 1:00 A.M., a group of men armed with knives, knobkieries and pangas barged into their shack demanding money.
>
> In the confusion they said they had none, hoping the attackers would leave, but the men rained blows on them, mercilessly beating them, the neighbour told "The Weekly Mail."
>
> While trying to ward off the blows, Khampane tried to protect her one-month-old daughter, holding the child close to her body. But she could not defend it from the blows, and the baby was struck on the head by a panga, leaving a gaping hack wound across her tiny forehead. She was lucky: she survived.
>
> All the while her terrified four-year-old stood hugging his father around

the legs, crying hysterically as he watched him being hacked to death. His "interference" by holding on to his father so angered the attackers that they hit him repeatedly, slashing the forearms and wrists before killing his father.

The boy is also in hospital, fighting for his life.

This family was the first to be attacked, but they were not the last.

Thus ends the first segment of the report. The next segment follows:

Vera Ndlela (19) was asleep when the men barged into her shack. They immediately began beating her, and demanded money from her. She said she was a student, and had no money. On hearing this, they told her that they wanted her 18 month-old baby to remove parts of his body. She tried to hold on to the boy, but repeated blows from knives and knobkieries forced her to let go. As the men took the boy, she broke away and ran. They flung him into the ruins and chased Vera among the dense reeds of a nearby stream.

For three days Vera lay in the smelly, marshy stream running alongside the squatter camp.

Unable to move after her severe beating, she remained stuck on the stream bank until she heard people nearby and let out a weak scream. Residents found her and took her to the Natalspruit Hospital. Her son is missing, and police do not know whether he is one of the injured in hospital, or a body in a morgue.

By Wednesday, five days after the attack, the police could not confirm the names or number of children injured or killed. The only incidents they were able to give details of were the cases of two children, both believed to be younger than one year, whose bodies are at Germiston mortuary. Both suffered "excessive burn wounds" and are thought to have died as a result of their burns.

More examples can be provided, altogether suggesting a rampant state of violence and an increasing inability of the public to be shocked. The recent events of Boipatong, in which the residents of the township were brutally attacked at random by unidentified people, is the measure of the prevalence and persistence of this kind of violence. Its history includes random killings of commuter train passengers; random shootings of mourners at funeral wakes; desecration of funeral rites by the police; ruthless taxi wars among rival taxi organizations; the bombing and burning of schools and churches; mass shootings of blacks by crazed whites puzzled by their sudden loss of power.

There has been much speculation about who is behind all of these events. Theories abound of a malevolent force consisting of special units of the apartheid army skilled in state-sponsored covert activities aimed at the liquidation of anti-apartheid activists. Are we seeing orchestrated attempts to create an atmosphere of terror, fear, suspicion, and despair in the general population in this time of transition? Is it all meant to engender a lack of confidence in the ongoing process of negotiation toward a new society? It is difficult to tell, but more revelations have been made in the press about government death squads, which seem to still be in operation. Some top cabinet ministers have been implicated.

It may be in order to ponder briefly on the above newspaper report itself. Its impact partly results from the implicit suggestion that the violence presently being exposed and confirmed is endemic in the country at the moment. That picture is correct.

There are some social facts referred to that have become integral to the political knowledge of South African society. These facts become reference points crucial to the forming of understanding. For example, in the piece as a whole, there is the almost casual reference to Zulus and Xhosas. The average South African is very likely to conclude that there is an underlying ethnic conflict. There is the suggestion that for some reason, as long as there are different peoples, speaking different languages, with different customs, such interethnic violence will follow. It is a sociological law that governs interethnic relations. There may be no possibility of probing further beyond this basic understanding, no suggestion that there could be other causes. This grammar of political understanding is the legacy of our immediate past, bedeviling every effort to think in new ways about the South African predicament.

In a slightly different category are some other graphic details of the incident. They underscore the irrationality and unspeakable horror of the events. They are described to ilicit horror and outrage, showing us how brute male strength is pitted against the vulnerability of women and children. They can enable us to ask some important questions about children and society. Beyond the horror and the outrage, what is there to be salvaged? What ought to be salvaged? How can such violence be prevented? On what basis can agreement be reached on such prevention? What value system can be brought into being to prevent such a tragedy? In a society constructed on the principle of difference, what chances are there to find common ground?

But these questions are soon rendered impotent when we notice how easy it is for the perpetrators of the violence to simply melt away undiscovered to continue elsewhere with their carnage. We wait, wondering where they will strike next. And then we will read yet another report.

From the report above we can gain an insight into how the reporting of violence has itself become part of the problem. The newspaper article, seeking to shed some light on a difficult and newsworthy phenomenon, reports it in a manner that reinforces the simplifications of popular South African political discourse already alluded to above. Produced by a newspaper that sees itself as being in opposition to apartheid, the report is unable to transcend the limits of social information and the interpretations of it as generated by the terrible drama of apartheid. It itself becomes another social feature of the violence: the reporting of violence. From this report, all of us and the children can conclude: things are the way they are because that is how they are.

I recall the horrible stories above not with the intention of shocking the reader, but rather with the wish to use them as an occasion for some painful reflections on the state of affairs in my country, South Africa. That children are at the center of these events—sometimes as victims, sometimes as perpetrators—is at the root of the problem, for our goal is nation building. What can we expect of children who have witnessed the death of parents; who have seen people being stoned, hacked with pangas and burnt to death; who have themselves been the direct targets and victims of this violence; and who have sometimes participated in these gruesome events?

I look at my country caught in this grip of violence and see nothing less than a breakdown of culture. Notwithstanding the impressive infrastructure of roads, railways, and harbors; the punctuality of airline schedules; the ups and downs of the stock exchange; the flurry of diplomatic initiatives and the opening of new embassies; trade agreements and investments; the technical sophistication of assembly line production; the abundance of electronic goods and commodities, the fact is that we have an industrial infrastructure, anchored on an overprivileged minority that, in spite of a presence of more than three hundred years, has never shed the mentality of being visitors. Consequently, the fruits of their achievements have no organic connection with the realities of the larger human environment in which they have occurred. We have a culture of technical achievement that is merely drifting forward by sheer momentum, without being informed by an overriding and creative sense of an inclusive nationhood. We are left with no other alternative but to strive to establish a more humane context for national reconstruction. We have to strive urgently to rediscover what it means to be a national community.

Where can we locate the metaphors of hope? No longer in children, for not only do we kill them, but they themselves have also killed. To return to education, let us look at what has happened in some of the schools. The young have taken over, hiring and firing teachers and principals. But how long can they do this meaningfully? Ultimately, they cannot run the schools or the educational system; they cannot run banks, businesses, or even churches. They cannot run nations. Yet, they have attempted to do so when, being on the firing line, they began to feel responsible for bringing the future into being. It is not for lack of ability or talent that they cannot perform such formidable tasks; rather, it is the limits of their experience. By assuming complex, adult responsibilities, they have striven after wisdom without the foundation of growth. They shed their childhood without having the pains and joys of learning from it. Effectively, we have witnessed the end of a childhood.

In a society without children, can there be a concept of innocence? The question implies that innocence has, over the thousands of years of human society, established a strong philosophical presence. For adults, confronted with all kinds of pressures, childhood innocence offers the possibility of refuge and redemption. Because childhood is vulnerable, we can be healed by offering it protection; in nurturing it, we confirm the need for culture, recreation, and creativity. That is why innocence has been such a powerful metaphor for social criticism. The loss of childhood signals the end of the metaphor. What is left is a world of instant adults with no experience of having lost something. If there is no sense of loss, there can be no sense of a paradise to be regained. To regain that philosophical paradise, in fulfillment of the yearning for a perfect society, we have to do no less than rediscover the child and childhood.

It may not be that easy for children, heroically transformed into adults overnight, to be their own redemptive metaphor, because the experience of compassion and the nurturing of conscience has not been a consistently informing aspect of their growth in recent times. Can they succeed in effecting a strategic distance from themselves for the purpose of moral reflection?

That we need their energy is beyond dispute. And so do we need their fearlessness and questioning attitude, which, under the circumstances, are welcome gifts of these terrible times. But where will the visionary authority come from that might harness that energy and assign a proper role to it in a new and infinitely challenging society?

Nor is childhood the only thing we need to rediscover. Adulthood itself has been threatened with destruction. The progressive loss of parental authority in the wake of the 1976 student uprisings was a significant sociological phenomenon. Hemmed in between children, on the one hand, and a hostile state on the other, black parents suffered an ontological crisis. Dismissed by children for having failed to protect them as well as having failed to bring about liberation, relentlessly bludgeoned into submission through the state repressive laws and other forms of state terrorism, the confidence of the black adult was seriously shaken. How can adults reestablish their roles in society?

Beginning with the recovery of childhood and innocence, there are so many other things to be recovered and even redefined: the family; the sense of autonomous and secure neighborhood engaged in purposeful collective action; the sense of interconnectedness of different aspects of society: politics, education, the economy; the sense of being part of a larger world in so many functional ways. It is a task of enormous proportions. But we have to locate the process of discovery in the child and genuinely believe in the newness that will come from that direction.

I have posed the issue of the recovery of childhood and innocence as a metaphor for the restoration of freedom and the range of human values that should go with it. Many of these have been eroded by apartheid. Those values will partly embody the meaning of the struggle against apartheid. Since apartheid largely succeeded in breaking up what held African society together, any attempt at rebuilding that society was by definition against the interests of the state. In this situation, the idea of reconstituting society becomes a principle of resistance. Consequently, the liberation movement, led by Nelson Mandela's African National Congress, has a responsibility to define a social order that will replace the repressive one.

The seeds of that alternative society are already there in social bonds developed within the broad liberation movement: the trade union movement; civic associations; self-help community groupings, such as burial and savings societies; and cultural, religious, educational, sporting, and taxi organizations. All these may be regarded as future organs of civil society. Political rallies organized in defiance of the state have served as bonding glue for the most liberating sense of solidarity. Democracy, nonracism, and nonsexism have been espoused as the framing principles of reconstruction informing the activities of all these social groupings.

From this entire context, it can be seen, then, that the recovery of childhood is something inextricably bound with the reconstruction of society. It will be the result of that reconstruction, rather than the cause of it.

Perhaps the way to end, since our way into this difficult subject was literature, is to ask whether South African writers will truly recognize their luck. How will they reflect a people struggling with the pains and joys of building a new society? A new society? The question suggests something that will itself have to be born, experience childhood, the rites of passage, and work toward wisdom. South African literature may itself be reborn and then grow the society of its preoccupation.

REFERENCES

Mofolo, Thomas, *Chaka: The King of the Zulus,* London, Heinemann.
Mphahlele, Ezekiel, 1955, "The Suitcase," *Drum,* February.
Mtshali, Oswald, 1971, *Sounds of a Cowhide Drum,* Johannesburg, Donker.
Mzamane, Mbulelo, 1982, *The Children of Soweto,* Harlow, Longman.

Appendix

The United Nations Convention on the Rights of the Child

Preamble

The States Parties to the present Convention,

Considering that, in accordance with the principles proclaimed in the Charter of the United Nations, recognition of the inherent dignity and of the equal and inalienable rights of all members of the human family is the foundation of freedom, justice and peace in the world,

Bearing in mind that the peoples of the United Nations have, in the Charter, reaffirmed their faith in fundamental human rights and in the dignity and worth of the human person, and have determined to promote social progress and better standards of life in large freedom,

Recognizing that the United Nations has, in the Universal Declaration of Human Rights and in the International Covenants on Human Rights, proclaimed and agreed that everyone is entitled to all the rights and freedoms set forth therein, without distinction of any kind, such as race, colour, sex, language, religion, political or other opinion, national or social origin, property, birth or other status,

Recalling that, in the Universal Declaration of Human Rights, the United Nations has proclaimed that childhood is entitled to special care and assistance,

Convinced that the family, as the fundamental group of society and the natural environment for the growth and well-being of all its members and particularly children, should be afforded the necessary protection and assistance so that it can fully assume its responsibilities within the community,

Recognizing that the child, for the full and harmonious development of his or her personality, should grow up in a family environment, in an atmosphere of happiness, love and understanding,

Considering that the child should be fully prepared to live an individual life in society, and brought up in the spirit of the ideals proclaimed in the Charter of the United Nations, and in particular in the spirit of peace, dignity, tolerance, freedom, equality and solidarity,

Bearing in mind that the need to extend particular care to the child has been stated in the Geneva Declaration of the Rights of the Child of 1924 and in the Declaration of the Rights of the Child adopted by the General Assembly on 20 November 1959 and recognized in the Universal Declaration of Human Rights, in the International Covenant on Civil and Political Rights (in particular in articles 23 and 24), in the International Covenant on Economic, Social and Cultural Rights (in particular in article 10) and in the statutes and relevant instruments of specialized agencies and international organizations concerned with the welfare of children,

Bearing in mind that, as indicated in the Declaration of the Rights of the Child, "the child, by reason of his physical and mental immaturity, needs special safeguards and care, including appropriate legal protection, before as well as after birth,"

Recalling the provisions of the Declaration on Social and Legal Principles relating to the Protection and Welfare of Children, with Special Reference to Foster Placement and Adoption Nationally and Internationally; the United Nations Standard Minimum Rules for the Administration of Juvenile Justice (The Beijing Rules); and the Declaration on the Protection of Women and Children in Emergency and Armed Conflict,

Recognizing that, in all countries in the world, there are children living in exceptionally difficult conditions, and that such children need special consideration,

Taking due account of the importance of the traditions and cultural values of each people for the protection and harmonious development of the child,

Recognizing the importance of international co-operation for improving the living conditions of children in every country, in particular in the developing countries,

Have agreed as follows:

Part I

Article 1

For the purposes of the present Convention, a child means every human being below the age of eighteen years unless, under the law applicable to the child, majority is attained earlier.

Article 2

1. States Parties shall respect and ensure the rights set forth in the present Convention to each child within their jurisdiction without discrimination of any kind, irrespective of the child's or his or her parent's or legal guardian's race, colour, sex, language, religion, political or other opinion, national, ethnic or social origin, property, disability, birth or other status.

2. States Parties shall take all appropiate measures to ensure that the child is protected against all forms of discrimination or punishment on the basis of the status, activities, expressed opinions, or beliefs of the child's parents, legal guardians, or family members.

Article 3

1. In all actions concerning children, whether undertaken by public or private social welfare institutions, courts of law, administrative authorities or legislative bodies, the best interests of the child shall be a primary consideration.

2. States Parties undertake to ensure the child such protection and care as is necessary for his or her well-being, taking into account the rights and duties of his or her parents, legal guardians, or other individuals legally responsible for him or her, and to this end, shall take all appropriate legislative and administrative measures.

3. States Parties shall ensure that the institutions, services and facilities responsible for the care or protection of children shall conform with the standards established by competent authorities, particularly in the areas of safety, health, in the number and suitability of their staff, as well as competent supervision.

Article 4

States Parties shall undertake all appropriate legislative, administrative and other measures for the implementation of the rights recognized in the present Convention. With regard to economic, social and cultural rights, States Parties shall undertake such measures to the maximum extent of their available resources and, where needed, within the framework of international co-operation.

Article 5

States Parties shall respect the responsibilities, rights and duties of parents or, where applicable, the members of the extended family or community as provided for by local custom, legal guardians or other persons legally responsible for the child, to provide, in a manner consistent with the evolving capacities of the child, appropriate direction and guidance in the exercise by the child of the rights recognized in the present Convention.

Article 6

1. States Parties recognize that every child has the inherent right to life.
2. States Parties shall ensure to the maximum extent possible the survival and development of the child.

Article 7

1. The child shall be registered immediately after birth and shall have the right from birth to a name, the right to acquire a nationality and, as far as possible, the right to know and be cared for by his or her parents.
2. States Parties shall ensure the implementation of these rights in accordance with their national law and their obligations under the relevant international instruments in this field, in particular where the child would otherwise be stateless.

Article 8

1. States Parties undertake to respect the right of the child to preserve his or her identity, including nationality, name and family relations as recognized by law without unlawful interference.
2. Where a child is illegally deprived of some or all of the elements of his or her identity, States Parties shall provide appropriate assistance and protection, with a view to speedily re-establishing his or her identity.

Article 9

1. States Parties shall ensure that a child shall not be separated from his or her parents against their will, except when competent authorities subject to judicial review determine, in accordance with applicable law and procedures, that such separation is necessary for the best interests of the child. Such determination

may be necessary in a particular case such as one involving abuse or neglect of the child by the parents, or one where the parents are living separately and a decision must be made as to the child's place of residence.

2. In any proceedings pursuant to paragraph 1 of the present article, all interested parties shall be given an opportunity to participate in the proceedings and make their views known.

3. States Parties shall respect the right of the child who is separated from one or both parents to maintain personal relations and direct contact with both parents on a regular basis, except if it is contrary to the child's best interests.

4. Where such separation results from any action initiated by a State Party, such as the detention, imprisonment, exile, deportation or death (including death arising from any cause while the person is in the custody of the State) of one or both parents or of the child, that State Party shall, upon request, provide the parents, the child or, if appropriate, another member of the family with the essential information concerning the whereabouts of the absent member(s) of the family unless the provision of the information would be detrimental to the well-being of the child. States Parties shall further ensure that the submission of such a request shall of itself entail no adverse consequences for the person(s) concerned.

Article 10

1. In accordance with the obligation of States Parties under article 9, paragraph 1, applications by a child or his or her parents to enter or leave a State Party for the purpose of family reunification shall be dealt with by States Parties in a positive, humane and expeditious manner. States Parties shall further ensure that the submission of such a request shall entail no adverse consequences for the applicants and for the members of their family.

2. A child whose parents reside in different States shall have the right to maintain on a regular basis, save in exceptional circumstances, personal relations and direct contacts with both parents. Towards that end and in accordance with the obligation of States Parties under article 9, paragraph 1, States Parties shall respect the right of the child and his or her parents to leave any country, including their own, and to enter their own country. The right to leave any country shall be subject only to such restrictions as are prescribed by law and which are necessary to protect the national security, public order (*ordre public*), public health or morals or the rights and freedoms of others and are consistent with the other rights recognized in the present Convention.

Article 11

1. States Parties shall take measures to combat the illicit transfer and non-return of children abroad.

2. To this end, States Parties shall promote the conclusion of bilateral or multilateral agreements or accession to existing agreements.

Article 12

1. States Parties shall assure to the child who is capable of forming his or her own views the right to express those views freely in all matters affecting the

child, the views of the child being given due weight in accordance with the age and maturity of the child.

2. For this purpose, the child shall in particular be provided the opportunity to be heard in any judicial and administrative proceedings affecting the child, either directly, or through a representative or an appropriate body, in a manner consistent with the procedural rules of national law.

Article 13

1. The child shall have the right to freedom of expression; this right shall include freedom to seek, receive and impart information and ideas of all kinds, regardless of frontiers, either orally, in writing or in print, in the form of art, or through any other media of the child's choice.

2. The exercise of this right may be subject to certain restrictions, but these shall only be such as are provided by law and are necessary:

a. For respect of the rights or reputations of others; or

b. For the protection of national security or of public order (*ordre public*), or of public health or morals.

Article 14

1. States Parties shall respect the right of the child to freedom of thought, conscience and religion.

2. States Parties shall respect the rights and duties of the parents and when applicable, legal guardians, to provide direction to the child in the exercise of his or her right in a manner consistent with the evolving capacities of the child.

3. Freedom to manifest one's religion or beliefs may be subject only to such limitations as are prescribed by law and are necessary to protect public safety, order, health or morals, or the fundamental rights and freedoms of others.

Article 15

1. States Parties recognize the rights of the child to freedom of association and to freedom of peaceful assembly.

2. No restrictions may be placed on the exercise of these rights other than those imposed in conformity with the law and which are necessary in a democratic society in the interests of national security or public safety, public order (*ordre public*), the protection of public health or morals or the protection of the rights and freedoms of others.

Article 16

1. No child shall be subjected to arbitrary or unlawful interference with his or her privacy, family, home or correspondence nor to unlawful attacks on his or her honour and reputation.

2. The child has the right to the protection of the law against such interference or attacks.

Article 17

States Parties recognize the important function performed by the mass media and shall ensure that the child has access to information and material from a diversity of national and international sources, especially those aimed at the promotion of his or her social, spiritual and moral well-being and physical and mental health. To this end, States Parties shall:

a. Encourage the mass media to disseminate information and material of social and cultural benefit to the child and in accordance with the spirit of article 29;

b. Encourage international co-operation in the production, exchange and dissemination of such information and material from a diversity of cultural, national and international sources;

c. Encourage the production and dissemination of children's books;

d. Encourage the mass media to have particular regard to the linguistic needs of the child who belongs to a minority group or who is indigenous;

e. Encourage the development of appropriate guidelines for the protection of the child from information and material injurious to his or her well-being, bearing in mind the provisions of articles 13 and 18.

Article 18

1. States Parties shall use their best efforts to ensure recognition of the principle that both parents have common responsibilities for the upbringing and development of the child. Parents or, as the case may be, legal guardians, have the primary responsibility for the upbringing and development of the child. The best interests of the child will be their basic concern.

2. For the purpose of guaranteeing and promoting the rights set forth in the present Convention States Parties shall render appropriate assistance to parents and legal guardians in the performance of their child-rearing responsibilities and shall ensure the development of institutions facilities and services for the care of children.

3. States Parties shall take all appropriate measures to ensure that children of working parents have the right to benefit from child care services and facilities for which they are eligible.

Article 19

1. States Parties shall take all appropriate legislative, administrative, social and educational measures to protect the child from all forms of physical or mental violence, injury or abuse, neglect or negligent treatment, maltreatment or exploitation, including sexual abuse, while in the care of parents, legal guardian(s) or any other person who has the care of the child.

2. Such protective measures should, as appropriate, include effective procedures for the establishment of social programmes to provide necessary support for the child and for those who have the care of the child, as well as for other forms of prevention and for identification, reporting, referral, investigation, treatment and follow-up of instances of child maltreatment described heretofore, and, as appropriate, for judicial involvement.

Article 20

1. A child temporarily or permanently deprived of his or her family environment, or in whose own best interests cannot be allowed to remain in that envi-

ronment, shall be entitled to special protection and assistance provided by the State.

2. States Parties shall in accordance with their national laws ensure alternative care for such a child.

3. Such care could include, *inter alia*, foster placement, *kafalah* of Islamic law, adoption or if necessary placement in suitable institutions for the care of children. When considering solutions, due regard shall be paid to the desirability of continuity in a child's upbringing and to the child's ethnic, religious, cultural and linguistic background.

Article 21

States Parties that recognize and/or permit the system of adoption shall ensure that the best interests of the child shall be the paramount consideration and they shall:

a. Ensure that the adoption of a child is authorized only by competent authorities who determine, in accordance with applicable law and procedures and on the basis of all pertinent and reliable information, that the adoption is permissible in view of the child's status concerning parents, relatives and legal guardians and that, if required, the persons concerned have given their informed consent to the adoption on the basis of such counselling as may be necessary;

b. Recognize that inter-country adoption may be considered as an alternative means of child's care, if the child cannot be placed in a foster or an adoptive family or cannot in any suitable manner be cared for in the child's country of origin;

c. Ensure that the child concerned by inter-country adoption enjoys safeguards and standards equivalent to those existing in the case of national adoption;

d. Take all appropriate measures to ensure that, in inter-country adoption, the placement does not result in improper financial gain for those involved in it;

e. Promote, where appropriate, the objectives of the present article by concluding bilateral or multilateral arrangements or agreements and endeavour, within this framework, to ensure that the placement of the child in another country is carried out by competent authorities or organs.

Article 22

1. States Parties shall take appropriate measures to ensure that a child who is seeking refugee status or who is considered a refugee in accordance with applicable international or domestic law and procedures shall, whether unaccompanied or accompanied by his or her parents or by any other person, receive appropriate protection and humanitarian assistance in the enjoyment of applicable rights set forth in the present Convention and in other international human rights or humanitarian instruments to which the said States are Parties.

2. For this purpose, States Parties shall provide, as they consider appropriate, co-operation in any efforts by the United Nations and other competent inter-govemmental organisations or non-governmental organisations co-operating

with the United Nations to protect and assist such a child and to trace the parents or other members of the family of any refugee child in order to obtain information necessary for reunification with his or her family. In cases where no parents or other members of the family can be found, the child shall be accorded the same protection as any other child permanently or temporarily deprived of his or her family environment for any reason, as set forth in the present Convention.

Article 23

1. States Parties recognize that a mentally or physically disabled child should enjoy a full and decent life, in conditions which ensure dignity, promote self-reliance and facilitate the child's active participation in the community.

2. States Parties recognize the right of the disabled child to special care and shall encourage and ensure the extension, subject to available resources, to the eligible child and those responsible for his or her care, of assistance for which application is made and which is appropriate to the child's condition and to the circumstances of the parents or others caring for the child.

3. Recognizing the special needs of a disabled child, assistance extended in accordance with paragraph 2 of the present article shall be provided free of charge, whenever possible, taking into account the financial resources of the parents or others caring for the child, and shall be designed to ensure that the disabled child has effective access to and receives education, training, health care services, rehabilitation services, preparation for employment and recreation opportunities in a manner conducive to the child's achieving the fullest possible social integration and individual development, including his or her cultural and spiritual development.

4. States Parties shall promote, in the spirit of international co-operation, the exchange of appropriate information in the field of preventive health care and of medical, psychological and functional treatment of disabled children, including dissemination of and access to information concerning methods of rehabilitation, education and vocational services, with the aim of enabling States Parties to improve their capabilities and skills and to widen their experience in these areas. In this regard, particular account shall be taken of the needs of developing countries.

Article 24

1. States Parties recognize the right of the child to the enjoyment of the highest attainable standard of health and to facilities for the treatment of illness and rehabilitation of health. States Parties shall strive to ensure that no child is deprived of his or her right of access to such health care services.

2. States Parties shall pursue full implementation of this right and, in particular, shall take appropriate measures:

   a. To diminish infant and child mortality:

   b. To ensure the provision of necessary medical assistance and healthcare to all children with emphasis on the development of primary health care:

   c. To combat disease and malnutrition, including within the framework of primary health care, through, inter alia, the application of readily available technology and through the provision of adequate nutritious foods and clean drinking-water, taking into consideration the dangers and risks of environmental pollution;

    d. To ensure appropriate pre-natal and post-natal health care for mothers;

    e. To ensure that all segments of society, in particular parents and children, are informed, have access to education and are supported in the use of basic knowledge of child health and nutrition, the advantages of breast-feeding, hygiene and environmental sanitation and the prevention of accidents;

    f. To develop preventive health care, guidance for parents and family planning education and services.

    3. States Parties shall take all effective and appropriate measures with a view to abolishing traditional practices prejudicial to the health of children.

    4. States Parties undertake to promote and encourage international co-operation with a view to achieving progressively the full realization of the right recognized in the present article. In this regard, particular account shall be taken of the needs of developing countries.

Article 25

States Parties recognize the right of a child who has been placed by the competent authorities for the purposes of care, protection or treatment of his or her physical or mental health, to a periodic review of the treatment provided to the child and all other circumstances relevant to his or her placement.

Article 26

    1. States Parties shall recognize for every child the right to benefit from social security, including social insurance, and shall take the necessary measures to achieve the full realization of this right in accordance with their national law.

    2. The benefits should, where appropriate, be granted, taking into account the resources and the circumstances of the child and persons having responsibility for the maintenance of the child, as well as any other consideration relevant to an application for benefits made by or on behalf of the child.

Article 27

    1. States Parties recognize the right of every child to a standard of living adequate for the child's physical, mental, spiritual, moral and social development.

    2. The parent(s) or others responsible for the child have the primary responsibility to secure, within their abilities and financial capacities, the conditions of living necessary for the child's development.

    3. States Parties, in accordance with national conditions and within their means, shall take appropriate measures to assist parents and others responsible for the child to implement this right and shall in case of need provide material assistance and support programmes, particularly with regard to nutrition, clothing and housing.

    4. States Parties shall take all appropriate measures to secure the recovery of maintenance for the child from the parents or other persons having financial responsibility for the child, both within the State Party and from abroad. In particular, where the person having financial responsibility for the child lives in

a State different from that of the child, States Parties shall promote the accession to international agreements of the conclusion of such agreements as well as the making of other appropriate arrangements.

Article 28

1. States Parties recognize the right of the child to education, and with a view to achieving this right progressively and on the basis of equal opportunity, they shall, in particular:

a. Make primary education compulsory and available free to all;

b. Encourage the development of different forms of secondary education, including general and vocational education, make them available and accessible to every child, and take appropriate measures such as the introduction of free education and offering financial assistance in case of need;

c. Make higher education accessible to all on the basis of capacity by every appropriate means;

d. Make educational and vocational information and guidance available and accessible to all children;

e. Take measures to encourage regular attendance at schools and the reduction of drop-out rates.

2. States Parties shall take all appropriate measures to ensure that school discipline is administered in a manner consistent with the child's human dignity and in conformity with the present Convention.

3. States Parties shall promote and encourage international co-operation in matters relating to education, in particular with a view to contributing to the elimination of ignorance and illiteracy throughout the world and facilitating access to scientific and technical knowledge and modern teaching methods. In this regard, particular account shall be taken of the needs of developing countries.

Article 29

1. States Parties agree that the education of the child shall be directed to:

a. The development of the child's personality, talents and mental and physical abilities to their fullest potential:

b. The development of respect for human rights and fundamental freedoms, and for the principles enshrined in the Charter of the United Nations;

c. The development of respect for the child's parents, his or her own cultural identity, language and values, for the national values of the country in which the child is living, the country from which he or she may originate and for civilizations different from his or her own;

d. The preparation of the child for responsible life in a free society, in the spirit of understanding, peace, tolerance, equality of sexes, and friendship among all peoples, ethnic, national and religious groups and persons of indigenous origin;

e. The development of respect for the natural environment.

2. No part of the present article or article 28 shall be construed so as to interfere with the liberty of individuals and bodies to establish and direct educational

institutions, subject always to the observance of the principles set forth in paragraph 1 of the present article and to the requirements that the education given in such institutions shall conform to such minimum standards as may be laid down by the State.

Article 30

In those States in which ethnic, religious or linguistic minorities or persons of indigenous origin exist, a child belonging to such a minority or who is indigenous shall not be denied the right, in community with other members of his or her group, to enjoy his or her own culture, to profess and practise his or her own religion, or to use his or her own language.

Article 31

1. States Parties recognize the right of the child to rest and leisure, to engage in play and recreational activities appropriate to the age of the child and to participate freely in cultural life and the arts.

2. States Parties shall respect and promote the right of the child to participate fully in cultural and artistic life and shall encourage the provision of appropriate and equal opportunities for cultural, artistic, recreational and leisure activity.

Article 32

1. States Parties recognize the right of the child to be protected from economic exploitation and from performing any work that is likely to be hazardous or to interfere with the child's education, or to be harmful to the child's health or physical, mental, spiritual, moral or social development.

2. States Parties shall take legislative, administrative, social and educational measures to ensure the implementation of the present article. To this end, and having regard to the relevant provisions of other international instruments, States Parties shall in particular:

a. Provide for a minimum age or minimum ages for admission to employment;

b. Provide for appropriate regulation of the hours and conditions of employment;

c. Provide for appropriate penalties or other sanctions to ensure the effective enforcement of the present article.

Article 33

States Parties shall take all appropriate measures, including legislative, administrative, social and educational measures, to protect children from the illicit use of narcotic drugs and psychotropic substances as defined in the relevant international treaties, and to prevent the use of children in the illicit production and trafficking of such substances.

Article 34

States Parties undertake to protect the child from all forms of sexual exploitation and sexual abuse. For these purposes, States Parties shall in particular take all appropriate national, bilateral and multilateral measures to prevent:

a. The inducement or coercion of a child to engage in any unlawful sexual activity;

b. The exploitative use of children in prostitution or other unlawful sexual practices;

c. The exploitative use of children in pornographic performances and materials.

Article 35

States Parties shall take all appropriate national, bilateral and multilateral measures to prevent the abduction of, the sale of, or traffic in children for any purpose or in any form.

Article 36

States Parties shall protect the child against all other forms of exploitation prejudicial to any aspects of the child's welfare.

Article 37

States Parties shall ensure that:

a. No child shall be subjected to torture or other cruel, inhuman or degrading treatment or punishment. Neither capital punishment nor life imprisonment without possibility of release shall be imposed for offences committed by persons below eighteen years of age;

b. No child shall be deprived of his or her liberty unlawfully or arbitrarily. The arrest, detention or imprisonment of a child shall be in conformity with the law and shall be used only as a measure of last resort and for the shortest appropriate period of time;

c. Every child deprived of liberty shall be treated with humanity and respect for the inherent dignity of the human person, and in a manner which takes into account the needs of persons of his or her age. In particular, every child deprived of liberty shall be separated from adults unless it is considered in the child's best interest not to do so and shall have the right to maintain contact with his or her family through correspondence and visits, save in exceptional circumstances;

d. Every child deprived of his or her liberty shall have the right to prompt access to legal and other appropriate assistance, as well as the right to challenge the legality of the deprivation of his or her liberty before a court or other competent, independent and impartial authority, and to a prompt decision on any such action.

Article 38

1. States Parties undertake to respect and to ensure respect for rules of international humanitarian law applicable to them in armed conflicts which are relevant to the child.

2. States Parties shall take all feasible measures to ensure that persons who have not attained the age of fifteen years do not take a direct part in hostilities.

3. States Parties shall refrain from recruiting any person who has not attained

the age of fifteen years into their armed forces. In recruiting among those persons who have attained the age of fifteen years but who have not attained the age of eighteen years, States Parties shall endeavour to give priority to those who are oldest.

4. In accordance with their obligations under international humanitarian law to protect the civilian population in armed conflicts, States Parties shall take all feasible measures to ensure protection and care of children who are affected by an armed conflict.

Article 39

States Parties shall take all appropriate measures to promote physical and psychological recovery and social reintegration of a child victim of: any form of neglect, exploitation, or abuse; torture or any other form of cruel, inhuman or degrading treatment or punishment; or armed conflicts. Such recovery and reintegration shall take place in an environment which fosters the health, self-respect and dignity of the child.

Article 40

1. States Parties recognize the right of every child alleged as, accused of, or recognized as having infringed the penal law to be treated in a manner consistent with the promotion of the child's sense of dignity and worth, which reinforces the child's respect for the human rights and fundamental freedoms of others and which takes into account the child's age and the desirability of promoting the child's reintegration and the child's assuming a constructive role in society.

2. To this end, and having regard to the relevant provisions of international instruments, States Parties shall, in particular, ensure that:

a. No child shall be alleged as, be accused of, or recognized as having infringed the penal law by reason of acts or omissions that were not prohibited by national or international law at the time they were committed;

b. Every child alleged as or accused of having infringed the penal law has at least the following guarantees:

i. To be presumed innocent until proven guilty according to law;

ii. To be informed promptly and directly of the charges against him or her, and, if appropriate, through his or her parents or legal guardians, and to have legal or other appropriate assistance in the preparation and presentation of his or her defence;

iii. To have the matter determined without delay by a competent, independent and impartial authority or judicial body in a fair hearing according to law, in the presence of legal or other appropriate assistance and, unless it is considered not to be in the best interest of the child, in particular, taking into account his or her age or situation, his or her parents or legal guardians;

iv. Not to be compelled to give testimony or to confess guilt, to examine or have examined adverse witnesses and to obtain the participation and examination of witnesses on his or her behalf under conditions of equality;

v. If considered to have infringed the penal law, to have this decision and any measures imposed in consequence thereof reviewed by a higher competent, independent and impartial authority or judicial body according to law;

vi. To have the free assistance of an interpreter if the child cannot understand or speak the language used;

vii. To have his or her privacy fully respected at all stages of the proceedings.

3. States Parties shall seek to promote the establishment of laws, procedures, authorities and institutions specifically applicable to children alleged as, accused of, or recognized as having infringed the penal law, and, in particular:

a. The establishment of a minimum age below which children shall be presumed not to have the capacity to infringe the penal law;

b. Whenever appropriate and desirable, measures for dealing with such children without resorting to judicial proceedings, providing that human rights and legal safeguards are fully respected.

4. A variety of dispositions, such as care, guidance and supervision orders: counselling; probation foster care; education and vocational training programmes and other alternatives to institutional care shall be available to ensure that children are dealt with in a manner appropriate to their well-being and proportionate both to their circumstances and the offence.

Article 41

Nothing in the present Convention shall affect any provisions which are more conducive to the realization of the rights of the child and which may be contained in:

a. The law of a State Party; or
b. International law in force for that State.

Part II

Article 42

States Parties undertake to make the principles and provisions of the Convention widely known, by appropriate and active means, to adults and children alike.

Article 43

1. For the purpose of examining the progress made by States Parties in achieving the realization of the obligations undertaken in the present Convention, there shall be established a Committee on the Rights of the Child, which shall carry out the functions hereinafter provided.

2. The Committee shall consist of ten experts of high moral standing and

recognized competence in the field covered by this Convention. The members of the Committee shall be elected by States Parties from among their nationals and shall serve in their personal capacity, consideration being given to equitable geographical distribution, as well as to the principal legal systems.

3. The members of the Committee shall be elected by secret ballot from a list of persons nominated by States Parties. Each State Party may nominate one person from among its own nationals.

4. The initial election to the Committee shall be held no later than six months after the date of the entry into force of the present Convention and thereafter every second year. At least four months before the date of each election, the Secretary-General of the United Nations shall address a letter to States Parties inviting them to submit their nominations within two months. The Secretary-General shall subsequently prepare a list in alphabetical order of all persons thus nominated, indicating States Parties which have nominated them, and shall submit it to the States Parties to the present Convention.

5. The elections shall be held at meetings of States Parties convened by the Secretary-General at United Nations Headquarters. At those meetings, for which two thirds of States Parties shall constitute a quorum, the persons elected to the Committee shall be those who obtain the largest number of votes and an absolute majority of the votes of the representatives of States Parties present and voting.

6. The members of the Committee shall be elected for a term of four years. They shall be eligible for re-election if renominated. The term of five of the members elected at the first election shall expire at the end of two years: immediately after the first election, the names of these five members shall be chosen by lot by the Chairman of the meeting.

7. If a member of the Committee dies or resigns or declares that for any other cause he or she can no longer perform the duties of the Committee, the State Party which nominated the member shall appoint another expert from among its nationals to serve for the remainder of the term, subject to the approval of the Committee.

8. The Committee shall establish its own rules of procedure.

9. The Committee shall elect its officers for a period of two years.

10. The meetings of the Committee shall normally be held at United Nations Headquarters or at any other convenient place as determined by the Committee. The Committee shall normally meet annually. The duration of the meetings of the Commitee shall be determined, and reviewed, if necessary, by a meeting of the States Parties to the present Convention, subject to the approval of the General Assembly.

11. The Secretary-General of the United Nations shall provide the necessary staff and facilities for the effective performance of the functions of the Committee under the present Convention.

12. With the approval of the General Assembly, the members of the Committee established under the present Convention shall receive emoluments from United Nations resources on such terms and conditions as the Assembly may decide.

Article 44

1. States Parties undertake to submit to the Committee, through the Secretary-General of the United Nations, reports on the measures they have adopted which give effect to the rights recognized herein and on the progress made on the enjoyment of those rights:

a. Within two years of the entry into force of the Convention for the State Party concerned;

b. Thereafter every five years.

2. Reports made under the present article shall indicate factors and difficulties, if any, affecting the degree of fulfilment of the obligations under the present Convention. Reports shall also contain sufficient information to provide the Committee with a comprehensive understanding of the implementation of the Convention in the country concerned.

3. A State Party which has submitted a comprehensive initial report to the Committee need not, in its subsequent reports submitted in accordance with paragraph 1 (b) of the present article, repeat basic information previously provided.

4. The Committee may request from States Parties further information relevant to the implementation of the Convention.

5. The Committee shall submit to the General Assembly, through the Economic and Social Council, every two years, reports on its activities.

6. States Parties shall make their reports widely available to the public in their own countries.

Article 45

In order to foster the effective implementation of the Convention and to encourage international cooperation in the field covered by the Convention:

a. The specialized agencies, the United Nations Children's Fund, and other United Nations organs shall be entitled to be represented at the consideration of the implementation of such provisions of the present Convention as fall within the scope of their mandate. The Committee may invite the specialized agencies, the United Nations Children's Fund and other competent bodies as it may consider appropriate to provide expert advice on the implementation of the Convention in areas falling within the scope of their respective mandates. The Committee may invite the specialized agencies, the United Nations Children's Fund, and other United Nations organs to submit reports on the implementation of the Convention in areas falling within the scope of their activities;

b. The Committee shall transmit, as it may consider appropriate, to the specialized agencies, the United Nations Children's Fund and other competent bodies, any reports from States Parties that contain a request, or indicate a need, for technical advice or assistance, along with the Committee's observations and suggestions, if any, on these requests or indications;

c. The Committee may recommend to the General Assembly to request the Secretary-General to undertake on its behalf studies on specific issues relating to the rights of the child;

d. The Committee may make suggestions and general recommendations based on information received pursuant to articles 44 and 45 of the present Convention. Such suggestions and general recommendations shall be transmitted to any State Party concerned and reported to the General Assembly, together with comments, if any, from States Parties.

Part III

Article 46

The present Convention shall be open for signature by all States.

Article 47

The present Convention is subject to ratification. Instruments of ratification shall be deposited with the Secretary-General of the United Nations.

Article 48

The present Convention shall remain open for accession by any State. The instruments of accession shall be deposited with the Secretary-General of the United Nations.

Article 49

1. The present Convention shall enter into force on the thirtieth day following the date of deposit with the Secretary-General of the United Nations of the twentieth instrument of ratification or accession.

2. For each State ratifying or acceding to the Convention after the deposit of the twentieth instrument of ratification or accession, the Convention shall enter into force on the thirtieth day after the deposit by such State of its instrument of ratification or accession.

Article 50

1. Any State Party may propose an amendment and file it with the Secretary-General of the United Nations. The Secretary-General shall thereupon communicate the proposed amendment to States Parties, with a request that they indicate whether they favour a conference of States Parties for the purpose of considering and voting upon the proposals. In the event that, within four months from the date of such communication, at least one third of the States Parties favour such a conference, the Secretary-General shall convene the conference under the auspices of the United Nations. Any amendment adopted by a majority of States Parties present and voting at the conference shall be submitted to the General Assembly for approval.

2. An amendment adopted in accordance with paragraph 1 of the present article shall enter into force when it has been approved by the General Assembly of the United Nations and accepted by a two-thirds majority of States Parties.

3. When an amendment enter into force, it shall be binding on those States Parties which have accepted it, other States Parties still being bound by the provisions of the present Convention and any earlier amendments which they have accepted.

Article 51

1. The Secretary-General of the United Nations shall receive and circulate to all States the text of reservations made by States at the time of ratification or accession.

2. A reservation incompatible with the object and purpose of the present Convention shall not be permitted.

3. Reservations may be withdrawn at any time by notification to that effect addressed to the Secretary-General of the United Nations, who shall then inform all States. Such notification shall take effect on the date on which it is received by the Secretary-General.

Article 52

A State Party may denounce the present Convention by written notification to the Secretary-General of the United Nations. Denunciation becomes effective one year after the date of receipt of the notification by the Secretary-General.

Article 53

The Secretary-General of the United Nations is designated as the depositary of the present Convention.

Article 54

The original of the present Convention, of which the Arabic, Chinese, English, French, Russian and Spanish texts are equally authentic, shall be deposited with the Secretary-General of the United Nations.

In witness thereof the undersigned plenipotentiaries, being duly authorized thereto by their respective Governments, have signed the present Convention.

About the Contributors

HAE-JOANG CHO teaches and writes about feminist and postcolonial theory and praxis in Seoul, Korea. She is professor of sociology at Yonsei University and a member of a feminist group called Tohana-ui-munwha (The Alternative Culture). She is the author of *Women and Men in Korea* (Seoul, 1988) and *Reading Books, Reading Lives in the Post-Colonial Era* (Seoul, 1992).

MANUELA CARNEIRO DA CUNHA is currently professor of anthropology in the Department of Anthropology, University of Chicago. Previously she was professor of anthropology at the University of São Paulo, Brazil. She has conducted research on Brazilian Indian ethnology and history and has studied the return of Yoruba Brazilian emancipated slaves to the Gulf of Benin in the nineteenth century. She has written extensively on Indian rights and on ethnicity.

NORMA FIELD was born and raised in Japan. She currently teaches Japanese literature, contemporary culture and society, and gender studies in the East Asian Languages and Literatures Department of the University of Chicago. She is the author of *The Splendor of Longing in the Tale of Genji* (1987) and *In the Realm of a Dying Emperor* (1991).

KATHLEEN HALL is a postdoctoral fellow at the Chapin Hall Center for Children at the University of Chicago. Her research in England and in the United States has focused on issues of race, class, and education.

MARILYN IVY teaches in the Department of Anthropology at the University of Washington. She is the author of *Discourses of the Vanishing: Modernity, Phantasm, Japan* (University of Chicago Press, 1995).

MARY JOHN, a developmental psychologist by training, is a full professor at the School of Education, University of Exeter. Her research is largely with minority-rights groups on issues relating to the transformation of power relationships. She has worked as an expert adviser to the Centre for Educational Research and Innovation, Organization for Economic Cooperation and Development, Paris, and with the European Commission in Brussels on policy issues relating to disability. In September 1992, she ran the first World Conference on Research and Practice in Children's Rights, which actively involved children in the planning and proceedings.

RUTH MANDEL is an anthropologist who received her Ph.D. from the University of Chicago. She currently teaches in the Department of Anthropology at University College London. She has done field research in Germany, Turkey, and, most recently, central Asia.

NJABULO SIMAKAHLE NDEBELE was born in 1948 and grew up in Western Native Township in Johannesburg and later in Charterstown, Nigel. He holds an

M.A. from Cambridge and a Ph.D. from Denver University. His collection of short stories, *Fools and Other Stories,* received the Noma Award for publishing in Africa in 1984. Until 1990 Ndebele was the pro vice-chancellor at the National University of Lesotho, where he lived and taught from 1975. In 1991 he became professor of African literature at the University of the Witswatersrand, and in 1992 was appointed deputy vice-chancellor of the Western Cape. He is now vice-chancellor and principal of the University of the North.

PAMELA REYNOLDS is senior lecturer and head of the Department of Social Anthropology at the University of Cape Town in South Africa. She holds B.A., B.Ed. and Ph.D. degrees from UCT, as well as a Me.D. from Harvard and a M.Litt. in Anthropology from Delhi. Her doctoral dissertation was published as *Childhood in Crossroads: Cognition and Society in South Africa.* She has also done extensive research in Zimbabwe, resulting in two books: *Dance Civet Cat: Child Labour in the Zambezi Valley* and *Lwaano Lwanyika: Tonga Book of the Earth* (with Colleen Cousins). A book on traditional Zimbabwe healers will be published shortly. Her current research is on youth and political involvement.

SAYA SASAKI SHIRAISHI was born and raised in Japan. She received her Ph.D. in anthropology from Cornell University in 1992. Her research on Indonesia and Japan has focused on the politics of culture, education, and childhood. She currently teaches "Children, Literature and Society" and "Ethnology of Island Southeast Asia" in the Department of Asian Studies and the Department of Anthropology at Cornell University as a visiting professor. She also edited *Reading Southeast Asia* and *The Japanese in Colonial Southeast Asia,* both of which are translations of contemporary Japanese scholarship on Southeast Asia.

SHARON STEPHENS received her Ph.D. in 1984 from the University of Chicago and has since held positions in the anthropology departments of the Johns Hopkins University and the University of Chicago. She is currently assistant professor in the Department of Anthropology and the School of Social Work at the University of Michigan, as well as senior research associate at the Norwegian Centre for Child Research in Trondheim, Norway (where she worked from 1991–95 helping to develop a new international and interdiciplinary research program on "Children and Environment: Local Worlds and Global Connections"). Her earlier research focused on Sami (Lapp) cultural history, with special interest in pre-Christian Sami religion. Her current work focuses on the social consequences of Chernobyl fallout in Norway and, more generally, on international debates about the nature and significance of low-level radiation.

VIVIENNE WEE was born and raised in Singapore. She dropped out of school at the age of thirteen and did not return to formal schooling until she went to the University of Minnesota at the age of eighteen. After taking her first degree in music, she went on to study anthropology. Her master's thesis, completed at the University of Singapore, was on Chinese religion in Singapore. She did her Ph.D. at the Australian National University, with a thesis on the Riau Malays of Indonesia. She has lectured at the National University of Singapore and is currently programme director of ENGENDER, a research center aimed at generating perspectives and policies on development processes so as to address issues of gender equity and environmental sustainability.

Index

Page numbers in boldtype indicate where to locate main discussion.

The History of Everyday Life: Reconstructing Historical Experiences
and Ways of Life *edited by Alf Lüdtke*

The Savage Freud and Other Essays on Possible
and Retrievable Selves *by Ashis Nandy*

Children and the Politics of Culture *edited by Sharon Stephens*